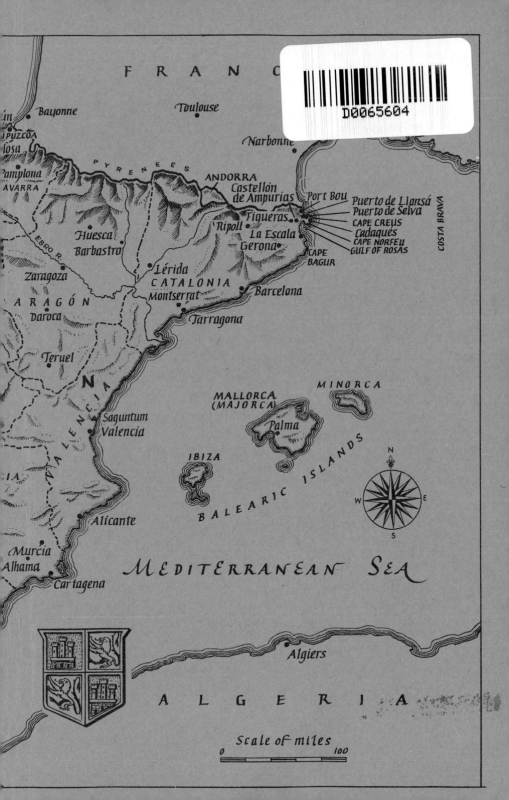

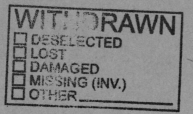

Please return or renew by
latest date below

An
Explanation of
SPAIN

A N

Explanation

O F

SPAIN

by

Éléna de La Souchère

TRANSLATED FROM THE FRENCH BY
ELEANOR ROSS LEVIEUX

Random House　　　　　　　NEW YORK

FIRST PRINTING

© *Copyright, 1964, by Random House, Inc.*

All rights reserved under International and Pan-American Copyright
Conventions. Published in New York by Random House, Inc., and
simultaneously in Toronto, Canada, by Random House of Canada, Limited.

Manufactured in the United States of America
by H. Wolff, New York

Designed by Jeanette Young

Library of Congress catalog card number: 64–11990

Originally published in French as Explication de L'Espagne
© 1962 by Editions Bernard Grasset

CONTENTS

Fifteen: Young Spain

1. Motifs of discontent
2. The mid-century generation
3. The eyewitness novel
4. Young Spain facing the future

Introduction

The object of this study is present-day Spain, and the future latent within her. The past would have no bearing upon our inquiry had it not played so decisive a role. For, in fact, all the phenomena characteristic of the Spanish present—general scepticism, the lack of vitality of the working class, the absence of a political opposition—are realities that foster the day-to-day survival of an anachronistic social structure which can be explained only by the memories and the violence of the civil war. But this in turn poses more questions than it answers. During the nineteenth century and into the beginning of the twentieth, an observer might have believed that the material violences associated with a social war were the fatal denouement of the antagonisms created by production relations. But we note that now, within the great industrial powers of our time, the class struggle assumes new forms always swerving from pure violence. This permanent compromise, made inevitable by the increasing interdependence of professions and classes, demonstrates that social war is possible only in those societies where such links of interdependence are still feeble: in a word, in pre-industrial societies. Violence is both the symptom and the result of economic underdevelopment. And, indeed, every civil war of our time has occurred in underdeveloped regions: in the Mexico and the Russia of the first quarter of this century, in China, in Spain.

But why was Spain, during the nineteenth century, unable to bring about such reforms as have enabled other western European nations to step firmly into the great industrial era?

Thus the twentieth century refers us back to the nineteenth; the present to the recent past.

The Spanish nineteenth century, like the twentieth, was characterized by civil war. Three times between 1833 and 1939 the country was riven into two hostile camps: region against region, city against city, Spain against Spain. In one hundred and six years, Spain lived through thirteen years of civil war:[1] one year of armed battle for every seven years of covert struggle.

The two cycles of struggle which came into being, between 1808 and 1854 and between 1854 and 1898, exactly prefigure the historical cycle which was to be achieved in the years between 1898 and 1950. We see, first of all, how the abuses of an authoritarian government arouse a thirst for liberty, a desire for reforms: between 1808 and 1814, on the fringe of the war for independence against Napoleon's forces; then in 1854, during the reign of Isabella II; and, finally, in 1898, as a reaction against the political conservatism of the restoration. After a more or less long and desperate period of struggles between two tendencies, the reformists come to power: the liberal revolutions of 1835-37 and 1868; the proclamation of the second republic in 1931. But internal divisions of the reformist groups, as well as street fighting, provoked a reaction from the right, whereupon an authoritarian regime was established by means of a military *pronunciamiento*: the *coup d'Etat* of Narváez in 1845; the *pronunciamiento* of Martínez Campos, who restored the monarchy in 1874; the Sanjurjo-Franco *pronunciamiento* in 1936.

Thus, the first glance at the preceding century strips the civil war of 1936 and Franco's dictatorship of any clinging aspect of the exceptional, and shows these bloody pages to

[1] The two nineteenth-century civil wars (the Carlist wars) lasted, respectively, from 1833 to 1839 and from 1872 to 1876. The twentieth-century civil war spanned a three-year period, from 1936 to 1939.

be only episodes in an historical process whose dawn coincides with the dawn of the nineteenth century and the collapse of the Spanish Empire.

Is the disease from which Spanish society suffers today the same as that which attacks all great conquering nations at the decline of their domination? Must we believe that omnipotence engenders a public demoralization which, being the true cause of an empire's decadence, outlives the realities of domination and provokes revolutions, *coups d'Etat*, and all the disturbances which Rome knew in the centuries of her decline and to which Spain is likewise prey?

The nineteenth century has sent back only the echo of our questions, for the recent past refers us still further to the distant, imperial past. Observers of Spanish society, no matter how determined they be to confine their curiosity to present realities and provided they do not confine themselves to describing phenomena but seek explanations as well, are driven in spite of themselves further and further into the past of this land whose long history, fixed and indestructible, lives on in each present instant.

I I

In nineteenth- and twentieth-century Spain, the privileged minorities—aristocratic, bourgeois, and intellectual—have taken the initiative in all reform movements. Not until 1931 and the civil war of 1936 do we witness an alliance, fleeting in any case, between reform groups and the masses. Never, in the course of the hundred and fifty years that went before did the liberals come to power otherwise than by royal choice or by means of a military *coup d'Etat*. In nineteenth-century Spain, revolution came from on high and *pronunciamientos* from the left.

While the southern peasantry and the working population remained indifferent to the reformists' efforts, the northern peasantry rose against them. Three times in the course of the nineteenth century Spain afforded the spectacle of a spontaneous popular mobilization, a veritable human tidal wave which, carrying along whole villages and entire provinces, resulted in the assembly of peasant militia armed with scythes and cudgels. The first of these peasant mobilizations, aiming to repulse the Napoleonic invasion, was inspired by patriotic motives. But the population which fought Napoleon the invader also hated Napoleon the representative of the principles of the French Revolution. As for the other two mass uprisings, the peasants in the north answered a call to arms, a thousand times echoed from one village to the next, of "Viva Don Carlos!" [2] and "Viva Christ the King!" Strangely absent from the political life of the nineteenth century, the Spanish popular mass erupted onto the historical scene only to proclaim its abhorrence of the liberalism inspired by the English and the French. Again in 1936, the small peasant landowners of Navarre and Old Castile were to constitute the infantry of the counterrevolutionary army.

Had it not been for the resistance of the peasantry in the north the progressive minorities, despite the numeric weakness of the urban proletariat, would doubtless have succeeded in setting the revolutionary process in motion. Indeed, if the success or failure of revolutions depended upon the intrinsic force of progressive groups (intellectual minorities, industrial proletariat, great urban centers), we would be at a loss to explain the revolutions brought about in the last four decades in Eastern Europe and in the Afro-Asian world:

[2] The first Don Carlos (Charles V to his followers) was the younger brother of King Ferdinand VII. Upon the latter's death in 1833, Don Carlos refused to recognize as sovereign his niece, the Infanta Isabella, proclaimed Queen Isabella II. He claimed the crown for himself, thereby launching the first Carlist war. Forced to abdicate in 1839, he died in exile in 1855. In 1845, he had renounced his rights in favor of his son (Charles VI), who was unable to act. But an opportunity opened to the Pretender's grandson, similarly called Don Carlos (Charles VII), after the fall of Isabella II when the crown was offered to the Italian prince Amadeo. The second Carlist war began in 1872 under the ephemeral reign of Don Amadeo, continued under the first Republic (1873-74) and after the restoration of Alfonso XII, son of Isabella. When his partisans were defeated in 1876, Don Carlos left Spain and died in exile in 1909, leaving a son, Don Jaime, who died in 1931 without a male heir. Whereupon the Carlists rallied to Don Alfonso, the younger brother of the second Don Carlos. But this prince died in turn, also without a male heir, early in the 1936 civil war. Since then, several princes descended on the female side from the Dons Carlos have unsuccessfully taken up the Carlist claims. Most Carlists have rallied to Don Juan, son of Alfonso XIII and great-grandson of Isabella II.

that is, in societies far less evolved, from the socio-economic viewpoint, than was Spain even at the beginning of the nineteenth century. In reality, the phenomenon which at times permits and at times paralyzes revolutions is the relationship between conservative structures and the groups making demands of them. In underdeveloped countries, where the masses remain passive, progressive groups though weak in number triumph easily over still more restricted oligarchical minorities. This could have been the case in Andalusia, where the mass of agricultural day-laborers, at first passive, would undoubtedly have given *a posteriori* support to a revolution promising the parceling out of great landholdings. On the other hand, in northern Spain, within a far more evolved social structure, relatively strong protest groups succumbed to the greater strength of the wealthy peasantry and the bourgeoisie in the little rural settlements of intermediary Spain.[3] The Spain of the *minifundio* assures the continuation of the Spain of the *latifundio*.

Between these two Spains there stretches an historic frontier, staked out by the gradual tread of the Reconquest. The Spain of the great landholdings and passive masses is the Spain which, so long in bondage to Moslem conquerors, was late in being liberated or reconquered by the armies of the north. And the small peasant landholders of northern Spain are the descendants of the soldiers of the Reconquest. That gory dawn, that tragic and unforgettable infancy, the long religious war which gave birth to Spain, survives in the mind and in social structures. Once again, the past commands the present.

But the conservatism of the peasant landholders was accompanied, among the Carlists of the nineteenth century, by the clamor for individual and local liberty—the *fueros*—which the Spanish people had enjoyed during the Middle Ages and the classical period. The people of northern Spain who rallied to Don Carlos hoped to return to a form of

[3] "Intermediary Spain" is a term borrowed from Ortega y Gasset's *España Invertebrada* which serves to designate the population in settlements of 2,000 to 10,000 inhabitants.

government of the people by the people, to a typically Iberian legislation to which no foreign institution is comparable. The nature of this total democracy as well as the irrepressible need to revive it reveal exceptional psychological tendencies. Through the *fuero*, a race expressed its singularity.

And that thirst for liberty, which gave rise to the *fuero*, finds a thousand expressions in contemporary Spain. First of all, in the claim made by the autonomist parties, born with the present century, in the Basque country, in Cataloña, and in Galicia. And again, in the orientation of Spanish syndicalism. Gradually formed in the northern part of the country, from about 1850 on, this labor union movement was likewise characterized by a fierce individualism which found expression in anarcho-syndicalism.

Thus, at the end of the nineteenth and at the beginning of the twentieth century, the most active social groups in the north of the Peninsula were defending, each under its own flag—Carlist, anarcho-syndicalist, autonomist—doctrines aimed against the enemy State. Each group in its own way strove to limit governmental powers as far as possible, to transfer the greater part of authority to lesser collectivities linked directly with the people: regional organisms, municipalities, trade groups or guilds, unions, and workers' federations.

Informed by the tenacious ambition for total democracy and, at the same time, enlightened by the first failures of representative democracy, both Unamuno and Ortega y Gasset, leaders of the 1898 generation, amply understood that the Spanish temperament was incompatible with institutions which had originated among other races. There was a need henceforth to study the Spaniard and his specific leanings, in order to create institutions to fit him. *En Torno al Casticismo*,[4] *España Invertebrada*,[5] indeed all the masterworks

---

[4] *En Torno al Casticismo*, by Miguel de Unamuno (born in Bilbao in 1864, died in Salamanca in 1936), was published in 1895. Even more than the *Idearium Español*, written in 1897 by Ángel Ganivet (1862-98), Unamuno's work was the manifesto of the "generation of 1898." The noun "casticismo" means the purity (of the race, of a style), the quality of that which is "castizo," that is, pure from the point of view of race or style. These terms, "cas-

of contemporary Spanish letters, express the anxiety of a people in search of itself, striving to find itself or, rather, to rediscover itself. In this way, breaking with the abstract and universal vision of human nature which made no allowances for the diverse and never-static reality of man, the writers of 1898 reintroduced the concrete man, the Spanish man in a sociological outline. Forty years after the Marxist message, they inaugurated a new cycle in Spanish thought and today we cannot reflect upon the Spanish reality without being, in some way, their disciples. To be faithful to them, one must abandon them, leave them behind and go ahead on that road which they opened up. And no one can go back to a pre-Ortegan time, to a sociological analysis from which man would be missing. In Spain, concrete or actual man, with his specific temperament and tendencies, is as present in history as is the past in each instant lived.

III

In making room for man and for his history within our analysis, we envisage this analysis within a social and psychological evolution. Yet can we exclude from our study the event itself, the circumstantial happening? We could state, for example, that the currents of opinion and the existing socio-economic conditions which led to the civil war of 1936 already contained the germ of Franco's triumph and all its consequences. But a change in the government at London, the accidental death of Mussolini, or an increase in the arms supplies from France and England to the republican forces could have meant a Republican victory. The state of mind of the population, as well as the known socio-economic factors, would have been profoundly modified. Thus, a mechanism of interreactions is established among man, the conjuncture, and the event. Born of a psychological evolution and a given conjuncture, the event in turn works a change in them.

---

tizo" and "casticismo," apply to Castilian purity. "Casticismo" might be translated as "Spanishness," "Hispanicity."
5 *España Invertebrada*, essay by the philosopher José Ortega y Gasset (1883-1955), was published in 1922.

But the need to embrace the event within our considerations singularly complicated the matter. Blurred by the foibles of memory, deformed by prejudice, the event required clarification, formulation. And such reminders, brief though they might be, could not help but encumber our reasoning.

Have we succeeded in according their rightful place to the facts and in resolving the difficulties implicit in the ambition of our purpose? We are at least assured that no one today may look at the problems of Spain without inserting in the abstract development of socio-economic analysis that which is ineradicable in the past, specific in the race, determinant in the event.

PART ONE

The Presence of the Past

Chapter One

❦

THE SPANIARD
AND HIS SURROUNDINGS

TO WHAT EXTENT is the Spaniard conditioned by his geographic environment? If he is a forger of history, is he, in turn, forged by history or did he rather, from the beginning, present specific traits explicable in the light of ethnic factors?

If we were to draw an ethnographic map of the Iberian Peninsula, taking into account only the given conditions from the start of the historic era, we would divide it into population zones entirely separate one from another. To the Northwest, Atlantic Spain: Celtic in Galicia, Celtic and Germanic in the Asturias; to the East and the South, Mediterranean Spain: influenced by the Phoenicians, Carthaginians, and Romans, bearing the deep imprint, at least in the South—in Valencia and in Murcia—of successive waves of Berber and Arab invaders. Northern Castile and upper Aragon are Latin and Germanic. Southern Castile and Andalusia are at once Latin, Germanic, and Arabic-Berber. These diverse Spains would be utterly foreign to one another and, conversely, similar to foreign peoples of the same ethnic origin.

Behind the diversity of individual and local traits, we can discern certain specific characteristics common to all the peoples of the Peninsula and in no way reminiscent of any of the invaders. Singular among these is undoubtedly the matriarchal tradition which, foreign to all of the Indo-European races, was practically intact in the Basque-Pyrenees region until fairly recently. Today it persists in certain aspects of Spanish life, particularly in the inheritance laws, the most feminist in all Europe,[1] and in the exalted cult of motherhood which has reigned from the beginning of time in Spain. Excluded from political life, from the cafés, from the majority of professions, the wife and mother are invested with despotic authority in the home. Catholicism has undergone matriarchal changes to such a point that God the Father and God the Creator have been almost totally suppressed. On the one hand, God the Son is the incarnation of weakness, of the falling away and of death; on the other, the obsessive beating of drums underscores the majestic presence—on the altar or on the processional float slowly propelled by the throng—of the goddess-mother, sparkling with precious stones, the miraculous and omniscient idol polarizing all the mystic fervor of the race.

These rites and institutions contrast so markedly with the spirit of the three deliberately "masculine" civilizations implanted in the Peninsula at the historic epoch—the Roman, the Germanic, and the Moslem—that we can explain them only as the resurgence of earlier tendencies, the heritage of a race which must have occupied the greater part of the Peninsula before the Celtic invasion in the sixth century B.C. The classic theory, expounded by Humboldt, identifies the

---

[1] By Spanish law, a married woman keeps her maiden name, adding to it the name of her husband. The children bear obligatorily the names of both father and mother. When there is no brother as successor, all titles and entailed estates go to the wife; a titled woman gives her title to her husband. Similar are those provisions of Basque common law by which the eldest daughter, rather than her brothers, inherits the family home.

first inhabitants of Spain with the Iberians and states that this people, which came from the Caucasus, did not belong to the Indo-European group. Whether or not we accept this interpretation[2], we may be certain that at least the majority of the peninsular population of the prehistoric epoch was composed of tribes which differed greatly from all North African and European peoples. Gradually, they absorbed their successive conquerors and, at the same time, assimilated the superficial elements of their respective civilizations.

As early as the Roman period, the Celtiberian population, born of the union of the first inhabitants with the Celtic invaders, bore specific and strongly marked traits which differed only slightly from those of modern Spaniards. The Celtiberians carried to an excess that menaced public liberties a passion for personal freedom; even then they seemed keener on dying for their liberties than uniting for a common defense.

This innate individualism was to become more specific, emphasized by the environment and, from the first, by the long struggle of Spanish men against an arid land.

1. LAND WITHOUT WATER

Not that Spain is poor. No other western European country presents simultaneously both varied and ample agricultural possibilities and a like richness of subsoil.

Second in land area of all western European countries, Spain has 21,000,000 *hectares* (1 *hectare* = 2.47 acres), or forty-two per cent of her total land surface, under cultivation. This figure, only one-third lower than the corresponding figure for France—the richest country of western Europe—is more than twice as high as that for Great Britain. Considering the relatively scant population of Spain, the amount of cultivated land per person (91 *ares*, the *are* being the

---

[2] A contemporary theory, that of Pericot García, assimilates the original race to the Ligurians. By this same theory the Iberians, of African origin, influenced the primitive civilizations of southwest Spain, especially the civilization of Tartessos.

hundredth part of a *hectare*, or 100 square meters) is considerably greater than that in any other western European country.[3] The soil in Spain is among the most productive in the world. Wherever water is not lacking, the yield is extremely high. On the Atlantic coast—where excessive rains sometimes rot the wheat—the yield is equal to that of la Beauce, the fertile region just to the south of Paris: seventeen *quintals* (or about seventeen cwt.) per *hectare*.[4] When the soil is artificially irrigated, the yield varies between sixteen and nineteen *quintals* on the *meseta*, is about twenty in the Ebro region (Navarre, Aragon, Cataloña), and goes as high as twenty-three *quintals* in Sevilla, twenty-five in the *vega* of Valencia and the *huerta* of Murcia, and from twenty-five to thirty in the *vega* of Granada. The very low yield of most of the regions of the *meseta* (six to ten *quintals* per *hectare*) is explained by aridity alone. Indeed, the irrigated land (*regadío*) produces an average of twice as much as the dry regions (*secano*). The *regadíos*, accounting for scarcely a twentieth part of the land planted to wheat (250,000 *hectares* out of 5,000,000), yield one tenth of the harvest.

Water, rare in even the richest parts of the Valencian *huerta*, is rigorously rationed and controlled by the *Tribunal de las Aguas*. Water is the cause of more court cases and lawsuits than is the ownership of land. In certain Aragon communities, water is more expensive than wine. Only in the royal gardens is water used lavishly; hence, for the Spaniard, a fountain is the very image of luxury, symbol of a world of joy and ease. Everywhere except on the Cantabrian coast,

[3] The following statistics date from immediately before the civil war:

	Cultivated Land Area (1000 *ares*)	Population	Land Area Per Person (in *ares*)
Spain	2,100,000	23,000,000	91.3
France	3,000,000	42,000,000	71.5
Germany	2,500,000	65,000,000	38.4
Gr. Britain	900,000	45,000,000	20.0

[4] In the last few years, modern agricultural methods have greatly augmented these figures, particularly in France, in the United States, in Russia, and in China. Spain however is so far from practicing these methods that a comparison founded on the present situation would give a false notion of the natural productivity of Spanish soil. Therefore we have based our comparisons on figures valid immediately prior to the civil war.

prosperity is signified by nothing more than a victory over aridity. Thus, at all times in Spanish history, irrigation should have been the prime national objective.[5] But irrigation works, which were beyond the means even of the great landholders, required a large-scale collective effort, which could be achieved only by the State or, at least, by regional public agencies.

Similarly, the development of mineral resources was seriously impeded. The world's most important producer of mercury (sixty per cent of the global total) and foremost European producer of copper (third on a world-wide scale), Spain, at the beginning of this century, ranked sixth among the world's producers of iron, thanks to the lodes of the Basque country.[6] Rich in lead (Jaen, Peñarroya, Córdoba, Murcia) and in tungsten (the western regions), Spain also produces zinc (the Atlantic zone), manganese (Oviedo, Huelva), and sulfur (Teruel, Albacete). But the coal yield is very poor, in quality and in quantity, and it was this dearth which effectively braked the rise of Spanish industry in the nineteenth century when coal was the sole source of energy. The example set by Sweden proves, however, that the lack of coal need not necessarily prevent industrial development.

[5] Total irrigated land in 1950 amounted to only 1,500,000 *hectares*, against 18,000,000 *hectares* of *secanos* and 1,500,000 *hectares* of land in the rainy Atlantic region. Yet, according to plans drawn up in 1933, the irrigated area could be doubled: 3,048,000 *hectares* divided among the Ebro region and the eastern Pyrenees (853,284 *hectares*); the tributary basin north of the Duero, between the Cantabrian range and the river (1,022,100 *hectares*); New Castile and the Extremadura—the Tago and Guadiana regions (300,000 *hectares*), the Río Jucar region—Valencia—(167,200 *hectares*), the Río Segura-Murcia region (155,530 *hectares*), and Andalusia (449,885 *hectares*).

[6] The absolute and relative figures for the world's principal iron producers were as follows, on the eve of the Civil War in 1936:

	World Production (in tons)	World Rank	Prod/person (in kg*)	World Rank
United States	74,200,000	1	600	4
France	50,731,000	2	1,200	3
England	13,215,000	3	290	5
Sweden	11,468,000	4	1,890	2
Luxembourg	7,571,000	5	25,000	1
Spain	6,559,000	6	280	6

* 1 kg. = 2.2 lbs.

Sweden, whose iron production was still no more important than that of Spain in the early years of this century, was obliged to import all needed coal; yet she created a great modern industry. Undoubtedly Spain could obtain like results, but at the cost of developing production and fixing quotas for superfluous imports, in order to preserve funds for the purchase of coal and machinery. In short, there was need of a long-range systematic plan for the whole country. Just as in agricultural development, so too in industry and mining, the resources latent in Spain could be extracted and turned to good account only at the cost of a vast collective effort. Coordination, foresight, method: these were the conditions indispensable to the achievement of prosperity. And it was precisely these conditions which the Iberian character found the most repugnant. At the very root of Spanish poverty, there is a divorce between man and the soil, between the individual energies of men and the effort toward collective discipline required for cultivation of the soil. Hence, Spanish mineral deposits, sometimes neglected and more often ceded to foreign development companies, have enriched only foreign stockholders and a few Spanish businessmen. Today, after half a century of intensive mining, Spain's iron reserves are close to exhaustion and her veins of copper ore almost dried up.

Still more grave is the way in which agricultural resources have been laid waste. Deforestation and greedy cultivation of the soil without care for the future, with no other thought than the immediate yield, have made way for the scourge of scourges: erosion. Rains streaming over the bare soil drag along the fertile humus, uncover the stark rock, dig gullies in the fields, and cause landslides which in turn damage the paths of communication and dump sand in the waterways. This evil is apparent everywhere but is particularly evident along the Mediterranean shore,[7] an area in Spain distinguished by the longest history of human occupation and

[7] Eight inches of topsoil is eroded during a period of 174,000 years in forested land, 29,000 in the prairies, 100 on cultivated land, and 17 on fallow land. Today from thirty to fifty per cent of hitherto cultivated slopes in the Mediterranean region are abandoned.

simultaneously unfavorable natural conditions: uneven terrain, rare but torrential rains. Yet even in the Mediterranean region, few are the lands in which human destruction of nature is so extensive as in Castile. In every country man, when pitted against nature, demonstrates the barbarous mentality of an occupying army; it is the Castilian peasant who outstrips all others in his enmity to nature.

The Castilian peasant sullenly tenants the parched land and gazes toward the goal of immediate utility; hating all life foreign to man, he wages a war of extermination against the trees which protect his land and the birds which destroy harmful insects. Such sins bear their own punishment. Fierce rapacity destroys future gain by destroying the soil and the life it supports. And the destructive labor of man is completed by the greediness of the sheep. Throughout the Mediterranean region, in fact, sheep are among the chief causes of damage to the land; but the evil is greatest in Spain where for four hundred years, from the fifteenth to the nineteenth century, the herds of the Mesta, an association of sheep-raisers, were privileged to pass over all the land without any restriction whatever.[8] Not only did the hordes of sheep lay waste the year's crops but also by stamping on the ground caused its deterioration, grazed the land clean, and stripped the protective bark from the trees which thus vulnerable were not long in dying.

The ravages of the land, resulting from brutal human occupation, are aggravated by archaic methods of cultivation. The cultivator himself, whether small landowner or laborer, pushes over the drought-cracked land the ancient wooden plough used by his ancestors as early as the period of Roman domination. Such unfavorable conditions call for the utmost effort and labor; hence, in virtually no other country is the

---

[8] The privileges of the Mesta, granted in 1511, were abolished in the eighteenth century. The corporation itself was dissolved in 1835, by the government created by the liberal uprising. During the fifteenth and sixteenth centuries, the Mesta owned up to 7,000,000 head of sheep, divided into herds of 10,000. The overall number of sheep was to decrease considerably during the centuries that followed. The Mesta possessed its own tribunals which, both judges and parties in the cases contested between small farmers and big sheep-raisers, consistently reached decisions favorable to the latter.

farmer more sober and industrious. To a foreigner, the Valencian peasant appears rich and indolent; yet, to reach water, he must struggle to break the arid crust of the land. The Castilian peasant, thin and gnarled, continues in mute tenacity at his exhausting task, though rendered almost useless by the lack of equipment, the general disorganization, and the shirking of responsibility on the part of the authorities.

Thus, it matters little that the soil and the subsoil of Spain offer vast possibilities for development. The overriding factor in the past and at present is that poverty which may be imputed both to natural obstacles and to the Spaniard's inability to surmount them: A poverty which bears the stamp of man and which, in turn, places its stamp upon man, moulds him, deforms him.

2. INDIVIDUALISM AND THE TRAGIC SENSE OF LIFE

In this hostile atmosphere, there came into being a hard and willful kind of man, withdrawn into himself. And these characteristics, acquired in the course of constant struggle against the inclemency of the elements, were accentuated by a seven-year war against the African invader, a permanent *guerrilla* on no fixed front. Mounted on their fleet horses, the Moslem fighters might appear at any time just outside a village of the Castilian *meseta*. Merchants, artisans, peasants, serfs, each had to provide for his own defense. The common danger leveled social distinctions. Everyman in his fields became warrior and lord. Everyman was, above all, a man alone, faced with danger, with arid land, with death everywhere and ever present.

This long familiarity with death has marked the men of Spain. The taste for bloody spectacles—the *corridas*—proves that the perception of death is greater in Spain than in any other western European country.

And, assuredly, at the very instant when the death agony is expressed in the attention lavished by *aficionado* upon the arena, the man who is prey to this complex is not clearly conscious of the motives for his action. Were he to inquire into the nature of his penchant, the Spaniard would come up with trifling reasons; our minds secrete the rationalizations required by our passions. But the Spaniard does not question himself; his mind does not trace back the obscure plodding transmutations of the mind into the hidden root of his vital anguish. Thus it is difficult for an analysis to reveal the causes of this anxiety.

Must we believe, as does Unamuno, that the Spaniard is pushed toward the anguish of death by his ungovernable love of life, by the savor of life during those fleet hours of relaxation and joy in this world of ardor and color? Or is it rather that his love of life is strong because he senses that life is unstable, precarious, fleeting—because life slips out of his reach? It matters little where exactly the dividing line may lie if, by a symbiosis to which all literature bears witness, life and death nourish each other. From the *coplas* of Jorge Manrique[9] to Unamuno's *Del Sentimiento Trágico de la Vida*, from the *Sonetos* of Quevedo[10] to the *Don Juan* of Zorrilla[11] and to that other hymn to death which is García Lorca's *Llanto por Ignacio Sánchez Mejías*,[12] there is not an essayist or a poet, a novelist or a philosopher in Spain who could not speak these words attributed by Machado to García Lorca:

[9] Jorge Manrique (1440-78) is the great Spanish poet of the fifteenth century. His *Coplas a la muerte de su padre*, very popular in Spain, were penned in memory of his father, Don Rodrigo Manrique, Count of Paredes, master of the Order of Calatrava, who died in 1476. Manrique resembles his French contemporary, François Villon, by his choice of themes: fleeting time inducing anxiety, nostalgia for the past. . . . His *coplas* are distinguished by their pattern of two octosyllabic lines followed by a line of *pie quebrado*, that is, a short four- or five-foot line.

[10] Francisco de Quevedo y Villegas (1580-1645) is one of the greatest writers of the Siglo de Oro, Golden Century. Poet, whose sonnets are famous, he was also novelist (*El Buscón*), and author of *Los Sueños*, original works rather like pamphlets or essays.

[11] *Don Juan Tenorio*, written in 1844, by the romantic writer José Zorrilla (1817-93), is freely derived from the classic drama by Tirso de Molina, *El Burlador de Sevilla*, which dates from 1630. Zorrilla's romantic *Don Juan* is the most popular work in the Spanish repertory.

[12] This celebrated poem was written by Federico García Lorca in 1935 to commemorate the death of a young matador during a *corrida*.

Hoy, como ayer, gitana, muerta mía,
Qué bien contigo a solas, . . .[13]

Man cannot live with the idea of his annihilation. To live, he needs the illusion of a superlife. From the torment of his irresolution before death, he has wrought a *"Dios Inmortalizador."* [14]

The living man who instinctively aspires to continue, to persevere in his being, in fact secretes incantatory myths of death, just as certain animals, in their own defense, secrete certain juices and poisons. Man is never wholly the dupe of his myths: a doubt slips in behind the very core of the most deeply rooted faith; a gleam of hope survives amidst total negation. Forever torn between the need to believe in the survival of his "self" and the faculty of reason which cripples his hope, man lives in doubt. The essential doubt is the fate of our mortal nature revolted by its mortality. But this doubt is stimulating, creative. The notion of death is the thorn in our side, yet this thorn represents incentive as well as pain. Each consciousness aroused to exasperation by the sense of its mortality strives to sharpen itself still further, to affirm itself, to make itself irreplaceable, thus to prove that it did not deserve to die—to prove it by action and by works, in the writing of a book, in the reshaping of the world, in the laying of its stamp upon this world, in bringing forth cities, in battling with bulls. . . . Whether as a gratuitous single combat in the lists conceived for the purpose of permitting knights of the Middle Ages and the classic period, their lances pitted against the wild beast, to prove their strength and valor; or as a bloody spectacle offered to the multitude which, identifying themselves with the combatant, fell

[13] Antonio Machado, *El Crimen fué en Granada* (The Crime Committed at Granada), poem commemorating the murder of García Lorca.

> Today, as yesterday, gipsy, you: my death,
> How good it is to be alone with you . . .

Born at Sevilla in 1875, Machado himself was to be a victim of the civil war: he died at Collioure, in French territory, on February 22, 1939, of a pulmonary infection brought on by the retreat from Cataloña.
[14] Unamuno, *Del Sentimiento Trágico de la Vida.*

with their own arms the beast Death; the *corrida* is always a form, active or passive, of affirmation of being in the face of menacing death.

In this way the unconscious anguish of mortality takes on a thousand faces and arouses the most diverse reactions. It impels action and engenders spectacle. And the same phenomenon is at the origin of the Don Juan myth. Not in vain was this myth, although symbolic of a universal tendency, forged and developed in a country where the anguish over mortality is everywhere apparent. Of all our emotions, carnal love is in fact that in which love of ourselves has the greatest place. The person loved tests his power; he exercises it. Don Juan multiplies his conquests because each of them is a victory for the "self"—and any form of affirmation of being is a victory over death, that death which in Tirso de Molina's classic drama, as well as in Zorrilla's romantic *Don Juan*, is present on stage the moment the curtain rises.

It is symptomatic that the *Don Juan* of Zorrilla be played in all the cities of Spain around the time of All Saints' Day. The drama of Don Juan is part of the Spanish ritual of death. Don Juan is the symbol of the Spaniard, consumed by his anguish over mortality, vainly seeking to prove himself in victory and domination, that his irreplaceable "self" may not die, that he may always persist in the integrity of his being.

If we take as a basis the anguish over mortality, we may reconstitute the process of the Spaniard's psychological evolution. As long as Catholicism offered to Spanish society the certainty of the survival of being, individuals consented to subordinate themselves to the disciplines of the collective life. But the fifteenth and sixteenth centuries, when the passionate nature of Spanish Catholicism was to find its most spectacular manifestation, actually mark the beginning of a progressive weakening of religious convictions. At this time the spirit of the Renaissance made its way into the court and the large cities, in the wake of the officers and dauphin-soldiers returned from Italy where they had gone to fight from Ceresole d'Alba to Lepanto and from Naples to Taranto in the *Tercios* of the Constable Gonzalo of Córdoba or on the galleys of Don Juan of Austria. But at this moment the discovery of the New World presented to the Spanish a new task, a new enterprise. Scarcely ten months separate the moment when the Catholic Kings entered into delivered Granada from that other moment when the lookout of the "Santa María," spying the outline of the isle of San Salvador on the Caribbean horizon, cried "Land ho!" and Christopher Columbus and his crew went down upon their knees to offer thanks to God for a success whose significance they were, nonetheless, far from appreciating. One great enterprise was coming to an end; another was being launched. The Spanish people continued to live in the passion-charged tension of a great task, where each "self" found the chance for affirmation, a chance to blossom in the achievement of a collective design. In the abundant disorder of individual improvisations, in the tension which united individual energies or set them tumultuously against one another, a new world was to be forged with its distinctive features and its mode of living, its nonchalance and its vitality. Citadels erected upon the foundations of ramparts overlooking the Caribbean, cathedrals and palaces, *alcázars* and universities, an entire new Spain in stone thrust itself into the luxuriance of the tropics.

The conditions for living offered to the Spaniard at this time were those which Ortega y Gasset was to define, in our day, as the most propitious to a well-balanced society. In defining the collective life as a task proposed and assumed, a continuous "to do" oriented toward the future, Ortega formulated a social clinician's diagnosis; but he also expressed the Spaniard's desire or need, the state of mind of a man in quest of an objective, of a program for the future which could justify the individual effort. All energies focus and depend for their validity upon the future. Each time the program for the future proposed to the masses by an active minority was sufficiently attractive to justify their support, sufficiently probable to authorize hope, Spanish society attained a moment of equilibrium between communal disciplines and the liberty of individual inclinations. At that moment the task to be accomplished galvanized all energies. Anchored in his vision of the future, the Spaniard marched straight toward the target. In the grip of this impetuosity, he confined himself to the most rigorous asceticism. Failure was simply not taken into account. When Hernán Cortez debarked on the coast of Mexico with three hundred soldiers, he caused all his ships to be burned: to envisage the possibility of return whence he had sailed would have meant to accept failure. From that instant, the case was one of conquer or die.

No sooner does the target appear elusive than the high tension is interrupted, whether the target be reached or out of reach, debased or improbable. The most serious of these imbalances occurred toward the end of the seventeenth century and the beginning of the eighteenth. There was no longer a Christianity to defend, a New World to build. The sole problem which confronted the Spanish people—as indeed all the peoples of western Europe—was that of well-being, of arranging a life of greater ease, brought about by increased production and technical progress. The machine age was beginning. And in this new era, the Spaniard appears an exile.

Yet he is technically minded and has always favored scientific research with an intellectual curiosity so vivid that it is termed anxiety. In regard to the mysteries of nature, the Spanish intellectual is not only attentive and curious but he is also anxious. . . . The distance from pure science to applied technique is easily covered, and, indeed, for the past century-and-a-half, has had at its service as competent engineers and as efficient, qualified labor as have other Western nations; Spanish workmen are quite European in their ardent taste for mechanics. Whoever pauses a moment in the suburbs of a Spanish city toward the end of the afternoon will notice that every man is busy putting together, taking apart, inspecting, adjusting some bit of machinery, something obsolete perhaps: an old motor, a bicycle, an old blunderbuss left behind by the turn of the century.

But even at the highest pitch of pleasure in this pastime, the technical element is never promoted beyond its rightful, and modest, place. To a Spaniard, the material aspect of his existence, its comfort or its decor, is by no means a goal. To live fully, the race requires a new myth. Its greatness, like its misery, lies in its inability to burgeon in a climate other than the tense impassioned effort toward an end which overwhelms it. When the basis of a program for the future is lacking, when society no longer offers some thing which will allow his "self" to grow stronger while being of service, the Spaniard sags like a dismembered puppet or seeks escape in unbridled individualism.

The vacancy in which he begins to drown as soon as hope leaves him is only a temporary refuge. Sensing that each second is gnawing away at the substance of his being while moulding his personality, that life is eluding him and his "self" crumbling, he feels the need to assert his own individuality and to prove it to others. Finding no chance to act, to shine in a collective enterprise, he will strive to assert himself outside of or even against society—by chatter or insolence, by bragging or vice, by crime or destructiveness. For to destroy is one way to make a mark upon reality, to leave one's stamp upon it.

Thus, indifferent to the disciplines and the aims of the communal life, each man, withdrawn into himself (*ensimismado*), seeks by means only subjectively valid to create a microcosm where he will be the undisputed king. In this way, society fragments itself into a sort of fine dust of little subjective worlds which most often brush past one another in reciprocal oblivion but which now and then collide violently.

3. THE INDIVIDUAL IN THE SOCIAL CONTEXT

Despite his exaggerated individualism, the Spaniard is not isolated. In fact, one of his fundamental character traits is a sociability which at times opposes his individualism and at others feeds upon it.

Here, as elsewhere, the language is revealing. Spanish sociability is expressed in a word without equivalent in, for instance, French: *convivencia*—life in common, communal life. (The English word "conviviality" does not quite render this.) For the Spaniard, life is *convivencia*; life is open and shared with others—neighbors, fellow workmen, even passers-by, strangers, foreigners. No matter what his social status, the Spaniard is the habitué of a certain café where his *tertulia*, or gathering of friends, regularly takes place. The *tertulia* is more than a custom: it is an institution in Spanish life, the perfect example of a (free-spontaneous) society in which words are the links.

The compartment of a French or of an English railway carriage is simply a place where several individuals are juxtaposed. In Spain, the compartment is transformed into a community. The persons already seated move over to make room for those who come in later and soon a dozen or fourteen people are squeezed into an eight-seat compartment. Conversation becomes general. Each traveler must oblige his companions with the story of his life, and courtesy requires that his neighbors hear out his story in order that he will listen to theirs.

Abroad, Spanish people seek each other out and recognize each other before having spoken a word. If a Spaniard adopts a certain bar or restaurant, he is not long in bringing in his friends, and they in turn introduce other compatriots. The place is transformed into a meeting hall for the Spaniards of that city. Soon, there appear one after another the *cocido* (*pot-au-feu* or stew), the *jerez* (sherry), the *turrón* (almond nougat), as well as flamenco recordings and out-of-work guitarists. Beneath a foreign sky, a new miniature Spain has appeared; the Spanish immigrants to this other land have brought Spain with them—dishes and odors, language and customs, *tertulias* and *chistes* (epigrams or funny stories). Into foreign surroundings they have thrust the closed and intangible world they carry within their hearts. They may spend their lives in exile, yet never feel exiled. Having lived for years in another country, they know only the barest rudiments of that country's tongue. A young Madrileño was asked what he had learned in the course of a year's apprenticeship in Paris; the young man was one of those post-civil war children who grew up in the street, fatherless and school-less, and after a moment of thought he replied: "I think I have begun to learn to speak Spanish."

All the more sociable because of his individualism, the Spaniard must come in contact with his brothers, must become part of a group. Yearning to talk about himself, he must find a confidant, a witness; he must have an audience. The effect of individualism is thus to tighten the social ties of family, work, neighborhood, all the while heightening their formal nature. A society whose social ties are narrow and complex tends, in effect, to codify the attitudes and formulae befitting every circumstance of the communal life. Indeed, there are few countries in which formality is pushed to such an extreme. In Spain, there is a ritual of collective life the survival of which may be explained by the immobility of a society which, except in the large industrial centers of the north, has not been penetrated by modern technique.

Of all the countries of the West, it is in Spain we find the clearest statement of man's permanence through the ages. The traveler who crosses the Castilian *meseta* finds himself side by side with the peasants and soldiers, the students and monks, the mule drivers and serving girls whom Don Quixote knew in these same village inns. And everywhere reigns the same exquisite urbanity; even in the working-class suburbs of the big cities we may find a somewhat dimmed reflection of it. American tourists in search of "picturesque Spain" may wander at will among the *chabolas* (hovels) of Madrid's "slum belt" without risking an insult. The worker who meets the rapid fire of their questions with his disdainful courtesy proves that the civilization—i.e., civility—of a people has nothing whatever to do with its level of education or its material prosperity. If, as the Spanish are pleased to maintain, the modern world is full of *barbaros ilustrados* (learned savages), then the Spaniard is aware of being an ignorant civilized man. While it may take only a few months to train a good technician, man in the most noble sense, a precious and precarious sketch of the civilized human, is the product of several millennia of history and the rarest conjunction of fortune and misfortune.

Social formalism is one of the major aspects of this civilization, so ancient that civilization has become flesh, blood, and instinct; has become the man himself. Undoubtedly this formalism is sometimes a source of disturbance and disorder: the need to defend the "self" brings on arguments, quarrels, brawls, revenge. But, more often, formalism is a source of order and harmony. It moves the most impoverished and crude of Spanish peasants to welcome the traveler and foreigner into his home, to put his house at the disposal of the passer-by for an unlimited time. This rite of hospitality is stronger than the harshness of the most miserly peasant or the most unruly character. The man who considers that he has been insulted under his own roof would also consider that he made himself mean were he to forget the calm dignity custom demands in such a situation. His chief care is *quedar proper*—to remain proper—to abide by the prescribed attitude. By "remaining proper" a man earns his self-esteem. He shows that he can rise above others and above circumstances. To "remain proper" is one form of affirmation of the "self."

This somewhat dramatic conception of social life, by which a man considers himself the principal actor in a play, either drama or comedy, confers upon the interlocutors and witnesses a secondary role; that of satellites of the "self." The term "satellite" should not be taken as referring to a social hierarchy. If the action by which a man seeks to assert himself is political, he will undoubtedly look for subordinates in the social sense of the term. If the action is rather literary or artistic, the individual may wish for ministers, princes, kings, to praise and patronize his achievements. But no matter how eminent the social position of the witnesses, they inevitably play a secondary role in any action involving the "self." This tendency constitutes a predisposition to intolerance. Indeed, while he pays his respects to another through the formulae of refined courtesy custom demands of him, at that very moment the Spaniard is miles away from even conceiving of the other person's point of view. This mental impermeability turns every dialogue into a misunder-standing, not likely to be resolved, because each party to it—walled within himself and speaking for his own benefit—pays very little attention to the arguments which are opposed to him. If he were to accord awareness to the disagreement which places him in opposition to others, he would be as offended by it as by an attack upon his inner world, his personality. And certainly he would be right in thinking an insult had been offered to all that he holds most dear: to the illusion that is indispensable to him. The world must be as his vital need of the world depicts it.

Thus, the Spaniard is tempted to refuse to make those concessions demanded by the social *convivencia*, while his natural sociability and craving for self-assertion compel him to multiply the number of his contacts and to become in-tegrated into diverse groups, whose existence and continua-tion require, in return, a certain willingness to abandon the pretensions of the "self." Usually, this fundamental contra-diction is resolved by the similarity of tastes and opinions which exists among the members of these lesser groups, in which the individual may easily find companions whose men-tality, hopes, and interests differ but little from his own.

All minor groups, whatever their separate natures and aims—cities or labor unions, associations or *tertulias*, ath-letic clubs or political parties—contain a common characteris-tic: each of their members plays a personal role. The indi-vidual takes part in discussions of problems with which he is familiar and upon whose solution his personal interest may depend. Even if the individual is not one of the group's leaders, he knows the leaders personally. He speaks with them at the café or in the street, and can bring to bear on them a certain pressure or influence. In this lies the satis-faction of a need for personal action, an "activism" which to the Spaniard is the first corollary of individualism and manifestation of the personality; by belonging to minor groups, he manages to have an impression of acting, of having some control over happenings and over other people.

On the other hand, in the case of the individual's relationship with the State, the constraints enforced upon the personality outweigh the satisfactions obtained from individualist feeling. It is not surprising that the most significant acts in the life of the average voter are those of renunciation. The individual is urged to delegate his powers to a deputy, to be self-effacing before a representative he knows scarcely or not at all and who nonetheless is going to act, to play a role, to shine on a distant and remote stage, beyond the surveillance of the voter or the militant. The individual does not feel that he has any control over the apparatus of the State —that so distant and complex mechanism, so difficult to grasp. The State is constantly manifest to him in the form of orders, prohibitions, obligations which the authorities force him to respect.

Perhaps that realism which is one of the essential traits of the Iberian character, when joined to individualism, causes the Spaniard's profound non-comprehension of the notion of the State. He grasps easily enough the advantages and implications of a situation related to his region or his profession, hence one immediately perceptible. But when he has only an abstract image of other interests and relationships, his conception of them is imperfect. The Spaniard is gifted with a lively imagination. But it is a visual imagination, nourished by the concrete and operating with difficulty in the abstract.

In his inability to grasp the abstract notion of the State, the individual has trouble distinguishing it from the concrete personality of the leaders of the day. Hence he tries to remove himself from the scope of the limitations and obligations which, to his mind, emanate from an oligarchy of spoils-reapers. The latent anti-Statism of the Spaniard, his mistrust, extends to the political party: the group whose objective it is to control the levers which command the State. Ordinarily, Spanish political parties are minority formations, whereas the masses turn toward local or corporative organisms more concretely apparent to them: town councils, unions, fellowships. . . .

Thus on the fringe of the State, or in opposition to it,

thrives a number of lesser collectivities, village or corporate, each microcosm directed toward its own goal, each one exhausted by the central power in an incessant centripetal movement, reassembling, incorporating into an overall plan, into a program for communal life.

Chapter Two

SPAIN AND
THE SEVERAL SPAINS

IN THE PAST, people spoke of the several Spains; today, of
Spain. Between the plural and singular stretch centuries of
struggle: struggle which in the nineteenth and twentieth
centuries, at the time of the awakening of peninsular na-
tionalisms, was often undertaken to safeguard the extant
fueros (charters) or to revive abolished *fueros.*

The term *fuero* has only recently come to mean a
charter granting to racial or linguistic minorities certain
rights in opposition to the arbitrary force of the central
power. This new interpretation of an old word grew up
gradually in the Spanish consciousness between the seventeenth and nineteenth centuries, during a period in which the
fueros were already disputed, threatened, or abolished. While
they were endowed with legal force, the *fueros* ruled over the
relations between various collectivities, and between such
groups and individuals. They constituted the common law of
ancient Spain, guaranteeing to individuals as well as to lesser

collectivities—town councils, corporations, regions—liberties
ample enough that the diverse aspirations and personalities
of ethnic and cultural minorities might find room.

Why did this juridical system, the most original expression of the Iberic temperament, collapse between the seventeenth and nineteenth centuries? And by what historical
process did the decline of Spanish civil rights lead certain
peoples of the Peninsula to rise up against Spain so as to
assert their specific personality?

1. FORAL DEMOCRACY

The original "foral" law, the law of the *fueros,* was so far
from being a defense system directed against a central
power that at the moment when the *fuero* was born of
Iberian custom, Spain was still only a memory and a project;
conceived by the Asturian dynasty and sprung from the
recollection of a Roman administrative district.

The aspirations toward liberty of the Iberian peoples
grew ineluctably from the struggle against Mohammedanism.
Once the Moslems had triumphed, the Asturian dynasty was
too feeble to exercise any real power over the territories in
northern Spain subject to its nominal suzerainty. By breaking
the Roman-Visigoth framework of the State, the African
invasion was indirectly to foster the resurrection of a primitive civilization, formerly victim of the Roman and Germanic
conquests. Called upon to play a leading role in the Reconquest, the Celtiberian peoples who, dug into the mountains of
the north of the Peninsula, had escaped both Romanization
and Germanization, were not only to preserve but to perfect,
and even to bring back to the other parts of the country their
particular institutions and customs.

These customs differed from one region to another, but
beneath the diversity are certain common principles. During
the period of the *fueros'* crystallization, assemblies met at
more or less regular intervals in the Cantabrian and Pyrenees
villages. The serfs—who lived on the domains of the great
landholders, *los ricos hombres,* the rich men—were excluded

from these assemblies; but even the poorest free man sat as an equal with the *ricos hombres* in the local assemblies, which named magistrates invested with executive and judiciary power. From their decisions inspired by ancient customs, arose the common law: the *fuero*. The Arab threat obliged the village assemblies to select their magistrates from among the *ricos hombres*, gentlemen who had transformed their country houses into fortresses. Thus, the lords of primitive Spain exercised both a feudal power over their domains peopled by serfs[1] and a political power over the communities of

---

[1] The emancipation movement, begun in the twelfth century, achieved its goal in the late fifteenth century. While the number of serfs dwindled steadily during this period, the lot of those who remained in serfdom grew progressively less harsh. (It was forbidden to sell serfs with the land, tasks and periodic charges were stipulated, a serf's right to marry without the lord of the manor's consent was recognized.) Various factors influenced emancipation: intervention on the part of the Church or the sovereign; serfs' rebellions; arrangements arrived at between the serfs and their masters—who were either humanitarian or else aware that the yield from labor freely consented to is greater; and the right of asylum accorded in the city to a serf who made good his escape. But that factor which most favored emancipation was the Reconquest. Kings, *seigneurs*, governors who required soldiers and farmers to defend and people the newly reconquered territories accorded the status of free men to all who came forward as volunteers, regardless of their origins. The new horizon revealed by this possibility incited many serfs to escape their masters' lands. Their example was followed by a goodly number of *Mozarabes* (the term is a contraction of *Mozos de los Arabes*, that is, servants or serfs to the Arabs, and applies to the Spaniards who were reduced to serfdom by the Moslem invaders). The emancipation movement therefore made more rapid headway in the areas situated at the vanguard of the Reconquest: in León, then in Castile. As early as the end of the twelfth century, Alfonso XII, King of León, granted to serfs the right to leave their manors and to take along their cattle and belongings. Theoretically valid within the limits of León only, this permission, which spelled the end of serfdom (since those who remained on feudal manors did so of their own free will and hence could impose their own conditions), was quite often carried over into Castile as well. By her decision of October 28, 1480, Isabella the Catholic extended this right to the remaining serfs in the Castilian States—the two Castiles, the Asturias, León, Galicia, and the greater part of Andalusia. Emancipation came about more slowly in the States of Aragon, where numerous revolts by *payeses* (serfs) occurred in the fifteenth century. Ferdinand the Catholic, by a sentence handed down at Guadalupe, limited seignorial rights in the extreme and gave serfs the right to buy their freedom. The last traces of serfdom in Spain disappeared in the first half of the sixteenth century. It may be noted that, exceptionally, Christians were never held in serfdom in Valencia, reconquered from the Moors by the monarchs of Aragon. In this region, serfdom was reserved for Moslems, but must not be confused with the slavery which was reserved for Moslems who were taken prisoners of war.

free men possessed of legislative assemblies and a common law. During the ninth and tenth centuries, this political power, at first elective, became hereditary. Simultaneously there occurred a territorial reconstitution or collectivization. In most cases, the lesser lords or free communities agreed to subordinate themselves to a greater lord the better to defend themselves. This explains the birth, in the Atlantic and Pyrenees regions over which the Asturian dynasty claimed to have a [merely theoretical] sovereignty, of a series of little States which were actually independent: Kingdom of Galicia, Seigniory of Vizcaya, Kingdom of Navarre, Earldom of Barcelona, and the Earldom of Sobrarbe which was to become Aragon.[2]

Throughout this formative period, from the eighth to the tenth century, the *fueros* had retained their nature of oral customs. Beginning in the eleventh century and continuing until the thirteenth, the codification of the *fueros* was achieved in parallel to territorial reconstitution.[3] These codes,

[2] It is significant that almost all of the princes of these little States tried to legitimize their power by asserting that they descended from tribal chiefs of the period preceding the Roman conquest or the Visigoth kingdom. On the other hand, the Asturian kings justified their claim to sovereignty over these little princes by asserting that they descended from Visigoth monarchs.
[3] As early as the start of the eleventh century, the Asturian kingdom (which had conquered León in the ninth century) united with Castile. The latter had begun a military advance under the late-twelfth-century Asturian-Leónian monarchs. But the counts (governors) of Castile had become independent in the tenth century, under the reign of Fernán Gonzalez. Joined by a dynastic marriage to the Asturian-Leonian kingdom, Castile continued the Reconquest. In 1085, the troops of Alfonso IV returned to Toledo, the historic capital. Halted by new African invaders (the Almoravides and the Almohades), the forward march picked up again after the great victory in 1212 of Las Navas de Tolosa. The Castilians liberated Sevilla in 1248 and the greater part of Andalusia. Throughout this era, Galicia enjoyed a liberal *de facto* independence under the sovereignty of the Asturian-Castilian monarchs who had also come to rule over three Basque provinces (Alava, Guipúzcoa, Vizcaya) detached from the Kingdom of Navarre. The Kingdom of Aragon (arisen from the Earldom of Sobrarbe) liberated Saragossa, its natural capital, in 1108, and in 1137 was joined by a dynastic marriage to Cataloña. In the next century, the Cataloñan-Aragonian monarch, Jaime el Conquistador (1213-76) liberated the Balearic Islands (1229), Valencia (1238) which had been conquered in 1092 by El Cid's Castilian army and then reoccupied by the Moslems, and finally Alicante. From mid-thirteenth century until the end of the fifteenth, there were two great States (Castile, Aragon) in the Iberian Peninsula and

fruit of the sovereigns' effort—particularly that of the Asturian-Castilian monarchs—amounted to a synthesis between the written Romano-Germanic law (*fuero juzgo*) which the sovereigns tried to impose, and the popular *fueros* which they were obliged to recognize. In the texts of this period, popular law in fact greatly outbalanced written law. At the end of the thirteenth century, Alfonso el Sabio (Alfonso the Wise), King of Castile, explicitly stated the superiority of common law over written law by declaring in the *Código de las Siete Partidas*: "From usage springs custom, and from custom, the *fuero*." [4]

In rural communities as well as in cities, the *fuero* decreed a certain number of guarantees in favor of the governed: no free man could be subject to corporal punishment or imprisonment without trial; the domicile was inviolable. The *fuero* of Vizcaya provided for temporary freedom in certain cases, and stipulated that no one could be imprisoned for debt. Several *fueros* inaugurated a procedure of judicial appeal: in the Basque country, a condemned man could demand a second hearing, this time beneath the tree of Guernica[5]— an oak symbolic of Basque freedom. In several regions, the judicial power was separate from the executive. In Aragon, particularly, separation of the three powers was practiced five centuries before Montesquieu formulated its theory. At the summit of the judicial organization was a supreme justice— *Justicia mayor*—irremovable, fully independent of the executive, and having the power to bring up all cases, upon request of the parties involved, and to protect these parties by ordering their transfer to the prison of the *manifestados* at Saragossa.

At first very limited, the range of application of the *fueros* widened constantly. The *fuero* constituted in effect the

---

three small ones: Navarre, the Moslem realm of Granada (corresponding to the three present-day provinces of Granada, Málaga, and Almería), and Portugal.
[4] The *Código de las Siete Partidas* combined written laws and customs. Alfonso el Sabio, who ordered his jurists to compile the Code, reigned over Castile and León from 1252 to 1284.
[5] See note 19 of this chapter.

privilege of free men; gradually this privilege was extended to all serfs as they attained freedom. On the territorial level, the *fuero*, born of immemorial usage of the peoples in the northern Peninsula, was to become implanted in regions where this usage had long been interrupted. Indeed, among the most venerable and most perfect of codified *fueros* were those of León (1020) and Old Castile (early eleventh century). In these regions, conditions created by the permanent *guerrilla* against Moslem invaders fostered emancipation. Whether free men (soldiers or merchants) from the north, serfs escaped from the glebe-land to which they had been bound, or *Mozarabes* (Christian Spaniards escaped from the Moslem zone), those who had made their way to the wooded-palisaded parade ground of a *castillo* (castle) on the gentle Castilian plains were reluctant to leave this shelter and venture out into a countryside exposed to Berber raids. To enjoin them to settle on the advance posts of the Reconquest, the kings granted such men not only territorial concessions but also *cartas-pueblos* conferring upon them the power to govern their own communities and to designate their *alcaldes* (mayors) and judges.

Similarly, in southern Castile, local enfranchisement was born of the struggle against Mohammedanism. At Toledo in 1085, for instance, Christians who had organized themselves secretly to combat the occupying forces rose up at the approach of the troops of Alfonso VI and opened the city gates to the liberating army. The King was thus confronted by a community forged in struggle and comprised of active, enterprising men who sought complete liberty of action and were desirous that this liberty be guaranteed by a *fuero*. And indeed, the *fuero* of Toledo was considered in the Middle Ages to be the most complete and liberal of all municipal *fueros*.

The foral movement was considerably delayed elsewhere in New Castile. In the twelfth century other regions had been ceded to the knights of Alcantara and Calatrava in return for protection against the new African invaders—the Almoravides and Almohades dynasties. Toward the end of the fifteenth century, some two and a half centuries after the victory of Las Navas de Tolosa (1212) which ended the Moslem invasions, the tyranny of the decadent fighting orders gave rise to the movement of communal revolt connected with the celebrated episode of the insurrection at Fuenteovejuna.[6] Isabella the Catholic, who had relied upon the Communes' support in order to gain power,[7] was in favor of the movement for emancipation. At this moment, then, a considerable number of small southern-Castilian villages obtained their *fueros*.

Fueros were similarly granted to certain of the large Andalusian cities. But municipal life languished in this region and the *fueros*, abjectly copied from texts in use elsewhere, particularly in Toledo, inspired not one whit of enthusiasm among the population.

The *fuero*, born of municipal practice, crystallized the latter and defined it. The two eras of the *fueros'* codification (from the eleventh century to the thirteenth) and territorial extension (from the thirteenth to the early sixteenth century) coincided with the periods of vigor and the apogee of municipal life. From the municipal organization came the *Cortés* (tribunals) in the late twelfth and thirteenth centuries. In certain areas, especially in the Basque country, a regional institutional apparatus had been created, parallel with territorial collectivization. Delegates of the diverse local communes had grown into the habit of meeting in general assembly. Where this custom did not exist, the *Cortés* were born: apparently, on royal initiative; actually, because of the

---

[6] The small town of Fuenteovejuna, on the border between New Castile and Andalusia, is now part of the province of Córdoba. Early in the reign of Isabella the Catholic (Queen of Castile in 1474), the inhabitants rose up against the order of Calatrava and assassinated the commander, Don Fernán Gomez de Guzman. After a long inquest, Doña Isabel and the king-consort, Ferdinand of Aragon, extended their protection to the insurgents. From this episode, Lope de Vega drew inspiration for one of his most celebrated historical plays. Written between 1604 and 1618, *Fuenteovejuna* appears in the twelfth part of the Comedies of Lope de Vega published at Madrid in 1619.

[7] On the death of her brother, King Henry IV of Castile, Isabella the Catholic was faced with a rival: the late monarch's daughter, the Infanta Doña Juana, whose legitimacy was contested. While Doña Juana was supported by certain important feudal lords and by the Portuguese, Isabella allied herself with the cities.

treasury's needs and the will of the communities, which were, in fact, the sole tax-paying group—the clergy and the feudal domains were exempt from all tribute. Hence the sovereigns had come to convoke the communal delegates—*procuradores*—to solicit their financial participation.[8] The power to grant or to withhold a tax became, in the hands of the communal delegates, a powerful means of bargaining and pressure. In this way they succeeded in establishing that the sessions be convened periodically. In addition, the delegates began to present petitions. Aside from this right of initiative, the *procuradores* appropriated, in Aragon particularly, the right to criticize royal politics by presenting *quejas* (grievances). In several regions, the *Cortés* came to exercise full legislative power. In Aragon, royal decisions could be enforced only if the *Cortés* ratified them unanimously. In the Basque country, royal orders were passed in review before a sort of jurists' council; if this body considered that the measure ran counter to the *fueros*, the *Cortés* of Guernica pronounced: *Se obedece y no se cumple* (we obey but we do not execute), a formula which effectively suspended execution of the royal decree in Basque territory. Providing for the recess between sessions, the *Cortés* of the various regions named a permanent delegation which, in Cataloña, was called delegation of the General Assembly or, more simply, *Generalidad*.

As representatives of the population, the *Cortés* made themselves guardians of public liberties. Each king, upon his accession, swore before the assemblies to respect the *fueros*, although this practice did not in any way signify a conquest over popular representation. The memory of an era when the

---

[8] The first meeting of the Cataloñan *Cortés* dates back as far as 1064. But the composition of the assembly was not settled and these *Cortés* met only at long intervals. They took on their definitive form beginning with the session at Villafranca in 1218. For the *Cortés* of Navarre, the case is similar: having first met in 1094, it was not until the end of the thirteenth century that the assembly met regularly. The *Cortés* in Aragon met first in 1163. In León and Castile, the first sessions date from, respectively, 1188 and 1250. In Aragon, the *Cortés* met every year, even if the King did not convoke the session, and the session had to last for at least forty days. In Castile, on the contrary, the *Cortés* met only upon royal summons—but custom demanded that the King convoke the assembly every two years. In Vizcaya, the *Cortés* met twice yearly; in Guipúzcoa, once a year; and in Alava, every other year.

population enjoyed greater rights, particularly that of electing its sovereigns, lived on in Aragon's ritual formula of coronation: "We who, each man apart, are worth as much as you and who, all together, are more than you, we make you king. . . ." When the royal power became hereditary in the various States of the Peninsula, the *Cortés*—at least in Aragon, where rules governing succession were rather vague —retained the right to intervene in and decide certain disputed successions. On the death of Martín I, a commission composed of delegates from the *Cortés* of Barcelona, Aragon, and Valencia met in the little town of Caspe, in Aragon. In 1412 they handed down a decision in favor of Don Fernando de Antequera, a decision famous in the annals of Spanish history as the *Compromiso de Caspe*.[9] But even in cases where the succession did not involve any difficulty, the hereditary princes of the Peninsula's various States became kings with full powers only after having taken an oath to respect the *fueros*. In Spanish law, the oath created the power, and violation of the *fuero* effectively freed the subjects of their duty to obey. When a sovereign violated the *fuero* revolt almost always ensued, and sometimes the prince who had thus broken his covenant with his people was dethroned. At the end of the thirteenth century, the nobility and communes of Aragon tried to institutionalize this practice by compelling King Alfonso I to countersign a document which granted the *Cortés* the right to depose a sovereign in the event of violation of the *fuero*. This charter was nullified in 1248, after a long period of upheaval, by an energetic and authoritarian monarch, Peter IV.[10] The Basques of Vizcaya, on the

[9] Don Fernando was descended from the elder branch of the House of Aragon on the female side. His rival descended from the younger branch on the male side. This sort of situation always gave rise to difficulties in the Cataloñan-Aragonian kingdom. Aragon, before uniting with Cataloña, observed the matriarchal tradition honored in virtually all of the Iberian regions. But Cataloña, marked by Roman and French influences, would not allow a woman to inherit the crown. To avoid separating the two regions, it was understood that the women did not rule but transmitted their rights to their sons and descendants. The commission which met at Caspe thus confirmed this custom by deciding in favor of Fernando de Antequera.

[10] The arbitrariness of royalty was for a long time checked and mitigated in Aragon, for the cities united with the nobles in a league called *la Unión*,

contrary, succeeded in deposing their sovereign, King Henry IV of Castile, who had tried to force them to pay a tax for which the *fueros* did not provide. They then recognized as Countess of Vizcaya the Infanta Isabella, heir to the crown. Thus Isabella the Catholic reigned over the Basque country for eighteen months before the death of her brother made her Queen of Castile.

The *fuero* did not merely limit the arbitrary aspect of authority. It was also maker of kings in that total democracy which, founded on the irrevocable character of an immemorial custom, was six centuries ahead of contemporary democracies.

2. IBERIAN CENTRIFUGISM AND CASTILIAN CENTRALISM

Beginning in the sixteenth century, foral democracy was progressively to disappear in the center and the south of the country. In the north the *fueros* underwent a change of character, becoming guarantees of local particularism against the State.

This evolution was not due to the progressive regrouping of peninsular kingdoms under the same scepter.[11] In fact, at her apogee—from the late fifteenth to the middle of the seventeenth century—Spain constituted a federation of kingdoms which, united in their common sovereign, maintained their respective personalities, governments, laws, currencies, armies. But the balance between power centralism and re-

whereas the cities of Castile backed the king against the feudal lords. Nonetheless, Peter IV of Aragon triumphed over *la Unión* with the aid of a mercenary army. It is said that his rage was so uncontained that, in slashing the charter providing for deposition of sovereigns in certain cases, he wounded himself at the wrist with his own poniard. In Aragonian history, he is still known by the epithet, "Peter of the poniard."

11 The marriage of Isabella (Queen of Castile, 1474; died, 1504) and Ferdinand (King of Aragon, 1479; died, 1516) united the two great States of the Peninsula. Their joint forces conquered Granada in 1492; and in 1512 Ferdinand annexed that part of Navarre which lay to the south of the Pyrenees. The daughter of Isabella and Ferdinand, Juana-the-Mad (proclaimed Queen of Castile on the death of her mother in 1504), was unable to reign. It was therefore her eldest son, Don Carlos (the future Emperor Charles V) who, in 1516, reunited—for the first time under one throne—all the kingdoms of the Peninsula, with the sole exception of Portugal.

gional centrifugism was soon upset. Whether King of Castile at Toledo or at Valladolid, King of Aragon at Saragossa or King of Navarre at Pamplona, the monarch aspired to be King of Spain. This desire for unification, which met with various kinds of often prolonged resistance, is at the root of one of the most singular features of the sixteenth-century Spanish monarchy: its itinerant nature, its flight from one capital to another. The central power was fleeing local opposition, searching for solid ground: Carlos I, for instance, fled Toledo and set up his capital at Valladolid. Historic capital and symbol-city of the Romano-Germanic unitary conception, Toledo was also the city of the perfect *fuero*, which, early in the reign of Carlos I (the Habsburg Charles V), had been the center of the revolt of the *comuneros* (Castilian communes) against the first absolutist efforts of the central power. But again in the new capital, Valladolid, the Castilian communal past was still too present for the taste of the successor to Carlos I. Philip II required a capital of his own invention, that he might model it to suit his taste. From this will to unify was born Madrid, artificial city which, like an imperial thought, surged up in the geometric heart of the Peninsula.

Toledo and, in lesser measure, Valladolid represented at this time the most formidable obstacle to royal power: the Castilian communal liberties. By limiting regal power, Castilian democracy prevented it from weighing too heavily on the peripheral regions. Paradoxically, Castilian democracy obstructed, in this manner, the effects of the "Castilianization" which was beginning to be felt in all the branches of the State.

The decline of municipal life in Castile was to pave the way for a rupture in Iberian equilibrium. Already the progressive enlargement of urban centers had begun to prepare for a climate of political indifference. This enlargement was expressed through the disappearance of the old general assemblies composed of all free men; these were replaced by elected councils, a cruel evolution for an activist race. The indifference became more pronounced in the sixteenth century, under the influence of class struggles within the cities. The first symptom of these conflicts was the revolt of the *comuneros* (1520-1522) which marked the culmination of Castilian communal sentiment. At its inception, the revolt was strictly political: the insurrectionists aimed to defend the bourgeois Castilian democracy against the infringements of Carlos I who, educated in Germany, wanted to introduce into Spain the feudal methods still in practice in the rest of Europe. But social upheaval was grafted onto the stout root of political uprising. The Emperor, inaugurating a method of divide-and-conquer often adopted since by the Spanish State, was successful in disarming the bourgeoisie not only by guaranteeing the continuation of the *fueros*, but also by exploiting the fears inspired in leading figures by the popular agitation.

In the course of the next hundred and fifty years, the Castilian bourgeoisie became increasingly remote from the lower classes. City-dwelling notables—*hidalgos* and rich bourgeois—strove to take over municipal offices. Weary of electoral corruption, the poorer voters—shopkeepers and artisans —turned their backs on municipal affairs. Oligarchical factions quarreled over power. And from then on the *corregidor* (representative of the king) played the role of arbiter of opinion in these quarrels and pushed into the municipal magistrates' posts the most pliable candidates—those most subservient to the royal will. The Castilian municipalities, now creatures of the royal power and of certain oligarchical factions, lost all authority and independence.

The economic situation was also unfavorable to the Castilian cities. Industries and, consequently, the Castilian cities of this period (late sixteenth and early seventeenth centuries) were ruined by continuous inflation and foreign competition, and by the psychosis which urged so many Spaniards to desert mercantile offices and manual labor to enter the bureaucracy, to play the gentleman, or to seek their fortune in the army or in the Americas. The decadence of the Castilian cities brought about that of the *Cortés*. No sooner had the *procuradores* ceased to be the representatives of an authentic force than their duties lost all prestige. These

Cortés, which no longer represented anyone, no longer played any but an imaginary role; their sessions were held less often, so that the royal decree of 1665 doing away with the *Cortés* of Castile, was merely rendering official a *fait accompli*.

Power, henceforth absolute in Castile, found all the more irritating the barriers intact against it in other regions.[12] Whereupon it set out to reduce the prerogatives of the regional assemblies and Castilianize the peripheral populations.

The government at Madrid was aided in this task by a powerful bureaucratic and military apparatus whose composition was almost exclusively Castilian. For the caste of Castilian *hidalgos*[13] furnished the administration and the army with the majority of both its officials and its personnel.

In addition, the State's centralist aims were favored by demographic conditions. The assimilation, the "re-Hispanization," of the Andalusian populations had attached them to the central homogeneous group formed by Castile and the regions of similar culture (Santander, Asturias, León) which,

[12] The celebrated "Pérez affair" of the late sixteenth century is typical of the precarious equilibrium established at that time between the central power and the already mistrustful regions. Guilty of malpractice and suspected of murder, Philip II's Secretary of State, Antonio Pérez, was in possession of State secrets which in any other European country at the time would have earned him imprisonment without benefit of trial, and death in some dungeon. Availing himself of the guarantees granted by the *fueros* to accused persons, Pérez obtained temporary release and fled to Saragossa, where he appealed to the *Justicia Mayor* of Aragon, Juan de Lanuza. This appeal caused the accused to be transferred to a prison which did not fall under the *Justicia Mayor's* jurisdiction. Philip II then called in the Inquisition, habitual auxiliary of royal trespasses. Made to appear before the Holy Office, Pérez had no further refuge —for the Inquisition's tribunal was the only one in Spain before which an accused man could not invoke the judicial guarantees provided by the *fueros*. Aroused by the violation of Aragonian franchises, the people of Saragossa rose up in rebellion: under cover of the excitement, Pérez was able to escape to France. The *Justicia Mayor*, who had undoubtedly given clandestine encouragement to the revolt, was decapitated in 1592. But to appease the populace, the King was obliged to confirm the *fueros*. The Crown was as yet too weak to abolish them.

[13] In the broad sense, *hidalgo* refers to any member of the nobility and even to those notables having pretensions to nobility. But in the narrower sense, *hidalgo* is used to mean an impoverished gentleman, as opposed to the great titled lords (*ricos hombres*). In the Aragonian *Cortés*, the *ricos hombres* and *hidalgos* sat separately. Here we have used *hidalgo* in the sense of impoverished gentleman.

long subject to the feudal tyranny of the Moslems, was predisposed to submit docilely to the arbitrary central power and to cultural Castilianization. The precarious demographic equilibrium established at the time of the Spanish hegemony, between the Castilian-Andalusian masses and the peoples of the periphery, was overthrown once and for all when Portugal [14] withdrew from the Iberian community during the first revolt by the Iberian nationalities in 1640-1643.

A policy of unification which easily triumphed over indistinct local differences could not but give rise, in Spain, to determined resistance. The geographic isolation of the various surrounding regions, the rapid maturation of their civilizations under the stress of permanent struggle and with the impetus of constant exchanges between Islam and the West, had contributed to heightening the respective personalities of those regions. If we take a nation to be the juridical and cultural personality combined with the territorial delimitation, then Aragon, Navarre, Cataloña, Galicia, Portugal, the Basque country, the kingdom of Valencia were so many nations each with its historical traditions, its language, its culture.[15] By trying to strip them of these aspects of their

[14] Portugal was created at the end of the eleventh century by Alfonso VI of Castile (liberator of Toledo and the unjust suzerain of the Cid). At that time, the central and southern areas of present-day Portugal were occupied by the Moslems. The northern territories, between the Bino and Mondego rivers, were related to Galicia by their racial stock (mainly Celtic) and their tongue, and were political dependents of the Castilian-Leónian kingdom. Alfonso VI elevated them to the status of an earldom and gave them to his younger daughter, the Infanta Teresa, as a dowry. The Infanta's son, Don Alfonso, proclaimed himself king in 1143, under the suzerainty of the King of Castile. His successors, however, became fully independent and shook off the Moslem domination of the areas which today form southern and central Portugal. In 1580, Philip II of Spain took up the rights he had inherited from his mother, Isabella of Portugal, and was recognized King of Portugal.

[15] Many conflicts arose from the central power's attempts to impose the Castilian tongue, which stemmed from the Santander dialect brought to Old Castile during the Reconquest (between the late ninth and late eleventh centuries) by the soldiers and settlers from that area. Of Latin origin, the dialect contained a large number of Arab words introduced into Old Castile by the Mozarabes (Christian Spaniards, escaped from the Moslem zone). While the inhabitants who came from the north were soldiers, farmers, merchants or civil servants, the Mozarabes had arrived without the least resource and were artisans or building workers. This accounts for the Arabic origin of most trade terms, particularly those having to do with construction. This language,

personalities, the central power tempted them to secede. In 1640, the unifiying policy of the prime minister, Olivares, stirred up a revolt of the Portuguese and Cataloñans. With the help of England, the Portuguese became independent of the Spanish Crown. Having opened the gates of Barcelona to French forces, then at war with Spain, the Cataloñans lost no time in calling again for the Castilians. Indeed, alongside French centralism, that of Castile appeared all the more benign since the Habsburg dynasty promised to give back to Cataloña its traditional *fueros*. Thus the peoples of Cataloña and Aragon, once the war of succession had been ignited by the death in 1700 of Charles II, were obliged to take arms against the French pretender, Philippe d'Anjou.[16] This international dynastic war, in reality the first Carlist war, already opposed the centralists to the defenders of the *fueros*. It is not surprising that, after the victory of the French pretender, Cataloña and Aragon were deprived of their *fueros*. The traditional institutions survived only in certain small regions: Navarre and the Basque country.

There was no longer the slightest link between the inorganic population and the State. Unsupported, the apparatus of royalty was unable to resist the slightest shock and in fact, early in the nineteenth century, it was to collapse in a few

---

wrought at the outposts of the Reconquest, forced its way into use, from the eleventh to the fifteenth century, in the lands reconquered by the Castilians (southern Castile, Andalusia), and even gained ground in Aragon and in Navarre. In the sixteenth century, early in the period of unification, a linguistic map of the Peninsula would have shown four zones: in the center and the south: Castilian; to the west, the Atlantic zone, where Galician or its derivatives were spoken, Galicia and Portugal; to the east, in the Mediterranean zone, the lands speaking Cataloñan or its derivatives, Cataloña, Valencia, the Balearics; to the north, Euskera-speaking lands, the three Basque provinces and part of Navarre.

16 The weak and sickly King Charles II (great-grandson of Philip II) had designated as his heir the grandson of his sister, Infanta Maria Teresa, and Louis XIV of France. The new king, Philippe d'Anjou, came in conflict with the claims of Archduke Charles of Austria. The ensuing war (1700-1713) was at once a Spanish war between partisans of the two pretenders and an international war between France, Austria, and their respective allies. By the Treaty of Utrecht, Philippe d'Anjou was recognized King of Spain but he agreed to renounce claims to Gibraltar, which was occupied by England, the ally of Austria.

days under the blows of Napoleon's army. The isolated State identified with the king and a few courtiers' factions. The administration, the army, everything emanated from the king and depended on him. Hence, all that was necessary to ensure the immediate collapse of the entire administrative and military house of cards was the imprisonment of the king and dispersal of the courtiers.[17] The liberal minority, leading the struggle in the south, strove to create a new royal apparatus and to re-establish a link between the State and Spanish reality by creating representative institutions.[18] But in the south the masses remained indifferent, whereas in the north they were generally hostile to the representative system. The "foralists," in the majority in both regions, considered that individual and minority liberties could not be fruitfully guaranteed by texts which, proceeding from the State, were liable at any moment to be repealed or suspended by the State under the pressure of an active minority or, at best, of the majority. In the foralist conception, a balance between authority and individual liberties could be nothing more than a balance of forces, obtainable only through a union of individuals into strongly structured communities.

The conflict between supporters of total democracy and representative democracy along French lines was to last nearly a century. In 1833, at the accession of Isabella II, it took a sharp turn. Under cover of influences brought to bear

[17] The French army had occupied Madrid almost without resistance in 1808. King Charles IV, who had agreed to meet Napoleon at Bayonne in French territory, was considered a prisoner as was his eldest son, the future Ferdinand VII. When the people of Madrid rose up against the invader on May 2, 1808, and were answered by the horrible repression of May 3 (the inspiration for the most famous of Goya's works), the beginning of a national popular war was signaled. While the *guerrilla* was organized spontaneously in the occupied northern provinces, new authorities (a provisional government and a *Cortés*) came into being at Cádiz in the unoccupied zone. The struggle was continued with the aid of an English expeditionary force, and resulted in the great 1813 victory at Vitoria (in Alava), in the restoration of Ferdinand VII, and in the invasion of French territory—Anglo-Spanish forces entered Toulouse in 1814. [18] The liberals, who formed the majority in the provisional government and in the Cádiz *Cortés*, voted a liberal constitution in 1812 and abolished the Inquisition. Upon his return to Spain, Ferdinand VII nullified these measures. The next nineteen years (1814-1833) saw bloody struggles between Ferdinand's reactionary government and the liberal opposition.

upon the Regent, the liberal party seemed about to gain power. Its program was well known: legislative unification, abolition of the last *fueros*. Should non-Castilianized peoples of the north accept the language, the law, and the religion which prevailed in the Castilianized areas? Was that abstract liberty promised by the ideologists thus fatal to real liberty, that modest but inalienable right of every man to remain himself, to defend his personality, to speak his own tongue?

Rejecting the chains with which others sought to bind them in the name of liberty, the peoples of Galicia and the Basque country, of Navarre, Aragon, and Cataloña, declared themselves in favor of the pretender, Don Carlos. Its prerogatives were threatened by the liberal movement, the old Castilian right, which was centralist by historical vocation; they nonetheless implored the support of the particularist provinces. This temporary collusion gave birth to the first Carlist uprising.

A vast assemblage of peasants marched on Madrid. In the outskirts of the capital they fell victim to the technique and discipline of a professional army. The vanquished Carlists, divided and discouraged, were obliged to surrender arms, and the liberalist government decreed the abrogation of the last *fueros* in 1839. This accentuation of centralism was, in turn, responsible for the second Carlist movement. But the resumption of hostilities would not have been possible had not the liberals' return to power after the 1868 revolution and the abdication of Isabella II, provoked a new impulse of the old Castilian right toward the particularist provinces. Yet after the second defeat of the foralists, in 1876, the triumph of centralism was still more complete in that the reconciliation of liberals and Castilian conservatives facilitated the adoption of a program for unification. The former kingdoms, split into provinces, would have, henceforth, one law, one language.

These centralist reforms brought about a decisive evolution in the way of thinking of the northern masses which had considered themselves linked to Spain and supporters of that vast federation of diverse nations. But in a unitary Spain which was neither more nor less than a Greater Castile, non-Castilianized peoples felt out of place. Their active élite envisaged only two possible solutions: to secede from Spain; or, to be granted, within the framework of the unitary State, recognition of the exceptional status of an autonomous regime.

The problem inherent in the political structure of a community of Hispanic nations had, by a singular detour, become a problem of national minorities. And the minority populations which now felt themselves foreign to Spain were precisely those which, devoid of all ethnic mixture and with weapons in hand, had brought Spain into being.

A natural factor, the lack of coal, was to concentrate peninsular industry in the areas near sources of water power, in the Pyrenees and the Cantabrian mountains. Wealthy and overpopulated, the Basque country and Cataloña were to assume the leadership of the minority movement for emancipation. But the centralist intransigence of the right, in power at Madrid, constrained the autonomists to seek out the support of the new forces on the left. Thus, Iberian centrifugism, which had identified with the extreme right during the entire nineteenth century, veered to the left in the twentieth century. And in 1936 the descendants of the Carlist soldiers were to fight, for the most part, on the Republican side.

THE TREE OF GUERNICA[19]

The Basque country is the only region in which the *fueros* remained in force until the nineteenth century. This unsevered tradition, transmitted by the Carlist movement, fa-

19 The veneration accorded the Guernica oak is perhaps a vestige of some pagan cult. The Celts worshipped oaks and a similar cult may have existed among the Basque peoples of the proto-historical era. In support of this theory, it may be noted that the Basque provinces observe a time-honored custom of planting a "May tree" (in Euskera: *mayatza recha*). The feast of Saint John, which perpetuates the pagan feast of the summer solstice, is similarly marked by the planting of a tree. There is reason to believe that the first gatherings beneath the Guernica oak go back to remotest antiquity. The first such recorded meeting occurred in 870 A.D., at a time when the Basques were not

vored the rising of the current of Basque nationalism in the last years of the nineteenth century. In addition, the people felt a deep resentment at the destruction wrought by the second Carlist war.

Having suffered this, the Basques felt themselves foreign to Spain, and the superiority complex which they had nurtured since the Middle Ages was reinforced. One of the *fuero* documents proclaims, to this effect, that the Basque "is noble by his blood"—a principle which explains why always in the past and still today, Basques of all social levels take great pains to join the nobiliary particle, *de* (of), to their names.

A certain text of the late fifteenth century throws some light upon this notion of superiority. A message, addressed by the assembly of Guernica to King Henry IV of Castile[20] states: "The Basques are the representatives of the Iberic nation. In the cause of Spanish liberty we have shed our blood against Carthage, against the Romans, and against the Goths." [21] The Basques' feeling of superiority rested, at this time, upon the purity of their blood, upon their superior degree of "Hispanicity."

In the present day, the motive of the feeling has changed but not the overall nature of the sentiment. The Basques are

yet converted to Christianity. On this occasion, the assembled notables elected the first lord of Vizcaya, Lope Zuria. The event is confirmed by oral tradition, later by various chroniclers in the Middle Ages and by two historians of the Siglo de Oro, Gonzalo Argote de Molina and Esteban de Garibay y Zamalloa. These several authors add that Lope Zuria's successors were also elected in Guernica and that, when the Seigniory became hereditary in 1105 and later when the province was acquired by the crown of Castile in 1370, both lords and kings took their oaths beneath the Guernica oak. When the original tree died, it was replaced by a young oak grown from an acorn of the original.

[20] Vizcaya, like Alava and Guipúzcoa, was originally placed under the suzerainty of the King of Navarre. Alava and Guipúzcoa, dissatisfied with this ruler, broke away and voluntarily attached themselves to Castile in about 1200. As the result of a dynastic marriage, Vizcaya too was joined to Castile in 1370. Navarre itself was annexed in 1512. The people of Navarre were displeased by the policies of a dynasty in fealty to France. Taking advantage of this feeling, Ferdinand the Catholic caused his troops to enter the country and the re-allegiance with Spain to be approved.

[21] Cited by Manuel de Irujo, *Inglaterra y los Vascos*, p. 205. He stipulates that he quotes from Garibay's *Crónica general*, Book XVII, ch. 9.

prone to believe that they belong to an original race, biologically different from that of all neighboring peoples.

Whether the Basque people do belong to a racial nexus foreign to the Spanish milieu or whether they be the sole heir of a specific "Hispanicity" which was modified, elsewhere in the Peninsula, by other ethnic importations, their temperament does differ profoundly from that of their neighbors. It exhibits a robust optimism which finds its outlet in songs of a surprising buoyancy, in rhythmic pantomimes, satiric transpositions of scenes from daily life. The Basque makes a vocation of happiness. Yet he is able to discipline himself to do the hard methodical labor which enriches man and his community, and which guarantees civic peace in an atmosphere of respect for individual liberty.

The equilibrium of the Basque temperament is promoted, furthermore, by a temperate climate and the fertility of a soil bathed in the rains that sweep in from the Atlantic. Thus, the standard of living has been consistently higher in the Basque country than in most of the Iberian regions. The rapid expansion of industry in the area around Bilbao was made easy, during the early years of this century, by propitious natural factors: iron resources and the relative proximity of the Asturian coal mines.

Blast furnaces and factories soon were built in the environs of Bilbao. Along the shores of the Nervión River warehouses, arsenals, and shipyards were created. Metallurgy became the springboard for other, transformational, industries. The Bank of Bilbao and other banking associations appeared. Vigorous production made foreign trade essential and thus brought about the development of merchant shipping. Ramón de la Sota, a Basque, became the Peninsula's greatest shipowner and, at the time of World War I, held nearly half the merchant tonnage of Spain.

This industrialization gave rise to interests which diverged from those elsewhere in Spain. Because the standard of living of the masses in the south and center of the Peninsula was low, Spain offered few outlets to Bilbao production while the duties imposed on the Bilbao area were among the heaviest in the world, reflecting the unwieldy nature of the bureaucracy which imposed them.

The industrialists who bore the brunt of these taxes and whose expansionist ambitions were countered by Spanish protectionism showed their eagerness to loosen the tie between Euzkadi (the Basque country) and the Spanish State. Whereupon the great industrial magnates of Bilbao, as well as the bankers and shipowners, used all the means at their command to further the Basque nationalist movement. This had been founded in the last years of the nineteenth century by Sabino de Arana y Goiri,[22] the son of a former Carlist fighter. Influenced by the prevailing moral and economic factors in the Basque country of the early twentieth century, a whole structure of forces, inspired by Sabino's doctrine, was to come into being: The Basque Nationalist Party, *Emakumes* (women's sections of the Party), Solidarity of Basque Workers (church-oriented unions), cultural institutions, newspapers.

The Basque nationalist movement had not had to develop its economic and social doctrine; at its inception the movement had found its doctrine in the Papal Encyclicals, *Rerum Novarum* and *Quadragesimo Anno*. Indeed, Basque nationalism and the social doctrine of the Church were, in Euzkadi, two indissoluble terms. For this reason, at the end of the monarchical period and on the eve of the great reversals and drastic overthrows of the second quarter of the twentieth century, the Basque movement presented a solid front, a coherent whole of doctrines and forces which drew the ma-

---

[22] Arana's works—twelve books in defense and illustration of the Basque language, written in Spanish or in Euskera, and many newspaper articles—caught the eye of the police. Imprisoned several times, he had to go through trial after trial. In spite of severe attacks against the Spanish State, he was acquitted several times by the jury. He was condemned only once—after sending a congratulatory telegram to the President of the United States, at a time when the anger caused by Spain's defeat in Cuba in 1898 had not yet calmed down. In fact, Sabino was not congratulating McKinley on having defeated Spain but, rather, on having stated his intention of making Cuba politically independent. But given the wrathful atmosphere of that moment in Spain, these subtleties were not appreciated. Sabino died shortly after his condemnation, at the age of 39, exhausted by his repeated terms in prison and by the exacting labor to which he had driven himself.

jority of the population in the Basque maritime provinces—
Vizcaya and Guipúzcoa.

The aim of the Basque Nationalist Party was to introduce into the modern State a system of juridical guarantees
and distribution of power, founded upon the foralist principles. In addition, what linked the claims of Basque nationalism to the ancient *fueros* was more than implied in the motto
of the party: *"Jaungoikoa eta lagi zarra"* [23]—God and the
ancient laws.

The maritime Basque country had made efforts to adapt
its particularism to the structures of the modern world. Navarre, land of mountain pastures, had evolved scarcely at all
since the end of the first Carlist war. Typically, the people of
Navarre, faithful to the letter of the foral law, rejected any
modernized version of it. Burning to set their Faith and their
King over all of Spain, they accused the Basque Nationalists
of separating their cause from that of Spain insofar as their
movement broke with the Carlist tradition of the armed
Crusade and also to the extent to which, while respecting the
will of the other peoples of the Peninsula, it sought to
establish in exchange respect for the Basque personality under
the protection of a statute of autonomy. In 1936, when it
was evident that the Basque nationalists would not join a
new Carlist Crusade, the people of Navarre looked upon
this neutrality as treason. And in July of that year, on the day
of the *pronunciamiento*, the *Requetes* (Carlist volunteers)
of Navarre took up arms and threw themselves upon the
maritime Basque country.

The Basque nationalists then wished to underline, by a
stunning ceremony, the significance of the combat in which
they were obliged to engage. On October 7, 1936, José
Antonio de Aguirre, elected president of the Basque Region
—which had recently been granted a statute of autonomy by
the Republic—descended the steps of the *Casa de Juntas*[24]
at Guernica preceded by a herald at arms in medieval cos-

---

[23] In Euskera, the Basque tongue; in Spanish, *"Dios y los fueros."*
[24] Houses of Parliament; the neo-classical edifice is without historical interest.
It was spared in the 1937 bombardment.

tume; arrived before the historic oak, the president swore the ritual oath of fidelity to the *fueros:* "As I stand on Basque land and in the memory of our ancestors, I vow to respect the *fueros. . . .*"

4. THE LAND OF GAY SABER[25]

While Basque nationalism is rooted in a racial conception, Cataloñanism arises from an obstinate and nearly heroic loyalty to a culture born of the intermingling of races in the Mediterranean world.

From the Phoenicians to the Greeks and from Rome to Carthage, all the Mediterranean civilizations have left their imprint on Cataloñan soil. Until the twelfth century, the country had ignored the Iberian peninsula. Cataloña was oriented, culturally and commercially, toward the Languedoc region—the south of France and northern Italy. Mountains and sea, far from acting as frontiers, served as hyphens between the *langue d'oc* principalities ranged at varying levels on either slope of the Pyrenees and along the Mediterranean shores. The union effected between the Cataloñan littoral and the Aragonian back-country, under the aegis of a dynastic marriage in 1137,[26] was not to distract Cataloña from its *langue d'oc*-Mediterranean destiny. For this reason, when the feudal forces of northern France launched their attack on the Languedoc region and the Comte de Toulouse, on the pretext of stifling the Albigensian heresy, King Peter II of Aragon and Cataloña hastened to the aid of his neighbors. He was killed at Muret in the great disaster which, on September 12, 1213, destroyed the *langue d'oc* armies.

---

25 "Gay Saber" is a Cataloñan term, meaning the poetry of the *langue d'oc.* [*Langue d'oc*, the soft tongue in which *oc* meant "yes," was the language of the troubadours in medieval France. The language, in which Provençal has its origins, was spoken south of the Loire. (*Cf.*, *langue d'oïl.*)—Ed.]

26 This marriage—between the Infanta Petronila, heiress of Aragon, and the Count of Barcelona—is an example of subjects' intervention in a question of royal succession. The notables (a genuine *Cortés* did not exist as yet) forced King Ramiro of Aragon to break his daughter's engagement to an Infante of Castile and to give her in marriage instead to the Count of Barcelona. These same notables had elected King Ramiro three years earlier, after setting aside his predecessor's will.

This date, which marks the downfall of the *langue d'oc* world, is of capital importance in Cataloñan history. For, after Muret, Cataloña turned from the *langue d'oc* regions of the French *midi* to orient itself toward southeastern Spain and southern Italy. The decline of Toulouse and Provence, the bright flame of whose art and poetry had long since been reduced to ash, left Cataloña solitary on the cultural level and, at the same time, stimulated the blossoming of the Cataloñan personality. Chroniclers and poets no longer wrote in Provençal; and Cataloñan, heretofore looked upon as merely a popular dialect, was promoted to the dignified rank of a literary language.

Between the end of the fifteenth century and the beginning of the sixteenth, Cataloñan, like the greater number of the coastal countries of the western Mediterranean, was to pass through a lengthy period of eclipse brought about by the Turkish invasions which ruined Mediterranean trade, and by the phenomena which abruptly turned the "spice route" toward the Atlantic. Several factors were involved in the decline of Barcelona: the union with Castile, the new orientation of trade toward the ocean and the Americas, the privilege of Atlantic trade which had long been reserved to the port of Sevilla. Thus, in 1640, when the Crown was strengthening its centralist tendency, the Cataloñans tried to secure their independence with the aid of the French. But the annexationist goals of the French forced the Insurgents back toward Spain. From that moment on the temptation to lean upon France, at least in political matters, was so utterly wiped out that the Cataloñans stood against France on every possible occasion. Early in the eighteenth century, Cataloña declared its opposition to Philippe V of Anjou; and his accession brought about the abolition of the *fueros*.

Toward the late eighteenth and early nineteenth centuries, a liberal movement under the doctrinal influence of the French Encyclopedists grew up among the bourgeoisie of the coastal cities. The mountain regions, remaining faithful to traditional beliefs and customs, rallied to the Carlist movement of 1833. Both tendencies were crushed, between 1939 and 1942, by the central government. Their common frustration was to set in motion, in Cataloña, a wave of exacerbated particularism which, in the beginning, took on the aspect of a reaction toward the *langue d'oc* cultural sources.

The transmutation into nationalism of this cultural particularism took place under cover of the great industrial boom of the late nineteenth and early twentieth centuries, influenced in turn by two essential factors: on the one hand, the harnessing of water-power, abundant in the Pyrenees; on the other, the completion of the Suez Canal, which once again placed the Mediterranean at the center of important commercial currents.

Barcelona was henceforth in control of communications between Africa and western Europe, between the Mediterranean and the Latin American worlds. The advent of the steamship and the airplane brought in their wake the travel agency, the shipping company, the de luxe hotel, the currency exchange bureau. . . . Those bankers and moneychangers who had kept shop in the little streets off the Via Layetana set up offices in sumptuous buildings, and the *lonja*—the stock market—became the center for all peninsular transactions.

About the medieval city—the "Gothic quarter"—grew up a vast modern city with broad, straight avenues. Under the impact of Gaudi's architecture, embodied in his *Sagrada Familia,* a neo-Baroque style was born in Barcelona about 1900, while the turn-of-the-century statuary which encumbered the opulent edifices of the Paseo de Gracia and the neo-Corinthian façades of the Tibidabo attested to the glory of the textile magnates. The city took great strides, adding suburb after suburb the length of the valley of the Llobregat, bristling with smokestacks. Barcelona became a confederation of industrial complexes linked by a metropolitan network.

From the earliest years of this century, the city's industrial growth gave rise to a twofold immigration of peasants, from the agricultural areas of Cataloña as well as from the provinces of southern Spain. Of these, Murcia provided the highest number of immigrants to the city, emigrants from hunger; hence, to a Cataloñan, all laborers from the south were labelled *Murcianos*. To the *Murcianos* fell the most menial tasks, those spurned by the Cataloñans dazzled by the prospect of jobs as office workers, qualified laborers, shop assistants. The *Murcianos* become pariahs, encamped in their huts, filling the enormous suburbs of Barcelona, an extra-mural plebeian force supplying the anarcho-syndicalist C.N.T. with the majority of its adherents. In the evenings, this uprooted mass, like the sailors on shore leave, had recourse to the bars, the music halls, and brothels which proliferated near the docks. This *barrio chino* spread like a tumor in the bowels of Barcelona.

The industrial evolution of Cataloña had begun in the normal way, with small and moderate-sized industries of transformation: manufactures of food products, textile weaving, silks, cottons, laces, glass, chemicals. By a system of integration, a series of associated activities (dyes, artificial leathers, finished work) accrued to the looms and spindles. In this way, there emerged those immense textile complexes strung along the Llobregat which absorbed bales of raw cotton and, at the end of a complicated network of operations, ejected cotton cloths and artificial leathers, carpets and imitation silks. . . . Barcelona would have asked for nothing better than to become the center of the textile industry; but how to mass-produce clothing and shoes in a country whose southern peasants have a standard of living so low that food purchases absorb virtually all of their resources?

A genuine capital, in contrast to the provincial aspect of Madrid, Barcelona arose like a monstrous head on the bloodless body of the Spanish economy. Henceforth, the conflict for which the Basque country had been the setting was to continue with greater intensity on Cataloñan soil.

Cataloñan industry had practically no outlets within the country and, at the same time, customs duties, the purpose of which was protection of local industry, had the effect of provoking reprisal measures harmful to Cataloñan exports. Furthermore, the machinery of the State weighed heavily upon the country. Cataloña occupies one sixteenth of the territory of Spain; her population is one eighth of the country's total; yet in the last years of the reign of Alfonso XIII, Cataloña was paying one-quarter of the nation's taxes.

Insistently slowing the evolutionary process, these limitations and duties prevented Cataloña from entering into the ultimate stage of genuine heavy industry. This steady braking determined an anti-Spanish reaction, an autonomist movement within the social structures born of industrialization. But while acting as an obstacle to the development of heavy mass production in Cataloña, the resistance of the Spanish milieu had yet another effect: it made impossible a drop in manufacturing costs and, consequently, for the rise of the workers' standard of living. The effect of these phenomena was, in turn, to prolong dangerously the most acute phase of social conflict in Barcelona, the same phase experienced in western Europe in the late nineteenth and early twentieth centuries. And finally, these internecine conflicts, dividing Cataloñans against each other, entailed the collapse of the autonomist movement.

This process was inaugurated, in Cataloña as in the Basque country, in the revolt of industrial management against the Spanish State. Weary of the obstacles the Madrid government placed in the path of Cataloñan industry, the great industrialists—who had fostered cultural Cataloñanism[27] since the mid-nineteenth century—created a new party, politically Cataloñan and socially conservative: the *Lliga*.

Cataloñan propaganda found a welcome in the new social levels which grew with industrial expansion. Shopkeepers, artisans, white-collar workers, the petit bourgeois or lower middle class whose numbers increased consistently were recruited from among the old Cataloñan stock and they too felt themselves wronged by the obstacles to economic

---

[27] Certain great industrialists were patrons to the Floral Games of Barcelona, inaugurated in 1858. This annual poetry competition (so named because the winner was awarded a gold flower) bridged an interruption of several centuries in the tradition of the "gay saber" competition: the medieval poetical jousts in which the most sought-after troubadours of the time took part. [*Cf.*, The Floral Games of Toulouse.—Ed.]

expansion. Among those Murcian immigrants who were hastily "Cataloñanized" there emerged a sort of Barcelonan
particularism. An atavistic anti-statism and the hate aroused
in them by the oligarchical control of the Spanish State
incited them, moreover, to support all forms of opposition
and all movements toward decentralization, whence the fact
that several times the *Murcians* voted for the Cataloñan
parties.

The new social classes thus worked in the Cataloñanist
movement alongside an upper bourgeoisie which they opposed on the social level. Social conflicts in fact grew more
and more acute at the start of this century and, in 1909 a
general strike degenerated into a riot. Barcelona became the
scene of genuine street fights. This *"semana trágica"* (tragic
week) began the trend which eventually led the oligarchies
to turn against the Cataloñanist movement they had created.

A new policy was adopted in Madrid in the wake of the
Barcelona riots. The indignation stirred up by their cruel repression forced Antonio Maura, unyielding centralist and conservative leader, to step down from the post of Prime Minister in favor of an opposition (liberal) spokesman, and also to
turn over party leadership to the director of its moderate
wing, Eduardo Dato. In 1913, Dato stepped into government leadership. Whether liberals or moderate conservatives,
the politicians who ruled Spain after the *"semana trágica"* in
Barcelona realized that the State could turn to its own advantage the great fear which held the body of Cataloñan employers in its clutches. It was henceforth possible, on the
other hand, to split the Cataloñan movement, to separate the
bourgeoisie from the proletariat by throwing certain sops to
Cataloñan feeling. A law worked out in 1912 by Canalejas'
liberal cabinet and enacted in 1914 by the moderate conservatives created a Cataloñan administrative authority, the *Mancomunidad* [28]—with very little power.

---

[28] The authority of the *Mancomunidad* extended to all of Cataloña. By
creating this organism, the State partially canceled the effects of a measure
adopted in the nineteenth century which divided Cataloña into four provinces,

The great Barcelona industrialists who were members of the *Lliga* wanted the *Mancomunidad* to be endowed with greater powers; but they were still more anxious to secure the protection of the State's military and police. The revolutionary strikes of 1917 which brought management's terror to an hysterical pitch hastened the reconciliation of the old Spanish right with Barcelona's upper middle class. Limiting its Cataloñan demands, the *Lliga* agreed, in 1917, to name representatives to the central government. Henceforth, the *Lliga* was associated with the monarchy's most reactionary measures. Hated more than ever by the workers, the leaders of this party, by acting hand in glove with Madrid's centralism, had managed to arouse the middle class against them. Office workers exasperated by the skimpiness of their salaries, shopkeepers wronged by the excessive prices forced upon them by wholesalers and middlemen, members of the liberal professions eager to take part in local politics—all of these representatives of the up-and-coming classes were as hostile to the upper middle class of management in Barcelona as to the Spanish State.

A parallel movement developed in the Cataloñan countryside against big agrarian capital which, in addition, was closely linked to industrial management. Subject to very severe conditions which were totally different from those prevalent elsewhere in Spain, the *rabassaires* (sharecroppers) wanted their regional problems to be treated in Barcelona by Cataloñan authorities and Cataloñan assemblies who would pay more attention to their grievances than did the *Cortés* of Madrid.

The ultra-centralist dictatorship of Primo de Rivera returned the *Lliga* to opposition status without, however, reviving its prestige. Thus, the gradual evolution begun between 1903-1923 and continued during the great silence imposed by that dictatorship eventually resulted in the alliance of the Cataloñan middle class and the sharecroppers. In 1930-1931,

---

each administered by State-named governors and having no administrative interrelationship. But the authority of the *Mancomunidad* carried only in matters of sanitary regulations, public welfare, and fine arts.

when the dictator's fall brought politics back to life, there emerged a new Cataloñan party representing both classes: *Esquerra de Catalunya* (Cataloñan left). The anarchist leaders contributed to the electoral success of the new party by advising their followers to vote for *Esquerra* in the 1931 elections.

We have seen how, when the long-term propaganda efforts of the *Lliga* were crowned by the granting of a statute of Cataloñan autonomy, the Cataloñan masses brought to power reform parties whose programs threatened management interests. And by throwing themselves back upon the Castilian centralist right to defend their endangered privileges, the Cataloñan oligarchies aided in the destruction, between 1934 and 1939, of the regional liberties they had sought to revive.

As in the Basque country, so in Cataloña the autonomist movement led to internal war: in the one case, social war; in the other, war of one province against another. In the light of this dual experience, the spirit of the oppressed minority, that deviation from foralism, appeared as a perhaps inevitable reaction of Iberian individualism against a centralism of foreign origin, but it by no means appeared to be a solution. Born of a common evil—the decadence of the Spanish "foral" institutions—both autonomist and centralist deviations resulted in chaos and the Civil War. Their common disaster demonstrated that no region, no class, no party could elude by any subterfuge no matter how fortuitous, the essential problem confronting the Iberian peoples: the elaboration of a new and modern formula for communal life which would revive the institutions peculiar to the Iberian race and which would allow harmonious relations to exist among the personalities and interests of the Spanish nations.

Chapter Three

꧁꧂

THE ROME
OF MODERN TIMES

ALTHOUGH THE SPANISH imperial cycle covers scarcely three centuries, its consequences still are felt today. The age of Imperial domination, prolonged thus interminably in the ills of the recent past and uncertainties of the present, had been slowly ripened by Spain's entire history of fertile initiative and freedoms.

In fact, the most striking characteristic of Spanish history is the precise coincidence between the periods of grandeur and the evolutionary process of public liberties. The formative periods of the State, as well as its periods of progress and conquest, coincide with those of the crystallization and apex of foral liberties. But once the majority of the Spanish people played no part in the history of Spain, Spain played no part in the history of the world. There should be nothing surprising in this coincidence. From ancient Greece and Rome to nineteenth-century England, revolutionary France, and the United States, experience teaches that, at least in the occidental era begun over three thousand years ago on Hellenic shores, the great powers that have dominated the world have been democracies and the decline of empires has always coincided with the decline of democratic institutions.

1. FROM RECONQUEST TO REVOLT
OF THE MASSES

Like all other essential realities of Iberian life, the Imperial cycle may be traced to the Reconquest. Castile was endowed with its dual personality of military march and militant democracy—two traits which bore a whole fatality of wars and domination—by the struggle against Islam.

The struggle did not require merely the methodical reoccupation of the land and the construction of fortresses (*castillos*) on each portion of liberated land. It was also essential to bring the fields of Old Castile, systematically ravaged by the Moors, back under cultivation. A colony of soldier-laborers must correspond to each fortress, a landmark in wood or stone, erected along the path of liberation. And if a colonialized people was to be persuaded to face the surprise of death which at each successive advance post of the Reconquest—Navarre, Aragon, Castile—could spring from ambush in the form of a party of Berber marauders, then this peasantry, drafted on a permanent basis on its own land, must know that the cause of the Spanish kingdoms was its cause as well; that liberty was not a privilege of the élite but the right of all. Constrained to ask assistance of the free men on their domains, the feudal lords were obliged in turn to confirm the old freedoms or to grant new franchises. For each acre of reconquered land, for each colony of colonists-laborers established about a *castillo* in the Castilian peneplain, there was a new municipal charter. Liberty marched in step with the Reconquest.

The height of democracy was reached at exactly the time of Spanish omnipotence. The movement of communal emancipation which helped Isabella the Catholic to power, continued under her reign. Supported by the cities, Ferdinand

and Isabella managed to subdue the great figures of the kingdom and to extricate southern Castile from the domination of the knightly orders.[1] In the hundred and fifty years (late fifteenth century to mid-seventeenth) during which Spain was at the summit of her power, although royal power had got the better of the feudal lords it was still too feeble to endanger public liberties and was the expression of three dominant forces: the communes, the poor *hidalgos,* and the peasant-landowners.

The dynastic situation, which worked in favor of the foundation of the Empire, has concealed from most historians the underlying causes of the Imperial phenomenon. Without the Habsburgs,[2] who brought to Castile their heritage and their megalomania, it would have been more difficult to build the Empire. But the way in which Castile soon took the upper hand over those states which chance, in the form of various marriages, had associated with its own destiny reveals a will to power which would have succeeded sooner or later in

---

[1] The territories belonging to the knightly orders were indirectly attached to the Crown when Ferdinand the Catholic proclaimed himself Grand Master of these communities of fighting monks, established to defend Spain against invasions of *Almoravides* and *Almohades.* The Order of Calatrava was founded early in the twelfth century, in the Ciudad Real region, by Saint Raimundo; the order of Alcantara was created in 1156 in the Cáceres region; and the order of Santiago was begun in the Leon region in the late twelfth century. Successors to Ferdinand and Isabella preserved the dignity appertaining to Grand Masters of these orders. The title *chevalier* became purely honorific.

[2] The Habsburg States were united with Spain by the marriage in 1496 of Juana the Mad to the Archduke Philippe le Beau (the Fair). By this time, Philippe possessed Flanders through his mother, Marie de Bourgogne (d. 1482). Through his father, the Habsburg Emperor Maximilian, he was heir to Austria. Upon his death in 1506, Philippe left Flanders to his eldest son, Don Carlos who became Charles V, King of Spain, in 1516. Having inherited Austria, he was elected Emperor of Germany in 1519 on the death of his paternal grandfather, the Emperor Maximilian. Austria was separated from Spain in 1555 when Charles V, weary of rule, decided to abdicate and enter the Yuste monastery in Extremadura. He left Austria to his younger brother, Ferdinand; Spain and Flanders to his son, King Philip II. After the Flanders revolt, Philip II had to recognize the independence of the northern part of that country (present-day Holland); the southern part (Belgium) remained an annex of Spain until the early eighteenth century. At the end of the war of the Spanish Succession the French pretender, Philippe d'Anjou, acknowledged King of Spain, had to cede Belgium to the Austrian Habsburgs by the treaties of Utrecht and Rastadt, 1713-1714.

any case. The King was the first conquest of the military advance. Born German, Charles V died Castilian, Carlos I; his successors were born and lived in Castile. Having assimilated the monarch, the military thrust "Castilianized" the State; in its turn, the State set about subjecting associated peoples to the rigors of forced assimilation. From the Low Countries to Andalusia, from the States of Aragon to Portugal, from Milan to Naples,[3] every one of the States which had entered the Habsburg Empire as an equal was soon to change its rank and become a fief of Castile: a mere nursery of troops and vault of cash to maintain the wars of conquest launched in Europe and in the New World.

Castilian supremacy was assured at this time by the temporary conjunction of technical progress with a social structure the origin of which lay in the Castilian vocation for war. Indeed, although the entire population had been exposed in the Middle Ages to Moslem incursions, and although men of every social condition had been called upon to repulse them, the chronic *guerrilla* had given rise to a superabundant military caste. For the most part, these *hidalgos* were so needy that they formed a particular social class, related to the titled nobility in its pretensions and military vocation but close to the peasantry in its mode of life. When the Moslem foe began to weaken, to fade away from the horizon of battle and from the seas, the impoverished *hidalgos* found themselves without work; since they would not stoop to work in trade or industry, they were obliged to invent new adversaries, not only across the seas but in Europe itself. The fate of any military vocation is to turn against those it protected.

Castile was thus doomed to perpetual war, and the more than sufficient numbers of the military caste gave them the means to victory. Late in the fifteenth century and early in the sixteenth, *hidalgos* thronged to sign up with the *Tercios* of

[3] Naples and Sicily had belonged to the House of Aragon from 1284 when Peter III, the Great, took possession of the country in answer to an appeal from the inhabitants who had risen against their rulers—of French origin— and massacred all the French in Sicily (massacre of the Sicilian vespers, 1282). Milan was conquered by Charles V in 1535. By the treaties of Utrecht and Rastadt, Philippe V d'Anjou renounced all claims to the Italian territories.

the King; too poor to keep horses, they fought on foot. Other important states were still organized along feudal lines and so had an indifferent infantry, one ready to break up at any moment. Only in England—still poor and underpopulated—and in Switzerland did the communes enjoy liberties sufficient to imbue the bourgeois and the peasants with a feeling of citizenship and a desire to fight for their country. Hence, Castile was the first of the important countries to be enhanced by an infantry force at the very moment when the invention of the *arquebus* (a light hand-gun with match-lock or wheel-lock mechanism) made the medieval horseman an anachronism and gave mastership of the battlefield to the infantry. From Pavia to Rocroi, for over a century and a half, the heavy *Tercios* of pickmen and arquebusiers who manoeuvred under fire just as they did on parade, trampled the major roads of Europe and the New World and the gory pavement of subjugated capitals.

In the realm of science and technology, the Iberian universities[4] alone were in a position to confront the accepted achievements of western Christianity with the wisdom of Oriental antiquity introduced into the Peninsula by Arab scholars, doctors, architects. Thus Spanish scholars had made advances in mathematics, in cosmography, and in naval construction[5] which placed Spain roughly a century ahead of all other nations. Christopher Columbus was, in fact, obliged to place his boldness and his reckonings at the service of the Catholic monarchs simply because there were none but Spanish vessels and Spanish pilots equipped to venture out onto

4 The first Spanish universities were founded in Valencia (1212), Salamanca (1220), and Valladolid (1250). In Italy at that time, there were eleven universities; in France, four; in England, two. In Germany and elsewhere, there were none.

5 Between the ninth and fourteenth centuries, Spanish mathematicians perfected modern arithmetic and were the first to apply algebra and trigonometry. At Salamanca, Alfonso X, *el Sabio*, King of Castile from 1252 to 1284, caused the first astronomical tables to be drawn up, showing latitude and longitude. The island of Majorca, meeting point of the western and Arab worlds, was, from the thirteenth to the fifteenth century, a particularly active center of mathematical and naval studies, marine cartography, and the manufacture of compasses and astrolabes. The first practical manuals of navigation for captains and pilots were published in Spain in the late fifteenth century by printers established between 1474 and 1478 in Valencia, Barcelona, and Saragossa.

the Atlantic. From the discovery of the New World in 1492 to the disaster which struck the Armada in 1588, squadrons of Spanish galleys and galleons made the Spanish peace reign over all the seas.

But in Spain as in all of the great conquering democracies, omnipotence and the tide of colonial riches began, in the last years of the reign of Philip II (late sixteenth century), to determine the sociological phenomenon which Ortega y Gasset termed the "revolt of the masses." [6] The people-king acquired the classic mentality of the heir apparent, the spoiled child. Forgetting that the benefits of democracy and empire had been achieved by hard labor on the part of their ancestors, they looked upon these goods as gifts of nature which it was their rightful lot to enjoy without effort or sacrifice. In seventeenth- and eighteenth-century Spain, every man wished to be a gentleman[7] and to line his own pockets with the treasure of the Indies. The court and the ministries were besieged by spoils-seekers. While the State, needy in the best of times, drained its resources to support a horde of useless bureaucrats, pensioners, and prebendaries; sycophants of all sorts—cohorts of beggars, of counterfeit gentlemen and unemployed squires, *pícaros*,[8] starving bohemians—existed by what expedients could be found in the big cities. The land was abandoned as were trades. To live well with the least effort, was hence-

[6] Ortega y Gasset does not take "masses" in the sense of "proletariat" but rather quantitatively: the psychosis in question is a collective ill, an evil from which the majority of the population suffers. But men of every social level are affected by it.

[7] The psychosis which led a crowd of persons, none of whom had any right to do so, to claim to be of the nobility; and the real dimensions of the nobility and of the caste of *hidalgos*—both are revealed by the censuses of 1768 and 1787. The first shows that some 722,794 out of a total population of 9,159,999 belonged to these castes. The second census, which required authentic proof, found only 480,589 persons of the noble castes, in a total population of 10,268,150. It was proven that at the time of the 1768 census, at least 242,205 persons had usurped the title to nobility. Nonetheless nearly one million Spaniards—one in twenty—belonged by right to the nobility and hence refused to consider manual labor and even industry or trade—except for maritime or colonial trade, in which the *hidalgos* could engage without losing face.

[8] *Pícaro* means rascal, scoundrel. From this word comes the adjective "picaresque," referring to the literary genre treating of *pícaros*. [See for example, *Gil Blas* (Lesage), *Moll Flanders* (Defoe), or *Tom Jones* (Fielding).—Ed.]

forth the motto of all social classes. All branches of the government and all jobs sank into a routine of indolence, negligence, venality. This social decomposition was reflected in the picaresque novel (see note 8 above) which, introduced in the mid-sixteenth century in *Lazarillo de Tormes*, took a more sarcastic and bitter turn between 1599-1630 in the hands of Mateo Alemán and Quevedo.[9] Science was contaminated by the social demoralization. Encouraged in laziness by the neglect of their professors, students aimed for nothing more elevated than the painless winning of the diploma which would open to them a lucrative career, and the decline in the spirit of research entailed a decline in technique. By the end of the fifteenth century, Spain had discovered the New World, thanks to her maritime supremacy; in 1588, Spain was defeated at sea, because of the unwieldiness of the Armada whose vessels—overloaded, ill-balanced, ill-commanded—were unable to destroy the light English embarkations and resist the autumn tempests in the English Channel and the North Atlantic.

In the cities of Castile, interest in public affairs dropped off. Expecting everything to come from the Providential State, *hidalgos* and bourgeois alike petitioned for lofty posts—for employment at court, in the administration, or in the colonies. Municipal duties, mandates of the members of the *Cortés* once deserted by the most capable men were seized upon by coteries which saw in them a means to money. And from the decline of the cities there necessarily followed that of the Castilian *Cortés* which, stripped of all real responsibility, ceased to function altogether after the mid-seventeenth century. The State was now in the hands of a few courtiers, whose factions struggled for power.

The rush toward an American El Dorado had not only

[9] Published anonymously in 1554, *Lazarillo de Tormes* is generally attributed to the diplomat and historian Diego Murtado de Mendoza (1503-1575). Mateo Alemán (born in Sevilla in 1547, died in Mexico in 1610) published his picaresque novel, *Vida y hechos del pícaro Guzmán de Alfarache*, between 1599 and 1602. Francisco de Quevedo (1580-1645) published *El Buscón*, his best picaresque work, in 1626. Also included in this genre is "Rinconete y Certadillo," one of the *Exemplary Stories* published by Miguel de Cervantes in 1612.

depopulated the rural areas and the factories; but it also had removed from the mother country the most active and daring of the younger generation. Their absence calmed social tensions, for social structures ossified without the stimulus of frustrated ambition.

Colonization likewise brought about harmful economic conditions. From the start of the sixteenth century, the flow of precious metals caused an inflation which, like a malignant fever, undermined the economy. For the State treasury was not alone importing gold and silver; private individuals engaged in fraud. The inevitable monetary depreciation nibbled away at fortunes carefully kept in carven chests, while prices soared,[10] forcing the government to resort to new taxes, and to dig into its hard money reserves thus swelling the volume of fiduciary circulation still further. The salaries of workers, office employees, and civil servants lagged far behind price increases. A minority of profiteers made a scandalous show of luxury, but the far greater part of the population saw purchasing power diminish; decreasing consumption finally ruined industry, already hurt by foreign competition and scanty man power. The decline of the mercantile cities of the Castilian *meseta* and of certain Andalusian cities—especially Granada and Córdoba—dates from this era.

In other countries, inflationary crises almost always result in the bankruptcy of the State and in a currency devaluation which deals the *coup de grâce* to the once-affluent classes. The introduction of a sound new currency, day-to-day consumer needs, and food shortages stimulate production anew. In this way, inflation's cure is found in the very disaster toward which it tended. But the Imperial Spanish State was sheltered from bankruptcy by the constant influx of gold and silver from the New World. Thus, Spain's inflationary crisis continued for three centuries, and every Spanish activity withered to the root.

Spain could no longer support the American colonies or

10 In the century following the discovery of America, prices in Spain rose about 1,000 per cent. For the 1560-1613 period, the chronicler Garcilaso noted an increase in the ratio of 1:5. A pair of shoes that cost one *real* in 1560 cost five *reales* in 1613.

absorb their production, yet she forbade them all trade with other nations. The duties of port and frontier surveillance entailed by this prohibition were reserved to officials from the mother country, and all participation in public affairs was denied to the rich Creole (*criolla*) aristocrats. Under the reigns of Isabella the Catholic, Charles V, and Philip II, the government officials were intended above all to defend the Indians against the excesses of the *conquistadores* and the greed of the wealthy *encomenderos*—the great feudal lords, heirs of the *conquistadores*, who held a power of life and death over the Indian serfs on their landholdings. But in the seventeenth and eighteenth centuries the Indians' state, having made some progress, ceased to be a source of conflict between the Crown and the *Criollos*.[11] On the other hand, the *Criollos* found that the Castilian trade monopoly[12] became an increasingly heavy burden; and every attempt on their part to get around it incited the Spanish government to adopt ever stricter measures—which could be carried out only by Spanish officials. In this way, a monopoly on trade, centered elsewhere than where the real interests lay and counter to new economic currents, necessitated a monopoly on positions of responsibility. Therefore, from the end of the eighteenth century, an autonomist movement among the *Criollos* became discernible. Indeed, the emancipation movement in the American territories was characterized neither by an insurrection of subject peoples, nor by a resurrection of pre-Columbian civilizations. "Indigenism," or native nationalism, did not appear until the twentieth century and then, furtively and in vain, as a reaction against the tyranny of the *Criollos* and the *métis*. But

11 *Criollos* were pure-blooded Spaniards born in America, as opposed to the Spaniards born in and arrived from the mother country, and the *métis*, those who had a mixture of Spanish and Indian blood.
12 The monopoly on trade with the Americas was reserved for subjects of the Crown of Castile. The prohibition on trade applied not only to foreign nations but also to those associated with Spain (the Low Countries, Naples, Milan) and, to some extent, to subjects of the Crown of Aragon. The latter could emigrate to the Americas and send merchandise there—but both travelers and goods had to make the crossing on Castilian vessels setting out from Sevilla and, after 1717, from Cádiz. The Sevillian monopoly in fact ruined Barcelona for three hundred years.

at the end of the eighteenth century and early in the nineteenth, the revolt was of Spanish colonists against a mother country which refused them their just part in the government of the Empire.

The invasion of the Peninsula by Napoleon's forces[13] hastened the emancipation of the Empire. With the collapse of the monarchy and the occupation of a great part of the mother country's territory, the Spanish colonies gained a *de facto* independence between 1808 and 1813; henceforth all trade by the Hispano-American world turned toward the Anglo-Saxon nations.[14] It was too late to try to revoke this independence. In any case, after the restoration of Ferdinand VII, the Spanish State would have had to grant a large measure of autonomy to her realms across the ocean and make a mighty effort, in restoring the peninsular economy, to recreate a real economic link between the mother country and her Empire. But instead, she completed her own ruin through civil discord, and the centralist pretensions of the Crown provoked a colonists' uprising.

The only remnants of the Spanish Empire were Cuba, Puerto Rico, and the Philippines. But the demoralization which, engendered by omnipotence, had caused its disappearance, survived. At the end of an historical curve identical with that of Rome, Spain presented the phenomena typical of Rome or Byzantium: circuses and the latent insubordination of the pretorians.

13 In 1804 Spain was obliged to cancel her monopoly, for communications between the mother country and the Americas were practically interrupted by the English blockade. To punish Spain for having concluded a peace with revolutionary France (Treaty of Bâle, 1795) and to maintain neutrality in the London-Paris duel, the English fleet harried Spain's merchant vessels. To break the blockade, Spain allied herself with France. But the Spanish fleet, along with the French, was annihilated at Trafalgar in 1805. The only way Spain could re-establish her maritime communications was to come to an agreement with England. Her so doing resulted in Napoleon's invasion.

14 Before 1804, the overall turnover of trade between Spanish America and the United States amounted to only $3,000,000 yearly, this, in contraband goods. During the period of *de facto* autonomy, 1808-13, the figure rose to a yearly average of $21,000,000.

2. PANEM ET CIRCENSES

Beginning in the eighteenth century, the uprooted and somewhat indolent masses who pushed into Madrid and Sevilla conceived a passion for the arena. Bullfights, which until this time had been occasional single combats for the pleasure of the knights-combatant, now were transformed into periodic spectacles; the professionals of the arena reappeared, the type of the ancient *bestiarius*. These games were the response to a deep-rooted psychological need. The people had ceased to participate in public life and the psychologically passive plebeians refused henceforth to take any risk or assume any effort; nonetheless, they craved a chance to demonstrate their aggressive instinct. The passive body could be assuaged only through the arm of an active being. In Madrid, as formerly in Rome and Byzantium, the people continued to fight and to triumph but through an interpreter—an appointed slayer-of-beasts—with whom they could identify. When a thousand outstretched thumbs or a blossoming field of white handkerchiefs force the presiding official to decide the battle accordingly, when rhythmic chants cause spectral horses to spring out of the *corrales*, when a gale of whistles makes the *matador* hasten to encounter the beast—the multitude imprisoned by its own unemployed legions exults in a brief illusion of power, believes that it is still the forger and destroyer of civilizations which once reigned over the seas, still the people-king which sowed cities over continents remodeled in its own image, and caused the silver entrails of the mountains to flow in ingots. The throat burns from shouting so vehemently, the ears buzz with commingled noises, the spectator does not hear the silence of the forum. The arena is the last forum of subject peoples.

But this torpor in the midst of servitude shot through with dreams of power is a makeshift shelter. The *corrida* in fact completes the destruction of the conditions which gave it birth. The games of the circus are costly, voracious. There is not enough bread—and the wheat fields lie fallow as far as the eye can see, giving graze to the *corrida* bulls. The farmer trudges behind his antique wooden plough: the bullock is a luxury, reserved for the minority of wealthy cultivators. Thousands of bulls are sacrificed each year to the arenas. The circus devours the unsown harvest, the bull unharnessed to plough the scanty soil, the glebe land, which is the raw material of bread and of man's labor.

Each village should awaken from the torpor into which all have fallen. But the *corrida* is an obstacle in the path of the necessity which orders man to work. This torpor is born of and nourished by the perpetuation of man's resignation. Every Sunday, the circus games sap his vital energy: the intensity of a prolonged and repeated emotion summons all his energies, gathers them, strains them to paroxysm, breaks them by an abrupt relaxation, knots them together once again, breaks them once again, to the rhythm of the bull's charge and retreat, charge and retreat. In this impassioned catharsis, the active energy of a people becomes so many nervous sparks strewn on the sterile sand of the arena. Becoming accustomed from an early age to the death-spectacle, the dolorous diversion, destroys the sensitivity of the human being. Henceforth, he is predisposed to any abuse, any cruelty. Familiarity with bloody spectacles goes a long way toward explaining the sadistic abuses which have marked the revolutions and the civil wars in nineteenth- and twentieth-century Spain. By tolerating the arena games, by promoting them and allowing children to witness them, the Church and the public authorities have shown to what extent they submit to the *terratenientes*, landowners, who raise the bulls; and they show once again how indifferent they are to their essential task: education of the masses.

On the other side of the ledger, the idolatry of these circus games has been condemned by all the great figures of late-nineteenth- and early-twentieth-century liberal Spain, from Blasco Ibáñez to Pío Baroja and Ortega y Gasset. In that era all of the progressive forces, particularly the liberals and the anarcho-syndicalists, were alarmed by the psychological effects of the *corrida*. Their alarm was all the more pronounced because the ravages of the arena, physical ravages first of all, are felt most in the lowest classes: each Sunday during the bullfight season is marred by several accidents.[15] But the *corrida* perverts even more than it kills. Its false prestige has demoralized generations of young workers; in presenting a gilded mirage and factitious universe it tempts their appetites for luxury, for vainglory, and instills in them a disdain for useful work. Yet the majority of apprentice *toreros* have not even a chance to prove themselves in regular *corridas*. While casting about for engagements they subsist on shady deals.

A varied fauna buzzes about the walls of the arena: ticket-hawkers, unemployed *banderilleros, puntilleros* who finish off the clumsily killed bulls, *"monos sabios"* ("wise monkeys") who sew up wounded old jades to keep them going. Sickly and spitting, these down-and-outs perhaps were once the hopes of a season; ever suppliant, they cling to the neighborhood of the plaza in low taverns filled with the stench of refried oil. The adolescents who hang about the arena in search of work will join them one day. And others, and still others. . . . The arena wins. It spreads out. It eats into the city, as an ulcer eats into healthy flesh; the ulcer is devouring the city.

3. THE TIME OF THE PRETORIANS

The pretorian revolt is a classic phenomenon of all periods of imperial decadence; it results less from a military appetite for power than from the alteration of social structures.

In all countries and at all times there have been ambi-

---

[15] In a special issue, September-October, 1962, devoted to bullfighting, the Madrid magazine, *Índice*, published the complete list of Spanish *toreros* killed in the arena since the end of the eighteenth century. Listed were the names of some 278 victims between 1900 and 1962; in other words, considering the brevity of the bullfight season (from Easter to the autumn), one death every six weeks. Even so, *Índice* deliberately omitted the accidents which occurred during unofficial *corridas* at private parties or in fields. The *Índice* list included only professional *toreros*, omitting amateurs, *vaqueros*, and arena seconds. Nor did *Índice* mention the non-fatal accidents (sometimes resulting in serious disabilities) which occur at the rate of two or three every Sunday during the bullfight season.

tious generals willing to use the means of action with which the State has entrusted them to force their own wishes upon that State. But these ambitions can flourish only under cover of two phenomena common to the decline of empires: the survival of a heavy military system and the psychosis of the "revolt of the masses." The psychosis in turn takes on a double form: massive indifference to public life, and a mobilization of egos and ambitions. Professional and economic pressure groups strive by any and all means to make their interests prevail. Political parties, whose every member wants to become the leader, split into a flock of factions and into factions of factions. There is no chance for public opinion to act as arbiter of these quarrels because public opinion is indifferent and inorganic. Force is the only arbiter of political battles. If the ambitious generals did not of their own accord offer to achieve, through violence, the goals of a given faction, the political leaders would come begging for their intervention; and in nineteenth-century Spain, every party and every faction had a military coterie at its disposal.

The first of the *pronunciamientos,* made in 1820, came from the liberal officers. Military anarchy was fostered by the excessive number of officers who rose from the ranks during the war for independence against Napoleon's forces. Anxious, embittered, stopped short in their advancement, they watched the rapid promotion of the young and aristocratic officers polished by their military academy in Toledo.

Of middle- or lower-class origin, those officers risen from the ranks were needy men who felt bullied by a conservative government and the oligarchies in power. It was natural, then, that their resentment lead them toward the parties which stood for social renovation. The army was a progressive force; and the *pronunciamiento* was issued in support of the liberal revolution.

The conservatives, in turn, felt the need for pretorian backing at a time when a new generation of career officers, accustomed to the privileges of the class to which they were born, were stepping into important posts. From this time on, rightist *coups d'Etat* match liberal *pronunciamientos.* In turn, royalty, various regimes, governments and ministers were brought to power, overthrown, called back, banished—all to the alternating rhythm of the *pronunciamientos*. Conspiracies of officers' *"casinos"* or messes, barracks plots, abortive schemes, victorious *pronunciamientos*, generals' *coups d'Etat*, sergeants' uprisings—over a hundred military revolts succeeded each other in the hundred and sixteen years of Spanish history between Riego's[16] *pronunciamiento* of 1820 and Franco's *coup d'Etat*.

In each case these eruptions of the military branch onto the political scene coincided precisely with a slight change in the relative strengths of various minority factions quarreling under cover of mass political indifference. Some light is thrown on this coincidence by the history of the two important cycles of *pronunciamientos* in the nineteenth century. At the outset, both times there was a slight tendency toward the left on the part of the urban bourgeoisie irritated by the abuses of a conservative and clerical government. These conditions occurred simultaneously in 1836, when an uprising of sergeants of the royal palace of La Granja brought the liberal government of Calatrava[17] to power; and again in 1868, when the *coup d'Etat* brought off by Admiral Topete and General Prim[18] forced the abdication of Isabella II.

As in 1835-36, the parliamentary government installed by the army in 1868 was marked by factional quarrels and street fighting. Since a military coterie identified itself with each po-

[16] Rafael Riego (b. 1784), was a liberal general whose 1820 *pronunciamiento* forced Ferdinand VII to turn the government over to the liberals. A French army, led by the Duc d'Angoulême, invaded Spain to uphold the conservative right. Commander of the liberal forces besieged in Cádiz by the French, Riego had to surrender and, on Ferdinand VII's order, was hanged in Madrid in 1823. Riego's name was given to a liberal anthem which was the national anthem from 1931 to 1939.

[17] J. M. Calatrava (1781-1846), liberal *homme d'État*, followed to power another liberal leader, M. A. Mandizábal. The Queen Regent (for Isabella II) having dismissed Mandizábal in order to bring the moderates to power, the sergeants compelled her to summon Calatrava.

[18] Juan Prim, liberal general born in 1814. Member of the provisional government after Isabella II abdicated in 1868, then government leader after the *Cortés* elections. Since these elections showed a preference for a constitutional monarchy, Prim offered the crown to Prince Amadeo of Italy. Prim was assassinated on the very day in December, 1870, the new King sailed for Spain.

litical faction, the disputes begun in the assembly were continued by gunshots in barracks and public squares. During this phase of the process, *pronunciamientos* followed one another like so many links on a chain. Among the bourgeois liberals the need for order was stronger than the need for liberty; and this slight tendency back toward the right created propitious conditions for a *coup d'Etat à la Bonaparte*, intended to re-establish order and, simultaneously, safeguard the results of the revolution. It was at this stage of the evolutionary process that Generalissimo Espartero[19] gained control of the government in 1840, and that General Pavia threw over the first republic and set up the dictatorship of Serrano[20] in January, 1874. But the conservative oligarchies beginning to feel reassured, hence they and the bourgeois liberals who aspired to an orderly regime were not long in establishing a *modus vivendi*. The conservatives' *rapprochement* with the established regime caused it to lean to the right, and the way was then open for a *pronunciamiento* from the right: that of Narváez[21] in 1843 and that of Martínez Campos, in 1874, restoring the monarchy.

Suddenly, and for nearly half a century after this date, military agitation ceased as if by magic though the army was ridden by the same ambitions; only the political conditions had changed. As alarmed by the military anarchy as by incipient labor agitation, the conservative oligarchy had been reconciled with the liberal bourgeoisie and both had agreed to a certain number of common principles: constitutional monarchy, legalism excluding all recourse to force, and a parlia-

19 Baldomero Espartero (1792-1879), liberal general risen from the ranks during the war against Napoleon, commander-in-chief of Isabella's army against the Carlists (1833-39). He dismissed the queen mother and took over the regency in 1840 only to be overthrown by Narváez in 1843.
20 Francisco Serrano (1810-1885), moderate liberal general. As government leader in 1869, he was Regent in the interim before Amadeo's arrival. He served as minister several times during the reign of King Amadeo (1871-1873) and was ousted by the republic in 1873. He became Chief-of-State after the *pronunciamiento* which overthrew the republic in 1874, and was overthrown in turn by Martínez Campos.
21 Ramón María Narváez, a conservative general who, having overthrown Espartero in 1843, governed until 1854 with the title of Prime Minister or through an intermediary. Between 1854 and 1868—a period marked by the struggle between conservatives and liberals—he was government leader several more times.

mentary regime based upon bipartisanism. No sooner had a semblance of national unity been re-established than a pretorian rebellion became impossible.

During the third decade of the twentieth century, however, the *pronunciamiento* was to be born again—born of political disharmony, of the decomposition of the political system, and of the growing acuteness of social conflicts. In 1923, the *coup d'Etat* effected by Primo de Rivera opened a new cycle of *pronunciamientos*. Once again, experience proved that civil discord ushers in rebel generals.

Chapter Four

❦

THE "HOLY WAR"
FOREVER BEGUN ANEW

IN EACH OF THE political struggles of the nineteenth and twentieth centuries, the Church played the role of belligerent. Whether victim of violence or its instigator, the Church is always to be found at the heart of the conflict.

Three times in one century, the men of the little Navarre parishes took up arms, under the leadership of their curates, to cries of "Long live Christ the King!" (*"Viva el cristo Rey!"*). And since the start of the nineteenth century, each of the political convulsions which brought the left to power made bonfires of churches and was punctuated by scenes of blood and sacrilege. Yet nine times in ten the assassins of priests, the iconoclasts, were pupils of a Church which, in Spain, except for the brief period between 1931 and 1933, has never relinquished its monopoly on education. Why do many young Spaniards come away from Christian schools with such a vocation for violence? Would such crimes have been possible if the Church had brought to bear against cruelty—the veritable original sin of humankind—one tenth of the ardor which she has lavished for two thousand years on preaching against the most benign infringements upon property rights and the most natural tendencies of the flesh? When indeed has the Church of Spain, that Church which has shrunk morals to the dimensions of a practical code of sex and property, condemned violence?

Have not the men of the Church themselves often set the example by resorting to force in order to impose their doctrines? At the end of the eighteenth century and at the start of the nineteenth, when anticlerical liberalism was born, the Inquisition had prisons at its disposition and a populace of judges, policemen, guards, bailiffs, torturers. . . .

In the more remote past, in the Golden Century, when mere municipal magistrates were legally empowered to suspend the execution of a royal order, the most opulent of bourgeois knew that they risked their very lives when, double-locking the doors of their studies, they hovered over the writings of Erasmus or read the Bible in the vernacular. As early as medieval times, enemies of the King and common-law criminals alike, conspirators and rebels, enjoyed all the judiciary guarantees that other peoples were not to know until the eighteenth and nineteenth centuries. But at the end of the sixteenth century, any Spaniard could be thrown into a Church prison on the strength of a denunciation, real or faked, could be kept for an indefinite time in a dungeon and tortured merely at the whim of the Inquisitioner, would be given no choice by the Inquisitioner-Judge than that between "confession" of imaginary crimes or death by fire—inevitable reward of his obstinate denials. The land of total democracy was also that of total theocracy.

If we are to understand how this theocratic despotism, which weighs still upon the Spain of our day, was born and was able to gain strength and to last in a country which has for so long been devoted to political liberty, we must again plunge back into time, back to the long religious wars which gave birth to the Spanish nation.

1. THE STAGES OF INTOLERANCE

The psychosis of intolerance was formed slowly during twelve centuries of evolution and four historical cycles.

The seed of the spirit of intolerance was sown during the first cycle, that of the invasion from Africa and of the Reconquest. There awoke in the Iberians a Christian conscience, acid and rebellious. The Moslems' fanaticism and all in their behavior which bore the stamp of pre-Moslem tribal notions, drove the Iberians to the limit of their endurance. Spain underwent not so much an Arab invasion as a series of Berber invasions.[1] Both aridity and demographic expansion moved precipitate and successive waves of Moroccan invaders to crash against the rich granary that was Andalusia. In this opulent region, the tribes from the Moroccan desert found themselves abruptly transplanted into the framework of Roman life with its cities and aqueducts, baths and amphitheatres, roadways and irrigation canals. After their initial astonished and dazzled reaction the Berbers gradually grew accustomed to their new existence, became civilized and Hispanicized. The era of destruction and pillage was succeeded by the establishment of a markedly hierarchical society, theocratic and feudal, which placed terrible pressure within upon the subject Christians and multipled its aggressions without against the Christian realms in the north of Spain. But the invaders softened and lost their combative virtues. Similarly the regime forced upon the Christians softened until the softness of the occupying powers encouraged other Moroccan tribes to attack them and to reintroduce war and intolerance into Andalusia.

Even during the periods of relative calm, however, coexistence between Moslems and Christians continued unequal. In the country, the Christians were serfs on their own land, now distributed among the Moslem conquerors; in the

[1] Those Arabs, whether military chiefs, architects, or merchants, who had come from Baghdad or Damascus to the court of the Emirs at Córdoba, were so few in number that the Moslems themselves considered them foreigners and called them "the Syrians."

cities of the Moslem states of Spain, where they were relegated
to special zones—veritable ghettos—overwhelmed by taxes,
and given access only to the most menial jobs, the Christians
led an existence entirely comparable to that of the Jews in
the Christian states of Europe. The renegades themselves, although freer, were not entirely exempt from the status of inferiors. The Berbers who were converts to Islam and superfi-
cially "Arabized" could neither accept nor even understand
the theocratic society conceived by Mohammed, a society
founded upon a community of religious beliefs. No matter
how converted they were they regarded all those born outside
of their tribes as foreigners, inferiors, serfs; hence the renegades, obliged to pay a special tax—less burdensome, it is
true, than the monthly tribute extracted from the Christians
—were at the same time excluded from public office.[2] The
advantages offered them did not compensate for the risks to
which conversion made them liable in a society where the
least sign of a return to the Christian faith was punishable by
death.[3]

While the remains of the tribal concept discouraged conversion, there proceeded from the enforced inferiority of the
vanquished and from the alternating periods of tolerance and
persecution a sharpening, an accentuation of their personality,
and an exasperation which urged them to revolt. Ostensibly
persecuted because of their faith but in fact because of their
race, the Christians of occupied Spain (dupes, in turn, of the
equivocal nature of the holy war) considered as enemies all
who held other religious beliefs and as brothers all fellow
Christians whether serfs to the invaders or subjects of the
Christian princes. In this way, during a period of political
comminution, Christianity became the Spaniards' first com-

[2] Nonetheless, there were a certain number of departures from this principle,
when several small Moslem states were born of the decadence of the Caliphate
at Córdoba.
[3] The most celebrated instance of this is the case involving St. Eulogio. In
851, when he was elected archbishop of Toledo, the Arabs occupied that city
and he was unable to take up his duties; such was the persecution aimed at
him. In Córdoba, where he lived in hiding, he was accused of having recon-
verted to Christianity a young renegade girl formerly converted from Christianity to Mohammedanism. Both prelate and girl were put to death.

mon fatherland. Relations were secretly maintained between
the Christian realms in the north of Spain and those Christians who clung to their faith clandestinely. Castile was re-
peopled, defended, built with the aid of Christians escaped
from the Moslem zone; and the Christian armies were always
guided by secret agents in occupied land. It was thanks to the
support of the renegade Christians of Valencia that El Cid
succeeded in taking that city in 1094.

Certainly the long war of religion favored the confusion
between the spiritual and the temporal. But the persistence of
the holy war had not succeeded in stifling the liberal instinct
of the Iberians in religious matters. After the great victory of
Las Navas de Tolosa in 1212, when the Castilian, Navarrian,
and Aragonian armies liberated the major part of the Peninsula,
a *modus vivendi* intervened between the Christian states and
the little kingdom of Granada, last retreat of Islam on Iberian
soil. In the Spanish kingdoms reigned an unequal coexistence
modeled on the Moslem practice but working now to the
benefit of the Christians and the detriment of the Moors. Yet
in the Middle Ages the subjugated Moslems suffered neither
the periods of acute persecution which in Moslem Spain had
coincided with the eruption of new invaders nor the exclusion
caused by the survival of tribal traditions. Rather, new converts
were incorporated by law into Christian society; they had
nothing to fear even from the Inquisition. For the Inquisition
—born in the Languedoc early in the thirteenth century amid
the bloody convulsions of the Albigensian Crusade, codified
some years later by the Papacy and the Holy Empire, and
which had covered all Europe from Flanders to Italy with
blood and burnings at the stake—was not able to plant itself
firmly in Spain until the last years of the fifteenth century.
The Spanish *Cortés* had ruled out the summary procedure of
the Inquisition because it contravened the guarantees accorded to the accused by the *fueros*.[4]

The second stage on the way toward intolerance was

[4] In 1327, the *Cortés* of Aragon declared that the procedural methods of the
Inquisition were illegal and in contradiction of the *fueros*.

reached at the end of the fifteenth century, through an event stimulated by an external threat as well as by a profound social evolution. The external threat was in the form of Turkish invaders who, masters of Constantinople since 1453, were completing their conquest of the Arab world and assailing Christianity in the Balkans and the western Mediterranean.

The Spanish knew that the invaders, once established in Morocco, would penetrate into the Peninsula easily enough by the bridgehead of Granada and, once there, would find secret agents, guides, and spies in all the cities of Christian Spain, in the Moslem communities, and even among the *Conversos*.[5] It was as a preventive measure against the dual threat that in 1492 the Catholic monarchs, Isabella and Ferdinand, stamped out the last Arab stronghold, Granada. For the same reason, in 1478, the Inquisition had been authorized to establish itself in Spain.

At that time the Inquisition functioned as a tribunal of public safety. The peoples in the north of Spain, never having known an African invasion and remote from the new danger, were hostile to the Holy Office,[6] which consequently never became fully active in these regions. But Sevilla was the advance post of the holy war and here a frenzy of terror and espionage took hold of the population. Denunciations rained upon Torquemada's tribunal and the condemned went to their torture amidst cries of hate from the merchants and the populace of Sevilla. This climate of collective terror and popular consent explains the extent of the inquisitorial repression[7] and the measures of expulsion directed against the Jews, traditionally considered by the masses as the accomplices

[5] *Conversos:* Moslems converted to Christianity.
[6] In 1484, the first Inquisitors sent to Barcelona were expelled *manu militari* by the city's militia. Torquemada himself went to Barcelona to establish the tribunal of the Holy Office. In Aragon where, after long resistance, the *Cortés* at last accepted the presence of the Inquisitors, their chief, Pedro de Arbues, was massacred in Saragossa in 1485.
[7] Between 1482 and 1494, while Fray Tomas de Torquemada was Grand Inquisitor, some 80,000 various sentences were handed down. As to the number of persons actually burned at the stake, historians' estimates vary between 2,000 and 8,000.

and secret agents of the Moslems.[8] Ferdinand the Catholic lived surrounded by Marranos;[9] but under pressure from both the clergy and the communes, he agreed to promulgate the decree by which the Jews were to be expelled, thus making the first departure from the practice of coexistence.

The center of gravity in Spain had shifted from north to south and from the nobility to the bourgeoisie; this double transformation fostered religious fanaticism. By their demographic bulk, the peoples of the south who, snatched from Moslem domination, still loathed their former oppressors, outweighed the peoples of the north. And although, for their part, the great feudal lords had attempted to defend the Jews, who were useful to them as moneychangers, and the Moors who were a source of cheap agricultural labor, their attempts were futile. In addition, as members of a caste devoted to war, they could not very well hate the adversaries who had brought perpetual war to Spain. But on the other hand, to the merchants and the peasants, to the eternal victims of campaigning armies, war was the basic evil; and its instigators were, in their eyes, the Moslem and his Jewish accomplice. The latter was the object of additional bourgeois and peasant hate in his role as usurer, moneychanger to kings and lords. Furthermore, the mercantile class and the peasantry, less cultivated than the aristocracy, was more easily led by the clergy. For these reasons, the victory of bourgeois democracy was simultaneously the victory of intolerance.

In the seventy-five years following the first rigorous measures adopted by Isabella and Ferdinand, the consolidation of democracy and the permanence of the threat from outside aggravated the condition of the Moors and the Conversos. Spain the conqueror and holder of dominions was in fact incessantly threatened with invasion until the October day in 1571 when the immense armada, under the orders of Don

---

[8] So considered because of the part played by the Jews during the first Moslem invasion, in the eighth century. Persecuted by the Visigoth rulers, the Jews had risen in rebellion and opened the gates of certain cities to the Moslems.

[9] Marranos: converted Jews.

Juan of Austria,[10] sank three hundred battleships—the entire Turkish-Barbarian fleet—off Lepanto, and at last smashed the offensive apparatus of the Turkish Empire and rescued Europe from the Afro-Asian peril.

Until that moment, the possibility of a new Moslem offensive had encouraged the Moriscos of Granada to conspiracies and revolt. Whether converted or not, the descendants of the invaders had cause to look back longingly upon the period of Moslem domination, for now they were harassed in all sorts of ways. The treaty signed when Granada surrendered had guaranteed freedom of worship to the vanquished. But in spite of official proclamations of tolerance, Christians liberated from the Moslem yoke and civil servants themselves seized every occasion to vex and humiliate the Moriscos—who rebelled. After holding out at Albaicin, they were forced at last to ask for mercy. The violence of this revolt and the cruelty of its repression whetted hatred to a fine edge. Thus, at the beginning of the sixteenth century, after ten years of coexistence, the two communities were more hostile to one another than at the end of the siege. This disappointing experience moved the sovereigns to abandon the policy of coexistence in favor of one of forced assimilation. The decree of 1502, which commanded the Moriscos to accept conversion or exile, was not enforced before 1569 until which time the Moriscos retained their names, their customs, their modes of dress, their quarters, their fountains—and the majority of them continued clandestine practice of their religion. But new taxes were laid upon them; these and new arrests and executions ordered by the Inquisition provoked violent reactions. The leaders of the Moorish community established contact with the external enemies of Spain—the Turks and the English—while suspects, sought by the Inquisition, turned *guerrilla* or informer to the Barbary pirates who raided the

[10] Illegitimate son of Charles V, Don Juan (born in 1547) was entrusted by his half-brother, King Philip II, with the task of putting down the rebellion of the Moriscos (Moors) in Granada (1569), then with the command of Spanish forces in the Mediterranean against the Turks. He died suddenly before Namur, at the age of 31, amid circumstances which lend weight to suspicions of poisoning.

Spanish coast. These alternate acts of violence, at the time of the Turkish offensive toward the western Mediterranean in 1569, resulted in a general uprising of the Moors; quickly quelled, it was punished by decrees of expulsion, renewed forty years later under the reign of Philip III.

With the leaders of the Moorish community in exile and hope of an Ottoman offensive dashed at Lepanto, the spirit of revolt no longer found sustenance; the invaders' descendants, dispersed and equipped with Spanish names, lost themselves little by little in the mass. The systematic destruction of any documents accrediting the Jewish or Moorish affiliation of the new Christians extinguished their memories and their nostalgia, at the same time making them secure from persecution and blackmail. By losing their religion, relinquishing their personality, Jews and Moors had acquired Spanish citizenship and full equality of rights with those who had long been Christians; to such equality no religious dissident in any other theocratic society could lay claim. And, from the Orient to the Occident, what society of the time was not theocratic?

One might suppose that the disappearance of the African threat would in turn cause the disappearance of the Inquisition. But the Holy Office turned its attention instead to the Protestants. The five great *autos da fe*[11] early in the reign of Philip II struck his contemporaries by their sinister solemnity. But the number of victims was uncommonly low, as may be seen by comparison with the figures noted in other Occidental countries at the time. This difference is due to something other than the numerical weakness of Spanish heretics —Protestants or disciples of Erasmus. Intolerance was then less acute in Spain than elsewhere in Europe. Whereas in England the mere fact of attending Mass was punishable by death and in Paris, Henri II was devising a plan to massacre the Huguenots—a plan which his son was to carry out thirteen years later on St. Bartholomew's night in 1572, Philip II refused, at the beginning of his reign, to join the anti-

[11] Two in Valladolid, one in Sevilla in 1559; one in Toledo and another in Sevilla in 1560.

Protestant crusade proposed by the French monarch and for a long time strove to maintain cordial relations with Protestant England. But under the influence of purely political factors, the Spanish government took a further step on the path to intolerance.

Foremost power in the world, Spain was a threat to so many interests that the fanaticism, the fear, the hate she aroused formed a coalition to defeat her. The Huguenots of Holland rose up in defense of their faith, and the Catholics of Belgium in defense of their liberty. Protestant England supported the Flanders war, but the French Catholics warred against Spain in order to remove Belgium from Spanish influence. Philip II could split this coalition only by supporting the Catholic crusade in opposition to Elizabeth I who, on every occasion, was the champion of Protestantism. The Huguenots would not hate Spain any more deeply, and the Catholics would never dare take up arms against the defender of their faith. Having long retreated from the risks a new crusade would entail, the Spanish king nonetheless summoned the supporters of the Holy War to his government in 1578.

Spain was actually following the English example—just as, seven centuries earlier, she had adopted the usages of the Moslem holy war—when in order to safeguard its imperiled hegemony, Spain turned the concept of the crusade against Christian Europe.

By appearing as the champion of Catholicism, the Spanish monarch indeed managed to disarm the Flemish Catholics and, for the moment, to conserve Belgium. But the very mechanism of the crusade required Spain to support Catholics whenever they were in danger, to combat Protestantism wherever it showed itself. When this excessive war, having decimated armies and drained finances, came to an end—on the sea, by the sinking of the huge *armada* launched against England, and on land, by the evacuation of France, which had been momentarily occupied [12]—Spain was bled and

[12] Philip II had intervened on the side of the League (Catholic alliance) in the civil war in which this group was pitted against the Protestants led by the Pretender to the Crown, Henri de Navarre (the future Henri IV). Spanish forces, commanded by Alejandro Farnese, entered Paris in 1593. But, weary

ruined, and remained at the mercy of the enemies she had not been able to conquer. In fact, scarcely half a century later, on the battlefield at Rocroi, a reconstructed France was to seize from Spain the domination of the world.

More than eight centuries of victories had done, this defeat without a battle which in the late sixteenth century terminated the anti-Protestant crusade aggravated the complex of intolerance. Far from realizing that Spain's military impotence resulted from the decline of her cities and their manufactures, from the departure of her labor supply and from her public demoralization, her people maintained that their misery and all the humiliations to which they were henceforth subject were the consequences of Spain's failure —the failure of the champion of Catholicism—in her struggle against powerful enemies of the Faith. From this moment on, the identification of the nation with the Faith was absolute. Whosoever presumed to criticize the clergy or to express the slightest doubt in religious matters was instantly accused of adopting English or French notions, of being an accomplice of the enemy, henchman of anti-Spain. Religious heterodoxy became an insult to one's country.

Together with the extent to which it paralyzed the nation's evolution, the psychosis of imperial decadence contributed to the continuation of intolerance. In a ruined country where, after the middle of the seventeenth century, science and technology made only the slowest progress, and almost always with the aid of imported ideas, the way of life, social relations, mores and hence morals and ideas, all indicated that Spain was lagging farther and farther behind the other countries of the West. Until then, in spite of the singular conditions in which the Moslem invasions had placed her, Spain had passed through the various theocratic phases proper to the childhood and adolescence of societies at about the same rate as had those other countries. But in a western Europe arrived at spiritual maturity, the survival in Spain of ways of

---

of Spanish occupation, Frenchmen of both religions regrouped about Henri IV, who had converted to Catholicism.

life and of beliefs proper to vanished eras constitutes a pathological case of non-evolution.

2. COMMUNAL CONSTRAINT

Crystallized in the seventeenth century, intolerance has not been reduced since. But methods of material coercion, abandoned one by one, have given way to an insidious moral pressure, a communal constraint.

The Inquisition, dormant since the eighteenth century, was in fact no more severe for the times than were foreign tribunals dealing with misdemeanors of thought. We seek in vain among the annals of the Sevillian Inquisition for traces of a trial as iniquitous as that of the nineteen-year-old Chevalier de la Barre, beheaded and burned in France in 1766 on charges of having mutilated a crucifix.

But in the Spain of 1750, mores, beliefs, and state of mind had lingered at the level of those of France or England in 1650. At the end of the eighteenth century, this gap provoked the first conflict between the Church and intellectuals. Masonic lodges and "Societies of Friends" [13] appeared in the larger cities. But this minority movement came to life in protest against the Spanish milieu. Those young aristocrats or "enlightened" bourgeois who, struck by the decadence of their country, began to formulate doubts and to criticize met the disapproval of their fellow citizens. They were obliged to turn away from them and look abroad, where they could find encouragement and support. But when, in turn, they sought to spread the good, encyclopaedic word among their fellow citizens, the foreign origin of their arguments became a new argument against them. Spied upon by the entire population of his little city, instilling such fear into children that they crossed themselves when he passed near, pursued in his own home by his wife and his maidservant

[13] The most famous of these Societies was that of Azcoitia in the Basque country. Its members, the *caballeritos* (little chevaliers) of Azcoitia, undertook to study various aspects of public life: agriculture, customs duties, currency, finance, communications routes.

whom the priest had transformed into spies, the freethinker came to loathe the Spanish milieu.

The conflict between the liberal minority and the Catholic majority became still more grave after the Napoleonic invasion. Whether the liberals, being more patriotic than partisan, had borne arms against the invader, or whether, preferring their principles to their country, they had been in the service of Joseph Bonaparte,[14] all professed his ideas—whence their suspect and vulnerable position. And public opinion must have been easily excited against them by the clergy which, on the contrary, had gained in prestige by directing the *guerrilla* in the occupied areas of the north. The major result of the war for Independence was, indeed, a strengthening of the traditional identification of Fatherland and Faith. In the Catholic way of thinking, the liberal and the Freemason were the ultimate successors of the Infidel. Furthermore, the believer talked himself into believing that it was his duty to avail himself of violence against this new enemy of the Faith and of Spain. The historic reflex of the crusade, reawakened in Spanish souls, stirred the malcontent peasant of the northern provinces to take up arms twenty years later in support of Don Carlos, in this way transforming a particularist agitation into civil war. For more than a century to come, religious passion was to complicate all political conflicts and to endow them with the character of fatality and inexorable cruelty inherent in religious wars.

Nevertheless, though thoroughly beaten by the first Carlist war and persecuted by the liberal government which had come to power in 1835, within ten years the Church had won back a considerable number of her prerogatives. By turning the liberal bourgeoisie toward the right, the revolutionary excesses had played into the hands of the clergy. A concordat of reconciliation between Spain and the Holy See was signed in 1851. Since the greater part of its possessions had been sold to private individuals the clergy could not have them back but, as compensation, priests and bishops henceforth were to re-

---

[14] The Emperor Napoleon had tried to secure recognition of his brother Joseph as King of Spain.

ceive regular emoluments; in return, the Vatican recognized the State's right to presentation of the prelates.

Denounced after the liberal revolution of 1868, the concordat was once again put into effect in 1874 after the restoration of the monarchy. Thus began a truce in the religious war, which was to last over a half-century, due to the rapprochement brought about between the conservative oligarchy and the liberal bourgeoisie. The liberals conceded that Catholicism had the status of a State religion and, in return, secured freedom for dissident sects.

A new form of collaboration was established between the State and the clergy. By means of the confessional, of general spiritual guidance, and of the religious press, the clergy could sway and control a goodly portion of the electorate. The Church had at its disposal in the remotest villages a docile network of priests, monks, sacristans, and parishioners—a network which was in fact the implement of the Conservative Party; and precisely because the Conservative Party had this reliable network, it remained in power almost consistently during the half-century of the constitutional monarchy. Obliged to handle the Church with delicacy, the State, however, had certain powerful advantages over her. Invested with the right to present bishops, the government reserved the most responsible ecclesiastical positions for those priests who had proven their servility. By means of the episcopacy, the State passed its commands down to the lower clergy. The priestly office was becoming an offshoot of public office.

No sooner was the State in the hands of certain important interests than the politics of the Church became identified with those of the oligarchical castes. This collusion undermined the prestige of the clergy among the working classes and brought about a de-Christianization of the masses which is in fact the essential phenomenon of the history of Spain in the late nineteenth and early twentieth centuries. The Spanish bourgeoisie had constructed a perfect city from which the plebeians, kept beyond the walls, enveloped the clergy in the hate they bore the institutions and the castes which were admitted to that closed city.

Early in the nineteenth century, when the masses were still steeped in Catholic traditions, the liberal movement had appeared as an almost purely aristocratic and intellectual movement supported by a fraction of the middle class and by the army. But henceforth the situation was reversed: confronted by a people hostile to the Church, statesmen and Freemason or atheist military leaders were brought to collaborate with the Church for the sake of social defense.

The progress of popular atheism was furthered by the emigration of farm workers to the industrial centers where they fell under the spell of leftist propaganda. But de-Christianization was no less evident in the agricultural areas of central and southern Spain. The bureaucratization of the sacerdotal function and the elimination of colleges of theology in the universities were instrumental in lowering the moral and material level of the clergy and their effect was most pronounced at the bottom of the ecclesiastical hierarchy—at the level of the country priest. The pay provided by the treasury assured him lifelong security in poverty and was simultaneously an alibi for the avarice of rich parishioners. As a government employee committed to the State religion, the country priest dispensed prayers and rites with the surly indifference of any ill-paid civil servant. The friendship with which the great landowner might honor him publicly merely made him suspect in the eyes of the day laborers who were still less willing to pardon him his direct control over the minds of their wives and the indirect control which, consequently, he had over their homes.

The less influence the clergy retained over the masses, the more it gained over the ruling classes. By the end of the nineteenth century, religion had become the sign of the well-educated bourgeois, the perquisite of proper people. Those who did not haunt the churches were, in the eyes of their peers, no better than *turbas*—the ordinary people, the masses. There could be no question of entrusting such dissidents with the lowest public offices. If a freethinker was a lawyer or doctor, he saw his clientele drift away; if he was a shopkeeper, he saw the proper people go out of their way to avoid treading the sidewalk before his door. At school, Protestant or unbaptized children were hazed by their schoolmates.

So it was that members of the bourgeoisie and the middle class were refused, by the prejudices of their class, the freedom of thought and expression which the law, notwithstanding, had just granted for the first time to all Spaniards.[15] Toward 1898 a neo-liberal movement was to be born of this insidious constraint, and it was this movement which resulted in the proclamation of the second republic thirty years later.

3. SCHOLARLY TREASON

Spanish intellectuals have always been obliged to manoeuver around the power of the Church. Men whose vocation it has been to think could not live a life free of trouble and anxiety in a country whose tradition allowed all liberties except the liberty of thought.

Beginning in the eighteenth century, this underlying scholarly resistance underwent a mutation and emerged as overt rebellion against clerical domination, a revolt which was to lead to conflict with the Spanish milieu. Isolated and subject to the narrow limits of a community dominated by the Church, freethinking intellectuals were driven to seek their teachings and support in Paris or London at the end of the eighteenth century and into the nineteenth. Similarly, later generations turned to Germany or Russia. The fate of Spanish intellectuals at home is to gaze forever beyond Spain and to be forever foiled by the same resistance when they attempt to implant in Spain their adopted foreign doctrines. Generation after generation, they have been defeated by the fierce obstinacy of a people shut up in itself, impervious to English constitutions, French doctrines, German or Russian philosophies. By his thought, citizen of a foreign country,

15 At the end of the nineteenth century, civil status and family organization ceased to rest upon confessional bases. The code of civil law of 1889 had created civil marriage; and the recording of birth certificates, formerly the exclusive right of the clergy, came into the jurisdiction of civil magistrates.

the Spanish scholar lives as an exile within his native land, empathizing with all those who live or have lived on the fringe of Spanish society—those Moors, Jews or Aztecs, Moslems or Protestants, infidels or heretics who were opposed and deposed by Christian Spain. Henceforth, it matters little that medieval and Renaissance Spain was by no means a monstrous exception in areas where there were none but theocratic societies and intolerance was universal. Historical truth counts for very little with hunted beings the passion of whose own fear and wrath illumines and colors the ashen shadows of the past. Today, factions carry on their debates in a medieval or purely conventional sixteenth-century atmosphere; in the midst of all discussions looms Philip II.

These polemics have more than a retrospective interest. Since the history of Spain knows no institution, no custom, no memory which is not marked to some degree by Catholic influences, the anti-conformists were goaded into refusing the entire legacy of the Spanish past, into cutting themselves off from their national roots. To some extent this refusal of history compromised the results of the great inquiry into *casticismo*—the essence of Spain—undertaken by the writers of the 1898 generation and their successors.

A quarter-century after the inauguration of the constitutional monarchy, Spanish intellectuals had to admit that parliamentary institutions simply did not take root in Spain. But what regime would suit the Spanish temperament? To find the answer, it was imperative to study the Spaniard, the concrete man, his tendencies and the contingencies of his life. But although this investigation inspired some brilliant works, it came to contradictory and disputed conclusions, insofar as contemporary scholars gave their attention especially to the most rudimentary forms of racial expression, those most subject to lyric and impassioned interpretations: folklore, peasant customs, popular legends. Molded by several generations of liberal thinkers, they dared take on neither history nor traditional institutions thereby depriving themselves of the only clues which might have guided their inquiry into the more profound tendencies and aspirations of the race. For it was not in contemporary Spain, unable to find a way of life genuinely her own and hence reduced to imitating foreign ways, that the ultimate expression of *casticismo* was to be found, but rather in the active and creative Spain-that-had-been during centuries of vitality. Too biased against the institutions which had marked the Spanish past to take them seriously, nineteenth- and some twentieth-century intellectuals failed to understand either the originality or the importance of the Iberian, total democracy. So the precursor of the "generation of '98," Ángel Ganivet, saw in the *fueros* only texts of strictly local bearing, out of place in the modern world.

By deserting their mission the scholars, whose duty it was to transcribe the principles of total Spanish democracy and transform them into a formula for living applicable to the present day, handed over to the manipulations of the rightist oligarchies the most active part of the Spanish people: that which consciously experienced a nostalgia for the traditional liberties. Since the intellectuals spurned the heritage of Spanish thought and, instead, drew inspiration from the lessons taught by foreign teachers, people with long memories turned to men who appeared to champion the traditional institutions. These were the priests or princes, aristocrats or industrialists, the sincere or the cynical; at every turn they strove to preserve intact against every onslaught, against all reforms, a social status quo which was kind to their power, their vested interests, or their convictions. While the supporters of total Spanish democracy were opposed to those of representative democracy in the French or English manner, the sole effect of their fruitless conflict was the reciprocal neutralization of these two active liberal minorities; the solution was delayed infinitely, while social immobility and oligarchical rule were prolonged from one day to the next.

It was in this condition that Spain, boxed in by a false dilemma, and torn apart by civil wars which were in the last analysis all religious wars, found herself in the twentieth century and the great industrial age without having accomplished a single one of the reforms which all the other western nations had realized in the preceding century.

Chapter Five

❧❀❧

MEN WITHOUT LAND

THE INCREASING gravity of social conflicts in twentieth-century Spain may be accounted for by the conjunction of two phenomena: demographic expansion and the concentration of workable land in the hands of a rigid oligarchical minority. In other words, by increased need within an immobile agrarian structure.

Although a universal phenomenon, demographic expansion has nonetheless been less remarkable in Spain than in neighboring countries. But, in Spain, it was not accompanied by those compensating phenomena which occurred everywhere else in Europe: an increase in the global volume of consumer goods and their redistribution through salary raises, progressive taxes, and, most importantly, by a form of land distribution or at least by shares in agrarian revenue. In other western nations, industrial development was indeed preceded and conditioned by agrarian reforms which had been achieved everywhere between the end of the eighteenth century and the start of the nineteenth. The capital fact isolating Spain from these other nations and which, stretching across the Pyrenees an invisible frontier called Technical Progress, casts her back into the huddle of underdeveloped countries, is the failure of each attempt to parcel out the great landholdings in the southern part of the Peninsula.

1. ONE REVOLUTION BEHIND

The Spanish agrarian problem, in both *minifundio* and *latifundio*, is more nearly the work of History than of Nature. In northern and southern Castile natural conditions—continental climate, aridity, low yield per acre—are roughly identical and all factors work in favor of the great landholding. Yet the manner in which the soil is divided is noticeably different: to the north of the Sierra de Guadarrama, the small landholding predominates; but to the south, the *latifundio* is the rule.

There are to be found, in northern Castile as well, vast domains of from five to ten thousand *hectares*. But these semi-*latifundios* are the exception in regions sworn to the average, the small, or the very small landholding. Similarly, the *minifundio* abounds in the south, but as the corollary of the *latifundio*—the voracious *latifundio* of thirty, fifty, or even eighty thousand *hectares* characteristic of the southern part of the Castilian peneplain and Andalusia.

The frontier dividing these two zones of agrarian distribution coincides with that which, throughout most of the Middle Ages, divided Christian Spain from Moslem Spain. To the north of this frontier stretched two natural and historical zones: the Atlantic coast, the Pyrenees area, and northern Cataloña, the maritime or mountainous zone which had never known invasion and favored the small landholding; on the other hand, northern Castile which, after long years as a tragic no man's land because of Moslem raids, was methodically repopulated by colonies of soldier-laborers.

Again in the south, in the district of the *latifundios*, are two distinct historical zones: in southern Castile, the origin of the *latifundio* is ecclesiastic, for this area was conceded in fact, during the thirteenth and fourteenth centuries, to the fighting monastic orders charged with defending it against Moslem incursions. After Ferdinand the Catholic decreed that each King during his reign was to be Grand Master of the various orders of chivalry, their huge domains were almost entirely allotted to the Crown or the important lay feudal lords. Similarly, in Andalusia, the distant origin of the *latifundio* is to be found in the Reconquest: officers in the Christian armies were rewarded with lands confiscated from their Moslem feudal owners.

As for the clerical domains, whose global extent far outmeasured that of the lay *latifundios* until the nineteenth century, they were to be found as well in the north as in the south. Constituted from generation to generation by donations and legacies *in articulo mortis*, by the thirteenth century they had become a source of anxiety for the temporal power which had tried several times to limit their extent. Despite these attempts, the land in mortmain had come to include a very considerable part of the surface of the country.[1]

Eighteenth-century liberals had based their campaign solely upon *"desamortización"*: sharing in the goods of the Church. The question of the large lay properties was relegated to a place of secondary importance in the Agrarian Law (*Informe sobre la Ley Agraria*) of Jovellanos, a major work which was to serve as the basis of all nineteenth-century reform programs. The problems of agricultural yield and peasant promotion, however serious they appeared to the founders of the liberal movement, were overshadowed by what was taken as the essential objective: the struggle against the Church. The early liberals felt that, in any case, once free of the rule of mortmain, the great landholdings would be divided up within a few generations by the sharing of inheritances.

All of the liberal advisers to the enlightened despot, Charles III—Aranda, Floridablanca, Campomanes, Jovellanos—had included the division of ecclesiastical wealth in their

---

[1] According to a study made in the middle of the eighteenth century, some 23.52 per cent of the arable land in the province of Álava (Basque country), for example, belonged to the clergy.

program. Made prime minister in 1766, the Count of Aranda took advantage in 1767 of schisms within the Catholic community to banish the Jesuits from the Spanish territories. But he could not break down the resistance of the other orders and the secular clergy. By 1788, on the advent of the devout Charles IV, the liberals, henceforth stripped of influence in government circles, had accomplished only the *"colonización"* [2] of a few districts.

During the war for independence, the partisans of *desamortización* returned to power. For in the south, free of all foreign occupation, a new governmental system and a new army were forged in the struggle. Both were of liberal inspiration—a phenomenon explained, in large part, by the influence of England whose support was essential if the war were to be continued. The *Cortés*, meeting in Cádiz, reflected the state of the mind of the urban bourgeoisie in the south which was strongly influenced by the liberal movement. But the tasks and vicissitudes of war did not permit the liberal leaders to put their agrarian program into action and, after the liberation, King Ferdinand VII succeeded in removing the reform party from the center of power by falling back upon the classic forces of social conservatism: the Church, the majority of the aristocracy, the middle class of the more important market towns, and the peasantry of Old Castile.

In 1833, Ferdinand's death temporarily reversed the ratio of strength between the conservative social groups and the reformists, bringing the liberals to power and allowing them to set in motion a primitive reform which upset the agrarian structure without putting an end either to the *latifundio* or pauperism.

As is always true in Spain after a period of rightist authoritarian government, youth and part of the bourgeoisie of the great urban centers aspired toward a more liberal regime. In addition, the secession of the colonies and the temporary suspension of emigration to the Americas filled Spain with

---

[2] *"Colonización:* parcelling out of land among the peasants and distribution of the farming implements, seed, and livestock needed to let them put the land to profitable use.

stranded, young and ruined *hidalgos*, with cadets without patrimony, petits bourgeois without futures, uprooted peasants without jobs in the city—in short, with all the classless malcontents who formerly had gone across the seas to seek their fortunes. Their presence swelled the ranks of the clamoring reformists.

By recognizing Ferdinand's heiress, the young queen Isabella II, the conservative elements of the north would have forced the Regent to deal with them. But by rising up in 1833 in favor of the pretender, Don Carlos, these forces excluded themselves from the resultant system of power. And the Regent, henceforth the captive of her military and liberal defenders, was obliged to concur in the formation of increasingly liberal Cabinets. The moderates of the party, Martínez de la Rosa and the Count of Toreno, gave way to Juan Álvarez Mandizábal who, in February and March of 1836, decreed that the goods of the Church be put up for sale. This measure was still more actively carried out by the still more resolutely anti-clerical Cabinet formed in the autumn of 1836, under Calatrava.

Three years later, when the Carlists, chased from one position to another, were forced to surrender arms it seemed that the liberal revolution had triumphed in Spain. But the revolution had come and gone without the day laborers in the south having gained a single rod of soil. The greater part of the possessions of the Church, indeed, had been put on sale directly after the promulgation of the law. But, renewing the error committed by the French revolutionaries in 1790, their distant disciples in Spain also achieved a collapse of land values. Whereas in France, this depreciation had allowed the peasant class to accede to the status of property holders, the consequences in southern Spain were diametrically opposite. The day laborers of this region lacked numerical strength, while the Spanish nobility had escaped the type of systematic persecution which, a half-century earlier, had decimated and ruined the French nobility. Hence the wealth of the Church was bought up at absurd prices by the aristocracy, the great property owners, and the rich bourgeois. In the last analysis, the sole effect of the revolution was to augment the lay *latifundios* at the expense of the ecclesiastic *latifundios*.

Having misfired, this revolution strengthened conservative elements. In the country, the sons of the important atheist lords and the liberal bourgeoisie, made wealthy forever by the spoils of the Church, could think only of consolidating the social order and, to this end, of mobilizing the immense influence of the clergy. In the cities, the liberal middle classes, frightened by the disorder of which Madrid had been the scene in 1835 and 1836, once again opted for order and the consolidation of the social status quo. All necessary conditions for the conservatives' return to power were assembled.

At the end of the reign of Isabella II, military and clerical pressure brought on a new revolutionary crisis which returned the reform party to power in 1868. But the implementation of a reform program was obstructed, once again, during the short-lived republican period, by factional struggles, governmental instability, and contradictory *pronunciamientos*.

The political system established after the 1874 restoration, which was to continue unaltered for more than a half-century, seemed destined to clear the way to a reform process. Indeed, the 1876 constitution had introduced a parliamentary system on the English model, characterized by bipartisanism, the opposition-collaboration of the Conservative and Liberal parties. But this bipartisanism resulted from a tacit compromise between the conservative social elements and the liberal bourgeoisie. The liberal leaders knew that by endangering the fundamental interests of the conservative oligarchies and primarily those of the caste of the great landowners, they would put an end to the established regime and re-open the era of chaos. So they refrained from launching the agrarian issue. After more than a hundred years of sterile struggles, the country was to enter the twentieth century with a medieval agrarian system.

2. PEASANT PAUPERISM AND
GREAT MIGRATIONS

Spain counted nine million inhabitants when for the first time, at the end of the eighteenth century, the agrarian philosophers of Jovellanos' group voiced the question of *desamortización*. At the end of the nineteenth century, the population had exactly doubled and was to reach 23.5 million in the last years of the reign of Alfonso XIII.[3] The number of mouths to be fed had increased by 14.5 million, and the immobility of the agrarian structure hampered the rise of production. There were two and a half times as many workers as at the time when Jovellanos published his plea in favor of the agrarian law, but the proportion of land monopolized by the great landholders, had not diminished appreciably. Yet the number of entailed estates accounts for only a small part of the cultivated land surface. Thus in the long run, successional distribution would seem to guarantee the parceling out of the *latifundios*. But the prime factor in the preservation of the large properties is the low birth rate among the leisure classes. In addition, the effects of a slow current of successive sharing are compensated by another current of agrarian "reconcentration" whose origin lies in the splitting up of the small landholdings, a very rapid splitting because of the elevated birth rate in the peasant class and the decline in infant mortality. When successive sharing left for the final heirs only such plots of land as were too negligible to be profitable (the *minifundios*), these landowners were obliged to eke out their resources by work as day laborers. And if work was not to be had these small property owners, after going into debt, resigned themselves to selling their crumbs of land and going off to the city. In most cases, the buyer was the nearest great landowner. Once again, Spanish experience has demonstrated that beyond a certain physical extent the great landholdings have a specific faculty of self-reconstitution.

And in fact the global surface covered by the great landholdings was to remain, again, practically unchanged between

[3] The census of 1768 revealed 9,159,999 inhabitants; that of 1797, 10,541,221; that of 1900, 18,594,405; and that of 1930, 23,563,867.

1900 and the civil war, while the average-sized holding lost ground to the advantage of the smaller, and the small holdings continually were broken up until all possibility of profitable cultivation disappeared. Hence, in the last years of the reign of Alfonso XIII, the *latifundios*—500 *hectares* or more —still occupied over one-fifth (21.91 per cent) of the land surface of the southern provinces; the only ones, moreover, which have an ordnance survey. Over one-third of the surveyed land (precisely 35.72 per cent) was divided into very small farms of less than ten *hectares* and into unprofitable lots. Whereas an infinitesimal minority of great landholders (0.97 per cent) of the overall number of landholders counted in the census) with an annual revenue above 5,000 pesetas totaled 42.05 per cent of the *cadastral* revenue, the remaining 99.03 per cent of the overall number of landholders, or 1,789,488 small farmers, shared the remaining 57.95 per cent of the *cadastral* revenue. Nearly a million of these, exactly 987,548 farmers, obtained from their field a daily revenue of not even one *peseta.*

Since the great holdings in the south were devoted above all to two types of farming which require only a limited number of hands, the breeding of livestock—particularly of bulls for the arena—and large-scale cultivation, the oversupply of labor and competition among landless day laborers and the small landowners who were obliged to work for others, since they did not own enough, gave rise to unemployment and the depreciation of wages. In fact, at the beginning of this century, demographic density had reached a level of saturation beyond which it was impossible to continue without totally upsetting agrarian distribution and methods of cultivation. While the birth rate remained remarkably high in the country and the mortality rate went down, the overall total rural population remained practically stationary between 1900 and 1930,[4] for throughout this long period, the excess of the rural labor force

---

[4] The figures for active population in the rural zone have varied only slightly during the twentieth century. The number of agricultural workers (in all categories: landowners, farmers, sharecroppers, day laborers, men, women) reached 4,500,000 in 1900, and 4,400,000 in 1930. (This total was again to reach 4,500,000 in 1940 and to drop to 4,300,000 in 1950.)

was drained off to the cities and abroad. It was in about 1900 that the chief phenomenon of the Spanish twentieth century, the great migration, began. In 1900, some 56,000 people emigrated to the Americas; and the number was to grow from year to year until the First World War—reaching 194,000 for instance, in 1912. Thereafter, the migratory current toward the Americas was slower. But the annual average was 72,000 emigrants during the *quinquenio* 1921-1925. Over two million emigrants in all, mostly from the rural zone of the south, left Spain between 1900 and 1931.

Within the country a vast exodus, its pace alternately quick and slow but never stilled since the beginning of the century, carries the superfluous agricultural labor toward Madrid and the two industrial zones in the north. The percentage of urban population (of cities with more than 10,000 inhabitants) in relation to the total population of Spain rose from 32 per cent in 1900 to 43 per cent in 1930, and was to reach 51 per cent in 1950. All in all, the urban population was increased by 4.5 million persons between 1900 and 1930.

Had this figure been accompanied by a proportionate industrial development, it would have been by no means excessive. But when agricultural unemployment caused a massive population rush toward the urban areas, the pauperism of the southern peasants limited demand and consequently slowed industrial development.

Hence these massive interior migrations, stimulated more by demographic saturation and underdevelopment in the country than by the attraction of the city or by its capacity of absorption, were translated into an excessive supply of unqualified labor in the cities. The peasant exodus, worsening urban problems, condemned city workers to lower salaries and to insecurity in their jobs. Furthermore, it created chronic unemployment which, at certain moments, was rendered acute by fluctuations in outside markets. Thus the problems of the rural areas entered the cities with the immigrants from the south and there created pre-revolutionary conditions. The political struggles of the nineteenth century emerged as the social struggles of the twentieth.

PART TWO

The Defeat
of Representative
Democracy

Chapter Six

⚭

THE TIME
OF LOST CHANCES

IF WE SET ASIDE the brief period of the dictatorship of Primo de Rivera, we see that Spain lived from 1874 to 1936 under parliamentary rule. This age of representative democracy is divided, in turn, into two phases: one monarchical, along English lines; the other, republican, on the French model.

During the fifty-seven years of the first phase—which corresponds to the reign of Alfonso XII, to the regency of Maria-Cristina, and to the reign of Alfonso XIII [1]—Spanish society underwent spectacular transformations. The relative rise of industry and the rapid growth of cities gave a false impression of the condition of the country. But beneath the

---

[1] Alfonso XII, son of Isabella II, was only 17 when General Campos' *coup d'Etat* caused him to mount the throne. Being young and amiable, he was very popular. Dead of tuberculosis at 28, in 1885, Alfonso XII left Queen Maria-Cristina of Habsburg pregnant with his child, the future Alfonso XIII. Until the young king reached his majority, in 1902, the Queen-Mother, Maria-Cristina, exercised the regency.

glittering façade of the *belle époque,* each of the problems handed down by the past remained intact. The gravity of social conflicts and the political indifference of the masses were to cause progressive decay of the parliamentary machinery, to call the pretorians back on stage, and bring about the downfall of the regime.

1. LA BELLE ÉPOQUE

The reconstruction of the constitutional monarchy was achieved largely because of an exceptional political stability, for the disturbances of the preceding era had engendered general lassitude. Military adventurers no longer found support or partisans. The majority of the population still had no part in the established order, but that majority remained inorganic. This was the case of the agricultural day laborers and even of the greater part of the urban proletariat. The inorganic minorities of the opposition—intellectuals, unions, and labor parties—were still too feeble to be influential in public life.

Great landholders, members of the middle class, landowning peasants—all of the controlling classes had become part of the established order and had come to an agreement on certain fundamental points. The liberal bourgeoisie admitted the monarchical form of government, the social status quo, the great agrarian landholding, and the officialization of Catholicism. Clerical domination of teaching and the schools was in fact the only question to stimulate controversy between the liberals and conservatives. For their part, the conservatives accepted the parliamentary system and tampered with it to their own advantage.

Within roughly fifteen years during this truce, the governments and parliaments of the Restoration constructed the administrative and juridical framework which still exists in Spain today.[2] Judiciary reorganization and the creation of the

---

[2] The Civil Code was promulgated in 1888. The penal Code (1879), the Code of civil procedure (1885), and the commercial Code (1886) date from the same period.

jury assured Spaniards of an independent justice, while new laws concerning freedom of press and of assembly restored to these aspects of life some of the former liberties.

Also during this period, the industrial infrastructure was created to equip a country which, because of earlier disturbances, found itself at least two decades behind the other western European countries.[3] The development of Spain was above all the fruit of private enterprise. Indeed, private, and for the most part foreign, companies built the Spanish railways and developed the mining resources: iron in the Basque region, copper, from the Río Tinto, mercury from Almadén.[4] Production of these ores reached its peak in the early years of the twentieth century and began to decline toward 1910 as certain reserves were exhausted. But progress in agriculture continued. Between 1910 and 1929, industrial production increased threefold; but the ceiling reached in 1929 in virtually all fields was not to be reached again for some twenty-five or thirty years, and then only with difficulty. Similarly, national revenue rose 32 per cent during the fifteen years which separate the *quinquenio* of 1911-1915 from the last *quinquenio* of the Monarchy. In spite of exceptionally rapid demographic growth,[5] due to an elevated birth rate and a drop in the rate of infant mortality, the average income per person rose from 884 to 1031 *pesetas* a year during this period. Thirty years later, Spain was still living on her inheritance from this pe-

[3] The first railroads appeared, in France and in England, between 1820 and 1840; the first in Spain—laid between Barcelona and Mataro—was inaugurated in 1848; and the link between Madrid and Aranjuez was established only in 1851.

[4] Upon its advent to the throne, the Monarchy found the subsoil already mortgaged by the diverse governments which had succeeded each other between 1868 and 1874. The lease of the Linares reserves dated from 1869; that of the mercury of Almadén, from 1870; and that of the Río Tinto, from 1873.

[5] In 1870, Spain had 16,320,851 inhabitants; in 1931: 23,563,867. The average rate of birth at the start of the twentieth century was 35.13 children born alive for every 1,000 inhabitants. This rate was to decline progressively to an average of 27.2 per 1,000 in 1931-36. It has been estimated that in 1901, 18.59 per cent of the children born alive died before reaching the age of one year, and 34.68 per cent before the age of five. In 1931, these statistics had fallen, respectively, to 11.65 per cent and 18.73 per cent.

riod: three-quarters of the industrial equipment in use in 1958 dated from 1931.

The interior rehabilitation was then attested to by a rehabilitation of diplomacy, the explanation of which lies also in the psychological shock attributable to the disastrous war of 1898 against the United States: Spain lost Cuba and the very last remnants of her colonial empire.

Alfonso XIII, although only thirteen at the time of the war, was marked by this defeat like all of his contemporaries; throughout his reign he directed his efforts to rebuilding the navy and to ensure that Spain would regain her former rank among the great nations. His design was, paradoxically, furthered by the weaknesses which prevented Spain from declaring imperialistic intentions. No sooner were other nations assured that Spain had no appetite for revenge than memories of her past grandeur returned and placed that nation on unparalleled moral heights, allowing her to mediate the disputes of the "great nations." Hence, in 1905, when Wilhelm II had made his spectacular debarkation at Tangiers and war appeared a certainty, the Madrid government was able to take the initiative in bringing together at Algeciras representatives of the great powers. During the First World War, the Spanish position was neutral, because opinion was so divided that the government was condemned to immobility, and this position brought immense diplomatic and commercial advantages. Following the war, eight years of successful arbitration gave Spain a permanent seat on the council of the League of Nations alongside the "greats" of the time.

The rapidity of Spain's rise in the early twentieth century is recorded in the structure of the big cities which, as exemplified by Barcelona, passed almost without transition from the eighteenth century to the twentieth. In Madrid, artificial city, administrative city, bureaucratic continuity made the evolution less abrupt. But the provincial and old-fashioned Madrid of 1880 still had the skeleton given it by Charles III at the end of the eighteenth century; and the contours of the Madrid of the *Siglo d'Oro* were clearly to be seen, the narrow streets and little squares, the palaces and arcades, the bell-towers squeezed between the *Alcázar* and *Puerta del Sol*, or about the *Plaza Mayor* or the balcony of the *Panadería*, that minuscule heart of the city from which Kings, *alcaldes* and *corregidores* had presided in turn over the presentation of Lope de Vega's plays and bullfights, religious festivals and pageants. On the fringe of this initial city, the eighteenth century had erected another metropolis, with baroque churches and neo-classic palaces, sordid slums and residential areas, a city open on every side to the Castilian peneplain: westward, beyond the Manzanares, open to the *Pradera* of San Isidro where the *romería* of the fifteenth of May attracted a crowd in holiday mood, courtiers and *grisettes*, artisans and great ladies, *majas* and *manolos*; eastward, the *Calle Alcalá* and the "salon" of the Prado, broad avenues lined with gardens were furrowed with carriages and gentlemen on horseback rode toward the *Buen Retiro*. The romantic age, drawing students to the famed Alcalá de Henares University near Madrid, had brought cabarets and bookstalls to the old *Calle San Bernardo*. Life had drifted away from the *Plaza Mayor* and adopted the *Puerta del Sol*, bordered with taverns where gathered a quarrelsome and bearded little throng of chroniclers, students, actors. The omnibus had appeared, soon to be replaced by small tramways drawn by mules trotting to the rhythm of their miniature bells. The first gas-lit street lamps shone in the Madrileño night, filled with the slow psalmody of the Galician *serenos*. Everything was changing—except the plan of the city which remained circumscribed in the limits fixed by Charles III: the *Palacio de Oriente*, a little Versailles built upon the ruins of the old Alcazar; the Arch of Triumph of Alcalá; Retiro Park, the *Paseo* of the Prado.

But in the last years of the nineteenth century, a new metropolis with rectilinear avenues sprang up from the peneplain on the rim of old Madrid. The population had not reached a half-million by the end of the century; in four decades it was to double. The city annexed neighboring villages on the way: Cuatro Caminos, Ventas, Vallecas, Carabanchel—peripheral communities emptied and repopulated each day by the shuttling subways and double-deck buses which carry the workers to and from their jobs in the stores and offices of central Madrid. Here, all along the *Calle Alcalá* and near the *Puerta del Sol* there suddenly appeared immense buildings bristling with colonnades, capped with cupolas, and coiffed with horses, chariots, warriors, all proclaiming the glory of the Bank of Spain or the Bank of Bilbao; while on the *Plaza de Cibeles* arose the huge post office, looking very much like a gigantic Neo-Gothic pastry confection—"Our Lady of Communications." Between 1916 and 1930, the central areas were split open to form a long diagonal: a *Gran Vía* lined with hotels, department stores, and skyscrapers, dominated by the geometric mass of the Telefónica: vast edifices of concrete and glass which give the capital the air of an old-world Buenos Aires. Above them, movie theatre marquees and luminous billboards dazzle the night.

Literature and the theatre bore the imprint of the social evolution. During the "Isabeline" epoch, almost all of the theatres of Madrid were devoted to the *zarzuela* (operetta) or to can-can shows with satiric interludes spoofing Sor Petrocinio[6] and political figures of the time. These were the spectacles which suited a middle class with little education and an aristocracy more preoccupied with equine than intellectual questions. But the rapid increase in the ranks of the bourgeoisie, who grew more affluent and more cultivated, brought forth new and typically bourgeois types of theater —dramas and comedies—and revived classical tragedy. In the first years of this century, the *Teatro de la Comedia* and the old Zarzuela hall offered the Andalusian *sainetes*, or farces, of the brothers Álvarez Quintero and Benavente's[7] first comedies of manners; simultaneously María Guerrero was reproducing the tragedies of Calderón on the very boards on which they

[6] A nun who exercised a strange sway over Queen Isabella who liked to surround herself with a court of visionaries, healers, and charlatans.
[7] Jacinto Benavente, born in 1866, author of about a hundred plays and comedies *Los Intereses Creados, La Malquerida, La Comida de las Fieras, Lo Cursi*), and recipient of the Nobel Prize.

had first been created at the *Teatro Español* in the *Calle del Príncipe*.

In those early years of the twentieth century, two generations were face to face in literary Madrid. The first—that of Juan Valera,[8] of "Clarín," [9] and of Menéndez y Pelayo[10]—had been outstanding at the end of the nineteenth century and had striven to practice the doctrine of *"l'art pour l'art."* Illustrious survivor of a declining generation whose theories he had never, in any case, wholly championed, Galdós[11]—whose last *Episodios Nacionales* were not a great success—could meet in the cafés and *tertulias* of Madrid two young novelists recently arrived in the capital, Blasco Ibañez and Pío Baroja. Ibañez had already finished his Valencian cycle; Baroja, weary of his forlorn existence as a country doctor, had come to seek his fortune in Madrid and, in the more sordid taverns, had fallen into the world of bohemians, anarchists, *pícaros, golfos*, whose tribulations he had set forth in the romantic trilogy, *La Lucha por la Vida* (The Struggle for Life). Blasco Ibañez and Pío Baroja had in common a will to be the witness of their times. This will was the inspiration of other young writers who, with Baroja, were part of the generation of 1898: Unamuno, Antonio Machado, "Azorín," [12] and Ramiro de Maeztu.[13]

The theory of art-for-art's-sake was by then so bankrupt that no one dared defend it openly, not even the modernist writers who practiced it: the poet-dandy, Rubén Darío; the Galician writer, Ramón del Valle-Inclán; and the young Anda-

---

[8] J. Valera (1827-1905), celebrated novelist, known especially for his *Pepita Jiménez*.
[9] "Clarín," pseudonym of the literary critic, Leopoldo Alas (1852-1905).
[10] Marcelino Menéndez y Pelayo (1856-1912), historian and critic. His major works are *Historia de los Heterodoxos Españoles, Historia de las Ideas Estéticas en España, Antología de Poetas Líricos Españoles, Antología de Poetas Americanos*.
[11] The famed novelist Benito Pérez Galdós, born in the Canaries at Las Palmas in 1845, died in 1920.
[12] "Azorín," pseudonym of essayist and critic José Martínez Ruiz, born in 1876, author of *El Alma Castellana, Los Pueblos*.
[13] The journalist and critic Ramiro de Maeztu, born in 1875, was assassinated in the republican zone very early in the civil war (1936).

lusian poet, Juan Ramón Jiménez. Further, modernist writers and the *noventayochentistas* (those of 1898) were listed side-by-side on the tables of contents of the swarming, ephemeral little avant-garde magazines: *Madrid Cómico, Vida Nueva, Helios, Arte Joven.* . . .

The formal preoccupations of the modernists and the characteristic aim of the writers of 1898 to express national and popular realities, were also to be found in the musicians of the early twentieth century. In *Iberia,* and *Vida Breve* in the *Goyescas,* and in *El Amor Brujo,* Albéniz, Granados, and Falla, by translating the popular traditions of the races into a new style, reached the goal which their writer and philosopher contemporaries often sought in vain.

Two decades later, the national and popular tendency was to triumph, at least in the field of letters, over the surrealistic temptation dangled before writers and artists by the first canvases of Salvador Dali, and by Luis Buñuel and his film, *El Perro Andaluz.* Juan Ramón Jiménez, renowned since the publication in 1931 of his *Platero y Yo* gathered about him a circle of young poets: Salinas, Guillén, the ascetic José Bergamín, Rafael Alberti, and Federico García Lorca who was to gain fame overnight from his *Romancero Gitano.* The way had been laid for this work by the stylization of folk dancing achieved by La Argentina and by Falla's Andalusian opera. The *Romancero* was the fulfillment of the renaissance begun in 1898 of popular themes, popular values. Once more Spanish literature was putting down roots in home ground.

While the literary milieu of Madrid was still nineteenth-century in the originality of human types and in the custom of literary *tertulias,* the trend in the big daily newspapers which had multiplied during the first three decades of the new century—A.B.C., *La Epoca, El Debate, El Sol*—was toward science and technology. This was the time when Spain thrilled to the helicopter experiments of the engineer, La Cierva, and to the flight of the *Plus Ultra* which, piloted by Ramón Franco,[14] made the first crossing of the south Atlantic in January, 1926. In the mirage of the 1925-1930 period,

14 Ramón Franco, the *Caudillo*'s brother, died during the civil war.

Spain could believe that technology itself was back on her side.

But in the midst of a brilliant Restoration society, philosophers, novelists, artists of this new *Siglo d'Oro* had adopted an attitude of tart criticism. Aware of the gaps in Spanish evolution since the disastrous loss of Cuba and already exasperated by the limitations set upon them by their social surroundings, the men of the generation of '98 once again voiced doubts about certain values, basing their scepticism on the philosophic theories of Giner de los Ríos,[15] founder of the *Instituto de Libre Enseñanza*—Institute of Free Teaching. And they in turn were to forge the rebellious spirit of their younger brothers, those writers who entered the life of letters in about 1925.

At this time, Ortega y Gasset, the Benjamin of the 1898 generation, was the indubitable leading light of Spanish cultural life. Professor of metaphysics at the University of Madrid, guiding spirit of the daily *El Sol* and of *La Revista de Occidente*, during the last days of the monarchy he was to gather about him the entire intellectual opposition, from students to mature scholars grouped in the association, *"Al Servicio de la República"*—"In the service of the Republic."

2. THE DECEITFUL MIRROR

The intellectual opposition was born, in fact, of the realization that representative democracy had failed. As early as 1898 it was evident that the Anglo-French parliamentary institutions imported by Spain a quarter-century earlier were not taking root in the unfamiliar soil.

The development of civic life in Spain was diametrically

[15] Philosopher, jurist and teacher, Francisco Giner de los Ríos (1839-1913) contributed to the diffusion in Spain of the theories of the German philosopher Krause. In 1866 he won a competition for the chair of Professor of Law Philosophy at the Central University of Madrid. Dismissed and persecuted for his liberal ideas by the conservative government of Cánovas del Castillo, he founded the Institute of Free Teaching in 1876. His University chair was restored to him in 1881, but the Institute was maintained. It was this Institute which trained almost all of the intellectuals who played a role in Spain between 1900 and 1930.

opposed to that in England and Germany, where the masses had gradually penetrated the structure of parliamentary democracy. Their first members of Parliament caused social reform laws to be voted; and timid though these reforms were, they did augment the buying power and, therefore, demand, production, and urban population. These first results incited the workers and even the peasants to support the parties on the left. In these two nations, political democracy was the vehicle of a relative social democratization. But in Spain the masses continued estranged from political life. Indeed, electoral participation, which at no time exceeded 40 per cent of the registered voters, several times fell as low as 25 per cent.

Yet the political constitution and living conditions of the peasants—who made up the majority of the population —were identical in the three countries. The political rights granted by the Spanish Constitution of 1876 equalled or even surpassed those enjoyed by the Germans and the English at the time.[16] In England and Germany, just as in Spain, the great landowners—landlords or *junkers*—monopolized a large part of the arable land surface. It is true that the rapid industrial rise, and expansion of the urban proletariat—the two outstanding phenomena in late nineteenth- and early twentieth-century England and Germany—largely account for the political evolution of those two nations. And most sociologists of the Marxist school explain Spain's industrial lag in terms of Spanish political immobility. But the electoral abstentionism urged by Spanish labor unions and the fact that the number of abstentions was, throughout this period, higher among the urban proletariat than in any other sector of the Spanish population, lead us to believe that a rapid industrial development in Spain would not have altered the political conditions.

The widening of the urban area at the expense of "intermediary Spain" and the rural area, the growing numbers of the industrial proletariat[17] and urban bourgeoisie—none of

---

[16] Universal suffrage was inaugurated in Spain in 1876, nine years before the enactment, in England, of an electoral law which extended the right to vote in fact—and not in principle—to nearly all of the male population.

[17] In the 1900 census, industrial workers were found to account for 15.99 per

these sociological phenomena brought on by the economic growth between 1875 and 1930 would be translated into political terms until the last years of the monarchy. In the half-century between the Restoration and Primo de Rivera's 1923 *coup d'Etat*, the evolution of social structures paradoxically had favored political immobility.

Throughout this period, the urban proletariat abandoned its passivity only to launch into direct action. Its revolt added not one vote to the Liberal Party and threw the bourgeoisie back toward the right. The groups clamoring for reform were weakened, furthermore, by a renewal of emigration toward the Americas and by the social ascension of a popular and petit-bourgeois minority. Those members of the middle class who had made their way to leisure and those peasants who, having migrated to the city, had succeeded in buying a shop or a modest handicraft business, turned to the Conservative Party or brought to the Liberal Party their anxiety for social conservatism and their great fear of the proletarian revolution.

Spokesman for the conservatism of the small interest groups, the Liberal Party even took care not to attack the big interests represented in the Conservative Party, in order not to endanger the tacit compromise on which public order rested. Parliament, sterilized by the sterility of the Liberal Party, appeared ever less attractive to the workers and to the young. Social tensions, finding no release in Parliament, now more than ever expressed themselves in the street, in the form of direct action.

So, for the Liberal Party, the period of decline succeeded the period of immobility. Its rightist element was poorer by a part of its bourgeois clientele who were leaning farther and farther toward the repressive methods advocated by the conservatives. And in the left wing of the Liberal Party new parliamentary groups were born, representative of the reformist minorities (the radical, the republican, the socialist parties). From this time on, bipartisanism was doomed, and the

---

cent of the active population, or 1,049,000 persons. In the 1930 census, they accounted for 26.51 per cent of the active population, or 2,300,000 persons.

conservatives were in power more often than the liberals during the first two decades of the personal reign of Alfonso XIII (1902-1923).

The Conservative Party relied not only upon traditionally conservative elements (the bourgeoisie of "intermediary Spain," landowning peasants in the north), but also upon the forced vote of the day laborers in the south. In these areas, demographic growth gave the *terratenientes* new means to put pressure upon the peasant mass by creating an oversupply of labor, lower wages, and chronic unemployment. Fearing that they would always be out of work if they displeased the master of the land, the sole employer, the *cacique*, the day laborers voted for his candidate. Rarely did the *cacique* run for office in person; he designated a straw man, perhaps a member of his family, a son or more often a son-in-law. *"Caciquismo"* gave the country a *yernocracia* (government by sons-in-law).

Elected as a result of the vote of those who stood to profit from agrarian reform, the conservative majorities were radically opposed to any structural reform. In a time of economic expansion and mounting social tension, Parliament and the government transformed themselves into instruments for the preservation of the status quo. And the stagnating State progressively slowed economic and social evolution.

The immobility of the agrarian structure maintained the buying power of the rural masses on the lowest possible level, while the increased yield of the national income was monopolized by the urban bourgeoisie. And the lack of consumers forced a "ceiling" upon the transformation industries which had got off to an emphatic start in Cataloña and the Basque country. Their rise was further hampered by a deficiency of heavy industry and a dearth of energy. Conversely, development of energy sources and heavy industry would have required such capital as was out of reach of the opportunities for savings in so underdeveloped an economy.

In addition, the great interests which dominated society, Parliament, and the State, were hostile to the expansion of industry, insofar as their own prosperity depended upon the exportation of agricultural and mineral products. Mining companies and *terratenientes*, middlemen and exporters, feared that the development of national industry would cause imports of manufactured articles to dwindle and incite their producers—England, above all—to restrict purchases of Spanish iron and oranges by way of reprisal.

Furthermore, Spanish oligarchies were directly affected by the activities of foreign cartels established in the Peninsula. A certain number of Spanish capitalists were shareholders in the Basque-Asturian Mining Company and in the companies which brought out the mercury from Almadén or worked the ore deposits of Peñarroyo or the copper of the Río Tinto. Spanish ministers and Spanish generals sat on the boards of directors of these companies. This collusion between Spanish oligarchical forces and foreign capital guaranteed to the latter a *de facto* monopoly over the major activities of the Peninsula. This caused dividends to flow out of the country: once again the national income was reduced and, with it, opportunities for saving and reinvestment.

At the very time when the immobility of agrarian structures and demographic expansion propelled a mass exodus toward the large urban centers, the slowness of industrial development restricted possibilities of taking on labor. Low wages and unemployment, these two corollaries of surplus urban labor, were aggravated by chronic instability. Such an economy, its expansion restrained and its existence based upon the exportation of raw materials, was dangerously susceptible to every slightest fluctuation in the international market. Hence every crisis in sales volume and every drop in prices on the world market was translated, within the Peninsula, into periods of serious unemployment and semi-revolutionary agitation.

Conservatism not only created pre-revolutionary social conditions: but it also stimulated dangerous psychological reactions by strengthening the conviction shared by peasants and workers alike that the State and Parliament, by their very nature as instruments of the oligarchies, were unable to remedy the evils which plagued labor.

These simplified reactions were fostered and furthered by mass ignorance. Like all oligarchical minorities kept in power by the apathy of the masses, the conservatives were careful to cultivate illiteracy. Hence the progress of illiteracy was parallel to the progress of the Conservative Party. Although the disruptions of preceding years had prevented the enactment of the 1857 law requiring every community of 500 inhabitants or over to establish a school, the number of school-less children was not more than one million in 1887. But during the next thirty-five years, the rate of school construction did not keep pace with that of demographic growth, while at the same time many of the old buildings became dilapidated. And between 1922 and 1924 there were some three million children without schools. Witnesses have left us numerous descriptions of Spanish primary schools at the beginning of our century: insalubrious quarters nearly in ruins where poor ragged wretches, in mortal fear of the local curate, taught the alphabet, catechism, and a bit of Church history, while blows of the ruler rained upon their pupils' fingers and backs.

The frightened pupils and the children without any school at all grew into violent men, predisposed toward direct action. Between the Spain of the *belle époque* and the Spain of wrath, there could be only one sort of interpreter: the bomb or the revolver.

3. ANGRY SPAIN

Born of popular abstentionism, the immobility of the State justified, in turn, the political indifference of the masses. At the end of the nineteenth century and at the start of the twentieth, the Spanish labor union movement, indeed, turned its back upon political action.

The labor movement had begun in Spain in about 1840 at which time the first union was formed by the Cataloñan workers in the textile industry; a cooperative movement swiftly developed in Cataloña and Valencia. In the years following, the first labor newspapers appeared: *La Attración*, in Madrid, and *La Fraternidad*, in Barcelona. In 1854, the various workers' syndicates—the "class unions," sometimes tolerated, sometimes arbitrarily outlawed by the authorities—decided to come together in a federation. The following year, the first general strike, supported by 40,000 workers, inaugurated a period of merciless combat.

The liberal leaders brought to power by the revolution in 1868 proclaimed freedom of association; hence, beginning in 1870, the workers' federation included 25,000 members. After the Restoration, freedom of association was guaranteed by the Constitution of 1876. Eleven years later, in 1887, the law authorized the formation of unions without any formality other than a simple declaration.

In the eight years preceding this decision, the labor movement had been split into two groups. At The Hague congress of 1872, when the quarrel between Marxists and libertarian partisans of Bakunin broke the solid front of the First International, the Spanish movement had managed to salvage its unity temporarily. This difference of evolution is explained by the difference in the distribution of strength. At The Hague, the Marxists, in the majority in practically every country, had excluded the libertarians. But at the Córdoba congress in Spain in the same year, a considerable majority had voiced support of Bakunin; therefore it was up to the Marxists to take the initiative in withdrawing from the federation. But the Socialist Party was not to be founded until 1879.

During the next half-century the libertarian movement, on the decline everywhere else, continued to progress in Spain. We may readily grant that the loyalty of the Spanish working class to the libertarian doctrines was explained by the underdevelopment of industry and the dispersal of production and workers in a multitude of handicraft enterprises. This argument is valid when Spain is compared to other western nations in the same era. But in the Spain of 1930, where the libertarian C.N.T. still held sixty-three per cent of the overall number of union affiliates, industry was more developed and concentration greater than they had been in France and Germany fifty-eight years before, when the results of the congress at The Hague showed that the Marxists were already far more numerous than the libertarians in those countries.

The fact that the bosses and financiers had taken over the State actually had nurtured the atavistic anti-Statism of Spanish workers. To their way of thinking, whatever its type and tendencies, the State was essentially the tool employed by the privileged minorities to oppress the masses. Stalin's dictatorship and Soviet bureaucracy, in their time, seemed to the anarcho-syndicalists the most convincing proof that their analyses were correct. But in fact, every event appeared to them in the same light because the conviction that the State is the enemy had existed in their minds well before the formation of unions. It was futile to hope to conquer it and make of it the servant of the working class; thus, it was essential to overcome it, to smash the military and police apparatus in order to deprive the active minorities of the instruments which served to subjugate the masses. By proposing to replace the State with a series of workers' committees summoned to resolve the problems of economic life and of the national *convivencia*, the C.N.T. satisfied the decentralist tendencies which have placed their stamp upon the entire history of Spain.

A doctrine which trumpeted the need to destroy the machinery of government necessarily implied the condemnation of all political parties, since their precise aim is to conquer the State. Hence the libertarian movement counseled abstention from voting. The Socialists' efforts to induce the workers to political action had, in the beginning, but little success. The Socialist Workers' Party (P.S.O.E.) was founded in 1879 by Pablo Iglesias. The party newspaper, *El Socialista*, appeared first in 1886. And two years later the General Workers' Union (U.G.T.) was founded in Barcelona.

Yet in the last years of the nineteenth century, there were only 15,000 U.G.T. members. At this time, there were approximately four times as many libertarians. From 1882 on, the libertarian organization—the Workers' Federation of Spain—counted some 58,000 members, a number which thereafter was to rise slightly. But overall statistics for the period between 1888 and 1911 are lacking. After its voluntary self-dissolution, the Federation crumbled into a number of little groups whose only common link was a study and information center.

The libertarians thought that in this way they would escape a repression made all the more severe by increasingly violent direct action. Tumultuous strikes and assassination attempts were more frequent; in vain bombs burst about the King, who remained invulnerable and disdainful. But three Prime Ministers did fall under the anarchists' blows: the rightist leader, Cánovas del Castillo, in 1897; the liberal, Canalejas, in 1912; and the conservative, Eduardo Dato, in 1921. The State answered this violence by reinforcing the *Guardia Civil*—created in 1844 during the reign of Isabella II—by periodically suspending constitutional liberties and calling upon the army.

The multiplication of repressive methods and the growing complexity of the system of production forced the anarcho-syndicalist movement into new modes of action, into a regrouping. In 1911, the various anarchist unions came together from the National Confederation of Labor (C.N.T.).

During the First World War, demand from abroad and the influx of foreign capital in quest of a safe refuge, stimulated industry anew and, consequently, speeded the rate of growth of the urban proletariat. Among these proletarian concentrations, which the postwar ebb of industry was to drive back to unemployment, the two workers' confederations had no trouble in recruiting members. The membership of the U.G.T. rose from 129,000 in 1912 to 210,000 just after the war; but at the same time the C.N.T. had 800,000 affiliates. The anarcho-syndicalists were clearly in control in Barcelona and in Valencia. The U.G.T. was going forward in Bilbao and predominated in the Asturias. In Madrid, the *"ugetistas"* had a slight edge.

When Primo de Rivera solicited collaboration of the U.G.T. with the corporative Assembly he had just created modeled on certain of Mussolini's institutions, the U.G.T. split in two. Led by the socialist chief of Bilbao, Indalecio Prieto, one *"ugetista"* segment declined to collaborate with the dictator. But the group led by Largo Caballero agreed to send delegates to the corporative Assembly. Roughly ten years later, after the elections of February, 1936, Caballero was to succeed in putting into practice the theory of socialist non-participation in the republican government, in spite of Prieto's efforts. Although these two attitudes appear mutually contradictory, they are the attenuated echo of the libertarian theories: since the State is always reprehensible, always to blame, there is no need to distinguish between a dictatorship and a liberal, "bourgeois," government. Thus, under an authoritarian regime, labor groups could take part in the work of an assembly called upon to discuss only labor matters. But on the other hand, under no circumstances could labor leaders agree to play an active political role in a "bourgeois" government, no matter how liberal it might be.

The future demonstrated that the *"caballeristas"* were in the majority in the U.G.T., for Caballero, by taking subjective and impassioned stands on the issues at hand, was far more representative than was Prieto of the typical Spanish worker. The Spanish masses recognized their own image in this unpolished man, with his intense integrity, his ingenuous disdain for politics and the compromises which were its essence.

At the very time when the socialists, still imbued unconsciously with libertarian theories, were collaborating with the dictatorship of Primo de Rivera, the *Guardia Civil* and the informers in the scab unions were engaged in a struggle to the death against the anarcho-syndicalists held responsible by the dictator for all labor violence. Doomed to lead only a clandestine existence, the C.N.T. lost the majority of its members at this time.

Immediately after the fall of the monarchy, the central anarchist union, free to reorganize in broad daylight, could nonetheless count 525,000 members while the number of *"ugetistas"* was only 300,000. For the first time, several months later, the membership of the U.G.T. was to equal and even slightly surpass that of the C.N.T., for the socialists' participation in the republican government caused a great spring of political hope to well up among the workers. Membership in the U.G.T. rose from 300,000 in December, 1930, to 1,041,500 in 1932. At this time, the C.N.T. had nearly one million members.

After more than a half-century of effort, labor agitation had succeeded gradually in bringing public authorities and/or employers to enact a series of reform laws equivalent to those in force in the other nations of western Europe.[18]

But even with equivalent social legislation, the Spanish worker did not enjoy the same living conditions as did workers in neighboring countries. The working man's living conditions depend not so much upon the enforcement of social welfare laws as upon the country's level of economic development. Embittered by persistent poverty and judging, not without reason, that even had they refrained from the use of force and violence their condition would not be one whit better than in 1840, the workers credited direct action with all the merit attached to the laws made in their favor. Having come to this conclusion, they redoubled their violence.

On the other hand, labor agitation had induced a more and more pronounced defensive psychosis. Several employers' associations came into being in the 1910-1920 decade;[19] henceforth, a solid front of management opposed the unity of salaried workers. Strikes were met by lockouts, which led to boycotts and sympathy strikes. Then came the processions, the demonstrations broken up by the *Guardia Civil*. Gradually, social war, already in possession of men's minds, gained possession of the streets.

4. THE END OF A MONARCHY

The constitutional monarchy was not destined to fall under the blows of the rebellious proletariat: rather, the monarchy had borne death latent within itself, ever since the political

[18] The series of social welfare laws began with measures to protect female and child labor. There followed, in order: legislation on accidents while on the job, the eight-hour day and the forty-eight-hour week (1919); the Labor Exchange (1920); the Sabbath rest. The Labor Code of the Dictatorship, promulgated in 1926, made accident insurance at the employers' expense mandatory, and made provision for the collective labor contract.

[19] The Spanish Employers' Confederation was established in 1911.

system had ceased to mirror the reality of national life. The first symptoms of its failing appeared after 1902, when Alfonso XIII attained his majority. This process of internal decay was hastened further by labor agitation, pretorian intrigues, and the King's personal politics.

Although Alfonso XIII was thoroughly acquainted with the Europe of chancelleries and the Spain of electoral bargains, he carried ignorance of social realities to the verge of carelessness and looked upon Parliament as an intolerable affront to the Bourbon dogma of rightful royal pleasure. The power to nominate the holder of every post, the right to dissolve Parliament—in short, all the powers which a constitution based upon English usage granted to the Sovereign— were, in his hands, systematically transformed into means of bringing pressure to bear upon the Cabinet.[20] But if the King were to be the absolute ruler, it was imperative that no one party gain an absolute majority of the *Cortés*, so that no party could oblige the King to choose its leader.

The decline of the two major traditional parties was to play into the monarch's hands. Their disintegration had begun during the first decade of the personal reign of Alfonso XIII, when new political groups came to sit in the *Cortés*. The first republican deputies were elected at this time. And in 1907, the coalition of Cataloñanist parties was able, as the result of the workers' vote (a temporary departure from their habitual abstentionism), to carry forty-one of the forty-four seats allotted by electoral law to Cataloña. These new forces grew stronger, to the detriment of the old Liberal Party, split into several factions.

The disintegration of the traditional parties was made more evident in 1909 by the *"semana trágica,"* "tragic week," in Barcelona. A general strike had been called in protest

20 The alteration of the Parliamentary machinery under the personal influence of Alfonso XIII is attested to by mounting ministerial instability. In the space of sixteen and a half years, under the regency, there had been a succession of eleven prime ministers, whose average tenure was nineteen months. From the King's majority to the *pronunciamiento* of Primo de Rivera, in twenty-one years and three months, some thirty-three prime ministers passed in and out of office, their average tenure being seven and a half months.

against the calling up of Cataloñan reservists; under military provocations, it degenerated into a riot. The brutality of its repression by the army and the *Guardia Civil* was more horrible even than the rioters' excesses, and aroused great indignation in Spain and abroad. Thousands of persons came out in protest demonstrations in Paris, Brussels, Rome, Buenos Aires.

Held responsible for the army's violence, the conservative leader, Antonio Maura, was forced to yield the Prime Minister's post to Segismundo Moret, Liberal Party spokesman; he in turn was soon replaced by another liberal leader, José Canalejas. Apparently, the parliamentary left had profited greatly from the tragic events of July, 1909; the 1910 elections gave the leftist parties a wide margin. But certain circles which had backed the opposition until then withdrew. In Cataloña, part of the bourgeoisie turned back toward the right, while a great many workers took refuge in their habitual abstentionism. In other areas, the Liberal Party, triumphant in the 1910 elections, had received the votes of a considerable sector of normally hesitant or indifferent opinion which had insisted upon disapproving Maura's repressive policies. But these chance supporters were not long in abandoning the Liberal Party which, beginning in 1910, had also lost a number of supporters who had gone over to more clearly leftist parties. In this way, the alliance, formed after the 1909 incidents between socialists and republicans, had enabled the republicans to pick up thirty-nine seats. And in 1910, Madrid sent to the *Cortés* the first socialist deputy ever to sit in a Spanish parliament. The parliamentary left was more fragmented than ever, and this was to enable the conservatives to come back into power from 1913 on.

But the Conservative Party was also severely affected by the 1909 crisis. Maura, placed in the minority by the moderate conservatives, had to hand over party leadership to Eduardo Dato who realized the need of giving satisfaction to the opposition on certain points. Although the Conservative Party had salvaged its organic unity, it was—morally speaking—

split wide open. The King now had the choice of summoning either the official party leader or Maura, in whom the intransigents still placed their trust.

The third stage on the road to parliamentary disintegration was reached during the First World War, in 1917 and 1918. Massive exportations had induced a rise in prices which far outstripped the rise in salaries. The Russian Revolution had set the example, and a new wave of strikes, sabotage, and attempted assassinations swept the nation. Several months later, the socialists registered some important gains in the legislative elections. They were too weak as yet to rule; but their demi-victory awakened in the bourgeoisie a reflex of social defense. The Catalonian *Lliga* and the liberals themselves drew nearer to the Conservative Party, in which the moderates were opposed more than ever to the intransigents. The two big parties of former times were replaced by a considerable majority of social defense split into many factions. This new parliamentary conjuncture, making any government other than a coalition impossible, placed the King in the position of being able to choose his own prime minister from whom he could exact whatever he wished, and to govern under his own name.

Having incessantly played the army against the Parliament, the King soon found himself obliged to yield before his military allies. Hence, the pretorians' entry upon the scene was the logical corollary of the unreality in political life. No sooner were the reformists unable to pursue their ends along legal lines, no sooner were parliamentary debates replaced by street fighting, than the army, last refuge of the bourgeoisie, was promoted to the rank of indispensable protagonist in the life of Spanish politics. Indications of the pretorians' return appeared at the start of the twentieth century, when labor agitation took on a semi-revolutionary character. As early as 1906 the pretorians were strong enough to push through, over a liberal majority, a "jurisdiction law" by which those journalists who had written articles unfavorable to the army were court-martialed. In the years to come, military insubordination kept pace with social agitation. In

1909, after the "tragic week" in Barcelona, headquarters took advantage of the rights granted it by martial law to revenge itself upon the anti-militarist pamphleteers. It was in these circumstances that the anarchist leader, Francisco Ferrer,[21] was executed by a firing squad for his anti-military campaign, though he had taken no part in the riot. After the revolutionary strikes of 1917, which the army had been called upon to put down, "defense juntas," veritable officers' syndicates, were powerful enough from then on to place themselves successfully in opposition to the government.

At this time there had been hostilities for nearly fifteen years in the Rif, the Spanish zone in mountainous northern Morocco. The effect of this colonial war, undertaken early in the twentieth century at the instigation of the army, was to further military insubordination. After the Spanish defeat in Cuba, the army command were in need of an easy revenge; and the Spanish bourgeoisie, of balm for their *amour-propre*.

In 1912, the diplomatic obstacles which had so long held up the conquest were finally surmounted.[22] But Germany and France, ousted from Morocco thanks to England, surreptitiously armed the tribes of the Rif mountains (stretching parallel to the Mediterranean) and the pleasurable promenade of which the Spanish military had dreamed became a quarter-century of struggle. Everything worked in favor of the

---

21 Born in 1859 at Alella, near Barcelona, Ferrer worked first at various manual trades. He fell in with Freemasonry and anarchist unionism and, in 1886, had to go into exile in Paris. Upon his return to Barcelona, he founded the Modern School, which aimed to give rational instruction to workingmen's children. He was arrested in his native village a month after the "*semana trágica*" and was held responsible for all of the rioters' abuses, although it was never proven that he had taken part in the uprising. After a single hearing, which included not one defense witness, the court-martial handed down a death sentence. Ferrer was shot at Monjuich Castle (Barcelona) on October 13, 1909, without even having been allowed to petition the King for mercy.

22 By the 1902 *entente cordiale*, England, whose protectorate over Egypt was acknowledged, gave France free rein in Morocco. But she insisted that France, by the French-Spanish treaty in 1904, recognize the Madrid government's claims to the northern zone of Morocco. In 1911, Germany, realizing that England would not let her get a foothold on Moroccan soil, abandoned Morocco to France, in exchange for compensation in the Congo. Deserted by both England and Germany, the Sultan had to consent to the French protectorate (treaty of 1912). And France, to keep her word to London and Madrid, recognized Spain's protectorate over northern Morocco.

continuation of hostilities: the mountainous terrain was propitious for ambushes, the drafted men were apathetic, and there was embezzlement within the commissariat. Columns of eight or ten thousand soldiers, armed with out-of-date rifles, were held immobile for long periods by a few hundred Rif tribesmen perched up on the heights. This war, led on the Moroccan side by only a few thousand *guerrilleros*, required 121,000 Spanish troops as early as 1914; in 1923, that number rose to 217,000.

The nucleus of the *coup d'Etat* was formed gradually in the *guerrilla*. The new leaders, groomed on African soil, were permanently settled into this struggle which brought them high combat wages and rapid promotion. Since the great majority of the people were revolted by this war, the government was obliged to call upon mercenaries: Moroccan *Regulares* or *Tercio* Legionnaires. And these pretorian forces, recognizing no other authority than that of their officers, camped a scant few miles from the coasts of Spain: the mother country was now to live in danger from her own army.

But the bourgeoisie, alarmed by the high death toll and the costliness of the war, began to wish for a compromise in Morocco. Confronted with these partisans of peace, the officers of the African army were driven to defend, by all means at their disposal, their little foster-war. To this end, "defense juntas" had been created during the First World War. Soon these semi-secret organizations were able to bully officers unreceptive to their propaganda. When conflict broke out over this issue in 1919, the King supported the juntas and the Cabinet was forced to resign. Functional hierarchy was overturned.

The last step in the process, the army's gaining control of the government, was motivated by the pacifists' progress which obliged a number of deputies to fall in with their program which consistently gained in popularity. If a majority were to form in the *Cortés* to force a compromise in Morocco, once again part of the Assembly's prerogatives would be usurped by the King and the army. Only a spectacular success in the Rif could halt the gradual trend of opinion toward a compromise. Then the extreme right, resuming its normal domination of the middle class, would see to it that the war continued; and the King would continue to maintain an even balance between the army and the *Cortés*. It was then that Alfonso XIII, by a telegram of which the Ministry was unaware, ordered the brigade leader, General Silvestre, to commence an isolated operation. On July 21, 1921, the Silvestre column was ambushed and massacred at Anual.

Within a few days the uprising spread to all of the Rif tribes. In Spain, indignation rose so high that the *Cortés* dared not approve a new call of reservists without balancing it with the inquiry for which public opinion clamored. The conclusions of the duly named commission were to be divulged on September 16, 1923. But on the evening of September 12, it was learned that the Captain-General (or Marshal) of Barcelona, Miguel Primo de Rivera, supported by the army of the Rif and the Barcelona and Saragossa garrisons, had delivered an ultimatum to the government. Alfonso XIII, in league with the conspirators, hastened to ask the rebel general to form a government; symbolically, some of the *Guardia Civil* were picketed about the closed door of the *Cortés*. The parliamentary institutions which had governed Spain for more than a half-century had collapsed in less than twenty-four hours—and no one had lifted a finger to defend them. Indeed, everything had worked in favor of the military *coup d'Etat*: general dissatisfaction caused by the critical loss of sales following upon the industrial revival in countries ravaged by the First World War, anxiety among the bourgeoisie over the resurgence of social agitation, and the wave of anti-parliamentarism which was born in fascist Rome and inundated all Europe. Nonetheless, Primo de Rivera, frightened by the cost of the war and the pacifist current of public opinion, soon concurred in the necessity of evacuating the Rif. Uprisings in the French zone of Morocco, stimulated by the example of Abd-el-Krim, spared Spain another *pronunciamiento*.

To have done, once and for all, with a hotbed of trouble which threatened the whole of Morocco, the French government proposed a combined operation with Spain. The Spanish military was offered the chance of a rapid victory, just when the officers had come to realize that to prolong the war would be to give that sector of opinion which urged abandonment of the Rif a strength which the army would not be able to control forever; and, further, that the way to stay in Morocco was not to drag out operations but to bring them to a close. Preceded by the *Tercio*, led by young Colonel Francisco Franco, Spanish troops debarked at Alhucemas at the foot of rebel headquarters, and forced the Rif troops to withdraw from one position to another. The dissidence which had stymied the Spanish army for a quarter-century was wiped out, there being no possibility of defense, within six months.

This victory gave the dictatorship a respite during which it could pursue on a large scale its policy of economic expansion. Industrial growth, by reducing unemployment, calmed social tensions. Further, the working classes, in the grip of that magical terror invariably instilled in them by military regimes, dared not attempt their habitual agitation. But in 1930 the world-wide economic depression and the drop in demand abroad, which coincided with a spectacular increase in Spanish production, left that production without a market, and unemployment reappeared. Administrative corruption and the dimensions of projects undertaken by the dictatorship caused a disorderly swelling of budgets and the national debt and a sharp rise in the cost of living. Inflation and sacrifice sales irritated the bourgeoisie which, reassured by seven years of social tranquillity, no longer felt the need of a mighty military arm.

In addition, the single party and the corporative system which the dictatorship had brought into being on the Italian fascist model aroused no enthusiasm and answered to no reality at all. True enough, the *"Caballerista"* socialists had agreed to send delegates to the corporative chamber. But when unemployment furnished the opponents of the C.N.T. and Prieto's socialist wing with new ammunition, the *"Caballeristas,"* afraid of being overwhelmed, immediately joined the opposition.

Similarly, a considerable part of the army rose against the dictatorship. A monarchist and Catholic military *camarilla*, a sort of Privy Council, in power for seven years, could not help but be beaten by all the officers without ecclesiastical stipends. The most eager of these officers were those in the "scientific" branches (artillery and engineering) who felt they were bullied by the cavalry and infantry; eager too were those who, having received neither medal nor mention during the Rif campaign, wanted promotion to be based solely upon years of service. The malcontents united under the double banner of Freemasonry and of an anti-monarchical neo-liberalism. Their opponents had made of them the nucleus of a new tendency, and now the "defense juntas" were transformed into nuclei of conspiracy.

For Primo de Rivera, Spain had become barren soil. And the King, who had been lying in wait for an excuse to rid himself of this troublesome protector, demanded his resignation on January 28, 1930.

But the efforts of General Berenguer, the new governmental leader, to return to parlimentary normalcy were futile. It was demonstrated immediately that, alone among the classical parties, the Conservative Party had kept its political clientele. The others, particularly the Liberal Party and the Catalofian *Lliga*, were reduced to the status of headquarters without armies.

Alongside the fluctuations in daily political life a profound transformation had taken place. Aware of the impasse which trapped Spanish politics, a consistently growing sector of the urban bourgeoisie was desirous of a thorough renovation and tended toward a neo-liberalism. The university students, influenced by the intellectuals of the "generation of 1898," openly declared their opposition to the regime.

On the social level, the new lower-middle-class elements which had emerged from the economic expansion of the preceding twenty years were becoming more and more cognizant of the conflicts between themselves and the traditional oligarchies. From these new interest groups came two new parties: the Republican Left and the Catalofian Left. In addition, the growing numbers of the urban proletariat had facilitated the spread of the labor parties' propaganda and the "politicization" of the working classes. After the fall of Primo de Rivera, the leaders of the labor parties disbanded by the dictatorship and the founders of the new lower-middle-class parties, could rely only upon mild support. But the future would prove that they represented the unexpressed feeling of the majority.

Without denying its convictions, a part of the conservative Catholic upper-middle-class declared its irremediable hostility to Alfonso XIII. The gravity of these notables was affronted by the King's abrupt turnabout and by his manifold violation of the Constitution, at a time when the mere word "republic" no longer struck such terror into bourgeois hearts, reassured by repeated promises from the leaders of the little republican conservative group: Alcalá Zamora and Miguel Maura. Zamora, a renowned lawyer, had been a minister under the monarchy; Maura was the son of the former prime minister repudiated by the conservative majority because of his intransigence. The fact that these two important figures took the reins of the republican party meant that public order would have nothing to lose by the advent of a republic.

The liberal and Freemason military leaders vowed to maintain order. The Spanish bourgeoisie, which until then had believed that the Crown and the aristocracy were indispensable if the proletarian revolt were to be held in abeyance, suddenly discovered that with pretorian support it could live henceforth in security without having to live in servility under a monarchy.

No sooner had these nascent currents among the bourgeoisie and the army brought a republic into the realm of possibility than all those who were traditionally republicans—labor, as well as Basque and Cataloñan autonomists—threw themselves into the struggle with renewed ardor. The first group, instinctively anti-monarchical, blamed the King for thirty years of poverty and repression; the second hated him for his Bourbon blood, for two centuries of centralism, and for the longstanding identification of the Crown with the exporters of citrus fruits and raw materials, archenemies of industrial expansion.

On the official level, General Berenguer made futile efforts to set up elections; at the same time, all the anti-monarchical forces—the republican conservatives of Alcalá Zamora, the parties representing the new lower-middle-class elements, the autonomists and the labor groups—signed a secret pact at San-Sebastian on August 27, 1930. To bring them to power the opposition counted upon a *pronunciamiento*, the favorite expedient of the nineteenth-century liberals. The date had been set for December 15, 1930; but a last-minute order to delay could not prevent sporadic disturbances. The uprising of the Jaca garrison, in Aragon, was vigorously quelled.[23] The alert had been given, and the principal republican leaders were imprisoned.

General Berenguer attempted to profit from the opposition's disarray to precipitate the elections. But the leaders of the old dynastic parties, anxious to divorce themselves from a discredited sovereign who once had betrayed them in favor of Primo de Rivera, declared that they would have no part of the elections unless the new *Cortés* were to be a constituent assembly. There was nothing left for Berenguer to do but resign.

The King then asked an "apolitical" personality, Admiral Aznar, to organize a government of technicians whose task would be to engineer a progressive return to normalcy by means of three graduated elections: first, at the municipal level; next, provincial elections; finally, elections at the legislative level. All of the groups which had refused their participation in Berenguer's legislative elections agreed to the municipal voting.

On election day, April 12, 1931, the massive labor vote and the rallying of the urban bourgeoisie to the republicans gave that side the majority in Madrid, in Barcelona, and in forty-five of the fifty provincial capitals. But on the other hand, the pro-monarchical Conservative Party was victorious in the

[23] Two young officers shot at this time, the Captains Hernández and Firmín Galán, were looked upon as heroes and martyrs during the republican era.

small market towns of "intermediary Spain" and in rural communities. On the local level, the old machinery of the Church and of *"caciquismo"* had lost none of its efficiency. The monarchists had gained a narrow margin in the municipal elections which, in any case, by their very nature, could not endanger the regime. But those elected from the opposition, taking over their posts in all of the large cities, hastened to proclaim the republic, on April 13 and 14, 1931. The peasant uprisings which, on receipt of this news, broke out in Andalusia and in New Castile showed that the conservatives' success in those areas was due only to economic pressure.

In Barcelona, a delirious throng hailed the Republic of Cataloña. In Madrid, processions made up primarily of students and workers marched through the streets, singing the *Marseillaise* and waving flags with the republican colors. The majority of the Captains-General refused to act to re-establish public order. And General Sanjurjo, commander-in-chief of the *Guardia Civil*, let it be known that he was going over to the republic.

Opposition leaders, only recently released from the Model Prison in Madrid, had just installed a temporary government with Alcalá Zamora as president; they called upon the King to leave Spain as quickly as possible, in order to avoid more serious disturbances. At dusk on April 14, 1931, Alfonso XIII left Madrid by car, escorted only by a squad of *Guardia Civil*. He died in exile in Rome in 1941.

The Spanish Monarchy was dead of its own inability to solve the permanent problems of the nation. And the new reformist republic, born of a *pronunciamiento* by abstention, with the leftist military *caudillos*[24] as godfathers—Sanjurjo and Mola, Queipo de Llano and Goded—found its future assassins already grouped about its cradle.

[24] *"Caudillo"* means military chief, and is used to designate a leader occupying an elevated position in the military hierarchy or surrounded by a great reputation, having great prestige.

Chapter Seven

ॐ

THE PROFESSORIAL
REPUBLIC

NEVER DID any regime inspire as much hope as did the second Spanish republic. Two months after the fall of the monarchy, the people gave its new leaders carte blanche, by the elections of the constituent *Cortés*, on June 26, 1931. For the first time there was a massive turnout of workers and agricultural day laborers. So sweeping was the republican victory that the monarchists won but one seat in the Assembly.[1]

But two and a half years later the republican and reformist tidal wave of these premature elections returned a conservative majority to the *Cortés*. Five years after the ad-

[1] The electoral machinery of *"caciquismo"* had lost all its effectiveness when several monarchist figures went into voluntary exile. Further, the day laborers, expecting an agrarian reform to begin at any moment, would not have obeyed any orders. Disconcerted by the exodus of their leaders, many of the petit bourgeois in the monarchist tradition abstained from voting or voted for the rightist republican parties to check the advances of the left. The socialists won 166 seats. The various "bourgeois" liberals had 235 deputies; the Cataloñan and Galician autonomists, 60; the rightists and the Basque nationalists, also 60.

vent of the republic, the return to power of a reformist majority gave the signal of a civil war.

The pitiable outcome of the only reformist experiment in twentieth-century Spain may be accounted for, to a certain extent, undoubtedly, by the structural faults of the regime. Indeed, the constitution of December 9, 1931 deserves a choice place in the paradise of unworkable constitutions. Neither unitarian nor federal, this juridical monster created areas endowed with considerable autonomy within a centralized State. Heir to all the executive power of the dismissed sovereign, the president of the republic was nonetheless elected by a single Chamber equipped with full legislative power. Hence the constitutional text nurtured perpetual disagreement between the central power and the provinces, between the Chief-of-State and the Assembly.

Two factors increased the already outsized number of politically uneducated voters: the lowering of the legal voting age from twenty-five to twenty-three, and the enfranchisement of women. The irrational mass of voters was subject to abrupt changes of mind; and the electoral system itself seemed organized in such a way as expressly to exaggerate their vacillations, for the law granted eighty per cent of the seats in each district to that party with the greatest number of votes, hence the slightest edge over an opponent meant triumph. Between 1931 and 1936, Spanish political life was upset three times by these electoral tidal waves.

Moreover, most voters agreed to parliamentary arbitration only to the extent to which it helped their own interests. The possessor classes were ready to use force to defend their prerogatives, endangered by republican reforms. Among socialists, Prieto's political moderation was counterbalanced by Caballero's revolutionary intransigence. And the C.N.T., still aggregating half the urban proletariat, refused to appoint delegates to the government and to the *Cortés*. Since the breadth of its stern requirements by no means were confined to the reality of governmental tasks, the anarchist Confederation remained the expression of limitless demands.

The resistance of the privileged classes on the one hand

and the impatience of the masses on the other caused republican leaders to approach the reform problem with a timidity which disheartened regionalist forces and threw the working masses back on electoral abstention and direct action. While superficial military reforms caused republican generals to move precipitately toward the opposition, the ministers and the *Cortés* abandoned themselves to the intoxication of the anti-religious war, habitual deviation of Spanish liberals. A goodly part of the bourgeoisie, irritated by anti-religious persecution and still more vexed by social agitation, began to look again to the extreme right.

1. A "FEDERABLE" REPUBLIC IN SPITE OF ITSELF

The Spanish republic found itself burdened on the day of its birth with an older sister: the Republic of Cataloña, proclaimed several hours before in Barcelona by Colonel Macia, only a few days earlier returned from exile, and by Lluis Companys. The clandestine Catalonan left they had created, *L'Esquerra de Catalunya*, emerged triumphant in the municipal elections.

The leaders of *L'Esquerra* did not dream of creating a fully independent state. In his proclamation of April 14, Macia had urged the "brother peoples" of the peninsula to unite with Cataloña on new bases. The Catalonan leaders felt that all of the peninsular nations should follow the Portuguese example and recover their independence in order to be able thereafter to associate with one another by an act of free will. In their way of thinking, it was imperative to eradicate the root of the centralized state so that Spain might become once again a federation of free nations. They countered the idea of a Greater Castile with that of the United States of Iberia. But Macia's appeal awoke no answering echo except in the Basque country and in Galicia. Coming to terms with Madrid became indispensable.

The provisional government of the Catalonan republic made way for a *Generalidad* of Cataloña within the Spanish republic; and the republican government undertook to grant autonomy to Cataloña along lines which would be worked out in detail by the constituent *Cortés.*

On May 24, 1931, as an application of the compromise terms, the *Generalidad* requested that the municipalities designate the members of a regional Parliament. The new assembly worked out a bill which was submitted to the Cataloñan people for ratification on August 2. More than eighty per cent of the registered voters participated in this plebiscite, and the statute received unanimous approval.

Hence, when the constituent *Cortés* opened the constitutional debate on September 11, they were confronted with working autonomous institutions. Consequently, the centralization solution was out of the question, and the only problem which faced the *Cortés* was this: was Spain to be a federal republic or a theoretically centralized State in which certain regions, exceptionally, could obtain a statute of autonomy? The Cataloñan deputies and their allies threw themselves desperately into the fight for a federalist solution. But the majority of the representatives were doubly centralist, as representatives of "Castilianized" regions and as liberals. The French centralist theories with which they were imbued justified their traditional tendencies and their instinct for domination.

Discussion of the fundamental issues was slurred over in favor of a verbal joust. The republic was defined as "an integral state," a term without the slightest juridical meaning. But the "integral" State was declared "compatible with regional autonomy," which appeared to indicate that such autonomy contradicted the nature of the State. Further, the Constitution stipulated that autonomy would be granted to those regions which requested it, a move regulated by the strictest formalities.

This juridical slurring had made the non-"Castilianized" regions lose out, for the federalist thesis pleased the majority of the Spanish people by flattering their Iberian individualism. Virtually none but technical and administrative arguments, interesting to only a handful of specialists, could be invoked against the idea. But as soon as one region might dare present a petition for autonomy, orators of the old centralist right would rise outraged and speak mournfully in trembling voices of a fragmented fatherland and of the spirit of Carlos I.

The keynote of public hostility to the concept of autonomy was sounded in the discussion which opened in the *Cortés* during the summer of 1932, upon ratification of the Cataloñan statute. On the eve of the debate, the right had organized an intense campaign of agitation in Madrid and elsewhere; and the leftist majority did not care to let itself be outstripped by the conservatives where patriotism was concerned. Thus, furious attacks were launched against the statute by orators of the most divergent parties. Only the impassioned intervention of the Prime Minister, Manuel Azaña, who demonstrated the impossibility of denying the Cataloñan *fait accompli*, persuaded Parliament to ratify it.

But what was it in this autonomy which stirred such profound anxiety? The central government had reserved for itself matters of foreign policy, diplomacy, national defense, colonies, religion, the issuing of paper money, the border police, and customs. In other matters—penal law, civil status, marriage form, mortgage control, and social security— legislation was the responsibility of the State and its execution was incumbent upon the *Generalidad*. And it was in the province of the central power to establish the norms concerning the freedoms of press and of association which Cataloñan law was to respect. The *Generalidad* named the judges of all tribunals within Cataloña, but the sentences imposed by Cataloñan courts had to resort to the Supreme Court in Madrid for final appeal. The *Generalidad* was fully sovereign only in certain secondary areas: regional waterways and communication routes, public health and hospitals, museums and libraries. Public order was in the hands of both groups of police. But in time of crisis, declaration of a state of siege placed all police services, including those exclusively Cataloñan, under the authority of the captain-general, *i.e.*, marshal, who functioned under the central power. The most heated discussions in the *Cortés* had dealt with language and education; the outcome was that both languages were given equal status in the administration and in schools, as well as at the University of Barcelona. On the whole, the powers reserved to the *Generalidad* were slightly inferior to those which the United States Constitution reserves for each state under the federal government.

But this timorous return to the foral tradition had given rise to such rancor in the "Castilianized" regions that there could be no cordial understanding between Madrid and Barcelona. While the central government made use of all the constitutional powers at its command to further the ends of Cataloñan individuals and minority groups dissatisfied with the *Generalidad*'s politics, the majority of the Cataloñan people, overwhelmed by a sort of claustrophobia, were ready for any rebellious gesture against the State.

The centralist majority in the *Cortés* used all its power to delay the granting of the statutes of autonomy requested by Galicia and the Basque country. The anticlerical left, which dominated the constituent *Cortés*, felt a particular antipathy for the Basque nationalists who, fervent Catholics, had risen in protest against the anti-religious laws. Thus the plebiscite in the Basque provinces was adjourned on a variety of pretexts, and the proposed statute was not submitted for the approval of the Basque people until November 5, 1933, on the eve of the general elections occasioned when President Alcalá Zamora dissolved the constituent *Cortés*. The Basque nationalists hoped that the new majority on the right, which they had supported fervently, would ratify the statute which had been approved by eighty-four per cent of the registered voters in the three Basque provinces. But the new *Cortés* seized upon the high number of abstentions in the little province of Alava as a pretext for rejecting the statute. The Spanish right—having once, in its hour of shame, taken refuge among the Basque autonomists—now resumed its centralist tradition and, simultaneously, possession of the State.

Angered by this treachery, the Basque nationalists were little disposed to welcome the bellicose invitations from the Spanish right when this element was again placed in the opposition by the victory of the Popular Front in 1936. Their refusal incited the rightist conspirators to throw themselves on the Basque country, in July of the same year. And the result of this aggression was the approval of the Statute by the republican majority in the *Cortés*.

The Spanish left had every reason, indeed, to accommodate the unexpected allies pushed into their camp by the conservatives' centralist furor. Moreover, the Basque nationalists had already taken the lead in defending the region of Bilbao which, from the earliest days of civil war, had been virtually isolated from the rest of the republican zone. In the Basque country as in Cataloña, the republic, which had not dared be federalist, was obliged to bow before the facts of the matter.

2. AGRARIAN REFORM WITH THE BRAKES ON

As a whole, the people felt that the essential task of the republic was to bring about agrarian reform. To this purpose, an extraparliamentary commission had been named in May, 1931, to work out the plan of the agrarian law.

The reform presented serious technical difficulties. It would be mere illusion to distribute non-irrigated land to families with neither implements for its cultivation nor funds with which to buy them. Was it then necessary to allot land only when the irrigation works should be finished? Or was it preferable to decree immediate occupation of these lands?

When, after long hesitation, the agrarian law was voted on September 15, 1932, it represented a compromise between the two methods: it provided for a general inventory of the lands designated for gradual allocation within limits to be fixed by the government. The expropriable lands were those belonging to the King and the Spanish *Grandeza* (grandees)[2] the common lands usurped by the *caciques*, land which had

[2] The confiscation of the lands formerly belonging to the *Grandeza* was not provided for in the original plan but was decreed after Sanjurjo's would-be *pronunciamiento*, August 10, 1932, during the debate over the agrarian law.

been let lie fallow, and finally that part of the great land-holdings which surpassed 300 *hectares* of *secano*, 150 of vine-yards, 400 of pasture lands, and 10 of *regadío*. The lands of the *Grandeza* and of the King were confiscated without compensation; in all other cases, an indemnity was due the dispossessed owner. Expropriated lands were to be divided among needy peasant families, with preference given those farmers and sharecroppers already settled on the land. The execution of the law was entrusted to an Institute of Agrarian Reform.

A further measure provided for immediate occupation of certain domains appearing on the inventory of expropriable lands but, preceding the formalities of expropriation, such occupation was only temporary. If, after five years, expropriation had not yet been effected, its owner was to regain possession of his land.

The great landholders glimpsed a possibility of self-defense on the grounds of the September, 1932, law. And indeed, the next few months were to bring numerous cases of contested titles and discussions over the quality of the land.

During the twenty-seven months in which the agrarian law was applied at least nominally, a total of 116,837 *hectares* (about 290,000 acres) was distributed to the peasants,[3] whereas the *latifundios* of over 500 *hectares* occupied an overall land surface of 4,916,590 *hectares* (over 12,250,000 acres). At this rate, the completion of the agrarian reform would have required nearly a century.

To cancel the fear of long-term expropriation which weighed upon them, the great landholders began to finance the renascence of the rightist parties and, at the same time, there was a movement of "politicization" among the share-croppers and day laborers, and a return to the servitude of *caciquism*. The agricultural unions—most of them forming part of the socialist U.G.T.—organized in nearly every village attracted a minority of peasants, more courageous or better off than their fellows. But the majority of the tillers of the fields,

[3] Of this total, 89,137 *hectares* had been definitively distributed, while 27,700 were occupied on a temporary basis.

realizing that the *terrateniente* would be in control of land and employment for a long time to come, fell once again under his spell.

Similarly, the urban proletariat was drifting away from the government. The workers had believed the infant republic a paradise in which their every dream would come true overnight. Assured—or believing they were—of support from the new authorities, they felt that they could demand anything from their employers, and strikes commenced to break out all over Spain. During the first 20 months of the republic, there were some 30 general strikes and 3,600 partial strikes. But as months went by and the hoped-for reforms were still not effected, labor began once again to favor direct action. It was true that collective work contracts and salary increases had raised the general standard of living. But the world-wide depression was more and more grave, Spanish exports dropped and, in many Spanish firms, these two facts were translated in terms of diminished activity and reduced personnel. At the end of 1932, the number of urban unemployed had already risen to 600,000. Social agitation was gaining ground.

The government, threatened on all sides—by disturbances in the streets, conspiracies on the right—was obliged to take refuge in police measures. The forces of the *Guardia Civil*, object of popular hatred, were strengthened; further, they were backed up by a most modern militia: the Assault Guard, concentrated in the cities in order to be out of reach of the *caciques*. On October 21, 1931, the government was forced to promulgate a law suspending all constitutional rights. And when the applicability of this law had expired, it was replaced in July, 1933, by a "law of public order" which similarly endowed the government with exceptional powers. Thus, throughout her republican period, Spain lived under an emergency regime. The repressive laws, applied only exceptionally to the rightist conspirators, were consistently used against the anarchists. For the *"cenetistas,"* the C.N.T. members, exasperated by increasing unemployment and the reinforcement of the police, had recourse to the terrorist methods they had used under the reign of Alfonso XIII. An inexpiable war began between the C.N.T. and the pretorian militia.[4] The working class, convinced that the republican government, like the monarchist, was an instrument in the hands of the possessor classes, fell back upon its habitual tactic of electoral abstentions.

3. NEW EPISODE IN THE PRETORIAN REVOLT

The republican leaders had not the slightest suspicion that the peril to their own cause was the army. Fearing an uprising of the monarchist officers, they imagined that the republican officers would defend the new regime against conspiracies from the right as well as against street riots. But if the forces of public order were to play this role, they must be "republicanized," liberals must be placed in posts of command: in short, the army must be "politicized" somewhat more than it was.

But the republican leaders, who had so often charged flagrant waste in the matter of military allocations, were bound by their own criticisms: they had to set about working the military reforms demanded by labor and by the greater part of public opinion. In fact, the army had reached the last stage of disintegration. Phantom regiments justified the existence of superfluous officers: the ratio of officers to men was 1:5, or, 632 generals and 21,996 officers for 105,000 soldiers. A horde of useless agencies had been created by the successive Ministers of War, to give jobs to their friends and supporters. Temporarily detached officers, receiving full pay, were authorized by a 1930 decree to occupy posts in civilian ministries and hence to accumulate two salaries.

Manuel Azaña, Minister of War under the provisional government, calculated that to cut down the number of superfluous officers would be to take two healthful steps: remov-

---

[4] After a workers' uprising had been attempted in Figols (in the Province of Barcelona), in January, 1932, some 115 anarchists were deported to Spanish Guinea. Seizures of tracts and brochures, and domiciliary searches, often led to shots being fired between police and anarchists. In that same month, there were 400 killed, including 20 of the police, and 3,000 wounded.

ing officers who were not sympathetic to the new regime, and making handsome savings. So the number of divisions was reduced by half, from sixteen to eight, while the number of soldiers remained virtually the same. By a decree issued in April, 1931, officers who requested the move within thirty days could go into the reserves on full pay; beyond the thirty-day deadline, the war ministry could propose the dismissal of superfluous personnel. Azaña believed—rightly— that the monarchist officers, feeling themselves to be the particular target of this measure, would be the first to leave active service. In this way, the number of officers was reduced by two-thirds. The ministry also sought to wipe out corruption by closing functionless agencies and prohibiting the practice of simultaneously holding military rank and an administrative post.

Having driven the 14,000 dismissed officers into the opposition, the government proceeded to alienate those who were still on the active list. In the last years of the monarchy, there had been both republicans and monarchists in the army: after the decrees issued by Azaña, there were only malcontents.

The signal for rebellion was given by General Sanjurjo. Under his command, the *Guardia Civil* had put down labor agitation with singular brutality. The government, giving way to charges levelled by socialist deputies, finally removed the general thereby not only furnishing him with reasons for righteous rancor but also assigning him to a command in Sevilla, in the area of the *latifundios*, at the very moment when the *Cortés* was considering the agrarian law. The great figure of Freemasonry who had officiated at the birth of the republic entered into incontinent union with the monarchist and Catholic *terratenientes* threatened by agrarian reform. Proletarian disillusionment and bourgeois dissatisfaction seemed to build up an atmosphere favorable to a military *pronunciamiento*. The word was passed on simultaneously in Sevilla and Madrid, on August 11, 1932. But the revolt was so poorly prepared that the *Guardia Civil* and the Assault Guard were able to put it down without difficulty.

The disorganized army was at the mercy of a vast purge which would have placed the republic out of reach of its threat. But Sanjurjo, condemned to death by a court-martial, was given a reprieve by the Chief-of-State upon the urging of the ministers and the majority of the deputies; Sanjurjo's closest accomplices received light sentences. And those who looked into his case chose to overlook the contacts Sanjurjo had established with those officers who, living in momentary expectation of an uprising, waited only for certainty of the conspirators' initial success before joining their movement. Freemasonic brotherhood had worked in Sanjurjo's favor. The republic, relying upon the army to protect it against a proletarian revolt, handled the army with kid gloves.

From this point on, the regime was doomed. Officers accustomed to a long-term absence of discipline retained all of their means of action, while their rancor swelled at the affronts offered Sanjurjo and his accomplices.

Yet the republic lived on a while, thanks to a renascence of the parties on the right. The evolution of opinion was such that it was conceivable that a conservative government would come into power by legal means; once installed, it would annul the military reforms effected by Azaña. Hence the pretorians were to wager on the electoral hopes of the rightist element, whereas until now the right had appeared to interest only one of them: the director of the military academy in Saragossa. When that school was closed by Azaña's order—he considered it a hatchery for monarchists—the Academy's director delivered to his cadets a homily of Christian-Democrat sentiment which preached the gospel of submission to the established order, "even when it is in the wrong." This champion of submission to civil authority was Francisco Franco. How fruitful the application of these Christian-Democratic doctrines would be was revealed in 1933 when, after the triumph of the Catholic party at the polls, the future *Caudillo* was named army chief-of-staff at the age of 41.

4. NEW EPISODE IN THE "HOLY WAR"

Three weeks after a change of regime, brought about without the firing of a single shot, the religious quarrel invaded the streets after a banal dispute between some republicans and a monarchist group as they emerged from a private meeting. There was fear of a conspiracy of the aristocracy and the monarchist officers. Impelled by an ancestral reflex, the crowd went wild and threw itself upon churches and convents: Once again, on May 11, 1931, columns of smoke wafted toward the sky.

The latent anticlericalism of the masses needed but the slightest prompting in order to break loose. And the lavish anticlerical eloquence of political leaders and newspapers was an obvious invitation to violence. Yet the leaders of the new regime should have avoided religious polemics at all costs, since such discussion threatened to make Catholics—few in number but openly supporting the new regime—turn toward the opposition. The president of the provisional government, Alcalá Zamora, like most of the members of his party, was a practicing Catholic. The Vatican sanctioned a political rallying toward the republic. The director of the daily *El Debate*, Angel Herrera, who passed as spokesman for the Jesuits, had declared in an editorial published some weeks before the fall of Alfonso XIII, that Catholics would rally about the republic at the moment of its advent, "not too soon, nor yet a minute too late."

But men of the stamp of Azaña, former pupil of the Augustine brothers of the Escorial, were too haunted by memories of a cloistered childhood to resist the temptation to proclaim their new incredulity. Contemporaries of Voltaire strayed somehow into the twentieth century, they yearned to *"écraser l'infâme."* Hardly had they come to power when they commenced to secularize Spain, starting with the cemeteries. Indeed, the primary concern of a government which had before it the task of building a new Spain was to forbid religious burial—unless the deceased had stipulated in his will that a priest was to officiate at his funeral. Without this written word, families who believed that attendance at Sunday mass was the essential sign of social decency were obliged to bow their heads and follow a civil procession. The republic was a scant few weeks old and already in the heady grip of a holy war. In the smallest village, the curate was at close quarters with the schoolmaster, and the Freemason mayor with the associated fathers-of-families. In several towns in the Basque country, the two parties came to blows and left some of their number dead on the field.

In October, 1931, when the *Cortés* voted the anticlerical measures included in Articles 26 and 27 of the Constitution, those Catholics who had been ready to rally to the republic were driven into the opposing camp. Alcalá Zamora resigned from the presidency of the provisional government. This rupture did not prevent the *Cortés* from naming him, not even two months later, to the highest magistracy in the land: the gratitude due the founder of the republic had outweighed, in the minds of free-thinking deputies, their mistrust of the believer. But this admirable gesture had dismal consequences. The republic had chosen a leader who could no longer recognize in that republic the ideal regime he had conjured in his dreams. And when the authority of Alcalá Zamora, as Chief-of-State, covered an anticlerical policy abhorred by the man himself, the Catholics could no longer rally about him. They looked to parties with rightist sympathies.

All told, the "anticlerical" articles of the Constitution did not include any measure which could imperil freedom of religion. Catholic publishers and the Catholic press enjoyed the same latitude as did other publications. Religious practice within the churches was never endangered. But on the other hand, ceremonies on public roads or highways could not be held until permission was requested of and granted by the public authorities.

Divorce was recognized and illegitimate children were granted the same rights as those enjoyed by legitimate children. These two moves aroused impassioned protests. But the most fiery criticism was launched against the separation

of church and state. Yet, as Catholic jurists have since acknowledged, this measure entailed certain advantages for the
Church. The rupture of the Concordat meant, in fact, the
abrogation of the right to present bishops. The Church, freed
of all legal protection, was more than ever a state within the
State.

But the Constitution, while placing the Catholic Church
on the level of a mere "association," nonetheless made the
Church subject to surveillance from which other associations were exempt. For it was ruled that religious orders refrain from "acquiring and from preserving to themselves or
through the intermediary of other parties any goods other
than those destined for their lodging and for the achievement of their private goals." A further paragraph of the Constitution, providing that "the goods of religious orders were
subject to confiscation," was never put into practice. In the
matter of religious orders the Constitution was if anything
more liberal than the 1851 Concordat which authorized, in
theory, but three male orders in the whole of Spain. In fact,
all monastic orders were tolerated. The Constitution of 1931,
citing a certain number of cases of prohibition, appeared to
indicate *a contrario* that all orders were tolerated, apart
from enumerated restricted exceptions. The first of these re-
ferred to religious orders whose articles required a vow of
obedience to an authority "other than the legitimate authority
of the State." This stipulation was manifestly aimed against
the Jesuits—a singular paradox, since the republic was striking
at the sole religious order to have declared itself in favor of
rallying to the republic.

But the 1931 Constitution, less rigorous than the decree
pronounced by Charles III,[5] provided only for the dissolution of the Jesuits, not for their banishment. Most of them in
fact stayed on in Spain, living generally in groups of three or
four; and the property of their order, having long been regis-

---

[5] This decree, promulgated in 1767, had been abolished by Ferdinand VII
in 1815 and indirectly put into practice again in 1836, by the law dissolving
religious orders. The Jesuits have been officially tolerated since 1851 in Spain,
despite the restrictive statements in Article 29 of the Concordat.

tered under the names of dummy proprietors, was kept almost entirely out of reach of nationalization.

The measure which forbade religious orders to engage in trade and industry was to have consequences far more dire. Religious communities had indeed multiplied haphazardly, and many of them subsisted on some sort of handicraft work. One monastery might resole shoes, another turn out pottery. Deprived of these sources of income, the little rural religious communities foundered in a poverty equalled only by that of country priests. The first result of the separation of church and state was the elimination of the pay of these ecclesiastics and the faithful, used to looking upon their priests as functionaries of the State, did nothing to help them. Thus some priests were obliged to work as day laborers, and indigent monks and rural priests became propagandists for the parties of the right.

Further, members of the clergy were forbidden to teach on any level whatever. This measure, which threatened to deprive the Church of her most vital means of proselytism, aroused furious protests. In addition, a serious technical problem would ensue if the measure were put into action since, under the monarchy, education had been so neglected that the Church was almost alone in bearing the brunt of public instruction. Thus, if the religious schools were closed, hundreds of thousands of children would be bereft of any opportunity for learning. Notwithstanding, the republic had made remarkable progress in the field of education: in less than two years, it had erected 2,000 schools and trained the necessary personnel. Yet Azaña was obliged to acknowledge, in January, 1933, that to meet the most urgent needs created by the closing of the religious schools, the State would have to build 8,000 new schools—but that only a fifth of the necessary funds were available.[6] Nonetheless, the closing of the religious primary schools was scheduled for the last day of December, 1933. But some weeks before this deadline, the

[6] In Madrid, where the republic had built 185 schools in 18 months, only 37,000 children attended State schools; 44,000 were registered in Church schools, and 45,000 more found no room in any school.

Cortés was replaced by a new assembly in which Catholics were in the majority: the dissatisfaction evident on every social level had given President Alcalá Zamora the pretext he had been awaiting to dissolve the *Cortés*.

The anticlerical laws exasperated the peasantry in the north, the lower middle class of "intermediary Spain," and a portion of the urban bourgeoisie. The latter group was all on edge over social agitation and the economic depression. Business expenses grew as salaries rose. Funds allocated to teaching, to agrarian reform, to increased police expenditures, swelled the budget and inflated currency while a drop in exports brought about a drop in the value of the *peseta*.

These circumstances had favored the birth of two new rightist parties: the party of Spanish Renovation (monarchist), and the party of Popular Action, whose inception was religious and whose leader was a young professor in the University of Salamanca, former pupil of the Jesuits, and protégé of Angel Herrera: José-María Gil Robles. By taking the path toward opposition, the supporters of a rally to the republic remained faithful to themselves: never had they maintained that Catholics were obliged to submit to anticlerical legislation but rather that they could and should make their will known, and felt, by electoral means.

The new rightist parties gained the mass suffrage of the conservative voters who, two years earlier, had either abstained or given their votes to Alcalá Zamora's party. The majority of women, voting for the first time, obeyed priestly counsel and cast their ballots for the right; the anticlerical bourgeoisie voted for the Radical Party of Lerroux, who had adopted a policy of systematic opposition to the economic and social politics of the republican left.

A large part of the working class, disillusioned by governmental policies, forbore to go to the polls, and those among the day laborers who did not abstain despite the C.N.T.'s urging, were constrained to vote for the *caciques*. Thus, the Socialist Party lost half its strength, while the "bourgeois" parties on the left were virtually wiped out. The right gained 147 seats. In the center, the Radical Party was among the most triumphant. But while this party formerly had been allied with the republican left, it now mingled its votes with the right.[7] After the *bienio rojo* (two red years), Spain was to live the *bienio negro* (two black years).

5. RED OCTOBER

Following the elections in November, 1933, all of Spain believed that Gil Robles would be summoned to the Prime Minister's post and would immediately commence a reform of the anticlerical laws. But it was the radical leader, Lerroux, who was to perform the executive functions throughout almost the whole legislative session. One might have thought that the Catholic right had won the elections for the sole purpose of bringing to power the demagogue who, during the "tragic week" of 1909 in Barcelona, had unleashed the assault by that city's lower proletariat on the convents. The radicals in power were of course careful not to bring up the religious question and hastened to put into action a policy of social counter-reform.

This dramatic switch may be explained by various motives and, first of all, by parliamentary arithmetic. Neither the C.E.D.A.—the rightist coalition—nor the Radicals had an absolute majority in the *Cortés*. Hence their indispensable but unnatural union could be consummated only in the area of social reaction. Further, Gil Robles was anxious to avoid the direct responsibilities power involved, for to assume them would have been to expose the internal contradictions of the coalition whose leader he was. In fact, the C.E.D.A. linked a reactionary wing with a Christian-Democratic wing. The former, monarchist by principle, was resolved to defend the rights of the great landholders. The latter, indifferent to the form a regime might take, wished to effect a moderate agrarian reform. The Christian-Democrats accepted the parliamentary system; and the extreme right

[7] The left had 99 deputies (as against its 282 in 1931): 12 republicans (instead of 107), 61 socialists (instead of 116), 25 leftist autonomists (instead of 59), and one communist—the first ever to sit in the *Cortés*. The center won 167 seats (instead of 112), 104 of which were occupied by radicals. The right and the Basque nationalists together held 207 seats.

considered that the chance circumstances of an election, absurd and capricious by its very nature, had returned the conservatives to power only to facilitate a conservative *coup d'Etat* which would bring the republican experiment to an end.

Threats from the left supplied Gil Robles with a handy pretext for abandoning the responsibilities of power to Lerroux. Convinced that the C.E.D.A. coveted power in order to strike a strong blow. Largo Caballero had let it be known that the workers would rise up in revolt if the Christian-Democrat leader were summoned to form a cabinet.

These fears and threats were explained by the climate of violence which reigned throughout Spain. The impotence of parliamentary institutions, the gravity of social problems and a nostalgia for former grandeur incited the young Spanish bourgeoisie to welcome the bywords of totalitarian dogma emitted by Rome and Berlin. In October, 1933, José Antonio Primo de Rivera, presiding over the first public meeting of the Falange, preached to his few disciples "the dialectic of fists and pistols." Everywhere, the *encamisados*—the young people wearing uniform shirts—marched with rhythmic step and saluted in the Fascist manner. As yet there were but a few hundred members of the Falange. But the young Catholics of the Popular Action party, having similarly adopted a uniform shirt, began some impressive demonstrations. In Cataloña, the *Estat Catala*, super Cataloñan movement led by Dr. Dencas, sent out its green-shirted *escamots* in pursuit of anarchists. And the young red-shirted socialists, for their part, trod the city pavements while saluting with an upraised fist.

The masses were angered by provocations from rightist leagues and by the government's reactionary politics. The execution of the agrarian law was interrupted. The *terratenientes* demanded their back rent and expelled tenants unable to pay their debts. In the cities, the new governmental representatives on the mixed juries systematically awarded each case to the employer. Moreover, the suspension of the large-scale public works undertaken by the preceding legislature swelled the ranks of the unemployed. Where there had been one million jobless in 1933, there were a million and a half the following year. The proletarian frame of mind was receptive to every suggestion for strike or rebellion.

Tension mounted still higher after the Cataloñan Parliament voted a law which applied a typically Cataloñan solution to the *rabassa morta*, a contract by which the owner of a piece of land ceded it to a cultivator on condition that it be worked as vineyard and that each year the owner be paid a rent equal to one-half the harvest. The costs of production as well as taxes were incumbent upon the *rabassaire* (sharecropper). Destruction, disease, or sterility of the plants terminated the contract and the sharecropper received not the slightest indemnity for improvements he might have made on the land. Lluis Companys, a lawyer who had pleaded countless times on behalf of expelled sharecroppers, had founded the *Unio* (union) of *rabassaires* in 1921. Upon his election as President of the *Generalidad* of Cataloña when Macia died (December, 1933), the agrarian question took precedence over all others. In any case, faced with the double peril of anarchist agitation and centralist intransigence, the *Generalidad* had to rely upon the supernationalist *escamots*, to the right, and upon the *rabassaires*, to the left. Thus, Companys caused the regional Parliament to vote a law, on March 21, 1934, by which the *rabassaires* were exempt from taxes and were granted the right to reimbursement for necessary and useful maintenance expenses, in case of a premature expulsion. A review process for current leases was established. The law provided further that the sharecropper should have the right to buy the land he worked, and even to force the owner to sell, in certain defined cases. This rather moderate law was repudiated by the great landholders, who appealed it at the Tribunal of Constitutional Guarantees. This high court, controlled by representatives of the political right, declared that the Parliament of the Autonomous Region was not competent to legislate in matters concerning agriculture.

The issue at hand was no longer one of social justice but of Cataloñan liberty. The Parliament of Cataloña met in solemn session on the afternoon of June 12, 1934, to vote the promulgation of a law on farm leases, while a vast crowd filled the neighboring streets and chanted over and over and over again, "Weapons! We want weapons!"

All of the leftist parties were on the side of the Cataloñans. Throughout the summer and the harvest season, the two opposing forces held their positions, silently stockpiling arms and ammunition. Each awaited the rendezvous in October, crucial period in Spanish political crises.

Amid general astonishment, Gil Robles chose this moment of extreme tension to stake his claim to power. Having reason to fear conspiracy on the part of extremists within his party, he sought to bind them to the advantages—and the responsibilities—of government. By virtue of a compromise brought about by Alcalá Zamora, it was Lerroux nonetheless who formed a cabinet, in October of 1934, but with the participation of three C.E.D.A. members. Thereupon both labor confederations issued the order for a general strike. The miners of Asturia marched on Oviedo in out-and-out rebellion, while in Barcelona, Companys proclaimed "the Cataloñan State within the Spanish Federal Republic"; for if Cataloña were to be sure of enjoying full rights, Spain of necessity must be federal. And Companys believed that circumstances being as they were in October, 1934, the time had come to reach this essential goal.

He further thought that Azaña would form a "provisional government of the Republic" in Barcelona, the constitution of which would be approved *a posteriori* by President Alcalá Zamora, "liberated" from his reactionary majority, and by the new *Cortés*. In view of all this, Companys thought, the marshal of Barcelona, General Batet—a Cataloñan and a democrat—and the primarily Cataloñan troops under his command could not do otherwise than to go over to the side of the *Generalidad*.

But each of these forecasts was to be proven wrong by events. Azaña and the leftist liberal parties refrained from action. In Madrid, Largo Caballero and the entire Socialist Party leadership were arrested almost without resistance. Troops occupied all strategic points, thus quelling every attempt at rebellion even before its inception. The strike now had no meaning, and the workers returned to their jobs.

In Barcelona, the marshal led an all-out attack against the *Generalidad*. He had to move quickly if he were to cut off intervention by the anarchists—whom Companys had refused to arm—and by the *rabassaires* who, rising up in every Cataloñan village, marched on Barcelona. Caught short by the rapidity of the attack, the president surrendered in order to avoid a pointless massacre of the *mocos d'escuadra* (guards of the *Generalidad*) and of the *escamots*.

The struggle was centered at Oviedo. Under the miners' occupation, the city became the scene of such acts of violence as characterize all revolutionary eras: churches in flames, homes searched, hostages imprisoned, summary executions. Only after several days of hand-to-hand fighting was the African Army able to reconquer the Asturian capital. The unhappy city was sacked by Berber *regulares* and the international rabble of the *Tercio*. Over three thousand prisoners were executed without trial in the days following the capture of Oviedo.

The leftist groups were dissolved, their leaders taken prisoner, their newspaper seized. Martial law conferred all powers upon the army. Every condition which could foster a rightist *coup d'Etat* was present. Reporters thronged the steps of the *Cortés*, waiting for Gil Robles to emerge, shouting their question at him in every tongue, "Is it dictatorship?"

No, it was not. Lerroux continued to govern, with the aid of ministers representing the C.E.D.A. Only several weeks later did Gil Robles decide to take over the War Ministry himself. By refusing to carry out the *coup d'Etat*, he had doomed to failure the vast measures of repression which had been the dream of the extreme right. When martial law was lifted, the ordinary courts, overwhelmed by cases brought against the rebels, sentenced only thirty of these men to death.[8] Of these, twenty-eight were reprieved by Alcalá Zamora.

[8] Azaña and Largo Caballero were declared *hors de cause*. But Companys was given a severe sentence: thirty years' imprisonment.

The extreme right was infuriated by this show of mercy and by the "legalist" attitude of Gil Robles. The C.E.D.A. leader was thereupon obliged to offer certain guarantees on the social level. The Minister of Agriculture, Jiménez Fernández, had presented a most moderate program for agrarian reform. Attacked by the spokesman of the *terratenientes*, the minister cited what were to him unattackable references: the *Rerum Novarum* and *Quadragesimo Anno*, whereupon the deputies of the extreme right shouted down the words of the sovereign pontiffs. "If the minister persists in citing the encyclicals of the Popes," cried the traditionalist deputy, Lamamié de Clairac, "we, the defenders of private property, shall have no choice but to declare a schism."

Gil Robles sacrificed his agrarian program and his minister to the unity of the C.E.D.A.: Jiménez Fernández was replaced by a representative of the *terratenientes*, who caused an agrarian counter-reform to be voted. Peasant families, who had been made occupants of the land during the *bienio rojo*, necessarily had to turn to usurers in order to pay the back rents with which they, as "temporary occupants," were now saddled. The number of insolvent farmers expelled from the land grew apace.

The C.E.D.A. found itself in a ridiculous position. Elected to the parliamentary majority on a platform of abolition of anticlerical laws and creation of moderate social reforms, not once in two years had it dared assume control nor carry out its program. A sordid incident of bribery halted the day-to-day survival of a useless radical government. Every embezzlement, every shady deal within the radical clique was brought to light: scandal in the *Cortés*, prodigious scandal throughout the nation. Public opinion reacted by tending toward the left. If the agony of this impotent and degraded Assembly were prolonged, the masses might be sufficiently angered to see that justice was done—by violent means. Alcalá Zamora decided, then, to dissolve the Parliament.

Gil Robles, moved by a spirit of legalism or perhaps by optimism, agreed to the forthcoming elections, which yet portended disaster for the right. The Popular Front pact, signed on January 15, 1936, grouped the liberal parties of the left and the labor groups. To force the nullification of the anti-social laws and an amnesty of the October, 1934, rebels, the workers had decided to vote *en masse*. Besides, the C.N.T. had ordered its members to vote. The bourgeoisie, in Cataloña, for the most part, favored the left so that the statute might be reinstated.[9] A goodly number of former radical or C.E.D.A. supporters, disconcerted by the corruption of the former or the impotence of the latter group, abstained from voting or else cast their ballots for the liberal parties of the left. And once again, the electoral law, acting as a veritable bonus for the slimmest margin, turned a slight shifting of votes into victory for the opposition.[10]

The progress of the extreme left at the expense of the center-left, and the explosive tempers aroused by social conflict were the sole results of the Christian-Democrat experiment. And in the eyes of the proletariat, the Church was more than ever bound to the social reactionaries.

6. THE CONSPIRACY OF THE AGGRESSIVE RIGHT

The Popular Front victory was the signal for a polemic pitting Gil Robles against the extreme right wing of his movement which reproached him, not for having lost the election, but for having carried the battle onto the electoral field. For

---

[9] The Cataloñan *Generalidad* and Parliament had been dissolved after the events of October, 1934. But the administration set up by the *Generalidad* had been maintained, under the authority of a civil governor named by the government at Madrid.

[10] With 4,206,156 votes, the Popular Front won 258 seats (148 for the "bourgeois" liberals, 96 for the socialists, and 14 for the communists), or 1 deputy for 16,300 voters. With 681,047 votes, the center had 62 deputies, or 1 for 10,987 voters. The right had a total of 3,783,601 votes and 152 deputies, or 1 for 24,900 voters. The same instances of injustice due to the electoral law had occurred in November, 1933, but at the expense of the left. During the election, the Spanish press and foreign correspondents reported only minor incidents. If indeed pressure were brought to bear upon the voting public, it was brought rather from the right which, twenty-seven months in power, had placed its minions in all of the important posts and maintained the army and the *Guardia Civil* at its disposition, whereas the majority of the leftist groups were dissolved and many of the labor leaders were, if not in prison, in exile.

quite some time, in fact, the more aggressive elements of the right had dreamt of taking control by force.

The instrument of the plot was the "Military Union," a group led by Sanjurjo in exile, to which virtually all of the army chiefs-of-staff had lent their support. On March 31, 1934, one of these, General Barera, signed—alongside the Carlist leader Lizarra and the monarchist leader Goicoechea—the official minutes of the Rome treaty by which Mussolini undertook to send arms and subsidies to support an uprising against the republican government.[11]

At this time, the left was not in power. The president of the republic was a practicing Catholic. The *Cortés* was dominated by a majority on the right. Those generals who were to lead the July 18 uprising two years later, held complete sway over the army and the implements of repression. True enough, the right, in power, feared a proletarian revolt; this revolt erupted six months later, in October, 1934. But the bloody episodes of that period gave clear proof that the right controlled the governmental machinery and that this machinery was forceful enough to resist any labor revolt. If we are to understand the paradoxical attitude of a rightist element determined to conspire against the State it ruled, we must look to the account given by Calvo Sotelo. In an article published in the March 11, 1936, *Diario Vasco* of San Sebastian, after the February elections, 1936, the monarchist leader explained that the democratic system has a fatal tendency to bring to power the representatives of the masses. "The weapon of the left," wrote Sotelo, "is universal suffrage. The weapon of the right bears another name: it is called 'authority.'" Thus, if the left were to be prevented from coming to power, the parliamentary system must be undermined. And since this theory was counter to the convictions of President of the Republic Alcalá Zamora, and of Prime

[11] In the minutes taken down at the end of this meeting, the Spanish signatories declared that Mussolini and Balbo had given them a spoken promise "to aid by all necessary means the two parties in opposition to the regime currently in power in Spain, so as to allow them to overthrow it." This statement was discovered by the republican police, during the civil war, at the headquarters of *"Renovacíon"* in Madrid.

Minister Alejandro Lerroux, the first blows in the rebellion must be struck against these two men.

The aggressive right would not have asked Italy for arms had Gil Robles, official leader of the rightist coalition, been disposed to avail himself of every means of action (and they were considerable indeed) at his disposal in order to seize control of the governmental machinery by sheer force or by intrigue. But at the time of the Rome treaty, the extremists within the C.E.D.A. were already at odds with Gil Robles. This disharmony forced the Christian-Democrat leader to demand the War Ministry. For it was here, at this post, and only here that he could give his extreme right allies the impression that he was preparing a *coup d'Etat* and yet remain in absolute control of the decision of when, or when not, to give the signal for action. Further, upon taking over the War Ministry, he found that certain preparations had already been made by General Franco, chief-of-staff for the past few months. The future *Caudillo*[12] stated that Gil Robles had ordered him to "reorganize the army as quickly as possible." It is Franco himself who states the specific aim of these preparations when he writes that at the moment of the *Cortés'* dissolution, in January, 1936, the army "was not yet ready to strike a successful blow against the President of the Republic."

In other words, after nine months of accelerated efforts, army headquarters still did not have the two shock battalions needed to bring off a *coup d'Etat*. Only a disagreement between Gil Robles and Franco can account for such singular slowness, and for the rapidity with which Alcalá Zamora believed he should dissolve the *Cortés*. Everything happened as if the Chief-of-State, informed of the conspiracy directed against him, had known nonetheless that the right would not answer the dissolution order by a *coup d'Etat*, because the C.E.D.A. leader was willing to agree to hold elections.

After the victory of the Popular Front, General Franco

12 This quotation and the following one as well are taken from an article published in Paris on March 15, 1937, by the *Revue Universelle*.

strove to pressure Portela Valladares, last Prime Minister of the rightist legislature, into calling off the elections and suspending the rule of law, with the aid of the police. But Portela hastened to turn over authority to the leader of the new majority on the left, Manuel Azaña—who, in turn, forestalled the *pronunciamiento* by removing Franco from his command of the army.

Caught by surprise, momentarily disconcerted, the conspirators were to set about creating a new insurrectional apparatus, while international circumstances proved singularly propitious to their ends. The German-Italian alliance placed Europe, for the first time since 1918, in imminent danger of war; and if the Rome-Berlin axis were to win, it must obtain Spain's support. Spain was thus in a key position at the crossroads of the two essential axes of the Franco-British communications system: the north-south axis joining France to Northern Africa; and the east-west axis joining England and India via Gibraltar and Suez.

If Spain pronounced herself neutrally favorable to the democracies or even joined them, France would be able to disarm the frontier at the Pyrenees and then cross the Peninsula. This communication route, parallel to the maritime Marseilles-North Africa line, would endow the French military establishment with exceptional mobility, leaving the way clear for sizeable detachments to manoeuver between France and Northern Africa. If, on the other hand, Spain chose to be neutrally favorable to the Rome-Berlin axis, circumstances would be reversed. And indeed, when in 1934-40 this second possibility became fact, the threat of invasion by Franco forced the French to maintain part of their troops along the Pyrenees border. Some months later, the sealing off of this frontier was to prevent the defeated French army from falling back on North Africa to continue the struggle. If however Franco-British resistance were prolonged along the Maginot Line and in Belgium, Spanish air raids and submarines sent out from Spanish ports would endanger maritime communications between France and North Africa. Therefore, according to every conceivable hypothesis, Spain was the key to the success of the Axis, and the Axis must be assured of having that key in its hands before launching the decisive assault.

For these reasons, Mussolini had concluded an alliance with Primo de Rivera as early as 1926. Between 1931 and 1933, Mussolini made several futile attempts to open negotiations with the Spanish ambassador with a view to renewing the agreement. His verbal invitations were very likely reiterated after the elections in November, 1933. But Alcalá Zamora and Lerroux clung firmly to the dogma of Spanish neutrality. Only in March, 1934, when all hope of reaching an agreement with the Spanish government had faded away, did Mussolini consent to making some very specific promises in regard to the rightist conspirators. At this time, while drawing Spain into his camp, Il Duce was striving merely to elevate the efficiency of his military system to the utmost, with the purpose either of putting such pressure on France as to obtain concessions in North Africa or of negotiating a military alliance with the Reich. Mussolini had therefore nothing to gain from allowing his Spanish ally to appear on the scene. But in 1936, Italy effected a rapprochement with the Reich: war was inevitable, would come in the near future. At the same time, in Madrid, the pro-French left had returned to power and there was danger that Spain would return to the democratic camp. Whereupon the groundwork for Spanish intervention was laid hastily, not only in Rome but in Berlin as well.

7. GEARS OF VIOLENCE MESH

The conspiracy by the extreme right was also favored by circumstances at home: a feeble government and agitation by the extreme left.

Largo Caballero was of the opinion that the Popular Front pact had been concluded exclusively for the electoral period. Therefore his opposition prevented the Socialist Party from taking part in the cabinet formed by Azaña. When Azaña was elevated to the presidency of the republic, after the dismissal of Alcalá Zamora,[13] the socialists again refused to collaborate with the new Prime Minister, Casares Quiroga. These weak and timorously reformist governments, comprising only representatives of the "bourgeois" republican parties, went no further than to accord an amnesty to those condemned in October, 1934, and to reinstate the Cataloñan statute and the 1932 agrarian law. The insufficiency of these measures, the rancor accumulated during the *bienio negro*, the illusion that the new men in power would not dare to deal severely with the proletariat, and the example set by the progress of the Popular Front in France and in other countries, were circumstances all of which favored labor agitation. Throughout Spain strikes were called, churches turned into bonfires, streets made the scenes of stormy demonstrations. On the first of May, red-shirted Socialist youth paraded in the streets of Madrid, fists upraised, chanting: "For a workers' government, for a red army!"

This state of instability drove the bourgeoisie back toward the extreme right. In the five months between the elections and the civil war, the majority of Gil Robles' supporters and a certain number of Azaña's turned to the two bastions of counterrevolution: "Spanish Renovation" and the Falange. The influx of new members and the additional funds they brought facilitated the preparation of an armed uprising and were reflected in counter-agitation on the right. The Falange and the monarchists organized street demonstrations as so many retorts to the workers' parades.

Brought to power by the labor vote, the republican government could not very well break with the extreme left and entrust its fate to the pretorians who were making overt preparations to overthrow it. Yet it dared not dismantle the army, its last resort when in need of defense against the social revolution. Thus the government refused to discharge General Mola who, having come to terms with the Carlists, was busy placing Navarre on a war footing.

---

[13] By the terms of the 1931 Constitution, a president of the republic having twice availed himself of his right to dissolve the *Cortés*, could be deposed by the third, newly-elected *Cortés*.

The government flattered itself that it would obviate a proletarian revolt by threatening military reprisals—and cow the army by means of labor unions. But experience showed that for a government perched between two violent minorities, see-saw politics were the most dangerous for they set in motion a mechanism of interreactions whose natural outcome is civil war. Since the government dared not deal harshly with the military dissidents, labor groups prepared to defend themselves by silently stock-piling arms. Further, the permanent peril of an imminent military *coup d'Etat* had wrought the working classes to a high pitch of nervous tension. The slightest provocation, a false rumor, were enough to draw a mob in the street. Every demonstration degenerated into a fist-fight. Every faction provoked violent incidents, each of which gave way to a reprisal, each of which in turn stirred new violence. Those who had not yet taken sides, believing the civil war inevitable, hastened to enter one of the two camps to insure their defense. Similarly, many civil servants and policemen believed themselves obliged to choose one side or the other. The machinery of government was collapsing. The erstwhile extremist minorities had given way to two armies readying for battle.

The *pronunciamiento* was to occur on April 20. But General Varela, slated to lead the revolt, was transferred and the dissidents were forced to postpone their plan. After a good deal of dallying, the date was set for mid-July.[14] At this time, the rhythm of reciprocal violence created a *de facto* situation such that no further adjournment was possible. After a series of attempts on the lives of the political and unionist leaders, the terrorist element on the right, whose clandestine chief was Calvo Sotelo, had taken the police, the officers of the pretorian militia, and the magistrates as their targets. The aim of this new phase of terrorism was to dismantle the machinery of government by eliminating those in high places most devoted to the regime while paralysing the

14 On July 12, twenty-four hours before the assassination of Calvo Sotelo, José Antonio Primo de Rivera wrote (in a letter) to a friend, Giménez Caballero, "I think that it will not be many days before the way is completely cleared and ready."

others with fear. After the assassination of the socialist sympathizer, Captain Faraudo, came the assassination of Judge Pedregal, who had sentenced the killers of a socialist newspaper vendor. When violent rightist demonstrations took place in Madrid early in July, a certain José Castillo, lieutenant of the Assault Guard, was conspicuous for the brutality with which he led their repression. Several days later, José Castillo, in turn, was assassinated.

It was at this moment (July 13, 1936) that several officers of the Assault Guard, friends of Castillo, assassinated Calvo Sotelo.

Had the murderers been moved by a reflex for vengeance? Or had they acted, rather, in obedience to an order from the Communist Party?[15] In either case, the crime was complicated by an abuse of power: members of the police had placed at the service of their passions or their personal convictions the authority and the weapons which they held through the State. Certainly this abuse was not novel in Spain; Calvo Sotelo himself had striven to justify the abuses of power committed by the pretorians. During a debate with Gil Robles, Sotelo had held that the army was not merely an instrument of execution in the service of the State but that it was, on the contrary, the "backbone of the nation," and that it was incumbent upon the army "to save Spain" when the government did not do its duty. To defend this theory, the officers sympathetic to Calvo Sotelo were ready to unleash a civil war. The officers sympathetic to Castillo considered, on the other hand, that the salvation of the country had necessitated the death of the instigator of the rightist conspiracy.

The implacable character of interwoven acts of violence which, from murder to murder and revenge to revenge, were heading blindly toward civil war had struck down en route the man who had done most to bring them about. Calvo Sotelo fell on the threshold of a civil war which he had been

---

[15] The assassins, like Castillo himself, belonged to the Communist Party. On the eve of the murder, in a particularly stormy session of the *Cortés*, Dolores Ibarruri (*La Pasionaria*) had threatened Calvo Sotelo with death: "This," she told him, "is your last speech."

actively preparing for twenty-eight months, victim of that pretorian insubordination whose apologist he had been.

The anger ignited by this assassination probably hastened by several hours or several days the beginning of all-out hostilities. In fear of being outstripped or abandoned by the partisans they had armed, the chief conspirators were obliged to sound the call for action. The mock war with which conspiracy and direct action had experimented gave way to the reality of civil war.

Chapter Eight

REVOLUTION
WITHIN THE WAR

THE CIVIL WAR and the revolution which were the outcome of the miscarried *pronunciamiento* of July 19, 1936, did not merely put an end to all hope of structural reform for decades to come: they forged present-day Spain. In the republican zone, the war, breaking down all administrative structures, gave free rein to popular initiative. In the political vacuum were born—or reborn—certain communal and corporative structures which exposed, once again, the deep-lying tendencies of the race.

But the lessons taught by the civil war have been slanted by partisan interpretations. In conservative eyes, the victory of Franco's armies was the victory of Spanish nationalism over the forces of the Communist International; the republicans, for their part, explain away their defeat by Italo-German intervention on the Insurgents' side.

It is true that on four occasions foreign reinforcements

turned the tide. First, after the failure of the *pronunciamiento.*
Beaten in the important cities, the Insurgents held but a few
isolated bastions in all of Spain. The greater part of their
forces was in Morocco. If the army in Africa were to be
enabled to cross into Spain, the fragile bridgehead of Sevilla,
where General Queipo de Llano disposed of only a few detachments, must be consolidated. But the republican fleet
barred the Straits of Gibraltar. Then, Germany and Italy
saved the rebels from total disaster by placing at their disposal airplanes to fly the vanguard of the Rif army into
Andalusia. Three months later, the republicans were saved
by foreign intervention when the *Tercio,* Moroccan *tabors,*
and the *Requetes,* organic minorities, broke the resistance of
the republican militia. Discipline outweighed numbers. Madrid, in siege since early October, 1936, was about to fall.
Then it was that the first international volunteers arrived at
the front. In the first months of the siege, they were few; two
brigades, or 3,450 men. But some among them, having fought
in the First World War, taught the militiamen to dig and to
fortify trenches.

Thereafter, every decisive intervention worked in favor
of the rebels. In the spring of 1937, Italo-German reinforcements enabled the Insurgents to overwhelm the fortified de-
fenses of Bilbao. The following spring, a massive shipment
of heavy material of German origin gave Franco's forces the
upper hand, whereas they had been threatened by the creation of an arms industry in the republican zone. Leaving the
Huesca enclave, stuck like a ring-bolt into republican lines,
Franco's armored divisions broke through the Aragon front
and rapidly advanced toward the Mediterranean. The governmental zone henceforth was cut into two sections. Republican resistance could carry on for some time yet, but the republic had lost the war.

At this time the Italian expeditionary corps included
four divisions. If we count the Italian and German technicians and aviators, Moroccan volunteers from both zones, and
foreigners serving in the *Tercio,* we may consider that
Franco's army included some 80,000 non-Spaniards in the

last two years of the war. If we consider the Portuguese as foreigners, we may add to this the 20,000 Portuguese fighting on Franco's side. On the other hand, the total number of foreign volunteers in the republican army—between 1936, when the international brigades were formed, and November, 1938, when they were dissolved—did not exceed 40,000. In numbers as well as in organization and armament, the foreign aid furnished to Franco's forces greatly surpassed that received by the republicans.

Another aspect of foreign intervention in Spain is its progressive nature. In July, 1936, the arrival of a few detachments of the African army allowed Franco's forces to consolidate their bridgehead in Andalusia. In November, several thousand international volunteers saved the republican army in Madrid. But in spring of 1937, the Insurgents' army made use of two Italian divisions and some 138 of the most up-to-date German planes to batter republican resistance on the Bilbao front which was, after all, secondary. The romantic *guerrilla* of the first few months of hostilities and the street fights involving small groups of militia had given way to a conflict in the style of the First World War.

This period of alternate success and semi-immobility came to an end, in the spring of 1938, only because of the use of armored forces preceded by waves of bombers. The offensive launched at this time on the Aragon front was the dress rehearsal for operations to be led by German armored divisions on the French, Libyan, and Russian fronts. Within twenty months, the war in Spain moved from barricades in the style of those used in 1848 in Paris, to the trenches of 1916, from static warfare to the *blitzkriegs* of 1940.

The crescendo of foreign intervention on Franco's behalf corresponded to a geometric progression of governmental forces. At the outset of the war, the republic disposed of only a few tens of thousands of badly armed militia; beginning in the following year, the republic had managed to mobilize a half-million men and equip them with heavy arms. Despite their superior organization and armament, eighty thousand foreign soldiers, plus a few tens of thousands of men from the African army and from among the fanatic extreme right, would not have been able to make much headway against such numbers. And indeed, Franco's high command had succeeded in incorporating a half-million Spaniards between the autumn of 1936 and the spring of 1938. The supplementary forces furnished by the Rome-Berlin Axis tipped the scales in favor of Franco only because the two opposing Spanish forces were virtually equal.

What were the Francoist arguments, what were the republican errors which had driven so many pacific men, who had formerly cast their votes for the legalist right of Gil Robles or the "bourgeois" liberals of Azaña, into the camp of the aggressive and extreme right? Why did disharmony and discouragement undermine republican resistance? The republic had fought a losing battle in its own mind even before losing it on the battlefield. We must analyze this psychological and political process if ever we are to understand not only the triumph of the Insurgents but also the long-term disarray of the opposition and the tenacity of Franco's dictatorship.

1. DEATH OF THE STATE

Rebel headquarters had planned a classic *pronunciamiento*: a swift operation during which a few units of career pretorians and shock troops from the extreme right elements would seize key-posts in the governmental machinery—ministries, barracks, telephone headquarters. The operation was a success in Morocco on July 17 and 18; it failed in Spain on July 19.

But this failure was not due to the resistance of governmental machinery. The metropolitan army, for the most part, had withheld its support from the rebels; but neither had it come to the aid of the regime. Only fourteen of the fifty-eight garrisons "declared themselves." The majority of them stuck to the stand they had taken, for their commanders feared that their units would disband at the first shot; to maintain an appearance of strength, they decided not to employ them.

Most barracks presented the same spectacle: the banner of insurrection hoisted high above the buildings, the officers in a feverish huddle, the men confined to the base. And the government had refused to incorporate the labor volunteers who proposed to defend the established order. In the night of July 18-19, when the Moroccan zone was already in rebel hands, President Azaña and the "bourgeois" republican parties desperately undertook to avoid the establishment of popular militia forces by compounding with the rebel leaders. Summoned to form a government, Martínez Barrios, leader of the dissident radicals, as replacement for Casares Quiroga who had resigned, opened futile negotiations by telephone with Mola. The failure of this effort put an end to the most ephemeral of cabinets. On July 19, Giral, successor to Martínez Barrios, signed the decree by which the army was dissolved and a popular militia created.

Had the labor groups awaited this decree before intervening, all Spain would have fallen under rebel authority at dawn on July 19. But thousands of volunteers, men and women alike, answered the appeals of the U.G.T., the C.N.T., and the labor parties. Behind hastily thrown-up barricades, overalled and white-shirted figures elbowed the dark uniforms of the Assault Guard. Carbines and blunderbusses were to be found next to the guards' heavy Mausers. The first weapons came from the stocks accumulated clandestinely by labor groups and from pillaged arsenals. Additional weapons were stripped from corpses or taken from prisoners.

In the evening of July 19, the rebellion had been put down in Barcelona, Madrid, and almost all of the great urban centers. The Insurgents held only Navarre and a few insolated cities—Saragossa and Oviedo—where the army, in command of the center of the city, was besieged by miners. In Galicia and the agricultural provinces of Old Castile, areas supposedly on the Insurgents' side, rebel headquarters held only theoretical sway. Between the bastion of Navarre and the fragile bridgehead of Sevilla, Spain remained to be conquered.

The rebels could not withdraw. Their miscarried *coup*

d'État had unleashed a working-class violence which would not spare them in any case; the rebels could survive only by continuing the fight; and those zones nominally controlled by the army were similarly in the grip of such violence that the rebel leaders could not check it. War was inevitable in the context of revolutionary chaos into which an ill-conceived *coup d'État* had thrust the Spanish nation.

All political institutions had collapsed in forty-eight hours. The military remnants still under republican control were occupied in cutting down rebel centers. The Assault Guard opposed the *Guardia Civil*. The police force was, if not on the Insurgents' side, either destroyed or nullified. The *Cortés*, the central and provincial administration, the courts, were disrupted by defections or by opposing tendencies. The abstract hypothesis of the Death of the State had become reality. Dead in fact, the State appeared still to be legally alive. But the "bourgeois" government, with Giral at its head, had no means of action, no grip on reality.

The failure of the uprising throughout the country left the rebels as devoid of means of action as was the legal government. The generals' *junta* set up after the *pronunciamiento* was only a liaison instrument among the various armies, whose principal chiefs—Franco, Mola, Queipo de Llano—acted as proconsuls in their respective zones. Franco was not elected Chief-of-State by the other generals until October 1, 1936, and for a long time his title remained only theoretical. The creation of the actual machinery of government was the work of many long months.

In both zones, the collapse of disciplinary institutions gave the upper hand to violence. There were no longer any authorities, any police, any courts, any possible recourse. There remained no obstacle to the expression of hate, the wreaking of revenge. Armed minorities—Falangists and Carlists on the one hand, syndicalists of various leanings on the other—forced their authority upon the inorganic majority. With law napping and violence given free rein, the way was left open for the small terrorist factions. These minuscule political groups were swelled quickly by a mass of strays:

prisoners who had barely escaped from the penitentiaries under cover of the current chaos. All that had lain hidden in the dregs of society rose to the surface. These dubious elements were joined by adolescents drunk on high-sounding words and craving an escape from traditional authority. The humiliated were taking their revenge. Beggars brought down those who had given them alms. Fugitives from justice, gypsies, unemployed *toreros* who had once proclaimed their communist or anarchist sympathies, now killed for the Falange in the cities of Andalusia. In Barcelona, thieves escaped from prison turned themselves into anarchists in order to pillage houses.

In both zones, terrorist bands seized public buildings, liquidated hostile civil servants, and installed their own faithful in positions of command. These bands patrolled the streets and the outskirts of cities, requisitioned headquarters, cars, food, and improvised a sort of administration which issued safe-conducts and requisition warrants.

The most important business of the day was the liquidation of political adversaries. In the republican zone, soldiers taken while in possession of weapons, civil guards, important landholders, and real or suspected rebel partisans were often massacred by the mob—such was the paroxysm of terror and wrath caused by the *pronunciamiento*. Murder also visited the rebel zone, in the form of summary executions, as the army or Carlist or Falangist bands occupied successive villages. The chief victims were republican notables and labor militants. The orders issued by Yagüe were simple: "Spare the velvet trousers (peasants). Shoot the blue overalls (workers)." When columns of diabolic Rif fighters entered a village, they backed the workers up against a wall and shot them down on the spot. In New Castile, the *Tercio* also exterminated thousands of peasants affiliated with the "Federation of Tillers of the Soil," a socialist group. The phase of instantaneous massacre was followed by that of organized terror. Minorities which had seized power in either zone had their prisons and henchmen who carried out domiciliary searches and arrested suspects. Ordinarily, a parodied trial preceded execution. In the republican zone, the accused were judged by "popular tribunals" composed of representatives of labor organizations. In the rebel zone, makeshift courts-martial judged and sentenced without interruption. To give a veneer of legality to the assassination of civilians loyal to legitimate institutions, a rebellious soldiery paradoxically turned to its own account those articles of the military Code of Justice whose specific purpose it was to punish military rebellion.

But even these "legal" formalities were not always respected. In the general decay of authority, the leaders of the organized minorities were no more successful than anyone else in securing obedience. Thus, the extremists overflowing the extant "committees" assigned to themselves the task of speeding up the purge by making their adversaries take the classic *paseo*, or promenade.

The *paseo* invariably occurred at night. The killers went to pick up their prey either at their homes or in prisons where the inmates lived in constant fear of these nocturnal eruptions. The action then took place according to an immutable scenario: *a small truck bounces along pitch-black roads . . . at the edge of a field, a woods, a clearing, the motor of the stopped truck purrs loudly to cover the noise of shovels and pickaxes . . . a volley of shots . . . a few additional shots . . . the earth hastily shoveled over a heap of bloody bodies.* . . . On August 19, 1936, García Lorca was among the victims of the *paseo*. The killers came to get him, in the dead of night, in the prison at Granada into which he had been thrown only a few hours before.

2. FROM POLITICAL UPHEAVAL TO HOLY WAR

In the republican zone, priests were the principal victims of the killings which bloodied that summer of 1936, for the workers looked upon the priests as allies of the rebels. Certain concrete examples had confirmed that opinion. First of all, there was the attitude of the Navarre priests who had taken a decisive part in preparations for the uprising.[1] In Barcelona, it seemed, the Insurgents had compromised the clergy. On the evening of July 19, rebel groups had taken refuge in several churches in the Gothic quarter and in the Carmelite convent. The first republican militiamen who took the convent-*cum*-fortress by assault claimed to have found the cadaver of a monk killed, as evidence indicated, while manning a machine-gun. Perhaps the story was a mere fabrication, but broadcast on the radio, it made a deep impression nonetheless, one we cannot appreciate without knowing something of the mood of those early days of battle. The traditional freedoms of the Cataloñan people and the most moderate social reforms had been refused them by a party claiming to be the party of the Church. In Barcelona, as everywhere in Spain, the people had been living for several months in uneasy expectation of a new military uprising. The *pronunciamiento* had been made, a futile and absurd undertaking which had cost thousands of lives. The streets were still strewn with cadavers. Hospitals bulged, and the wounded lay on the bloody floors. And then the radio told the crowd already dazed by fatigue and noise: from within a convent converted into a fortress, the monks fired on the civilian population. The infuriated throng threw itself on churches and convents. Hundreds of priests and nuns were massacred. In the night, all of the churches in Barcelona were on fire.

In the days that followed, the work of systematic destruction was to be pursued, in Barcelona and the neighboring villages, by terrorist bands. Once the first instant of fury was passed, the people as a whole took no part in this persecution. Many persons—even liberals and freethinkers—harbored

[1] In his memoirs, the Carlist leader Lizarra reveals that the Navarrian curates of Caparroso, Esquiroz, Berriozar, and Traibuenas had, during the waiting period before July 18, turned their presbyteries into clandestine depots for hand grenades. The shipments of dynamite they received regularly from Bilbao were disguised as sacks of grain. In the village of Lezaun, the *Requetes* drilled under the command of the local curate. Certain presbyteries had sheltered conspirators; and the curate of Noain had installed a walkie-talkie in the belltower of his church.

priests or nuns in their homes.[2] All in all, 6,832 priests and nuns were assassinated in the republican zone.[3] Most of the churches had gone up in flames. No priest dared appear in ecclesiastical garb. Religious worship had to be observed in cellars, attics, or back of shops, as in the very earliest days of the Church.

These incidents justified the *pronunciamiento, a posteriori*, and gave the Insurgents an argument they were to use and abuse in their propaganda. Since the republicans were the enemies of the Church, those who fought against them were defenders of the faith, modern-day crusaders; their war was a holy war.

In reality, the preoccupation with religion was far from the rebels' minds on the day of the *pronunciamiento*. The manifesto issued at this time did not emphasize the defense of the Church. Most of the military leaders of the movement were notorious Freemasons. The Falangists, for their part, did not conceal their anticlerical feelings. And the behavior of the Insurgents in the Basque country showed how indifferent they were to religion.

Calvo Sotelo had written: "Better to have a red Spain than a broken Spain." This obtuse notion of centralism was shared by the Falange and by General Mola. The Carlists, on the other hand, who shared the decentralist ideas of the Basque nationalists, looked upon the latter as dissidents from the Carlist movement. Hence centralists and Carlists alike were agreed on a sort of St. Bartholomew's Day massacre whose designated victims were the Catholics within the Nationalist Party. On July 19, at Pamplona, the first places attacked and pillaged were the headquarters of the National-

[2] At the end of the first year of the war, there were about a thousand ecclesiastics hidden in private homes in Barcelona. When the struggle began, Companys was unable to prevent the sacking of Barcelona churches. The loyal *mocos d'escuadra*—the only militia of which he was sure—made a protective cordon about the Cathedral of Saint Eulalia, and a detachment was sent to Tarragona to protect the Cardinal Primate of Cataloña.

[3] The list of victims may be broken down this way: 13 bishops, 4,171 secular priests, 2,365 monks, and 282 nuns. (Estimate made by Father Montero, in his book, *History of Religious Persecution*, published in Madrid, 1961.)

ist Party and its newspapers, and of the Basque Christian unions.

After the *pronunciamiento*, the *Requetes* invaded Guipúzcoa. The inhabitants of San-Sebastian province were met by the spectacle of strange processions, bristling with rifles and bayonets, descending the Navarrian slopes in the summer dust. Amid the *Requetes* with their red berets were a few soldiers in khaki uniforms, a few Falangists in blue shirts . . . Sometimes two or three of the *Guardia Civil* in gray-green dress led the march, their headgear bicornes of *cuir bouilli*, their arms old Mausers slung over the shoulder. Scapulars and medals gleamed on every chest. The invaders were terrifying in masks of sweat and dust and, as they marched, they interspersed their marching songs with blasphemy, cries of death, and shouts of Long-live-Christ-the-King. Each village group was marked by the black splash of a clerical robe; sometimes the curate marched at the head of the column.

For their defense, their survival, the Basque nationalists had to arm and organize themselves. When the central government grasped that the creation of a regional autonomy was inevitable, it hastened to secure approval in the *Cortés* of the autonomy statute ratification of which had been sought for the past three years. An autonomous government was established in Bilbao. The Basque nationalists named a delegate to the central government. Perhaps they felt themselves to be in a position to demand an end to persecution of Catholics throughout the republican zone. If so, their hopes were dashed. But at least the Basque minister, Manuel de Irujo, could exercise a moderating influence on the repression.

The Insurgents, upon entering the villages of Guipúzcoa, had not awaited the establishment of the Bilbao government before proceeding with summary executions of militant Basque nationalists. Indeed, formation of the autonomous government inspired the rebels to new repression in the zone they occupied. Their fury was turned against the priests, who were generally in favor of Basque nationalism; the centralists reproached them particularly with delivering their sermons in *Euskera*. The first two Basque priests put to death, Abbots Albizu and Lecuona, were executed at Galarreta, in the Ernani quarter, on October 8, 1936, twenty-four hours after the new president of Euzkadi had taken the oath before the Guernica oak. More churchmen were executed in the days that followed. The Abbot of Aristimuno, who had incurred the wrath of the centralists by publishing (under a pseudonym, Aitzol) interesting works on Basque relics, was tortured in Ondarreta, to such an extent that he lost his eyesight, before he was finished off in the Ernani cemetery.[4] In the night of October 24-25, the archpriest of Mondragon and his two vicars were shot against the wall of the Oyarzun cemetery. On the same spot, the Abbot Celestino de Onaindia, vicar of Elgoibar, was executed in the night of October 28. Not the slightest semblance of judgment preceded these executions.

Some sixteen Basque priests had already been executed when, on November 6, a threatening telegram from Franco enjoined General Mola to put an end to the killing of ecclesiastics. This act was motivated, apparently, by pressure from ecclesiastical authorities. Since they had decided to raise their voices in protest, that was the end of the myth of the holy war. Henceforth the rebels spared the lives of Basque priests to be able to continue their propaganda offensive.

But the bombardments of Basque civilians continued. At Durango, churches and several convents were turned to rubble. One chapel was destroyed while a Mass was being

[4] The Abbot's last hours have been recounted by the French merchant, Pelletier, one of a number of prisoners led off in the night to the place of execution, who was spared at the last moment by one of the *Guardia Civil* who pointed out that the prisoner was a Frenchman, answered for by his consulate. Earlier in the day, Pelletier had seen Aristimuno emerge from the room set aside for the interrogatory: "He was unrecognizable, blinded by blood." That night, among the unfortunates being led to their death, Pelletier noticed the Abbot of Aristimuno pass by. "I can see the Abbot," he wrote, "his face black and swollen. He can no longer see clearly. Guards hold him up, drag him along . . . They are going to shoot him, in that condition."

said: the priest and his assistants perished in the ruins. Such destruction could not be accidental. Franco's bombardiers, in the absence of any anti-aircraft opposition, could cruise at low altitudes and choose their targets. At Guernica, the methods used during the bombardment on April 26, 1937, indicate that the goal was total obliteration.

The moment had been chosen carefully: market day, Monday. Some twelve thousand persons were therefore crowded into a town whose normal population was about seven thousand people. The first planes appeared in mid-afternoon. Then uninterrupted waves of *Junkers* broke over the town for nearly three hours. Flying at an altitude of less than two hundred twenty yards, the planes machine-gunned the inhabitants in the streets, pursuing along the roads and into the fields the women, children and even the cattle that tried to flee the center of the bombardment. When the town had been laid waste, a last wave of bombardiers rained incendiary bombs over the ruins.[5]

Following the fall of Bilbao and the capitulation of the Basque army at Santona, the *gudaris* (Basque soldiers), virtually all devout Catholics, and the chaplains themselves were treated as delinquents. A report presented by the Basque

[5] Since it was a notorious fact that the German squadrons did not obey Franco's command, certain observers suggested that they had destroyed Guernica as an experiment, without authorization from General Mola, commander of the northern front. But the Germans would have had no reason for choosing Guernica, holy site of *fuerism*, nor, having done so, for massacring the civil population, while respecting the historic oak and the *"casa de juntas"* (seat of the regional Parliament). But these contradictions are explicable if the bombardment order was issued by Mola. A wrathful centralist, he had declared on the radio: "We shall raze Vizcaya. We must destroy the capital of a perverted people which dares to oppose the irresistible cause of nationalism." Yet, despite his hatred of *fuerism*, it was logical that Mola give the order that the oak and the *casa de juntas*—objects of veneration to his Carlist allies—be respected. The world-wide indignation aroused by the destruction of Guernica alarmed Franco. His propagandists therefore claimed, in the face of all evidence to the contrary, that Guernica had been annihilated by the retreating Basque army. [Pablo Picasso drew inspiration for one of his most celebrated paintings which reflects, in sombre tones, his sense of horror on hearing the news. Conceived and executed within a short time after the bombings as a memorial tribute, "Guernica," together with sketches of its details, is in the Museum of Modern Art, New York.—Ed.]

priests to ecclesiastical authorities in December, 1937, included a list of 283 secular priests and 131 Basque monks imprisoned, sentenced to hard labor or exiled.

Cataloñan Catholics who were supporters of autonomy were dealt with equally rigorously. And even before Cataloña was occupied, the Cataloñan Christian-Democrat leader, Manuel Carrasco i Formiguera, who had fallen into the hands of Franco's forces, was shot on April 9, 1938, at Burgos, in spite of repeated efforts on his behalf by various Church authorities.

The overall conduct of the right was characterized by the way in which political factors took precedence over religious ones. Unlike the republicans, the Insurgents showed, certainly, that they had positive feelings toward the Catholic religion. They respected churches and objects of worship. Yet they did not hesitate to assassinate, as examples, certain priests who voiced political opinions divergent from their own. Similarly, the massacres of priests perpetrated in the republican zone stemmed from an aim for political order. Those priests who were assassinated, when they did not simply fall under the blows of mere evildoers escaped from the penitentiaries under cover of the *pronunciamiento*, had been victims of communist or anarchist labor groups which hated the ecclesiastics, not on doctrinal grounds but rather because they were accustomed to considering them defenders of the social status quo and because they saw in the churchmen accomplices of the Insurgents. Certain priests, such as the Abbot Lobo, who were known for their leftist political sympathies were not molested by the terrorist bands.

But those priests who supported the theses of the right outnumbered the "social" priests hostile to the uprising. Thus violence from the left accounted for more victims among the clergy than did that from the right. On the one hand, there were opulent ceremonies, the scarlet robes of the priests alongside the uniforms of the military; on the other, religious worship was forbidden, churches were reduced to cinders and priests pursued. In this way the myth of the holy war took on substance in Spain and abroad. Bound by their role as false crusaders, the rebels were constrained again and again to give in to the demands made of them by the clergy. And the clergy, hampered in turn by advantages gained in spite of themselves, had to close their eyes to the crimes committed by their impromptu defenders. Little by little an unbreakable chain of complicity tied the Church to the new regime, as it grew stronger on the battlefield. On the other hand, more than any other factor, the religious persecution unleashed over the republican zone helped turn the middle class toward the Insurgent side. The *pistoleros* of the extreme left who assassinated several thousands of churchmen brought down another, greater victim: the republic.

3. EXPERIMENTS IN AN UNFETTERED TIME

Revolutionary abuses were common to both zones but the revolution proper, the sudden and radical reform of institutions, was to be found only on the republican side.

Throwing off all confining elements, the military revolt had left popular initiative unchecked. In the country, day laborers took over the big plantations. In the cities, workers in every factory declared themselves collective owners of their respective enterprises.

A multitude of new structures sprang up in the administrative void: popular militia with elected officers, popular courts, village and provincial committees in place of mayors and governors, works committees in collectivized factories, agricultural cooperatives.

There was something prodigious about the speed with which these new elements had blossomed. Undoubtedly, it was the militant unionists who took the initiative, almost everywhere, in creating them. But on the village level, such a militant would be given only the most vague and intermittent of directives by his labor confederation—whereupon he interpreted, improvised. In this way popular action almost always goes beyond directives—when, indeed, it does not precede them. Leaders in union headquarters appeared to follow the revolution rather than guide it.

The many structures brought into being by the death of the State were very like those which the anarcho-syndicalists unceasingly had called for. But the workers in the U.G.T. also gave their support to the new elements. Only later influenced by their leaders and by the necessities of war, were they to turn in favor of restoring the power of the State. In July, 1936, *"cenetistas," "ugetistas,"* and the non-affiliated gave themselves over to that historical penchant of the Spanish people for grouping themselves in a multitude of minor collectivities, whether local or corporative.

In the space of a few days, these organisms took over the functions of government. Village committees caused the roads to be patrolled by their militiamen and issued safe-conducts. Certain of them coined money. Each committee in its village was second only to God. And every village was a republic which overlooked its neighbors. Economic norms varied from one village to another: here, collectivized land; there, the individual plot. To go from one commune to another, a safe-conduct had to be shown and money changed. The cultivators, whether sharing out the land or working it in common, formed cooperatives: the "collectives," to underwrite the purchase of seed and fertilizer and the sale of their produce. Industrial laborers, for their part, were often considered the owners of their factory; in other cases, they were only associates in matters of management and profits. But whatever the type of management, the enterprise functioned as a production cooperative attached to a professional union, *"ugetista"* or *"cenetista"*; these syndicates, in turn, took charge of the purchase of raw materials and the distribution of products. Merchants, even consumers, formed cooperatives attached to one of the two labor confederations. For the time being the syndicate was master and the isolated man was no-man and defenseless; therefore everyone sought the protection of a union. Without the C.N.T. or the U.G.T. "card," one was not safe. Very soon everyone had entered the cooperative circle. Even municipal public service organizations were run by one or the other of the two confederations, depending on the affiliation of the majority of the personnel. In Barcelona, for instance, the urban transport authority was in the hands of the C.N.T.

The workers' militias similarly were organized on a union basis. Though not every volunteer was necessarily a union affiliate in the beginning, the non-affiliated grouped themselves about a knot of militant unionists under the auspices of one of the two labor confederations.

From here on out there were three governments in the republican zone: a legal but impotent government; and two *de facto* governments, the central committee of the U.G.T. and that of the C.N.T.

The exclusively "bourgeois" nature of the legal government was the most apparent obstacle to unified action. Therefore, Largo Caballero, the socialist leader, was called upon, on September 4, 1936, to form a cabinet composed in the beginning of republicans and socialists, with little communist participation. When the anarchists entered the government in November, unity of control appeared to be re-established. But in fact, union headquarters and the labor parties were the only links between the government on the one hand, and the militia, the popular courts, the village committees and cooperatives, the works committees on the other. For a long while the Popular Front government had no executive means. Labor representatives in the cabinet made no all-out effort to restore to the State the full measure of its authority: the anarchist ministers because they were, by their very doctrines, hostile to the State under any form; and others, particularly the socialists, because they felt that the mass of the U.G.T. could be guided to governmental solutions only very gradually, and then not so much guided as driven by necessity. Furthermore, neither labor parties nor unions had any wish to release their grip on the controls they had captured while the central power was enfeebled.

When the Caballero cabinet was formed, a social and economic revolution already had been accomplished, the spontaneous work of the people, and a most extensive work it was. Agrarian reform, having occasioned so many struggles and so many futile polemics during a century and a half, had been achieved in a matter of days. A new law ruled the economy: the norm of the collective replaced that of private property. The worker henceforth was master within his own factory, an enterprise concrete and close at hand: his own, the factory he had joined before July, 1936, its walls and machinery long familiar to him. There was to be no question of going back to bossism, nor of yielding up possession for the sake of the State and of a red-tape bureaucracy which would manage, in their name, a multitude of remote and unknown goods while the workers, unable to check the State, would be reduced to only theoretical ownership. On this fundamental point, there was no divergence between the U.G.T. and C.N.T. members. For this reason the republican authorities did not attempt at any time to snatch the basic economic unit, the factory, from the hands of the little groups of employees who controlled it. The re-establishment of government authority was carried out on a higher echelon: that of the organisms which mould the economy and which the unions had momentarily taken over.

4. RESTORATION OF THE STATE

In the two enemy zones, there was a double, parallel struggle for the restoration of political power.

In the rebel zone, the office of Chief-of-State, conferred upon Franco on October 1, 1936, by the assembled generals, was originally more theoretic than real. The restoration of political power was achieved in two stages. The unleashing of violence on the individual level first drove the inhabitants to seek the protection of a military leader or a political party: regional bastions and military fiefs were then established with some rapidity. In Navarre, Mola and the Carlists, although natural enemies, were brought together in a marriage of convenience and constituted a state within the State. In other areas of the rebel zone, young people, galvanized by the frenzy of war, and leftist suspects in quest of a protective "card" registered by droves in the Falange. In but a few weeks, the little organic minority of former times had become a huge political force. The execution of José Primo de

Rivera[1] and benevolent protection bestowed by the Axis gave the party leadership to Manuel Hedilla, a figure of working-class origin who aspired to give the Falange a "social" orientation.

Inaugurating his see-saw politics, Franco made use of this new element to put off the extremists in the Carlist party. Enjoying more autonomy than ever Cataloña did within the Republic, they had managed to create their own "royal academy" at which cadets in the northern army were to receive a monarchist training. In December of 1936, Franco, abruptly losing patience, ordered the Carlist leader, Fal Conde, to leave Spain within forty-eight hours.

In fact, and as always, the *Caudillo* had chosen the propitious moment, for the haughty demeanor of Fal Conde no longer bore any relation to reality: the Carlists had already been eclipsed by the Falange. And in the next fifteen months, the Falange consistently gained ground. Only because of Italo-German matériel and reinforcements did the rebels advance on the battlefield, and the counterpart of these contributions was the granting of further strategic posts to the Falange. In the winter of 1936-37 it appeared likely that the Falange would absorb the new State. Manuel Hedilla nursed, perhaps, the hope of becoming the Mussolini of that Spain which was taking shape in its struggle against the republic.

But whereas the Falange extremists occupied the political stage, a far-reaching evolution was taking place, to Franco's advantage. Those among the peasant landholders and those members of the middle class who formerly had been pro-republic were rallying to the military party as frenzied propaganda worked upon them by exploiting the theme of "red atrocities" and mutilated churches. These further elements of support for the new regime wanted a rapid end to the war and calm restored to the streets. Tired of factional struggles and Italo-German intervention, they longed for a forceful State.

[1] Fallen into republican hands, he was condemned and shot in Alicante on November 20, 1936.

The swing of public opinion toward the new regime had made a large-scale mobilization possible. Henceforth the army was the foremost political element in the system, and its strength was dependent upon the Generalissimo who had taken care to place the most vital positions in the hands of those faithful to him. Having a monopoly on the promotion system, he was assured of the loyalty of the younger officers. Within this army devoted to its leader, the African units— swelled by mercenaries recruited in the two Moroccan zones —were a veritable bastion of ultra-loyalty.

Both Carlists and conservative groups, united in adversity, hated the Generalissimo. But they loathed still more the Italian and German interventions, the socialist tendencies of Manuel Hedilla, and the internal disharmony which would have played into the hands of the republic. So, all in all, they played into Franco's hands. Similarly many of the Falangists were put off by Hedilla's national socialism and by the arrogance of Italy and Germany. Hence, while they appeared triumphant, the Falangists of the Hedilla group were actually an isolated minority. On April 16, 1937, the Falange National Council, meeting in Salamanca, decided to replace Hedilla and conferred party leadership upon the moderates. Hedilla's shock troops answered with violence. The National Council was obliged to depose those newly elected and to bring charges against them. At this point Franco stepped in and had Hedilla arrested. If "Il Duce" and "Der Führer" gave Hedilla their support, an internecine struggle would be inevitable, and useful to the republicans. So they accepted the *fait accompli*, and Franco, backed by the army and upheld by public opinion, decreed the fusion of the *Requetes* and the Falangists to form a single party, under his personal control: the Falange of Traditionalist Spain. From this moment on, there was an omnipotent state in the rebel zone.

In the republican zone, the awakening of the Catañan *Generalidad* occurred prior to that of the State. As early as August 27, 1936, President Companys, supported by the middle class of the Esquerra and by the *rabassaires*, was able to issue an exceptionally bold decree. This decree, aimed at reorganizing Cataloñan agriculture, which had been upset by spontaneous collectivization, created within each commune a single agricultural syndicate, to be mandatory as well as unique and without any political affiliation. Grouped into a confederation, the syndicates were invested with both social and economic functions—insurance, on the one hand and distribution of funds, seed, and implements, and the sale of produce on the other. It was in sum an effort to cancel the influence over the peasant of the two extant unions. On October 24 of the same year, another decree legalized collectivization of factories. In theory, collectivization was indicated only when a factory employed over a hundred workers. Yet the *Generalidad* did not nullify the collectivization of smaller enterprises. It did grant an indemnity however to their dispossessed owners. In each branch of production, the works committees which supervised the various factories were placed under an "industrial council" upon which the *Generalidad* was represented. Hence control by the political authority was re-established on the upper echelon. And, in a speech made on December 18, 1936, Companys proclaimed the superiority of the political authority over the authority of the unions.

Three months earlier, Largo Caballero had taken up the fight to restore the State. His policy had two chief motivations: the satisfaction of the masses by ratifying the spontaneously achieved transfers of ownership; and the gradual retrieval of the keys to the economy which had fallen into union hands. The most important of the documents which crystallized the revolution was a decree issued on October 7, 1936, by which the agrarian reform was given *a posteriori* ratification.

In its struggle to regain control, the government was fortunate in the evolution of public opinion. The middle class, artisans and small shopkeepers, all bore with growing impatience the domination of the labor organizations. Those day laborers who had profited from agrarian reform and the workers, who had become master in their own factories, were less open to revolutionary slogans which in their eyes no longer had any purpose. By now the revolution was not to be accomplished: it was already a matter of fact. Now it was a question of consolidation and defense against the Insurgents. Union leaders lost ground all the more rapidly because they were held responsible for the economic chaos which began to be felt. Indeed, the fragmentation of economic structures, the wildly multiplied sorts of legal tender, as well as incompetence and red tape had made scarce basic commodities, devalued currency, raised prices.

Threatened by Insurgent strength, the State gradually brought to bear discipline and unified action. Caballero decreed the militarization of the militia and partial mobilization. The diverse military units—unions, parties, new recruits —were fused into one army, placed under the command of a Chief-of-Staff named by the government. The insignia of rank were reinstated. The few career officers loyal to the republic were placed in positions of command. On a lower echelon, the rank of elected officers was confirmed. In the new Spanish army, as earlier in the armies of the French Revolution, there was a swift renascence of military spirit. But the anarchists opposed the militarization of the militia, a move favored by republicans, Cataloñans, socialists and communists alike. In Valencia, the C.N.T. protested. In Barcelona, draftees demonstrated to cries of "Soldiers, no; militiamen, yes!" Durruti's celebrated iron column refused to melt into the new army. The Aragonian forces composed of Cataloñan and Aragonian *"cenetistas"* evaded governmental control until the great purge of 1937.

The militarization of the army was the key-reform, it made possible all the others. And indeed, in the months that followed, the government dissolved the political and unionist committees which had usurped provincial administration and in their place restored the traditional governors. The assault guard was reinforced; and the carabineers, whose numbers increased daily, took vigorous charge of transports.

Largo Caballero, believing himself competent to eliminate the last extra-legal powers without serious incident, sought to do away with the private police forces and prisons set up by the various parties and unions. In Madrid, the "defense junta" had forbidden civilians to appear armed in the streets. In Valencia, the government outdid this by ordering, on February 27, 1937, that the "rearguard militia" be incorporated into the regular army or dissolved. There was no longer to be a single armed group, at the front or behind the lines, which could elude the control of the State. The dissolution of the extra-legal militia could not help but lead to the disappearance of extra-legal powers and bring to an end the anarchists' reign, the latter group being the only one which claimed to counter the State with union strength in conjunction with certain attributes of government. The active, the ideological, minority of the C.N.T., endangered even in its final retreat, was to put up stubborn resistance. But it does not go without saying by any means that this civil war within the civil war would really have taken place had not the agitation of the most intransigent anarchists been upheld by communist provocation.

5. CIVIL WAR WITHIN THE CIVIL WAR

The progress of the Communist Party is one of the most singular phenomena of the civil war. In 1932, the Communist Party counted but 12,000 members; the Socialist Party, 75,000; the U.G.T., over one million. The victory of the Popular Front in February, 1936, following upon the persecutions of leftist organizations under the Lerroux-Gil Robles government, caused an artificial swelling of the various leftist groups without appreciably changing the ratio extant in 1932 among their respective memberships. But an invariable law proves that times of disorder and violence are propitious for organized minorities and allow them to gain the upper hand over the apathetic and divided masses.

Thus the progress of the Communist Party paralleled that of the Falange. Furthermore, by means of their infiltration tactic, inaugurated before the war, the communists were guaranteed a degree of influence higher than their actual numbers would seem to warrant. Upon the self-dissolution of the C.G.T.U. (a unionist confederation with communist leanings), its 180,000 affiliates had joined the U.G.T. While the new members tried to slip into the more important union offices, the Communist Party took advantage of conditions brought about by the war to place its men at strategic positions in the administration and the army. In Madrid, the small communist minority counted on two sources of strength: the international volunteers, most of whom were communist; and the Fifth Regiment, established after the *pronunciamiento* and which, as a unit of drill instructors, trained tens of thousands of men.

Beginning in October, 1936, the communists' progress was aided further by the international situation. Russia captured public favor easily enough by agreeing to sell to the republic, at steep prices, the weapons refused by the western democracies, in the name of the non-intervention pact, or supplied only in driblets.

The communist-dominated press cannily had played up this aid; and in fact, the flow of matériel and international volunteers, recruited by communist organizations, led the Spanish working class to believe that the communists were their only friends abroad. As Italian and German aid to the Insurgents was stepped up and the democracies continued to hesitate, Soviet aid to the republic appeared more and more precious every passing day. In Valencia and Barcelona, in Burgos and Salamanca, the foreign ally spoke authoritatively and used his influence to place ideological followers in the vital posts of political and administrative machinery.

The internal situation was no less favorable to the communists. Efficient insofar as they were organized, the communists had turned to good advantage the hatreds and fears which anarchist domination had aroused. The government, seeing in the communists a stabilizing force, willingly entrusted them with responsible positions. The communist party had grown mightier in the duel between political authority and anarchist unionism.

The communist leaders could not help but hope that the conflict would continue for it gave them the chance to combat the C.N.T., that prime factor in withholding the greater part of the Spanish proletariat from Marxist influence.

Barcelona was the focus of the battle. As early as December, 1936, the (communist) P.S.U.C.[2] had come in conflict with the (Trotskyite) P.O.U.M. The two parties, with few members, had been represented until that time in the *Generalidad*. The P.S.U.C. had insisted that the P.O.U.M. be excluded, whereupon the C.N.T. intransigents grouped in the "Friends of Durruti" association and their sympathizers in the F.A.I. and the P.O.U.M. were tempted to fuse the two enemies into one and to believe that the *Generalidad* was making common cause with the P.S.U.C.

After a series of incidents between the *Generalidad* and the unionist leaders, the extremist anarchists, after several weeks' efforts, at last succeeded in persuading the C.N.T. leaders to quit the autonomous government. Exploiting the discontentment aroused by the rise in prices and the scarcity of basic commodities, the anarchists sought to ignite a spark of agitation among the workers. The *Generalidad* enacted severe security measures. The P.O.U.M. replied with an appeal to the people. Incidents broke out between P.O.U.M. and C.N.T. militants, on the one hand, the police and P.S.U.C. militants on the other. On the first of May, the C.N.T. called a general strike. Hastily the Insurgents erected barricades in the streets.

But the C.N.T. delegates in the central government acted as mediators between the two parties.[3] Abandoned by the majority of the C.N.T., the intransigent anarchists and the P.O.U.M. militants were forced to surrender.

2 The P.S.U.C. (Unified Socialist Party of Cataloña) grouped both socialists and communists, but it was the latter who were in control. While the P.O.U.M. (Labor Party of Marxist Unification) refuted claims that it was "Trotskyite," it was strongly influenced nonetheless by Trotskyism. The F.A.I. included extremists in the anarcho-syndicalist movement.

3 The two *"cenetista"* ministers from Valencia—seat of the central government—sent emissaries to the two anarchist divisions from the Aragon front who were marching on Barcelona, to order them to do an about-turn. In Valencia, the C.N.T. newspaper, *Solidaridad Obrera*, blamed the Insurgents of Barcelona.

The political authority had got the better of the union authority. But the communists wished to take advantage of the moment to strike a significant blow at their P.O.U.M. and C.N.T. enemies and to bring about the fall of Largo Caballero. Having long aided the communists, the better to contain the anarchists, he realized that the tactic of communist infiltration in the army was endangering the regime, and attempted to combat their tactic. The political commissars, nearly all communists, named to the superior ranks only those officers who agreed to join the Communist Party. There was no advancement for those who had no party card.

Since Caballero was now trying to defeat these manoeuvers, he must be brought down. The two communist ministers, Urribe and Hernández, demanded that the P.O.U.M. be dissolved. Upon Caballero's refusal, they resigned from the government. The other ministers, driven to the wall, were forced to choose between the communist and the anarchist theories.

Must the P.O.U.M. be turned over to the "Stalinists"? If so, the government's political basis would be whittled down and resistance weakened. But if preference were given to the anarchists, there would remain the necessity of fighting the communists, and the republic would undoubtedly then be deprived of Russian supplies at a most critical moment. While shots rang out in the streets of Barcelona, the rebel army marched on Bilbao. Under the circumstances, the need for defense took priority over any other consideration, or so at least believed the socialist ministers and the "bourgeois" republicans. Their resignation drove Largo Caballero to back down, on May 16, 1937. The C.N.T. refused to take part in the new cabinet set up under the presidency of the socialist intellectual, Dr. Negrín. The enthusiasm with which the anarchists had struggled against the rebellion was forever dampened.

Early in June, the Russian embassy and the communists opened a punitive operation against their P.O.U.M. adversaries. The government, which had made use of the Communist Party to break the extra-legal sources of power, was not

merely forced to tolerate the fact that a communist organization, with its executioners and its clandestine prisons, was at
work in the Barcelona streets on behalf of the Russian Embassy. The government had also to decree the dissolution of
the P.O.U.M. and thereby "officialize" the vast purge con-
ducted by the "Stalinists" against that party's officials.

The implacable logic of war led the government to alienate the Cataloñans as well. Once the Basque-Asturian front
had fallen through, the creation of an arms industry became
indispensable to the continuation of the struggle. In October,
1937, the central government moved to Barcelona, in order
to be in the heart of the industrial area; and Indalecio
Prieto, Defense Minister, set about putting to war use every
resource the region had to offer. The *Generalidad* had to be
content with a role more apparent than actual; but the Cataloñans began to mutter under their breath.

It was not long before Prieto came into conflict with
the communists. Like Caballero before him, he became aware
of the danger inherent in communist infiltration into the
army and, with a stroke of his pen, he removed all army
commissars suspected of connivance with the communists.
They in turn resolved to oust Prieto. In spring of 1938, a new
military disaster gave them the opportunity for a new political victory. During the Insurgents' victorious offensive toward the Mediterranean, the Sagunto blast-furnaces, which
fed the entire metallurgical industry of Cataloña, fell into the
hands of the rebel army. Barcelona's arms industry was para-
lysed at the very moment when the stepping up of Italian
and German aid necessitated a total renewal of republican
armaments. Under the circumstances, only Russia could save
the republic from total disaster. The time had come to
demand that, in return, Prieto withdraw. Negrín and most of
the non-communist ministers gave in to this new instance of
blackmail. And Prieto, victim of those manoeuvers which
once he had encouraged, was removed from the government.

From this moment on, the political struggle between
communists and anti-communists became merged with
another conflict: that between partisans of resistance to the

bitter end and partisans of immediate peace. Azaña, Companys, and their followers felt that it was futile to prolong a hopeless resistance which obliged the republican authorities to give themselves over to the communists and the Russians only to elude, temporarily, the rebel and Italian-German forces. What could be the good of heaping ruin upon ruin, suffering upon suffering? Italian planes based on Majorca were bombing Barcelona daily. Hordes of refugees, from every province in Spain, were camping in barracks, churches, convents requisitioned for that purpose. The existence of several currencies at once had made the bottom drop out of the *peseta*. Refusing to work for depreciated paper, the peasant planted only enough for his own consumption. Once-opulent Cataloña was haunted by famine, by bands of ragged, red-eyed, swollen-bellied children roaming the streets. The houses of Barceloneta spilled their entrails of crumbled plaster and household utensils upon the pavement. Spectral dogs snuffled in the debris.

But Negrín believed that while the republic had lost the war in Spain, it could still win the battle on the chessboard of Europe. Admirably informed by his minister of foreign affairs, Álvarez del Vayo, Negrín knew that a second world war was bound to break out in short order—whereupon France and England would find themselves bound to supply the republic with the necessities of war to keep the Peninsula from falling to the Axis.

Hence the supreme goal of Dr. Negrín was to prolong Spanish resistance until the eruption of the world war. This singular person, who died in 1956 without having revealed his motives, reasoned, perhaps, that only a good war record could lead to a good negotiation, and that one must wage war if one is to conquer the peace.

But this calculation, although of impeccable logic, stimulated the most formidable of interreactions. With hostilities prolonged and misery accentuated every day, the pacifists' ranks swelled. The widening vacuum about him forced Negrín to count more and more heavily upon the Communist Party. In exchange for its backing, he had to give them guarantees which irritated the people even more and caused them to fall still further away from the government. Yet the more feeble it grew, the more rigorous its actions. Under the pretext of fighting defeatism the S.I.M. (*Servicio Investigación Militar*—communist-dominated military police) assigned to itself the task of eliminating all in Barcelona who hindered communist infiltration into the machinery of government. To rule on cases of espionage, the government created "Tribunals of Vigilance" whose cursory procedure accorded no rights whatever to the accused. Yet the S.I.M., feeling that even this procedure was not swift enough, carried out still more clandestine executions without benefit of trial.

Companys protested in vain. When the pressure of public opinion grew too urgent, Negrín spoke of withdrawing or stated that he was ready to open peace negotiations.[4] But every tactic which had been used against Caballero and Prieto was now brought into play against the opponents of the Prime Minister: pressure brought to bear by the Russian Embassy, threatened suspension of Soviet aid, press campaigns, accusations of "defeatism" and "treason," agitation within the army, menacing petitions and telegrams from communist military units. In August, 1938, for example, the communists went so far as to organize a parade of Russian tanks in the streets of Barcelona. Once again Azaña, horrified, called upon Negrín to form a cabinet. This last internal crisis resulted in the State's total takeover of Cataloñan industry completely and in the strengthening of S.I.M. power.

Part of the liberal or Cataloñanist middle class now wished Franco to win. It is true that the greater part of the population in the republican zone remained hostile to the Insurgents. Yet since defeat was certain, the blame for daily suffering could no longer be laid upon the assailant but upon the party which caused the futile resistance to drag on. Furthermore, a victory which would have been that of the centralist dictatorship and the Communist Party would have ap-

[4] Negrín's thirteen-point program, published on May 1, 1938, which could be interpreted either as a reminder of the war objectives or as a basis of discussion for a compromise-peace, seems to have been intended above all to appease public sentiment in the republican zone.

peared senseless to the majority of Spanish republicans. Franco had managed to place his authoritarian stamp upon his zone because many of his partisans wanted a "strong government," and because the others were willing to give up freedom in exchange for the social status quo and the restoration of order in the street. But the republic was supported by groups, by men for whom liberty was the supreme good: the "bourgeois" liberals, the anarcho-syndicalists, the defenders of regional autonomy. The very mechanism of war, by creating a dictatorial bureaucracy, had stripped them of any reason for fighting.

When the Insurgent army launched an offensive against Cataloña in December, 1938, the republic was in greater danger from popular apathy than from the military situation. Cataloña was exhausted by the pointless battle of the Ebro. Youths of seventeen had been called up to fill the vacancies. And when it came to weapons, the Insurgents had an overwhelming advantage. But Barcelona, in terms of its dimensions and its human density, presented a serious problem for the Insurgent army marching fearfully upon the city of revolutions, upon the entangled streets of its venerable districts, upon its vast working-class suburbs. If Madrid, as ill-defended at the beginning of the siege and with virtually no means of communications with the outside, had resisted for three long years and was still holding out, what could one not fear from Barcelona? But Negrín knew that the Cataloñans would fight no more. While the republican radio announced, in melodramatic tones, that the rebels would learn that Barcelona was a second Madrid, the government and the last detachments of the army were abandoning the city, drawing along behind them a rolling tide of human beings.

For three days the Francoists hesitated before slipping into deserted Barcelona. But the barrier that held them back no longer existed outside of their memories. Not a shot was fired from the capital of Iberian liberties as it submitted to the army of centralist dictatorship.

Negrín, having gone immediately to Madrid, was met there by the same longing for peace. Most of the officers, realizing that the people were exhausted and weary of communist domination, hoped for the opening of negotiations. Since Negrín demanded that the war be continued, the republican army proclaimed his deposition and formed a junta led by Colonel Casado. A counter-*pronunciamiento* issued by the communist units was stamped out. And while, one after another, the garrisons of the republican army rallied to Casado and to peace, Negrín, alone, unanimously abandoned, left the country by plane, accompanied by the upper echelons of the Communist Party.

Negotiations for peace demonstrated that the moderates had cherished false illusions in hoping that the Insurgents would offer them honorable terms. But by the time it became apparent that Franco was demanding unconditional surrender, it was too late to renew the battle: republican soldiers left the trenches to return to their homes. In certain sectors of the Madrid front, only the officers remained.

In Madrid as in Barcelona the people who, three years earlier, had risen up voluntarily against the military rebels, now on their own initiative put an end to the battle.

The new regime inherited every one of the complexes formed by the war and which had brought republican resistance to a halt: the disharmony which split the left, the overriding fear of working-class revolution which made the bourgeoisie the slave of the military, the terror of civil war. Spaniards of every party and every condition were convinced that even the most tyrannical of governments was preferable to the catastrophe of war.

PART THREE

While
Time Stood Still

Chapter Nine

DUALISM WITHIN UNITY

THE TOTALITARIAN STRUCTURE erected by civil war successfully halted Spanish evolution in its tracks for nearly a
quarter-century.

In rural Spain and in the little cities of "intermediary
Spain," the economic structures, the way of life, the mores,
did not change. Time itself seemed to stand still. But in
urban Spain a certain transformation did occur. In certain
cases, the regime was responsible for these changes. The rise
of heavy industry, for example, was fostered under the double
impetus of Falangist doctrines and big money interests. Elsewhere, changes were wrought by way of reaction against the
abuses of the regime. But in most instances, changes came
about imperceptibly, while the government was unaware of
them. While the immobility of institutions and structures
could slow evolution to a walking pace, it could not prevent
completely technical progress which in turn, although tardily,
entailed a transformation of manners and mores.

Foreign influences played a determining role in this
gradual and tardy transformation of the urban milieu. Ex-

amples set abroad and the pressure of international opinion necessitated a rejuvenation of phraseology and official doctrines. Reluctantly following the western fashion, the regime abandoned the Nazi totalitarian style and moved toward paternal authoritarianism. But beneath this timely camouflage, the armature of the Spanish system was as rigid as ever.

1. DEFEAT AND POSTHUMOUS SUCCESS OF THE FALANGE

The victors in the civil war were not those who had begun it; for the most part, the victorious coalition was comprised of one-time followers of Gil Robles and former supporters of Azaña.

Each of the groups within the "Francoist" coalition laid distinct claims: the Army intended to preserve its privileges, as proper to a ruling caste; the *terratenientes* wished to be spared a new agrarian law; the Church meant to dominate morals and education by means of the secular arm; the middle class was willing for the great landholders to be attacked, provided that the lesser landholders remained immune. And all of these elements insisted that civil order be maintained and strikes put down. The segmented right, a mixture of interests and fears, could put forward no common political doctrine, no common program. The middle class held vague hopes of regaining certain liberties; yet the specter of a proletarian revolution was enough to make the middle class accept the rigidities of dictatorship. The bourgeoisie had a certain sentimental leaning toward a monarchy, particularly, the better to assure social immobility, an authoritarian monarchy which would leave no legal way open by which the people could make themselves heard. Enjoying the security provided by totalitarianism, these "monarchists" were in no hurry to restore the monarchy.

Authentic monarchists, those who looked upon the monarchy as an end in itself and not as a temporary means to other goals, were but a splinter-minority at the end of the civil war. Supporters of Don Juan,[1] heir to Alfonso XIII, were few, while their Carlist rivals counted upon support from the peasants of Navarre. Everything—this localized strength, the existence of *Tercios* of *Requetes*, fear of an awakening on the left, the reformist exuberance of the Falange—encouraged the dispersed and uncertain elements of the classical right to regroup about the bastion of Carlism.

During this time and until the end of the Second World War, this classical right was eclipsed by the authentic Falange. Hitler's prestige was at its height. The hope of a Nazi victory, to which Spain would be linked, galvanized the sons of the Spanish bourgeoisie into action. Blue-shirted and red-bereted, adolescents and even ten-year-olds, they marched in step through the city streets.

But by the time the Falangist décor and slogans knew unlimited triumph, the real Falange was defunct. The moment when "national revolution" would have been feasible was irretrievably past—past in fact for years, ever since the Falangist leaders had agreed to take part in a civil war which, above all, was a social war. For the fundamental characteristic which sets authentic fascism apart from all contemporary political movements, whether of the left or of the right, is the rejection of class struggle and hence the rejection of social war. Fascism is an invitation to unity, an invitation addressed to antagonistic classes to participate in an effort to multiply national power, an effort which necessarily presupposes popular collaboration on a national basis. Without this total cooperation, a nationalist government eager to make good its claims could not surround itself with that vast nationwide unity which constituted the sole source of strength needed to gain the upper hand over the enemy abroad. The founders of the Falange had been sufficiently moved by this objective to outline vague projects for social reform, while the

[1] The two eldest sons of Alfonso XIII—Don Alfonso, Prince of the Asturias; and Don Jaime, Duke of Segovia, gave up their claims because of their physical incapacity. Moreover, Don Alfonso died in an accident in 1938. The King's third son, Don Juan, Count of Barcelona, came forward as the Pretender when his father died in 1941.

logic of their national ambitions left them no choice but to adopt a policy of industrialization at all costs, for industrial development was at once the prime condition of rearmament and the means of freeing Spain from subjugation by foreign capital. This industrialization, in turn, presupposed the creation of a mass consumer market by means of social reform and, primarily, an agrarian law: the party program indeed made provision for one. Had these projects been applicable, the Falange would undoubtedly have succeeded in rescuing Spain from the category of underdeveloped nations.

But the work of the party was to be compromised by, above all, the Falangists' impotence to banish the inherited prejudices of their class. Like José Antonio Primo de Rivera, the original Falangists belonged almost solely to the aristocracy or to the leisured middle class. Did they continue to be stirred, perhaps unconsciously, by a spirit of class war? Or was it rather their urge to snatch the working masses from the leftist organizations which led them to pose as enemies of those organizations? Whatever the reason may have been, from the time of its inception, the Falange launched a murderous small-scale gang-war against the leftist labor groups. The very nature of this conflict led the Falange to reach an understanding with the young extremists within the classical right and gradually dragged the Falange into open warfare.

With this in mind, the death of José Antonio Primo de Rivera appears to be both the symptom and the result of the party's essential failure. The Falange did not fail because its founder was dead, unforeseeably and accidentally. José Antonio was dead in a social war that was the negation of Falangist doctrine and the avowal of its incapacity to regroup all classes for a nationwide effort. The party had had to form an alliance with the aggressive right in an attempt to win, since it had not been winning enough to inspire.

The spiritual heir of José Antonio, Manuel Hedilla, nonetheless persisted, in 1938, in believing that authentic fascism could be achieved by means of a social war which diluted it. He believed that his party, swelled by a horde of "transfers" from the left in search of a protective card, could play the same role as that played in Germany and Italy by similar parties based, however, upon genuine massive acceptance of their doctrines.

But in Spain, the eleventh-hour "transfers" remained passive, and the young Falangists produced by the middle classes were indifferent to the social aspects of Hedilla's policy. If he were to emerge victorious over Franco, accomplish the "national revolution" of which José Antonio had dreamed, Manuel Hedilla would have needed the backing of the masses —the masses alienated once and for all by the participation of the Falange in the civil war. There was no longer any choice open to the party, separated now from the working class by so much spilt blood. Their common victory tied the Falange to the conservatives in the exercise of power. And indeed, from 1938 on, the majority of Falangists submitted to the inevitable results of the war. Hedilla, thus abandoned, was left open to Franco's vindictiveness. They agreed to join the conservative right as a single party. The single-party doctrine was borrowed from fascist doctrine. But the Falange, apparently successful in driving home its ideas, turned its back more than ever upon the realities of fascism. Unlike similar parties in Germany, in Italy, in Argentina, the Spanish single-party was not a living organism, the sum of a vast number of adherents joined by one doctrine, by a single political faith, by a common will. In Spain the single party was a rigid framework in which to hold and imprison a disparate throng of members often registered with the party against their will.

Far from being the expression of the general will, the party was rather a strait jacket fastened upon the people. Other fascist parties had won over the masses in order to hoist themselves into power on their shoulders. The single party in Spain had been placed in strategic posts thanks to the war; but the people were yet to be won over. Twenty years after the civil war, the "conquest of the street" was still the dream of the last of the "die-hards," a dream all the less likely to come true since, on the economic level, this composite party practiced an on-the-fence policy whose chief aim was to perpetuate the social status quo.

Falangists and conservatives disagreed over each and every plank in their platforms—taxes, salaries, income distribution. The single party emitted a constant undertone of complaints and anathemas. But both groups bowed before certain tactical necessities: maintenance of the "amalgam," Franco's personal authority, a policy of force to be used against the left, continued repression and permanent censorship. During two decades, all the internecine quarrels of the single party were restrained by the fear of undermining these fundamental needs.

2. DICTATORSHIP BY ARBITRATION

In making the amalgam hold firm, Franco had shown the strength of his personal position. This strength he owed, above all, to the army. Not only had the war devoured a great many men, but also it had eliminated the old generals, Franco's elders. Controlling the paths to promotion in rank, the *Caudillo* had placed new men in command who, owing him everything, were personally devoted to him. But the army was the arbiter of political life only insofar as the war had "atomized" public opinion, for the conquered masses were reduced to impotence. And within the victorious coalition, the two positive forces—the Falange and the extreme right— cancelled each other out with their struggles. Both the hatreds which made them opponents and the fears which brought them unhappily together cried out for arbitration. In the political vacuum created by the war there appeared an arbitration based upon armed strength.

Within the limits defined by the refusals and the *desiderata* of the various rightist elements, Franco's faculties for decision were considerable. What use was he to make of them? As an officer in the Foreign Legion, he had spent a good deal of his life among old offenders. His personality had been formed in the climate of the inexpiable Rif *guerrilla* which had pushed the legionnaires' natural brutality to paroxysms of passion. Officers were obeyed only if they proved themselves tougher, more intrepid than their subordinates. A vitally important account of this evolution has been given in *La Ruta* by the novelist Arturo Barea. Barea was a non-commissioned officer in the Rif army at this time. "When the *Tercio* was organized," he wrote, "the officers were like the others. But when they had to deal with the first *Bandera* [company of the Legion] they changed. No sooner had we arrived in Ceuta than we killed three or four officers. At bottom, they were afraid of us. But they were the bosses. They imposed the barbarous discipline that exists now. If a man refused to obey, they shot him. And now the officers have become brutes with us, with everyone, with everything."

Of all the officers in the *Tercio* the only one who managed to place himself above the legionnaires was the young Franco. Hence, at the age of 33, he was summoned to take command of the Foreign Legion. What explains this extraordinary ascendancy? Were the legionnaires conquered by Franco's mad bravado? But among the officers in the Rif army, bravado was the most common quality imaginable. No, the *Tercio* "toughs" were more impressed by the young colonel's cold gaze, his impassive demeanor, his silence.[2]

In Latin countries, where everyone talks volubly, the silent always inspire uneasiness. The other officers were as quick to feel pity as anger: a prayer, a sally of some wit could disarm them. But instinctively one felt that Franco, icy, unmoved by pity, would admit no let or hindrance—no moral rule, no other prejudice—and that he would go his way obstinately and one must either destroy him or submit to him.

Fine talkers and fine *sabreurs*, the other officers had at first disdained this young man of unimpressive stature and humble origin, a fellow whose silence was reinforced by his poverty, for he lacked the means that enable a man to shine and to please. But his influence over the legionnaires and the rapidity of his promotions obliged his peers, even his superiors, to take notice. They liked him even less than on the first day; but they had learned to fear him and to respect the antlike efficiency of his work.

2 "He looks at a guy calmly, and he says: 'Shoot him.' Then he does an about-face and walks away." (Arturo Barea, *La Ruta*.)

The young colonel who terrorized the "toughs" of the Foreign Legion is a long way from the elderly Chief-of-State who officiates at the celebration for a new dam and accepts flowers from a schoolchild's small hands as he smiles the immutable smile of the model grandfather. His ultra-determined assurance is masked by a paternal benignity.

From the time he was thirty, Franco became known for certain characteristics which maturity would serve to accentuate and primarily, by a singular self-control. From that period on, his passions were not strong enough to overrule his inclination to temporize. Neither anger nor imagination nor sensitivity could change the exactitude of his calculations. He measured his adversary's strength and his weakness. And when his infallible instinct whispered that the enfeebled enemy was at his mercy, he struck with unpitying sureness; no mercy tempered it, no scruple spoke against it. Let us observe his behavior in the years before the civil war. After the proclamation of the republic, he preaches submission to the established authority, while Sanjurjo and his friends ruin their own careers with a premature revolt. It would seem that Franco inclines to legalist scruples. But when Gil Robles rewards his moderation with the topmost position in the military hierarchy, Franco, chameleon-like, becomes the spokesman of the aggressive right. After the proletarian revolt in October, 1934, his calm voice, untinged by anger, demands that the leftist leaders be liquidated. Appearances to the contrary, Franco remains faithful to himself: only circumstances have changed. In 1932, the republic was strong: the wise course was to submit to it. But in October, 1934, the left is whipped, broken, at the victor's mercy. The right can dare anything at all; by wiping out the labor leaders it is assured of remaining in power for a long time. The man who never let slip any chance looks with disdain upon Gil Robles' vacillations. During the civil war, the *Caudillo* acts with the same opportunism. First of all he leans upon the Falange in order to destroy Fal Conde. Is he won over by Falangist doctrines? Not in the least. He allows Hedilla to go ahead incautiously. And when that Falangist leader is isolated, Franco smites him down in a single day. At forty-five he is master of the single party, master of the State, soon master of Spain herself. The lack of imagination which until then has been so helpful to him becomes the worst of handicaps as soon as it is necessary to act as an *homme d'Etat*, to build new solutions. In every field—religion, morals, politics—Franco adopts current notions. He strives to apply these concepts he has learned and apes the examples offered by History. In 1936, he fights the war of 1914 and only reluctantly does he accept the armored units advised by the German generals.[3] The colonial empire he dreams of establishing is that conquered by France and England in the nineteenth century under long since outdated circumstances. His failures do not move him to introspection, and he draws no lesson from his triumphs. This happy Chief-of-State is not to produce even a single meaty maxim on the art of governing men. All of his speeches are about particular circumstances; and when, exceptionally, he does rise to general ideas, he encounters only commonplaces.

But the very limitations of his character were marvelously suited to the times. A wider-ranging, more generous spirit would have attempted to resurrect national unity. But this was precisely the ambition which was unthinkable for the man who had led one half of Spain to attack the other. By alienating his supporters, he would not have disarmed his opponents. By reassuring the opposition, he would have put an end to that "atomization" of public opinion which, while it prevented him from being constructive, at least allowed him to last. No sooner was the only possible task that of perpetuating the domination of victorious classes over the defeated masses, a task which elevated repression into the indispensable and most constant activity of government, than the insensitivity with which nature had endowed Franco became the most precious of all his traits of character. Neither

[3] In his memoirs, entitled *Para Qué?* and published in Buenos Aires, an important monarchist figure, the aviation commander J. A. Ansaldo, who was Air Attaché in Paris and then in London during the Second World War, quoted the criticism made of Franco by the German military attaché: "A little colonial general who has only one brigade in his head."

pity nor the image of other people's misery had any power to ruffle his calm.

The only threat to his imperturbable equilibrium came from the dizzy heights of pride. An extraordinary photograph, published in the papers at the time of the civil war, shows him perched upon the throne of Carlos I: a stocky little figure under the colossal black eagles with widespread wings. He stated, he let it be known, that the *"happy circumstance"* of civil war, a war heavy with the burden of a half-million dead, was arranged by Providence expressly for him that he might seat his diminutive person upon the imperial throne. In this position he gave audience. The press, forced day after day to applaud the *Caudillo*'s ingenious foresight, had long since exhausted its stock of hyperbole.

Each of his failures was transformed into a triumph. On May 8, 1945, for instance, the press reported Hitler's surrender with enormous headlines along the lines of "Victory for Franco" (*Arriba*), "Man of the Moment: Francisco Franco" (*Pueblo*). To perpetuate the memory of his conquest over his fellow citizens, he caused a pantheon of granite, marble, and gold to be carved into the *Sierra de Guadarrama*, a monument larger than the Escorial and whose dome was loftier than that of St. Peter's Basilica in Rome. Yet all the while he gave way to this delirious megalomania, he kept a firm grip on his prudence. While part of his attention was turned to this monument, which is to house his earthly remains, another part looked to the security of his old age. Doña Carmen was the trustee of capital amassed through dealings in which the agent was Nicolas Franco.[4] In the intervals between masses and charity balls, then, that pious lady busied herself in placing the money with Swiss banks.

Somehow, no matter how drunk with himself, Franco managed to keep a cool head. With each passing year, habit perfected the mastery with which he made use of every little trick of sly politics. His silences, or his rare and suspended pronouncements, were calculated to mask the truth, to create

[4] Doña Carmen Polo de Franco and Nicolas Franco: wife and brother respectively of the *Caudillo*.

a false impression. He excelled in the tactic of "divide and conquer," in supporting the weak against the great, in calumny, in weeding out an opponent before striking down the isolated figure, in taking credit for a success and laying the blame for a reversal upon his ministers. His obstinacy was unequalled. His faculty for repetition tried the patience of his interlocutors, wore down the resistance of his opponents, exhausted even his collaborators.[5]

His favorite role was that of arbitrator. At any rate, circumstances did not permit him to play any other. For no man governs alone; and what dictator was more alone than Franco? José Antonio, Fal Conde, Hedilla all had their eager partisans. Franco had only those of other men or other parties, resigned to supporting him or calculating that it was in their best interest to do so. This being the case, his personal power could be anchored only in permanent arbitration between victorious factions and interests, and, at first, between the Falange and the conservatives. During the Second World War, he was artful enough to prevent the single party from leaning toward the Falangists. And no sooner did a German victory appear doubtful than he dismissed Serrano Suñer on September 3, 1942, charged with all the sins of collaboration with Hitler.[6] But the Count of Jordana, summoned to head the Ministry of Foreign Affairs, was by no means a newcomer: he had taken part in Franco's government during the civil war.[7] In naming him, Franco showed that he wished to avoid the precipitate reaching of turning points. When he reshuffled his Cabinet after the Allied victory in 1945, he summoned a Christian Democrat, Martín Artajo, to the Ministry

[5] In 1940, after the Hendaye interview, Hitler, who had just suffered through nine hours of uninterrupted *tête-à-tête* with Franco, declared that he would rather have three teeth pulled out than confer once again with his colleague from Madrid.

[6] Ramón Serrano Suñer, Franco's brother-in-law, was Minister of the Interior from February, 1938, to May, 1941, and Minister of Foreign Affairs from May, 1941, to September, 1942.

[7] Don Francisco Gómez, Count of Jordana, president of the "technical junta" from June, 1937, to February, 1938; acted as Prime Minister, Franco being Chief-of-State. Was Vice-President of the government and Minister of Foreign Affairs from February, 1938, to August, 1939. Returned to the government in 1942, he died in August, 1944.

of Foreign Affairs; and for the time left vacant the office of Minister of the "Movement." Falangists were not excluded from the government, and, when the balance of power dropped more and more toward the classical right, Franco, urged to sacrifice the Falange and to "liberalize" institutions, used all the resources of his dilatory tactic to veto these demands.

Had José Antonio Primo de Rivera lived and governed, the regime, dragged into the war on the Axis side, would have foundered in 1944. But a conservative general, provided he miraculously withstood the Falange assaults, would have hastened to call back Don Juan. And such a monarchical restoration would have opened the way toward a return to civil liberties. The regime was salvaged and prolonged for an unwarranted time only because of the seesaw politics of the *Caudillo*, the obstinacy with which he defended the simultaneously dualist and totalitarian structure of his system.

3. FACTORS OF IMMOBILITY

The *Caudillo*'s knowing political doses would have been less effective had not the social conditions of the time been so favorable to maintenance of the *status quo*.

On the morrow of the civil war, the middle classes, terrorized by revolutionary abuses, had pledged themselves wholeheartedly to the new regime. War, repression, and the black market had given way to a new class of profiteers. In fact all those who had belonged to a republican party before the war or who had held a government post, no matter how unimportant, during the civil war, had been in fact left destitute.

The result was a large-scale redistribution of jobs. Noncommissioned officers in Franco's army promoted to the ranks of civil servant or teacher, officers and policemen compromised by the repression, prebendaries of Falangist jobs, judges fearing to be judged, and speculators fearing investigation into the sources of their income—all of these creatures of the regime were resolved to preserve the status quo at all costs.

The workers, for their part, accused their former leaders

of having involved them in a hopeless affair, then of having abandoned them. Those who had known prison life returned to their homes broken in body and spirit. The recent struggles seemed to be only a rather wild adventure that had distracted them from the essential duty of supporting their families. The wives, heroines on the home front, had often had to provide for their children and see that their imprisoned husbands were fed; henceforth, the wife was the real head of the family. More than ever opposed to political action, which she had always blamed, she used her new-found authority over husband and sons to persuade them not "to get involved in things." The little labor minority whose convictions were still intact was deprived of leaders, for the leftist leaders who had not fallen during the civil war nor fled the country were shot immediately after the war. By exterminating two generations of labor leaders, the dictatorship paralyzed the opposition for fully a quarter-century.

Dissension within the resistance elements helped weaken them. The communists were at war with the other groups. Militants everywhere were haunted by fear of the *soplones* (police spies) whose ranks had swelled out of all proportion. Even when the *soplón* was not there, the opposition thought it saw him, and opposition members shrank from contact with persons unknown to their own close circle, from taking them into their confidence, from acting. They were convinced they would be denounced, imprisoned, prevented from making a fruitful effort, and that even should the impossible be possible and the revolt commenced, it would be put down. Mass executions would ensue. In this light, even hunger, police oppression, and all present evils were preferable to the risks implicit in action.

The war left behind it a general scepticism. The worker no longer had any faith in political action, convinced that it was bound to fail. The middle class no longer believed in bourgeois democracy, which appeared the inevitable victim of the proletarian revolution. Wistful for a change, but a nonviolent change and suspecting more evil in action than in the status quo, the dissatisfied remained passive. During the long dictatorial period, the factors creating immobility were reinforced or lessened, according to circumstances.

During the Second World War, the regime was more robust than at any other time. The middle class was more tightly held by its overweaning fear, based on still-fresh memories of the civil war. And the prospect of an Italian-German victory excited the Falangist fervor of the young people. Yet resistance was relatively active, a fact which appeared justified by the hope of aid from abroad. No one doubted that the defeat of the Axis would necessarily bring about the defeat of France. The larger loomed the Allied victory, the more the regime had cause to fear that resistance would grow fiercer and even that certain of Franco's collaborators would try to clear themselves of future blame for past responsibility by hastening to further the resistance. Certain generals did indeed offer to help the Allies overthrow the dictatorship; but their hopes of acting were crushed for lack of an internal climate or current which could support them sufficiently.

The resistance looked to the emigrants for the signal to act. But as much as three years before Hitler's fall, the second Spanish republic had already lost its sole chance of resurrection. In 1940-41, when England feared for Gibraltar, the republic could undoubtedly have obtained from the English Cabinet funds and material sufficient to establish a mighty network of resistance. The former Minister of Justice, de Irujo, tried to turn these favorable circumstances to good account. But he could not and would not speak otherwise than in the name of the Basque country. Furthermore, the disunited emigrants went about opposing this initiative.[8] And the Spanish commandos made up in England under the auspices of the exiled Basque government were dissolved in 1942 when Franco, disappointed by the Axis defeats, formally vowed to remain neutral.

[8] The Socialist Party was torn by the rivalry between Prieto and Negrín. The emigrants were especially split between an anti-communist majority (liberal republicans, Basques, Cataloñans, socialists, C.N.T., P.O.U.M.) and a communist minority.

War's end therefore found the opposition in chaos. Resistance groups were already weak and almost bereft of arms and of means of contact with the outside. Nonetheless, when they attempted to make firm contact with the emigrants, there was no republican authority, no constituted military force, no plan of action supported by the victorious powers. Under such conditions, action was impossible. And in fact, when some Spaniards who had fought in the French *maquis* attempted in 1944 to carry out an operation, the result was totally disastrous. In 1945, the emigrants managed to unite briefly and form a government; but the most foresighted diplomats in Spain and abroad had already conceived another solution. The inertia of public opinion, the helpless resistance (still further weakened by the disillusionment which came at the end of the war), and the loss of prestige by the emigrated leaders—all showed that it was futile to continue hoping that a popular revolution would overthrow the dictatorship. This being the case, the only hope of change in the regime lay in compromise. The elements which formed privileged castes under Franco's regime should not only agree to its fall but also they should take over the responsibility of overthrowing it. If they were to be persuaded to abandon Franco, they must be offered a political solution likely to safeguard all that was most precious in their eyes: order, property, and amnesty for the war crimes committed by the right. Without question, the monarchy was the solution most likely to reassure the privileged castes. Hence the more important socialist leaders were convinced, as early as 1946, that a reconciliation with the monarchists would prove inevitable; but they were prevented from leaving the republican government at this time by the resistance of their adherents. It was not until 1948 that the socialist-monarchist pact was signed.[9] Concluded under

[9] This document, actually countersigned by various socialist figures, was the work of Gil Robles and Prieto. The codicil added by the monarchists to the text of the October, 1948, agreement stated specifically that "the King was aware of, gave his approval to, and encouraged the pact." Furthermore, in his manifesto of April 7, 1947, and in an interview granted immediately after the signing of the agreement to the London *Observer*, Don Juan had voiced

the auspices of the English government, it provided for the amnesty, for the elaboration of a *fuero* guaranteeing the rights of the human person, freedom of conscience, incorporation of Spain into the Occidental diplomatic system, and the outlawing of all totalitarian parties whether on the right or on the left.

Most of the resistance networks established contact with the monarchist partisans of Don Juan, and in the next three years various plans were sketched to overthrow the regime; all of them called for the same scenario. Figures within diverse political elements (republican or monarchist) would form a transitional government, a "bridge-government" which would be aided by one or several of the foreign powers. The prospect of an imminent solution would bring out a rash of strikes and demonstrations. The bourgeoisie, threatened by these disorders, would be won over to the proposed solution. The army would withdraw its support of Franco and, if necessary, force him to fade out of the picture. The transitional government would then organize a plebiscite: the people would be asked to choose between a monarchy or a republic.

These plans rested upon two essential factors: aid from abroad and the active cooperation of the privileged classes. Neither presupposition materialized.

Between the end of World War II and spring of 1951, the democracies certainly did prove a number of times their hostility to Franco: repeated condemnations of his regime by the United Nations (1946), the closing of the French border. But these were purely moral encouragements, and the opposition leaders appeared to be hoping for more direct intervention: recognition of a government set up outside of Spain, the granting of material aid to this "junta," a note from all of the western powers together urging Franco to step down.

The opposition waited and expected in vain. What in-

---

ideas which were very close to those enacted in the pact: the wish to return to an *état de droit;* the plan of a thorough decentralization according to which "the activities which only burden the State unnecessarily will be transferred to the regions"; and the intention of organizing elections.

terested the western chancelleries was not the question of placing their top men in Madrid but rather that of knowing which negotiators Spain would force them to accept. While the opposition looked abroad, the chancelleries turned their gaze to the interior: they were on the watch for strikes, for street demonstrations, for the slightest signs which would allow them to foresee the tendency of peninsular evolution. For fifteen years, Spanish politics were to mark time within this closed circle.

It was evident that the Spanish privileged classes and the pretorians—absolute masters of the State—would not rise up against the regime which underwrote their privileges unless they were driven to do so by pressure from abroad or agitation in the street. Now that foreign intervention was not forthcoming, the leftist parties should have encouraged resistance. But the majority of the emigrated leaders, fearing that popular agitation would cause the privileged classes to turn back to the extreme right, saw to it that resistance was contained within the limits of non-violence.

From then on, a change of attitude among the privileged castes was all the more problematic since the proposed solution in no way gave a guarantee for the future. The "bridge-government" was indeed temporary, since its self-assigned mission was to prepare the way for a plebiscite. But a paternalist monarchy was the only mode of compromise which the privileged were willing to accept, and they did not care to run the risk of a plebiscite. For their own part, the leftist leaders, elected by the people, could not give up the exercise of popular sovereignty, and their supporters were so hostile to the monarchy that they could not even undertake to campaign for it. Under the circumstances, the plebiscite might return a leftist republic. And one would have to be very naïve to ask the privileged castes, who were not liable to any threat whatsoever, to overthrow voluntarily the regime which harbored them in order to launch an evolutionary process likely to lead to new revolutionary disturbances.

Nonetheless in the spring of 1951, the economic difficulties created by incompetence in the dictatorship and by the hostility of other nations were on the verge of pushing the regime over the brink. But this perilous situation was saved by the still more weighty factors of immobility.

4. THE WARNING OF SPRING, 1951

In the spring of 1951, the economic isolation of Spain and the insufficiency of production had taken on the obvious form of famine. The ballooning of prices was abetted by rampant inflation and speculation. The lower classes swelled with anger against the black market and a corrupt administration. Assuredly, the Spanish people had known darker days, between 1939 and 1944. But then, the leanness of those years had been justified by the civil war and the cross-blows of World War II; meanwhile, the people had waited in patient hope of a brighter future. Their hopes had been squashed. Twelve years after the last shot of the civil war had died away, rationing cards were still obligatory. Neither the power of the Falange nor fear of Italo-German intervention was able any longer to stifle the grumblings of the masses. Middle-class youth, jolted out of its dream of glory by defeat of the Axis, drifted little by little away from the Falange. Furthermore, a new generation which had lived unaware of the horrors of the civil war had just entered the universities, bringing a collective thirst for freedom. In sum, bourgeoisie, industrialists, businessmen, felt that the current regime prevented the resumption of exchanges with the West and cut off access to American funds, and favored the advent of Don Juan to the throne. Every condition conducive to a *pronunciamiento* was now present, and indeed plots were hatched in officers' *casinos*.

The Church sought to dissociate herself from an apparently foundering regime. In fact, for several months before strikes broke out, the ecclesiastical newspapers, *Tu* and *Razón y Fe*, had been campaigning against the racketeers and for reasonable salaries.

In such an atmosphere of popular agitation and churchly opposition, then, the Congress of Falangist Unions convened on March 6, 1951. Anxious not to be outdistanced by the Catholic movement, the delegates plunged into a veritable orgy of criticisms and demands for reform.

On the last day of the Congress, Spanish workers heard a broadcast message to them from Pope Pius XII; union leaders, in order that they might hear it, had assembled vast throngs of workingmen who lined up by union and factory, on the esplanade, ringed with loudspeakers, of every important city. The Pontiff confined himself to recalling the principles of Church doctrine: just wages, workers' participation in the management of the factory. But this simple reminder, resounding through the social tension of the spring of 1951, was heavy with meaning for the regime.

During all of February, there had been lively social agitation in Barcelona, in the form of a boycott of the tramways. Beginning on March 8, clandestine groups had distributed pamphlets urging the workers to come out on strike. The Pope's message had a stunning effect. Both the Church and the Falange, those twin pillars of the regime, appeared simultaneously to withdraw their support from the government. The way to action was open, and the proletariat of Barcelona took stormy advantage of it.

On Monday, March 12, the very day after the Pope's message, a general strike was called. Some three hundred thousand workers walked out. A huge crowd of workers from the industrial suburbs, marched down the *Paseo de Gracia* toward the *Plaza de Cataloña*. Tramways and automobiles were overturned. Everywhere, students appeared in the front ranks of the demonstration. Trainloads of troops and armed police converged on Barcelona.

But the next day, the city awoke as from a night of drunken delusion. The *Guardia Civil* and armed police patrolled the streets. The people observed that the regime remained intact, with its administration, its police, its threats. One more step and there would be open rebellion. No one cared to begin a contest of strength. But the underground organizations, now aware of their power, were to make methodical preparations for a series of strikes.

In April, the movement extended to the Basque region.

In San-Sebastian, in Bilbao, in Vitoria, as organized by the Basque Nationalist Party and by the clandestine leaders of *Solidaridad* (Basque Christian unions), the strike was upheld by the local clergy, by the Workers' Brotherhoods for Catholic Action (H.O.A.C.) and, in many cases, by the employers, who were in favor of Basque nationalism. On May 8, a general strike was called at Pamplona: thirty-five thousand persons, the entire working population, responded to the call. Processions moved through the streets. Fights broke out between demonstrators and police. After a dozen years of Franco's dictatorship, the red-bereted *Requetes*—the fighting élite of the anti-republican Insurgents—had become the most ardent of strikers.

Two weeks later, on May 22, ninety-five per cent of the population of Madrid supported the "white strike": the transport boycott. The Monarchists had promoted the movement by handing out tracts in which they demanded, among other measures, the dissolution of the Falangist unions. Obedient to the most anonymous of injunctions, students, workers, shopkeepers, civil servants, grand hotel *habitués*, Madrileños and passing provincials had all set about copying and circulating the tracts. In the space of a few days, the capital was swamped in clandestine leaflets passed from one person to the next.

The particular form of "white strike" had been chosen because of the need to avoid reprisals: Francoist legislation makes the strike a punishable misdemeanor, but no one can be made liable to punishment for not using the subway. This demonstration of will by abstention—a plebiscite by abstention—took the place of the positive demonstration, made impossible by police surveillance.[10]

Deaf to the clues furnished by the springtime strikes and to the general state of mind, the American government which had been negotiating unofficially with the regime for the past

---

10 One of the tracts passed out in Madrid declared: "The 'white strike' will constitute the exercise of the elementary right of all Spaniards to show in this way—since all other ways are forbidden or denatured—that the government governs badly."

year and a half, chose this moment to open the phase of official negotiations. In July, 1951, Admiral Sherman made a spectacular visit to Madrid.

To realize the full measure of importance of this intervention, we need only note the difference of tone employed by the Francoist leaders before and after Admiral Sherman's visit. During the six weeks which separate the "white strike" in Madrid from the arrival of the apostle of American aid, the regime went through a period of hesitation, of delaying tactics. Franco negotiated with the monarchists and the monarchists lent themselves to this game. By concluding a tactical alliance with the republicans, they hoped above all to intimidate the *Caudillo* and move him to abdicate. The monarchists' step backwards paralyzed the guiding "junta" of the Alliance of Democratic Forces,[11] the veritable clandestine government which, until this time, had led the strikes.

After Admiral Sherman's visit, the tone was different. The *Caudillo* proceeded to reshuffle his ministers and to purge his administration; everyone who showed weakness during the crisis was ousted. The new cabinet included not another authentic monarchist. In vain did the royalists, realizing they had been duped, register protest. It was too late. The American's visit had given rise to hopes, among the middle class and the industrialists, that a tide of dollars would soon reach Spanish shores. Not without anxiety, the possessor classes had seen in the bankruptcy of Franco's economy the beginning of a partial return to democracy. But no sooner had events shown the protection guaranteed by the dictatorship to the bourgeoisie to be compatible with economic aid from abroad than the floating mass of the classical right drifted back toward the established regime. And now that military conspiracy was no longer carried along on bourgeois fears, the plotting officers—torn between their eagerness to put favor-

---

[11] At this time the Alliance grouped all the republican forces acting clandestinely in Spain—but for the communists—and certain of the liberal monarchist elements.

able circumstances to good use and their fear of destroying the system of which they were the chief beneficiaries—fell back into the camp of obedience.

5. CONFLICTING TENDENCIES

In the decade following the danger signal of spring, 1951, aid from America and increased agricultural production—spurred by a partial return to free trade in grains—assured the urban proletariat of the bare essentials of life. Afraid of losing even this minimal well-being, labor as a whole abstained more than ever from involvement in political life. The alliance concluded between dictatorship and bourgeoisie in the days of illusion ensuing upon Sherman's visit was supported in the following years by meager, but concrete, American aid. But as memories of the civil war faded into a distant haze and social tensions relaxed, the ties of complicity and fright which had united the winning side gradually grew looser. The single party disintegrated. The dominant elements of the regime's first decade fell into swift decline, while new groups embodied the antagonistic interests fostered by the economic revival.

Spain is a kingdom from which the King is exiled. Generals and high officials, bankers, businessmen, great landowners—most of those in positions of power within the State—made great show of their royalist zeal but lifted not a finger to speed the restoration. Realizing that he had no means by which actively to oppose, for the moment, a regime whose inheritance was bound in the long run to fall to his dynasty, Don Juan detached himself from his allies on the left and drew nearer to Franco. Don Juan-Carlos, Prince of the Asturias, brought up in Spain according to the principles of the regime, was the pledge of this pact-on-credit. But the stalwart monarchists, those in favor of immediate restoration, were more than ever like a headquarters without an army.

Similarly, the Carlists were nothing but a divided and impotent little group. While some of them rallied to Don Juan, others remained loyal to the descendants of Don Carlos. But the peasants of Navarre grew daily more indifferent to both of the Carlists' essential themes: foralism and the dynastic question. These peasants, like those of Old Castile, are the present object of a struggle for influence in which the integralist clergy is pitted against Christian democracy.

Deserted by the new generation, the Falange was reduced to two small minority groups: the complacent and the bitter. Successful politicians, wily racketeers in Falangist jobs, bosses (*jerarcas*) of the vertical unions, shirkers—the prime objective of all was to prolong the life of the regime, source of their sycophants' stipends. But the younger men on the way up realized that it was to their advantage to steer toward other goals. Only the idealists among the new generation continued to be active in the Falange, and their numbers dropped steadily. Some, faithful to the word of José Antonio, blamed Franco and the conservatives for the failure of the "national revolution." Others dreamed of a radical reform in party doctrine and awaited a chance to slip away into the indifferent masses or to go over to the opposition.

To resist the pressure from the classical right, the unaffiliated Falangist leaders strove to win proletarian sympathies by affecting to champion an increase in salaries. The principal—and, since 1958, the only—stronghold of Falangism was the union organization; but that stronghold was undermined. The right to vote in union elections—a right partially granted to the workers in order to bring them over to the Falange—had enabled the (camouflaged) militants of the C.N.T. and of other leftist elements to get themselves elected as delegates to the works committees. The Falangist *jerarcas* at once encouraged and confined labor agitation. In this way, by its own decline, the party was led into such demagogic politics as brought down new conservative attacks upon it, while the party was denied the consolation of a firm hold on the masses.

Between 1951 and 1956, the up-and-coming element was Christian Democracy.[12] Under Jesuit auspices, the movement

12 The Christian-Democratic leader, Martín Artajo, had entered the Cabinet when given the Foreign Affairs portfolio in July, 1945. He remained at the same post after the reshuffling of 1951, when another Christian-Democratic leader, Ruis Giménez, was given charge of Education.

first made headway in the seminaries and among the younger clergymen, then gained adherents among all classes because of the distribution of various publications: important daily newspapers (*Ya*), magazines (*Razón y Fe*), parish bulletins. The H.O.A.C. (Workers' Brotherhoods for Catholic Action) drew a labor minority of the Christian Democrats. Peasant landowners in Old Castile and Navarre became the most dynamic element in these organizations. The membership of Catholic Action and of its youth groups increased steadily in the cities and still more in intermediary Spain. There was scarcely a single town in which the movement could not count upon a band of supporters: notaries, doctors, veterinarians, petits bourgeois, old maids devoted to parish works. But the principle of the single party was opposed to the gathering of all of these elements into a new political organization. The lack of overall leadership, the impossibility of convening assemblies, and of fixing a common mode and aim of conduct was to work in favor of diversity. In fact, the little coteries which influence Christian Democracy had greatly varied tendencies, some close to the regime and others to the opposition. Only later did the groups gathered about Martín Artajo and Ruis Giménez, both of whom were in the government between 1951 and 1957, practice a "constructive opposition" aimed not to destroy the system but to "liberalize" it. The H.O.A.C., for their part, laid the groundwork for strikes in accordance with the leftist groups, while the student networks of Christian Democracy worked clandestinely. The Christian Democratic left and sympathetic Cataloñan groups were allied, for the most part, with the opposition parties which had come over from the republican side. In the center, Gil Robles[13] and

13 The ex-leader of the C.E.D.A., who had fled Spain upon the outbreak of the civil war to escape the violence of his former extreme-right allies, chose to remain in exile during World War II and immediately after it. Deciding to return to Spain, he made a brilliant political comeback in 1956 as defense lawyer for the students prosecuted after the disturbances in Madrid. Only in 1960 was Christian Social Democracy definitely established. According to reliable sources, when Gil Robles went to Estoril to introduce his group's leaders to the Pretender, he declared that should the future monarchy be undemocratic, then Christian Social Democracy "would form His Majesty's Opposition."

his group of Christian Social Democrats, played the card of a
long-term monarchical restoration, along with an institutional
"liberalization." Riddled by the contradiction between its
ardently reformist minority and its politically amorphous and
socially conservative mass, Christian Democracy could take
only slow and unsteady steps. During the winter of 1953-54,
a third force[14] was born. And the public tended to confuse
this movement with a religious association which, thanks to
Papal approval, had just emerged from the shadow in which
it had been hiding for a quarter-century: *Opus Dei*. This
Third Order, founded at Salamanca in 1928 by Father Escriva, aimed to be to our century what the Jesuits had been
to the century of the Counter-Reform: a shock force which,
defending the faith by means of the intellectual weapons
forged by the times to use against the faith, would seek to
make its adherents familiar with the most modern techniques
and with the virtues of energy and self-discipline. Father
Escriva and his successors had therefore drilled a small team
of technocrats—economists, teachers, engineers—who were
admirably prepared to take over and control society.[15] The
Minister of Commerce, Alberto Ullastres, was the prototype
of these young leaders, combining medieval fanaticism with
twentieth-century technical training. *Opus Dei* did not form
a political party. But only slight differences could arise among
persons of the same social background—the governing classes
—and the same philosophic and moral education. Again, it
was natural that in government, in banking, wherever they
pursued their careers, members of this organization should
choose their colleagues among people whose thinking ran
along the same lines as their own. This was all that was

---

14 Fearing censorship by the Falange, Professor Calvo Serer, the theoretician
of *Opus Dei*, published the third force manifesto in a French revue, *Ecrits
de Paris*, 1954. The charges levelled by the third force's leading personalities
against the Falange's economic planning led the Falangist leaders to organize
the first national congress of their party since the civil war. But for the most
part, those who attended this massive reunion of "blue shirts" drifted away
from the movement in the years that followed.
15 Certain lay members of the *Opus* take the three vows: of obedience, poverty, and chastity. Other members are dispensed from the vow of chastity and
celibacy.

needed for the members of the Third Order to be accused of systematically giving preference to their co-religionists; this, in turn, was all that was needed for the ambitious, the climbers, to be attracted to the organization. The *Opus* through no wish of its founders was transformed into a mutual aid organ for the seizure of power, and gradually its members infiltrated into the responsible posts in the universities, in the administration, in finance and in the major industries. Soon the *Opus* had its education centers, its magazines (*Nuestro Tiempo, Arbor*), its national or local newspapers (especially the important evening paper, *Madrid*), and even its own bank, The Andorra Trust.

While the Third Order was the active wing of the third force, it was far from representing the entire third force, which was rather a coalition of big interests, an assembly of leading figures who, anticipating with alarm the *Caudillo*'s physical disappearance, were anxious to preserve the social status quo. Bishops or bankers, great landowners or industrialists, members or not of the *Opus*, the personalities of the "third force" look forward to a monarchy, not "liberalized" but authoritarian, which at the proper moment will come into its inheritance from Franco.

Discreetly supported by the American Embassy, the "third force," beginning in 1956, has leaned upon those officers irked by the results of the *Caudillo*'s "Arab policy." For the military caste feared that Ifni and Río del Oro would be abandoned as the Rif had been, and that the evacuation of African territories would be followed by the dismissal of a portion of the officers and a cut in pay.

With the exception of the Christian Democratic left, all of these groups had in common a desire to control or to amend the regime—but not to bring it down; to secure the inheritance from Franco—but not to cut short his reign.

The genuine opposition remained powerless and schismatic. The Alliance of Democratic Forces had disintegrated after their attempt had misfired in the spring of 1951. Isolated henceforth, the resistance networks established under the banner of the classical parties had nonetheless managed, in most cases, to hold on to their weak 1951 positions and even to advance a bit, while the disintegration of the Falange gave birth to a swarm of little networks.

In Euzkadi, the Basque Nationalist Party and the P.S.O.E. (Socialist Party) continued to hold sway over a goodly part of the population. Indeed, the Basque country is the sole region of Spain where the consistent alliance of two parties —the P.S.O.E. and the Basque Nationalists—succeeded several times in effecting general strikes, such as those in 1951, or localized ones, as in the Bilbao shipyards in the winter of 1954-55 or in the spring of 1958. In Cataloña, the *de facto* cooperation gradually established between the C.N.T. and two up-and-coming elements (Christian Democracy and the Cataloñan socialist movement) led to the creation, in 1959, of a "junta" comprising practically all of the clandestine groups under the banner of Cataloñanism.

In the country as a whole, the socialists controlled a small labor minority, made up especially of men aged 40 or over, and had won over a number of students. The Communist Party was advancing too, in intellectual circles, but in far smaller proportions.

Between 1956 and 1959, several student networks were formed in the universities. Some of these, such as the A.S.U. (university socialist group), are linked, ideologically if not organically, to classical parties. Others, like the F.L.P. (People's Liberation Front) are not part of any particular ideological current. Two other clandestine organizations, appealing to older intellectuals, appeared at about the same time: Dionisio Ridruejo's[16] Social Party of Democratic Action, which recruited its members especially among "repentant Falangists"; and the Christian Democratic Left.

But even the most sizable of these networks included at

---

[16] One of the earliest Falangists, the poet Dionisio Ridruejo was among those responsible for the words of the Falangist hymn, *Cara al Sol*. An officer of the Insurgent army during the civil war, then general propaganda chief for the regime, active in the Blue Division, Ridruejo broke with the dictatorship in 1942. After five years' enforced residence in a village, he lived for four years in Italy, as correspondent. Beginning in 1951, he campaigned in official circles for a liberalization of the regime. In 1956, he began overt opposition.

most a few hundred people. And the total failure of the general strike called for June 18, 1959,[17] showed that their influence at the time over the working class was virtually nil.

The masses were indifferent and sceptical. If their confidence were to be restored, there would have to be a "junta" of representative figures from all shades of opinion who would announce a specific political program capable of satisfying the workers and simultaneously of reassuring the middle class. This organism, its "brains" readily apparent from the outside and its executive arms hidden, would have had to organize propaganda from the inside, obtain aid from abroad, and coordinate the activities of the various networks. While the minorities would have set in motion all the means available to underground action, an ever-growing mass of sympathizers would have subscribed to the slogans of passive resistance. And in the long run the oligarchies would have been made to understand that while the opposition was in no position to take over power through an out-and-out struggle, neither could it be broken by repression and that only through compromise could a return to normalcy be achieved.

But not one of these conditions was fulfilled. Exiled since 1939, the leading figures of the left had lost their prestige, while the young leaders formed in underground activity had as yet no authority, no experience, and virtually no political training. In 1961 the Union of Democratic Forces emerged as the result of a partial regrouping. The coalition comprised the P.S.O.E. (socialists), the U.G.T., the Basque Nationalist Party, and the Christian Democratic Left. But these parties did not suggest any tactic for combatting the dictatorship. Whereas certain tiny factions, influenced by "castrism," were in favor of direct action, and whereas the Communist Party

---

[17] There were various reasons for the failure. First of all, the scale on which repression was carried out. Furthermore, the pro-strike propaganda, launched at the worst time of the year—June being a period of relative well-being for the workers—and monopolized by the communists, was openly opposed by the socialists and, surreptitiously, by the Basque nationalists and the C.N.T. Decimated by repression, the Cataloñan groups, student networks, and communists obstinately went ahead until the last moment. But desertions, which made a failure foreseeable, paralyzed the workers who had been in favor of striking.

championed "national reconciliation," the Union of Democratic Forces based its present-day calculations upon the realities of the 1951 situation. They believed that if Franco did not disappear physically in very short order, the economic contradictions within the system were bound to lead to a *pronunciamiento* and to a restoration of the monarchy, which would inaugurate the process of return to democratic normalcy. This being the case, there was no point in organizing clandestine resistance. Until 1956, most of the repentant Falangists and rebellious students, for their part, believed that the regime could be modified by public criticism. Thereafter, they came over to a semi-underground opposition, and are still against any form of violence.

With the masses indifferent and resistance impotent, the contradictions of Christian Democracy and the weakening of the Falange worked in favor of the seizing of control of the conservative extreme right. This was a four-stage process, each stage corresponding to a new forward leap of inflation, a new worsening of social tensions.

The signal for action was given in 1956 by the Madrid students in revolt against the S.E.U.—the Falangist university union. A Falangist student was seriously wounded during a skirmish between the two parties, at which point the Falangists threatened to massacre those Christian Democratic and monarchist leaders accused of giving secret support to the rebellious students. General Muñoz Grandes, then Minister of War, let it be known that he would take it upon himself to restore order if the government did not take the necessary measures. Franco dismissed both the minister who was Falange secretary, Fernández Cuesta, and the Christian Democratic Minister of Education, Ruis Giménez. The Christian Democrats were removed from the top university posts and gradually replaced by conservatives and members of *Opus Dei*. During the winter of 1956-57, the center of student agitation shifted toward Barcelona. There was labor agitation and once again a boycott of the tramways, not only in Barcelona but also in Sevilla as well. While the Marshals, met under the chairmanship of Muñoz Grandes, made known to the *Caudillo* the conditions they demanded, the Minister of Commerce, Arburua, presented the Cabinet with the ultimatum drawn up by the financial interests. In February and March of 1957, control of the economy passed out of Falangist hands into the hands of the classical right and *Opus Dei*. The Army, now controlling the Interior and the Police, held not three but five ministerial portfolios, and immediately moved to clamp down on the left.

The following year, Franco gave in to new conservative pressure and, before the *"procuradores,"* standing mutely at attention in the *Cortés*, he proclaimed new "organic laws," limiting Falangist action to the unions.

Finally, in the autumn of 1958, when galloping inflation raged through Spain and there was fear that Europe would be closed to Spanish exports, with the formation of the European Common Market, the monarchist leader Satrústegui delivered a solemn warning to Franco during a banquet organized by the Spanish Union at the Hotel Menfis in Madrid. This union, including whole-hearted Christian Democrats, ardent monarchists, and ideological "Europeanists" was, above all, the expression of all the interests wronged by the Falangist system. Disagreeing on the policy to adopt, the small industrialists outraged by economic planning, large concerns anxious for foreign capital to enter Spain, exporters of food and mineral products who wished to see Spain join the European community—all of these elements united against the Falange.

Faced by this new attack, Franco hastened to reassure the classical right. The government began to mull over the austerity program which, when enacted some months later, swept away the last scraps of the Falangist system: economic planning, "autonomous jobs," fixed quotas. The process had come full circle: complacent old conservatism made its comeback, scaling the ruins of the "national revolution."

6. THE LAST STAND OF THE FALANGE

The privation suffered by the working class as a result of the austerity plan stimulated a new current of complaints between December, 1961, and June, 1962. This cycle of strikes emphasized contradictions within the system by forcing Christian Democracy and the Falangist unions to give clearer backing to labor's demands.

Stands taken earlier by the Falange and by the Church encouraged the malcontents. In the Basque country, monsignor Gurpide's pastorals in favor of social reform provided new fuel for the labor movement. In addition, the collective labor contracts granted to workers in certain categories aroused legitimate jealousy among the others. The demands set forth early in 1962 by the Falangist unions' congress were a further encouragement. In the next few weeks, the hitherto sporadic strikes took so serious a turn that the authorities were alarmed.

Early in April, the movement reached the Asturian mining basin. Strikes continued in the Basque country, and a halt was called in certain of Madrid's factories, in the mines of Huelva province (Andalusia), and among the agricultural day laborers in the area around Cádiz. The authorities opened negotiations in an attempt to stop the spread of these disturbances. Certain strikers were given raises—thus, the workers found that not only could a strike be carried out with impunity but that it even "paid." And the authorities, by agreeing to deal with the strikers, had implicitly recognized that, contrary to what the law stated, a strike was legitimate. By the end of April and the beginning of May, most workers in the Asturias and in the Basque country had joined the movement.

It was too late for a governmental show of discipline. The workers, realizing their strength, refused to go back to work. It was now clear that the State could do nothing to put down a mass movement. Suddenly, the fear which had paralyzed the Spanish proletariat for two decades had crumbled and fallen away.

But by early June, because their financial reserves were exhausted and because labor contracts satisfying their demands had been signed, workers in nearly all of the industrial and mining centers had gone back to their jobs. Further, summer-vacation time was nearing and, as ever at that time of year, food prices dropped—two more inducements to relaxation.

These last factors would not have had much influence in a really "politicized" working class. But even in the Basque country, the Asturias and Cataloña—the three most politicized areas of Spain—underground parties and unions took in only a minority of the workers. These were the only groups in a position to distribute clandestine tracts establishing a timetable for work stoppages and keeping workers up to date on strike developments. (The authorized press did not make the slightest allusion to the strikes until May 5.) But union orders were followed only insofar as they corresponded to purely professional grievances, while the underground groups looked upon strikes as instruments in the political struggle against the regime. Political militants were the only victims of police action, thus giving the workers the impression that they could strike with impunity only so long as they steered clear of politics.

The opposition was not yet sturdy enough to lead revolutionary strikes. The bourgeoisie feared social agitation which could be restrained only by wage increases—an invitation to inflation. The established regime was in danger of losing the confidence of the property-owning classes. The time had come for the rightist opposition to soothe the bourgeoisie by offering an alternative or successor to Franco; hence, the Munich talks in June, 1962. Here, Gil Robles and other Christian-Democrat figures, the poet Ridruejo and the Spanish monarchist progressives (led by Satrústegui) met with spokesmen of the moderate republicans. Together they voted a motion enumerating the democratic reforms Spain must carry out if she were to be admitted to the Common Market; this motion was communicated to the governments of "Little Europe."

On their return from Munich, Satrústegui and his friends

were deported to the Canaries; Gil Robles and Ridruejo went into exile and collaborated, to some extent, with the moderate republicans. The Pretender broke with Gil Robles and the anarchists who had taken part in the Munich talks, thus emphasizing to foreign observers what every Spaniard already knew: that the Christian Democrats had gone over to the opposition. When Franco reshuffled his Cabinet in July, 1962, he had to take into account the dwindling political foundations of his regime. Since its only support came from two mutually hostile oligarchies—*"Opusista"* technocrats and Falange syndicalists—the army was once again the pivot of the regime. Muñoz Grandes was given the new title of Vice-President. This was a sop to the people who had been shaken by Franco's hunting accident: should the *Caudillo* die suddenly, he would not leave a political void. The government's "Europeanist" feeling was solemnly reaffirmed. The only Falangist Cabinet member was José Solis.

The successful spring strikes forced Falangist union bureaucrats to demand an increase in the minimum interprofessional wage and to come out against the conservatives. Social *juntas* (labor committees) within the vertical unions insisted that steps be taken against "monopolies and privileged interests." When these *juntas* later accused him of weakness, Solis carried the battle onto the political field by declaring, "We must present a firm and united front against political pressure groups."

The Falangist press then launched a virulent anti-bank and anti-trust campaign. Miguel Primo de Rivera, brother of José Antonio, directly accused the "pressure groups rooted in the *Opus*" of having "veritably sequestered the State." Another Falangist news organ stated that the monarchy is laden with the "failure of any potential revolutionary possibility" because "by its very nature it is the system of privilege." Other Falangist papers, broaching the question of Franco's successor, countered the formula of conservative monarchy with that of a presidentialist republic supported by the unions.

Franco tried to revitalize the moribund "Movement" (single party), less in an effort to provide for his succession than in an attempt to charm the Falange into giving him immediate backing. For only the old Falange could offset the conservatives, who began to feel that Spanish neo-capitalism was already so firmly planted that it could dispose of a dictator whom both the Spanish masses and western governments found hateful. So, in the era of liquidation and transition precipitated by the crisis of spring, 1962, the dying regime tried to revive the vocabulary and strength of its prime. Once again the old dictator used seesaw politics to prolong his personal reign, playing Falangists against conservatives.

Chapter Ten

❧❧❧

THE STRAIT JACKET

THE DICTATORSHIP could not dream of even a partial return to democratic freedoms. Although after the Axis defeat the pressure from abroad brought to bear upon the *Caudillo* did force him to "democratize" institutions, the ostensibly restored freedoms remained merely fictitious. Had authentic freedom of expression been restored to the opposition, public opinion would have found that the conspiracy of the extreme right was at the root of the war and had preceded the red "atrocities" of which it had claimed to be the result. To justify their having ushered in a war to which a thousand and one problems of postwar existence were a living testimony, the leaders had to remonstrate with the people and demonstrate unceasingly that at the time of the *pronunciamiento* Spain was threatened by evils far worse even than the most wasteful war. Only by accusing others could they excuse themselves.

But, in fact, far from attempting to appease the rancors left behind by the war, Francoist authorities set about perpetuating the invisible line of demarcation of spilt blood.

Each year the anniversaries of Franco's victories were marked with impressive military display. The press reminded its readers again and again of the "atrocities" of the republican period.[1]

The explanation is evident: if the bourgeoisie ceased to fear the "red peril" it would find the chains of dictatorship too heavy; if the little clans of control on the right were not held together by fear and hate, their disunity would hasten the transfer of power into the hands of other cliques. Had those responsible for the war gone back to the status of ordinary citizens, they would have every reason to expect retaliation. Thus they were defending not only their sinecures but their very existence, by aiming to remain in power until the end of their lives.

Such lifelong power presupposed an indefinitely prolonged suppression of all freedoms; totalitarian dictatorship in perpetuity. Having come to power by means of war, the victors could remain in power only by maintaining the animosities, the laws, and the spirit of war in time of peace.

1. ORGANIC DEMOCRACY

Immediately after the civil war, much of the middle-class youth had joined the single party with enthusiastic sincerity. But those who were genuine Falangists at heart were only a minority, as opposed to the numbers who had registered as Falangists because of resignation or obligation or because they were ambitious. These latter were weary or pessimistic republicans or petits bourgeois who calculated that this regime was the most benign of evils, men and women students obligatorily enrolled in the youth squads of the Falange, and politicians on the make who reasoned, correctly, that only the party label would allow them to succeed.

[1] Speaking at Pontevedra Villagrosa, in 1951, Fernández Cuesta, then the Falange's secretary-minister, used these terms to describe the relations between conquerors and conquered: "Between their Spain and ours, there is an abyss which may be bridged only by repentance and by submissive acceptance of our doctrine. Otherwise, let them remain on the far side of that abyss; and should they try to bridge it by clandestine means, may they perish."

The single party (or Movement) had a representative in every village, every urban neighborhood—a network of *jerarcas*, hierarchs: neighborhood, city-block or building bosses recruited from the ambitious and the fanatic, the *enchufados* and the *estraperlistas*.[2] If four citizens whose political loyalties were suspect met at the home of one among them, in some room or backshop, the "building leader" immediately tipped off the "block leader" and it was not long before the police were informed.

At this time the "vertical" unions were a mere arm of the Party, whose leaders, appointed by the State, in turn chose the national leaders of the union organization. The workers, although compulsory members of the Falangist unions of their respective trades, had no voice in the selection of their union officials. Thus, union leadership came under the heading of public office; and the unions chose from among the personnel in each factory or concern some "responsible" person who watched over his co-workers.

In this way the overwhelming majority of the population was drafted into the totalitarian system of the regime. The efficacy of this method has been proven by the success of the public demonstrations organized by Franco's government. Union or Party members had to take part in them as a block; each section or union was assigned its place in advance: the workers of one factory were to congregate in a given street before a specific number, while the workers of another were to do the same in front of the house next door. The "responsible" persons took note of the persons who were missing and of those who cried "Franco, Franco" with less than regulation ardor. This is how those vast throngs materialized in Madrid, a half-million men and women choking back their laughter, stamping enthusiastically and waving banners to welcome the Emir Abd-Ul-Ilah or King Abdalah or the Blue Sultan or the Caliph of Tetouan.

This large-scale scheme of encirclement, admirably suited to keeping the masses under the thumb of a minority of oligarchical groups, was still almost intact immediately af-

2 *Enchufados*: prebendaries; *estraperlists*: racketeers.

ter the collapse of the Axis, when Franco's leaders felt that they must erect a "democratic façade" in an attempt to enter into the good graces of the Allied powers. But in the next decade and a half, the younger elements fell away, disillusioned, and the classic right struggled against the authentic Falangists; both circumstances were felt in the disintegration of the Party mechanism. The Party could count no more than a few slender centuries of blue-shirt activists.

But the pseudo-democratic institutions thrown up between 1945 and 1947 in reality offer not the slightest means of legal expression. After "democratization" just as before, the opposition has had to choose between submission to the established regime and underground activity.

With the "succession law" of June, 1947, the Falangist definition of the State was replaced by a new, Catholic and monarchist definition: henceforth Spain was a "kingdom." But the "*Caudillo* of the crusade," assisted by a Council of the Kingdom whose members he selects from among the high ecclesiastical, civil, and military dignitaries continues to function as Chief-of-State, head of the government and generalissimo. The people are endowed with an utterly useless right of referendum, since the questions are phrased so imperatively that the voter's only choice lies between approval and abstention.[3]

Several other liberalization measures had been promulgated prior to the Succession Law. On July 13, 1945, the *Fuero of the Spanish People* granted civil liberties. Earlier, the Government had created a parliament with purely consultative powers (the law of July 17, 1942). Of the 318 *procuradores* in this assembly, 50 were appointed by the *Caudillo*, 112 by the vertical unions, and 18 by various other groups such as the Spanish Academy and the Lawyers' Guild. Furthermore, the *Cortés* included thirty-four legal members,

[3] A referendum was held on July 6, 1947, in order that the people might ratify the Succession Law. A negative response would have implied a preference for the preceding state of affairs. Many voters believed that the law was a forecast of monarchical restoration linked with a "liberalization"; for the others, the referendum was a mere formality. Of the 17,178,812 registered voters, 15,219,563 voted—and some 14,145,163 of these voted *sí*.

by virtue of their office, fifty-two representatives of provincial bodies (general councils), and finally, fifty-two delegates from municipal councils who were, for that matter, the only *procuradores* really representative of the people to some extent.[4]

Although mayors are still named by Franco's government, town councilmen are actually elected by the people, since the enactment of the law of July 17, 1945. But this law inaugurated a singular electoral system. The councilmen are elected by thirds: the first third, by "heads of families"; the second, by the vertical unions from lists approved by Francoist authorities and therefore including only Franco supporters in good standing; and the remaining third is appointed by councilmen already elected in these ways. Of these steps, only the first may be said to be accomplished by some measure of universal suffrage. But the lists of candidates must be approved by the governors, who are confidence men for the regime. Silence is so obviously the sole means by which one can express opposition, that a high percentage of abstentions is universally looked upon as a defeat for the government. For this reason the press is full of threats aimed at those who abstain. When the number of abstainers appears likely nonetheless to be too great, the governors have recourse to the ultimate device provided by Franco's law: they veto all but one of the candidates, and that one, having no opponent, is proclaimed elected, without there being any need to hold elections.

Nor can the aims and desires of the public find their expression through political parties. All of the prewar organizations were dissolved by the law of "political responsibilities"[5] and in accordance with the principle by which the monopoly of national representation resides in the single party, no new political organization may be formed. The groups on the extreme right are as clandestine as are the communists.

Certain rightist elements managed to circumvent the pro-

[4] The president and working committee-heads of the *Cortés* are named by the *Caudillo*; and the Assembly president, in turn, appoints committee members. The new law of December 26, 1957, did nothing to change these fundamental measures.
[5] Law of February 9, 1939.

hibition of new political parties by taking on the disguise of religious or cultural associations. Even so, all associations must be authorized by the government which may refuse authorization, at will, to any association formed by political suspects or leftist activists. Still less may protests be uttered aloud, in an assembly hall, for all meetings are or are not authorized at the discretion of the Minister of the Interior. In support of their application for authorization, the organizers of a meeting must not only indicate its purpose but also must present a copy of each scheduled speech.[6]

The press too is mute. Current laws make the newspapers entirely subject to the general press bureau. Only those papers espousing the ideology of the regime are authorized to appear,[7] yet even some of these have been suspended for having voiced criticism of certain aspects of official policy. In addition, if the government is dissatisfied with a publisher's attitude, it may turn his paper's direction over to someone else. The Marquis de Luca de Tena, for example, owner of the A.B.C., largest daily in Spain, was obliged in 1951 to accept a new director named by the general press office. This office often sends bulletins to all newspapers, informing them of the theme and conclusion of that day's editorials. The only authorized sources of information are the State-controlled news agencies.

Yet it would seem that even this encroachment by the State is not sufficient guarantee, since the regime does not dare do away with censorship. For the past quarter-century Spain, alone among western nations, has been subject to total censorship in time of peace.

Nonetheless, censorship has undergone certain changes. Until the 1953-56 period, it was very rigid. From agency dispatches to radio talks, from editorials to classified advertisements, from the big daily newspapers to the smallest

---

[6] Pamphlet of July 20, 1939.
[7] All republican newspapers were outlawed, their presses and offices put at the disposition of party publications, their journalists banned from the editorial staff. Editors are former journalists who have made a career in rightist parties or were pupils of the "National School of Journalism" established by the regime.

prospectus, no text intended for publication escaped the censor's eye.

From approximately 1953 until the time of the ministerial reshuffling in the summer of 1962, censorship was gradually eased. The dailies were authorized to discuss municipal affairs; similarly, in international matters, censorship was relatively lenient. This explains how, on January 19, 1962, alongside the editorials which are invariably favorable to the United States, there appeared in A.B.C. a philippic of unusual violence, entitled "Hypocrites," directed against the United States. But actually, only the rightist groups were in a position to take advantage of this lenience.

During this second phase, the weekly papers and the magazines were not so closely watched over as were the daily papers. The higher the price of a publication, the narrower its distribution—consequently, the more tolerant the censorship. For this reason, the literary review, *Índice*, was authorized to publish in October, 1961, a special issue devoted to agrarian reform. The facts revealed therein about the peasants' living conditions would not have been tolerated in a daily newspaper sold at 1 *peseta* 50: but this issue sold for 30 *pesetas*.[8]

Direct criticism of the *Caudillo*, his ministers, his policies, was never authorized even in a publication with limited distribution nor even from leading figures of the extreme right, nor was anyone authorized to question the structure of the regime or its institutions. Within this State—theoretically a kingdom—one of the foremost monarchical leaders, the Duke Gabriel de Maura, had to resort to clandestine publication, between 1947 and 1954, of brochures setting forth his followers' ideas. In a country where the Falange is a public institution, the Falangist leader, Luis de Arrese,[9] could

---

[8] Thirty *pesetas* were the equivalent of about 50¢—half the daily pay of the least well-paid qualified workers.
[9] Arrese was secretary-minister of the Falange from 1941 to 1945 and from 1956 to 1957, then Minister of Housing in 1957. When the austerity program was put into action, he knew that eventually the last Falangists would have to leave the government. His letter placed the responsibility for unemployment upon the conservatives.

distribute only covertly the letter in which, in March, 1960, he exposed the causes of his resignation. The only way open to the opposition was illegitimate, and that way was fraught with danger: any publication—whether newspaper, pamphlet or brochure—distributed without the censor's authorization, fell under the jurisdiction of the laws punishing "illegal propaganda."

But the danger was not equally apportioned. Whereas a de Maura or a Luis de Arrese ran no greater risk than that of seizure of his writings by the police, labor militants accused of illegal propaganda were brought up before a court-martial.

In the first post-civil war years, works of fiction—plays or novels—were accorded a greater measure of freedom. But, on the other hand, they were subject to the censorship of the Archbishopric and the fussy morality of the Association of the Fathers of Families. For the censorship of books, as apart from the censorship of the press, was controlled by an ecclesiastical super-censor, prey to an overwhelming fear of words —curses and blasphemy—and also of terms which, however remotely, might have something to do with sexual intercourse. In any case the novelistic universe was ruled by an infallible imminent justice which intervened in the final chapter, punishing wrongdoing and rewarding virtue.[10]

There was no stipulated criterion for censorship. Decisions depended on each censor's pleasure, on his zeal or his indolence, his sympathies or distastes. Some censors were on the monthly payrolls of the larger publishing houses—a fact which accounted for the disparity in their decisions. Some harmless manuscript might be suppressed, whereas a more daring comedy was produced without hindrance; a certain novel, although published in extenso by a magazine, might be forbidden in book form. Since there was no way to foresee the censors' verdicts, an author, unwilling to labor in vain, might conform to a self-imposed censorship more exacting

[10] The conventional edifying epilogue was so deeply rooted that translators of foreign novels had been obliged on countless occasions to modify final chapters which did not fit in with this fashion.

than the official one. The chaos created in literary life by these arbitrary decisions was exposed, early in the winter of 1960-61, in a collective petition by which writers demanded a regimentation of censorship.

After the ministerial reshuffling of July, 1962, the new Press minister, Fraga Iribarne, stated that censorship would be eliminated and that a new press law would shortly be enacted. All spokesmen for Catholic opinion—integrationists or Christian Democrats, ecclesiastics or laymen—had in fact demanded countless times that censorship be replaced by legislation designed to punish misdemeanors of the press. But they had never been able to agree on the sort of law needed. That which Iribarne promised never materialized. Censorship has been held in abeyance since he took office and replaced by an experimental system of "consultations" between Press ministry officials and editors. The latter, submitting to a sort of self-censorship, abstain from making any criticism of the government; while reporting only briefly upon the sentences pronounced by the courts-martial in the early months of 1963, they omitted to present the arguments for the defense. In regard to every current topic—the renewal of the Madrid-Washington agreement, the "crimes" with which Julian Grimau was charged, the "anti-Spain" campaign which developed abroad after this communist leader was executed—the dailies obsequiously printed versions obviously composed in the government's "smoke-filled rooms."

Where municipal affairs are concerned, the press is given total freedom. Similarly, any philosophical remarks or ideological articles couched in general terms without direct allusion to Spanish affairs, are now allowed. But even here, censorship sometimes makes an impromptu reappearance. For example, in the fall of 1962, barely a month after Iribarne had announced "liberalization" of the press, five studies which were to appear in *Indice* were censored. In late April, 1963, the censor made a temporary departure from the policy which, since the summer of 1962, looked tolerantly upon the foreign press: the *New York Times* and other papers which had reported on the Grimau trial were momentarily banned.

Nor has the government set up in July, 1962, completely relinquished the policy followed until then with regard to material published in Cataloñan or Euskera; the authorities, not content to abolish the statutes of autonomy, further attempt to prohibit or at least to restrict the use of regional tongues. In the Basque country, after the civil war, the authorities caused tombstones inscribed in Euskera to be scraped clean, as well as the façades of old manor homes whereon the family name was written in that language. Storefronts were "Castilianized," and the traditional given names no longer were accepted in the civil registry. Every "Miren" and "Inaki," for instance, became María and Ignacio. Even today, matter printed in the Basque tongue is tolerated only exceptionally. Cataloñan is too widely spoken for its use to be strictly limited. But at the end of the war, all publications in that language were forbidden, and the national dance, the *sardana*, remained the only means by which Cataloñans could assert their personality—indeed, never had the *sardana* been danced so determinedly in city or village squares. Since 1953, the authorities have tolerated the publication of volumes of poetry and novels in Cataloñan. Two small Cataloñan magazines were given permission to appear in Barcelona, in 1954 and 1956.[11] But Cataloñan is still banished from State schools, the administration, and daily newspapers.

2. PERMANENT REPRESSION

Oppression evolved at the same rate as political institutions, but it has never ceased completely.

During the three years immediately after the civil war, from spring, 1939, to spring, 1942, Spain lived under a reign of terror. Statistics reveal that the penal population, which varied before the war from a minimum of 6,000 to a maximum of 12,500 in 1934, after the Asturian revolt, rose to

---

[11] The drastically reduced number of items published in Cataloñan contrasts with pre-civil war figures. Between 1920 and 1936, there were 1,579 newspapers and magazines in Cataloñan.

270,000 in 1940, and, at the end of 1941, was still as high as 233,000.

Directly following the civil war, there were fourteen official prisons in Madrid, in addition to the clandestine prisons of the Falange. Schools and other public buildings had been converted into houses of detention. Five courts-martial sat in permanent session in the capital, and the accused were brought before them in "batches" of twenty-five and thirty. The percentage of those among them accused, rightly or wrongly, of "blood crimes" was minute. For the most part, the prisoners were charged with having belonged to leftist parties or of having held some office, in the republican army or the administration, during the civil war. On charges of "military rebellion," the Insurgent army tried those civil servants loyal to the republic. After a long speech by the *Fiscal* (prosecutor) and a brief collective plea by the defense lawyer, the military judges then rendered their verdict without leaving the hearing room. In most cases, they simply seconded the prosecutor's conclusions.

A number of prisoners spent months and sometimes even years on death row and, two or three evenings a week, were submitted to the anguish of hearing their names on the rollcall of men to be executed the next morning. In Madrid, during the first two years of the regime, there were at least three hundred men in every "batch." The condemned spent their last night in the prison chapel, standing, kneeling, or seated on the stone floor. At dawn, their hands were tied behind their backs and the lower parts of their faces were bound with rubber muzzles so that during their last trip, their chants and huzzahs! for the republic would not incite people to riot. Then they were bustled into trucks and taken to the cemetery where, in the chill fog of early morning, soldiers with sleep-heavy eyes waited and held their machine guns ready. In single file the condemned walked across a sort of gangplank, its wood already battered by previous machine gun fire. When the gunners had again polished off their task, officers with heavy revolvers leaped here and there over the every-which-way bodies, to deal the *coup de grâce* to those still breathing.

Courts-martial also met in the provincial capitals of the once-republican zone, and collective executions were carried out in these cities once each week. Repression was less bloody in Barcelona than in Madrid, but it was in Barcelona that the most consequential crime of the post-civil war occurred: the execution of President Companys. The Gestapo, disdaining the most elementary rights, had turned him over to Spain; and, in October, 1940, after a farcical trial, the President of the Cataloñan *Generalidad* was shot in the moat of Monjuich citadel. The murder was received with sullen indignation in all of Cataloña, even among Catholics and conservatives who had opposed Companys' policies. When you do away with a man who holds the supreme representative office of a people, you cannot do so with impunity. Even if only the man himself is the target, which was not the case in this instance, his office is insulted nonetheless and the entire populace aroused.[12]

It is difficult to state exactly the total number of victims of Franco's reign of terror. Official statistics for those dead of violence in the three years 1939, 1940, and 1941, give an overall total of 107,000; while in the three years immediately preceding the civil war, the total number of persons who died violent deaths was 22,500. The publication of these figures is tantamount to an implicit recognition of some 84,000 capital executions. Even so, this is certainly an underestimate of the actual case, and there is reason to believe that the official statistics listed in fact a certain number of executed victims under various headings of death from illness. From accounts given by survivors of the Madrid prisons, it is apparent that in 1939 and 1940, there were between five hundred to six hundred executions every week; thus, for those two years and for that city only, there were some sixty thousand victims. Furthermore, the overall number of deaths in the three

---

[12] Tracts secretly distributed, several times, by Estat-Catala on the anniversary of Companys' death, show a portrait of the president-martyr with the caption: "Shot by the secular enemy (Spain)."

years 1939, 1940, 1941, is greater by 220,000 than the corresponding figure for the three immediately prewar years.[13] In 1941, two years after the end of hostilities, figures show 484,000 dead, hence 100,000 more than the prewar average, and exactly as many as in 1938, that terrible war year (the year of Teruel and the battle of the Ebro).

Did all of these 220,000 surplus victims die before a firing squad? Certainly not. But there are no statistics which distinguish among the executed, soldiers whose wounds proved fatal, the victims of the famine which laid Spain low at this time, and the political prisoners dead of privation in government concentration camps. The prisoners were fed only a sort of sickly soup with vegetable cores and peelings afloat in it. Therefore, most prisoners were kept alive by their families. In the larger cities, a long line of women laden with provisions could be seen taking up its station each day before the prison. In penitentiaries far from any city, the inmates wasted away. Sanitary conditions were similarly deplorable. At the Dueso, a penitentiary in Santander province, at the very tip of a peninsula which becomes partly submerged when the sea is at high tide, the cells were intended to hold perhaps a hundred men: they held forty-five hundred, ten or twelve to a cell. When it rained—and it rains three hundred days in the year on the Atlantic coast of Spain—the inmates went sometimes ten or twelve days at a time without moving from their cells. Typhoid and tuberculosis were rampant in this fetid atmosphere; the doctors recorded four or five deaths every day.

Although they could scarcely stand up, most of the prisoners labored, either within the camps or outside, in factories or farms. Each day of work was counted as two days of imprisonment by the law regarding "the serving of sentences by working," a law adopted on the advice of the general prison chaplain, Father Pérez del Pulgar, whose intentions had surely been highly moral. But in actual practice the system

13 Immediately before the war, the number of dead rose annually to an average of 386,000. Now, immediate postwar figures show 470,000 deaths in 1939; 424,000 in 1940; and 484,000 in 1941 (according to the official *Anuario Estadístico de España*, Edición Manual, 1955).

proved an excellent bargain for the prison authorities, who pre-empted the greater part of the profit from the prisoners' labor.[14] By associating themselves with oppression, by cloaking injustice with their unbearable moralizing tone, the clergy became thoroughly discredited in the prisoners' eyes.

In 1942, the reign of terror was succeeded by an era of mitigated repression. A number of persons condemned for war crimes were accorded a reprieve. But each Axis defeat stimulated the birth of a resistance movement, which drove the regime to promulgate a new law, that of March 2, 1943, which grouped all political misdemeanors under the heading of "military rebellion." While the time of mass executions had come to an end, still some six or seven thousand persons were shot every year.[15]

Beginning in 1945, Spain entered a phase of semi-normalcy. As a token gesture to the victorious democracies, the regime granted *indultos* (pardons) to the overwhelming majority of political prisoners. As resistance gradually calmed down, condemnations and executions also tapered off.

But there were still some unreleased political prisoners, and that clause in the *Fuero of the Spanish People* which stipulated that anyone arrested either should be freed or legally charged within seventy-two hours after his arrest was violated constantly. Certain suspects, held in custody indefinitely and never brought before a judge, were subjected to torture.

Moreover, although the special law of 1943, which made it permissible to bring persons charged with political misdemeanor before a court-martial, had been tacitly repealed by the *Fuero of the Spanish People*, explicitly repealed by the new penal Code of 1944, by the new Code of military justice (Article 1,072), and by the preamble of the Order in Council of April 18, 1947, nonetheless there were courts-

---

[14] Each prisoner's work day was counted 15 *pesetas* to his employer. The prisoner received half a *peseta*; his wife had the right to two *pesetas*, plus one for each minor child, up to three children: the administration took in, therefore, at least nine and a half *pesetas*.

[15] Francoist statistics show a total of 77,000 victims of violent deaths in the years between 1942 and 1947—or 32,000 more than six times the prewar annual average of 7,500.

martial every year which issued a certain number of condemnations for acts of a political nature.

But at this time, there were few such suspects arbitrarily held in custody and few such accused brought up before a court-martial. For the most part, they were unknowns, and did not know influential people in high places, hence the co-existence of legal semi-normalcy and illegal practices.

In 1956, resistance came back to life and provoked sterner repressive measures. The opposition drew its greater numbers primarily from among university students, the bourgeoisie, intellectual circles. It became impossible to keep up the official fiction of semi-normal legislation when a considerable number of people who, this time, did have influential supporters in Spain and abroad were subject to illegal repression.

These new resistance members had been attacked primarily according to legal procedures. In 1956, for instance, the students accused in connection with university disturbances in Madrid were tried in civil courts. But gradually the government was led to produce new oppressive legislation. The decree issued on November 26, 1957, placed political misdemeanors within the jurisdiction of "a special military judge of subversive activities." And, contrary to juridical practice, the decree which created the post also named the person who was to hold it: Colonel Eymar, who was empowered to classify the misdemeanor. Two persons who had committed the same action—diffusion of illegal propaganda, for example—could be made to appear before two different juridical systems: the first might be tried by a civil court; while the second, more dangerous to the government, would be court-martialed, since Colonel Eymar had qualified the second man's act of illicit propaganda as "military rebellion." In the latter case, the Code of military justice was applied and the scale of sentences was far more severe.

On July 30, 1959, a new so-called "public order" law empowered the government to suspend the *Fuero of the Spanish People* at will.[16] Finally, a decree issued on Septem-

16 The *Fuero* had already been suspended, following the student demonstra-

ber 26, 1960, revalidated the special law of 1943, extending "military rebellion" to cover strikes "whose aims are political," and non-authorized meetings, lectures, or demonstrations which "create serious disturbances in the internal public order."

Oppressive judgments did not spare important names in the government. In 1958, the military tribunal of Madrid handed down a judgment by default of the son of the renowned novelist Rafael Sánchez Mazas—the earliest of José Antonio's disciples—and the nephew of General Kindelan, former commander-in-chief of Franco's air force during the civil war. The accusation stated that these young leaders of the socialist students' A.S.U. had been in contact with "exiled leaders" abroad and that "leftist" books had been found at their domiciles (July 17, 1958). In February, 1959, Dionisio Ridruejo was charged with having published, in the Cuban magazine *Bohemia,* so-called derogatory material about the Chief-of-State. Sentenced to twenty months' imprisonment, the author of the Falangist hymn, *Cara al Sol* was able to benefit from an *indulto* granted upon the election of Pope John XXIII.

In the past few years, there have been several court-martial condemnations for striking or for inciting to strike. In November and December of 1958, for instance, some sixty thousand workers who had played important parts in the strikes of the preceding spring in the Asturias and in Bilbao were court-martialed and given prison sentences ranging from six months to twenty years. Several of these persons were tortured; it was proven that one of them had been hanged for hours by one arm.

In the spring of 1959, the campaign for a general strike —planned for June 18—fell through completely, and repressive measures were strengthened. The police arrested 700 persons, and tortured many of them.[17]

The propagandists for this strike which did not take

---

tions in Madrid in February, 1956, and again in February and March of 1958, during the labor walk-outs in the Asturias and Cataloña.

[17] In Barcelona, a student named Helios Babiano was tortured, at police headquarters, before his mother's eyes. In an act drawn up by a notary, his parents

place were hauled up before a court-martial in "batches." In 1958, attention had focussed on A.S.U. leaders; now it was the communists' turn. One Abelardo Jiménez Lara, a student, was sentenced to twenty-three years' imprisonment for activities in favor of an imaginary strike.

One of the most widely discussed trials since the civil war, that of Julio Cerón Ayuso, opened on December 27, 1959. Cerón was the nephew of a high official in Franco's police and had served in diplomatic ranks himself. While Cerón was in Geneva when the pro-strike campaign began, confessions extracted by torture from F.L.P. (People's Liberation Front) activists brought to light the young diplomat's role as leader of this network. Called back to Madrid on the pretext of some routine matter, he was arrested at Barajas airport. Tried the first time before a court-martial, on November 9, he was sentenced to three years in prison. But when the Marshal of Madrid refused to ratify this overly-lenient sentence, Cerón and sixteen members of the network were made to appear again, on December 27, before the military tribunal. This time Cerón was given an eight-year sentence; the others, from one to four years.

In June, 1962, when the court-martial of Oviedo sentenced seven miners, it was only the beginning of the series of trials to which the organizers of the springtime strikes were submitted until April, 1963. By then, courts-martial had sat seventy-seven times since the first of January, 1958, an average of once every twenty-five days. Yet the civil war had ended two decades before and the country was absolutely calm. During this period, civil and military tribunals had handed down 711 sentences for political crimes, including 4 death sentences and 17 decisions ranging from 10 to 30 years' imprisonment.[18] On September 24, 1962, a court-martial in

---

stated that they had been held illegally and that their son had been tortured. (The act was drawn up by the notary, Don Luis Félez Costea, on May 29, 1959, in conformance with the regulations and in the presence of two witnesses and a lawyer, Maître Agustín de Semir.) The policemen involved were prosecuted for sequestration and violence; the case was dismissed.
[18] Among the most typical cases, we may note the following: a) the trial of

Madrid sentenced the communist leader Ramón Ormazabal to a twenty-year term.

Foreign public opinion had been indifferent to this profoundly abnormal state of affairs; it was awakened abruptly by the trial and execution of Julian Grimau. When he appeared before the military tribunal of Madrid, on April 18, 1963, he bore the marks of the ill treatment he had undergone and of his mysterious "accident" the preceding November.[19] The accused readily declared that he was a member of the central committee of the Communist Party, acknowledged that he had slipped secretly into Spain after several years' exile, and that he had made very active efforts to organize pacific strikes. But Francoist legislation provided for nothing more than prison sentences as punishment for this sort of "crime." In order to pronounce a death penalty on Grimau, he had to be accused of crimes dating back to the civil war— crimes he vigorously denied. The Prosecutor was obliged to formulate a new juridical conception: that of "continuous military rebellion." In conformity with the *sumarisma* procedure in use in courts-martial, not a single witness for the defense was heard. When the accused man tried to speak, the presiding judge cut him short.[20] Witnesses for the prosecution, whose testimony had been previously taken down in

---

the Falangist student, Francisco Urdiales, sentenced in December, 1960, to 12 years in jail for having shouted during a Falangist ceremony: "Franco, you are a traitor!"; b) eleven Cataloñan workers were sentenced to terms ranging from six months to two years on charges of "military rebellion by assimilation," *i.e.*, for having distributed tracts calling for an amnesty; c) Father Bailo, military chaplain, was sentenced in May, 1962, to an eight-year term, for having publicly proclaimed his solidarity with the Basque and Asturian strikers; d) an American citizen, William Bass, was sentenced by a civilian court to one year in prison, in July, 1962, for having ripped up a photograph of Franco; e) the *Premio Nadal* novelist Dolores Medio and seven other women intellectuals were sentenced in July, 1962, to twenty days in jail for having participated in a demonstration of sympathy for the strikers.

[19] Arrested in Madrid on November 8, 1962, Julian Grimau García fell, several hours later, from a window of police headquarters. It is difficult to know whether Grimau had made a suicide attempt to escape torture or whether the police had thrown him from a low window, not to kill him but rather to be able to attribute to this "accidental" fall the fractures from the blows they dealt him.

[20] The hearings theoretically were open to the public—but the police noted

writing, neither appeared in the court nor confronted the accused man. In spite of the courageous plea by the State lawyer assigned to Grimau's defense—one Captain Rebollo who, to everyone's surprise, acted as a genuine lawyer—Julian Grimau was condemned to death after a hearing which had lasted just over three hours. Thirty-six hours later he was executed in the Carabanchel prison yard; his firm serenity made a strong impression on all present at the dawn shooting.

Everyone had hoped for a last-minute commutation of his sentence; had expected, in fact, that the *Caudillo* would take into consideration the efforts made on Grimau's behalf by a number of persons in Spain and abroad. Furthermore, it appeared unlikely that the government would offer such an affront to foreign public opinion just when Spain was negotiating for her entry into the Common Market and for financial aid from France and other western nations. Several Cabinet members pointed out, the day after the sentence was pronounced, that Grimau's execution would have serious repercussions on these negotiations. The Minister of the Interior, however, was in favor of severity, and the *Caudillo* concurred for reasons of internal politics. The Christian Democrats were already on the opposition side; now the Conservatives too violently opposed the Falangists. To gather the fragmented right about him, Franco tried to revive the great fear which had gripped the bourgeoisie directly after the civil war by evoking, once again, memories of the war and of "red atrocities," and by declaring that the communists continued to attack the present regime. They must therefore be answered with firmness. If the "strong man" of the regime were to back down, if institutions were "liberalized," Spain would experience all over again the horrors of civil war, communist dictatorship, and working class revolution.

But Franco's calculations misfired. While most Spaniards remained indifferent to Grimau's fate, they were irri-

---

the identity of those who attended. Few people dared take this risk. The room was very small, and had been almost entirely filled, some time before the trial began, by plainclothesmen. Most would-be spectators could not enter.

tated by this inopportune reminder of the war. Catholic circles appeared more eager than ever to break with a discredited regime. The indignant reactions in other countries to Grimau's execution undoubtedly hastened the May 3 enactment of a law by which the courts-martial were stripped of most of their powers. For several months the *Caudillo* had been postponing the adoption of this measure which, although it did soften repressive policy, still did not constitute a return to normalcy. For the tribunal remained the arbiter in questions of terrorism, while a civil court was created to deal with political crimes: the old repression is merely clothed differently.

A certain number of opponents of the regime are still in prison. Official statistics group them with common law delinquents, so that their number is difficult to determine. Between 1959 and 1961 it was possible to identify roughly a thousand prisoners,[21] but there were certainly others, some of whom have since been released. On the other hand, new arrests have taken place. Reliable estimates fix the number of political prisoners between 1,500 and 2,000.

Many of these prisoners were sentenced for their resistance activities during the Second World War, and some of them had already been imprisoned for the first time following the civil war. The history of the anarchist poet, Cristobal Vega Álvarez, is a case in point. Jailed between 1939 and 1943, he was then released. Secretly, he passed over into France, where he fought in the *maquis* and, as member of one of the small groups of other Spanish *maquisards*, attempted to invade Spain in 1944. Fallen into the hands of the police, he was given a thirty-year sentence—which was afterwards prolonged by twenty years, because he had caused the manuscript of a work entitled *Penicillina* to be circulated within the jail. He has now spent nearly twenty-five years in prison.

---

[21] A petition signed by 357 political prisoners of Burgos penitentiary was presented, in June, 1959, to the penitentiary's director. In the spring of 1960, 120 political prisoners in Carabanchel went on a hunger strike. In El Dueso, 33 prisoners managed to get a message through to the conference in Paris in March, 1961, on amnesty in Spain. Certain prisoners in Saragossa, Valladolid, Ocaña, Puerta Santa María, and Alcalá de Henares (for women) have been identified.

When an activist's jail sentence is prolonged, it is not always because he represents a threat to the government. In 1960, among the political prisoners, were found one Félix Carrasquer, blind, and a paralyzed woman, Guadalupe Giménez. Both had been vegetating in prison for eighteen years.

In spite of calls for clemency, reiterated especially since 1959, the government has refused consistently to declare an amnesty, even of those persons sentenced for wartime actions.[22] In the past eight years there have even been ten further verdicts delivered in cases of acts dating back to the civil war. Therefore Grimau's case, in this respect, is not unique. And even the reassurances lavished upon the 1939 political emigrants, to induce them to return to Spain, have not always been respected. Lt. Col. Ricardo Beneyto Sopena, who reentered Spain with a regular visa in 1956, was immediately arrested at Granada, sentenced to death for his activities during the civil war, and executed.

Similarly, Franco's government has refused to grant an amnesty for acts of opposition committed after the war. In any case, a regime which subjects all meetings and associations, the press and all normal forms of expression, to Draconian limitations, and which is forced of necessity to hand out severe penalties to those judged guilty, could empty its prisons only in order to fill them with new inmates. While the government has been able to pardon certain categories of persons sentenced for acts committed long ago, it is difficult to see how the government could grant an overall amnesty to all opponents, including those sentenced recently, and yet maintain a repressive legislation in regard to all crimes of thought and expression. Permanent oppression is the inevitable corollary of totalitarian institutions.[23]

---

22 The *indulto* granted in October, 1961, to persons who had been in prison for twenty years and more had so many strings attached, in the form of qualifying conditions, that few prisoners were able to avail themselves of it.

23 In this chapter we have made no mention of a condemnation for terroristic acts, punishable under law all over the world. But in this regard Spanish practice is singular: those convicted of "blood crimes" are executed by the *Garrote vil*—a medieval torture in which a chain is placed about the doomed man's neck and tightened by a tourniquet. One of the Sabater brothers, famous Cata-

3. THE EVOLUTION OF LABOR UNIONS

The official system of unions also went through a certain change. But the issue of syndical unity has never been brought up again for there is only one union—the official Falangist syndicate—in each sector of production. Even the church-oriented unions were dissolved by the government. The official union brings together employer and employees. Purely labor groups are forbidden and so, moreover, are the federations which took in workers simultaneously from several branches of production. Employers, technicians, skilled or unskilled labor—all must belong to the sole and official union of their trade or profession. The official union is the only employment agency,[24] and the right to work, supposedly guaranteed in the "Labor Charter," [25] actually depends upon membership in the official unions; hence, these unions comprise the entire working population.

The union directors are named "from top to bottom." The Chief-of-State names the National Union Delegate who, from the loftiest post in the syndical system, designates the delegates (or directors) of the various professional unions. Each of these national delegates in turn appoints all of the provincial and local officers for his particular branch of activity. At every step of the hierarchy, these *jerarcas* are chosen from among the party's professional politicians. The State controls the party and the party controls the syndical system.

The role of these union officials is theoretically limited to bracketing the employers' and wage earners' respective representatives. On each level of the professional union (local, provincial, national), meetings do include an "economic committee" (the bosses) and a "social committee" (workers). But during the regime's first years, the Falangist *jerarcas* were undisputed masters of the unions.

---

loñan terrorists, was executed in this way. (The other two died while fighting the police.)
[24] Employers may place job offers as classified advertisements, but only if the union has been unable to supply workers in the desired category.
[25] Declared on March 9, 1938.

After the end of World War II and, still more, from 1951 on, the syndical system, like all other Francoist institutions, was subjected to a fictitious "democratization."

Henceforth the workers elected their representatives to the works committees (*enlaces*). Those chosen select the labor representatives to the provincial assembly who name labor representatives to the national convention of the particular professional group. But even at the lowest echelon of this hierarchy, the workers' choice lay only among the candidates on lists drawn up by union officials, hence among workers whom the party believed it could count on. In all events, the powers of the elected representatives are purely consultative; it is the union officials who exercise all real power—they call meetings, determine the agenda, draw up the minutes of the debates. No meeting may be held, no resolution adopted, no petition addressed to the public authorities without the consent of the Falangist *jerarcas*.

Most of the universities of Labor were inaugurated by the unions between 1950 and 1958. Their pupils were given technical training and general instruction, and the principal aim of these institutions was to train potential union administrators. The pupils' parents were drawn to the syndical system by the benefits their sons had received. Thus a small, privileged minority was formed within the proletariat and closely linked to the Falange. But the overall working population was only all the more dissatisfied. They compared the luxury of the universities of Labor to the dilapidation of the primary schools, and charged the unions with bestowing unduly large sums upon their universities, while most of the workers continued to live in hovels and had no schools for their children.

At certain moments of acute crisis, when the worker's standard of living fell even below that to which he was accustomed, those workers elected from among the cooperative, the docile, the resigned, were driven to act as spokesmen for the masses they supposedly represented. Similarly, union officials, overwhelmed by the tide, were obliged to tolerate their demands. This was the case at the time of the strikes in the spring of 1951, and in February-March, 1958. Moreover, certain long-time Falangists still hoped to conquer the laboring masses by demagogic politics. Other union leaders, officials without any illusion of a reactionary State, believed that it was advisable to give the masses the illusion of a certain freedom of protestation, the better to deceive them. Finally, certain young people who had gone over to the Falange after the civil war naïvely believed that the government and the union system were proposing to carry out the social reforms announced in José Antonio's program. It was not long before these young enthusiasts were disillusioned and left the party. In fact, pro-labor initiatives were stifled all the more easily by obedient officials because the workers gave no backing to the small clan of well-intentioned Falangists. Hostile and mistrustful, they voted apathetically for the officially appointed *enlaces*, for the vote was to them a mere empty gesture, and they had no hope at this time of ever making themselves heard by means of the vertical unions.[26]

In 1958 the evolution took a new turning. The office of minister of the Movement was combined with that of national union delegate. The Movement (single party) was now nothing but a fiction, and the syndical system took on new importance.

This period was inaugurated with the signing of several collective labor contracts which were drawn up, in minute detail, for workers throughout a particular branch of production. The collective contract for textile workers, drawn up in Barcelona in June, 1950, involved some 150,000 workers in 2,000 factories. The ceremony accompanying the signing lasted three hours, since each of the delegates had to sign

[26] The experience of a young Falangist union director, Francisco Farreras, is significant. Summoned to direct a training school for workers intended to sit on the "social committees," he tried in vain to become accepted by the workers, who looked upon him as an *agent provocateur*. And the union officials, for their part, considered the school a dangerous nursery for "deviationists." At the end of the term, Farreras listed the hundred students most suited to assume leadership: not one of them was placed on the officials' list of candidates from which the workers were to choose. Farreras resigned and engaged in open opposition. Pursued by the police, he secretly crossed the French border on May 2, 1958, and requested political asylum.

700 times. By then, nearly 300,000 wage earners had benefited from these agreements.

The active and ambitious minister-delegate, José Solis Ruis, organized a vast propaganda operation in September, 1960, at the time of the *enlaces'* renewal in various factories. Carried out, undoubtedly, with Franco's blessing, "operation Solis" aimed to restore some prestige to the union system, to counterbalance conservative and monarchist influence. The election balance-sheet was, at first glance, impressive: 1,000,000 registered voters in 11,500 factories; 80 per cent turnout at the polls; 26,000 elected. Candidacies were theoretically uncensored. In certain factories, three-quarters of those elected took their seats for the first time. The Falangist leaders themselves had launched the slogan: "Vote for new men." Union officials had made canny use of the current depression, the spectre of joblessness which haunted the salaried worker, to pressure any who did not vote and, moreover, who did not vote as required. Many workers felt, anyway, that under the circumstances, it was best to support the Falange, champion of workers' rights, against the employers who demanded abolition of measures which protected salaried workers from arbitrary dismissal.

Some months later, during the union convention held between February 27 and March 6, 1961, speakers addressing the 600 delegates presented some lively criticisms of the stabilization plan. Indeed, the authorities found it more difficult every day to check popular dissatisfaction, nourished by continual delay in industrial rebirth and by unemployment.

Even so, these critics would not have been able to express themselves openly had not José Solis taken the calculated risk of organizing this convention under conditions which necessarily implied the expression of certain complaints. To strengthen his personal position and that of his cohorts, he deliberately played the card of broadening the union basis. And, insofar as he sought to gain support from the workers, he was forced to give them in exchange a —relative—degree of liberty.

In fact, the minister vetoed a reform plan presented early

in 1962 by certain union leaders. The plan provided for the separation of labor groups from management groups and for the free election of leaders on every level. Jiménez Torres, the general secretary of the syndical system, who championed this reform, was obliged to resign; and the Congress of Unions, met in Madrid, rejected the plan, in March, 1962. The workers understood that, in this case, their grievances could not be expressed through the official union nor could the union obtain real support from the laboring masses.

Union impotence was stressed by the incidents which occurred in Beasain (Guipúzcoa) in late 1961. The underpaid workers[27] of the Auxiliary Railroad Company, while not daring to strike, placed a permanent picket about the factory gate. On Thursday, November 30, forty-eight hours after this silent demonstration had begun, a sizable detachment of the *Guardia Civil* took up position around the factory and their commanding officer caused all rifles to be loaded, declaring that he would give the order to fire if the workers did not disperse within five minutes. The demonstrators complied with this injunction, but all the workers in the area left their factories or their shops to join them. The demonstration, now counting some 3,500 persons, moved silently through the streets until charged by a detachment of the armed police. The workers withdrew, carrying their wounded off the field. In the next three days, the demonstration turned into a boycott of all public places—bars, restaurants, movies. At the noon break, the workers ate from their mess kits in the street, under the surveillance of the *Guardia Civil.*

All this time, the union representatives had made futile efforts to achieve an increase in wages and to see police brutality brought to an end. And when they urged the workers to stay home, they were driven off with shouts and catcalls. Several months later, in the Asturias and in Vizcaya, union delegates met with the same hostility. José Solís tried to mediate the tough bargaining between management and labor,

[27] They were paid between 268 and 400 *pesetas* per week ($4.40 to $6.60).

but the workers steadfastly refused to go back to work until given wage raises.

After a law decreeing "co-management," one which in fact did not give the workers any real part in management, the syndicates succeeded in obtaining slightly higher Social Security benefits and a very low sum of insurance for the farming day laborers who suffered seasonal unemployment. It took Solis six months of battle with the conservatives to wring from them even as small a rise in the minimum wage as from 36 to 60 *pesetas* a day (from about $.60 to $1.00).

By June 15, 1963, some 2,465 collective contracts had been signed, and applied to 4,838,475 workers in 997,082 factories. Those contracts signed after the strikes ended accorded further concessions: one granted the Riosa miners accident benefits equal to their basic wages; in 1963, another contract guaranteed the glove-factory workers in Madrid a basic daily wage of 125 *pesetas*.

Solis set up new, semi-free union elections in 1963; some 10,000,000 workers were able to name the occupants of the lower posts in the syndical hierarchy. But the cases brought against the *enlaces* who had taken the 1962 strikers' part show that these elections were quite futile. Some of the persons elected were jailed; others were fired, then rehired, but with a loss of tenure. If they try to fulfill their duties in loyalty to the workers who have voted for them, the elected officials are simply cut out of the organization. At the summit of the union hierarchy, eighty virtually irremovable officials try to become independent of the State which named them by relying upon mandates which, however, neither back nor trust them.

In spite of the recent "democratization," the "vertical" union is as yet one more fiction among so many others in that strange universe—where anything legal is fictitious and all that is real is clandestine.

Chapter Eleven

§◊§

THE CAPTIVE CHURCH

ONE MIGHT HAVE THOUGHT that Franco's victory would entail an immediate return to the Concordat of 1851 (unilaterally nullified by the republic in 1931) or else the signing of a new convention. But it was not until 1953, or fourteen years later, that a Concordat was signed.

Nonetheless a cooperation between Church and State developed at the close of the civil war, and the clergy played an increasingly vital role, drawing its strength from an enfeebled Falange.

The cooperation of the two estates is emphasized with pomp: at every official ceremony, the glittering uniforms of government representatives mingle with the purple or violet robes of ecclesiastical dignitaries. But behind this façade, their collaboration is difficult, even tempestuous. While availing herself of the secular arm to impose her credo, her teaching, her morality, the Church, alarmed by the dechristianization of the masses, strives to undo her solidarity with a reactionary regime. Most of the Spanish clergy is hemmed in by this contradiction. But the Basque and Cataloñan priests, at least, have managed to escape it and to gain new popularity by identifying themselves with their peoples' struggle against centralism.

1. THE REIGN OF THE CHURCH

While a Concordat was lacking, in the first post-civil war years, the Church and the State concluded a number of pacts on particular matters. The June, 1941, covenant ruled on the nomination of bishops. Sanctioning the established practice, a covenant dating from 1946 stipulated that parish curates be paid by the State, which had undertaken not to legislate without previously having reached an accord with the Holy See on *mixed matters* which might in some way involve the Church. Since there was, however, no general juridical document on the subject, relations of Church and State were somewhat fluid, leading to variations and vicissitudes under cover of which evolved certain *de facto* situations given *a posteriori* ratification by the 1953 Concordat.

During and immediately after the civil war, Francoist propaganda emphasized the Catholic nature of the regime, the better to take advantage of the unfavorable light in which the republic appeared because of its religious persecutions. But in fact, the Church was relegated to the background. The Falange ruled, and the role of the Church was defined by the twenty-fifth of the Falange's twenty-six points: "Our movement will incorporate Catholic feeling, of glorious and preponderant tradition in Spain, into national reconstruction. The Church and the State will give of their respective faculties, without there being question of any intrusion or any activity which would threaten the dignity of the State and the national integrity."

The Church was tolerated as an historical relic and at the same time feared as a threat to the omnipotence of the State. But no sooner were hostilities ended and the period of reconstruction inaugurated, than the field of clerical action was shown to be far more extensive than had been foreseen in 1939. The Falange had erected the framework of a totalitarian

State and was unable to fill it, lacking as it was in doctrine and in qualified personnel.

In the case of education, for example, teachers suspected of liberalism had been dismissed and sometimes jailed or shot. The State undertook hastily to train young instructors, many of whom, beginning to teach after a scant year of study, proved far inferior to their task. In village after village, it was found necessary to call upon priests and nuns. On the secondary level, the lack of schools and the quantitative deficiency of State personnel allowed the religious schools to grow increasingly important. Similarly, in higher education, ecclesiastics were called upon. While the Falange reserved to itself the fields of political training, military and athletic education, the Church acquired a *de facto* monopoly over philosophy, literature, science. In the matter of mores and personal morals, the Church launched an increasingly successful campaign of austerity against the Falange, which would willingly have introduced into Spain the sexual amorality so fashionable in Nazi Germany.

With the defeat of the Third Reich, Franco's government leaned closer to the Church, for only the Catholics could defend the cause of the regime abroad. So the 1947 "succession law" replaced the totalitarian definition of the State with a new definition which was not only monarchist but Catholic. The counterpart of the ever-widening powers accorded to the Church was—and had been since the 1941 covenant—the intervention of the lay power in the nomination of bishops.[1] The Catholic State was paired off with the State Church.

This union of the temporal with the spiritual afforded the clergy restrictive powers—and the temptation to abuse them. And indeed, never has there been such utter confusion between genuine belief and compulsory ritual. It is evident in a thousand places. Every Sunday, in every prison yard, the inmates are lined up and made to attend Mass as they stand at attention. The convictions of the individual have little weight: the rules require his physical presence and atti-

[1] In this, the 1941 covenant restored the principles of the 1851 Concordat.

tude. The civil servant and the salaried worker feel obliged, if they are to get ahead, to go through the motions of the faith: they go to Church and have their children baptized. No attendance at Mass, no promotion. All marriages are celebrated in church, by virtue of the law which replaces the civil formality by a canonical wedding, as the normal form for celebrating a matrimonial union. Only those who can testify under oath and in court that they have not been baptized may be married by a civil official.

But while canonical marriage is, for non-believers, only a vain formality, it has serious consequences for them: their marriage is indissoluble. The regime, taking over Catholic doctrine part and parcel, has also annulled the divorce law. And the *Fuero of the Spanish People* explicitly states: "Marriage will be one and indissoluble" (Article 22).

The Rota tribunal [2] is besieged by petitions for nullification of marriage. Their number is all the more exaggerated by the existence of countless irregular situations, the result of the civil war and of emigration, and they are rarely remedied by the most subtle interpretations of canon law.

Undoubtedly, the Church in Spain hoped that the attitudes required by secular officialdom would become reality, profoundly felt and profoundly lived, for a new generation brought up in the precepts of Catholicism. Hence the monopoly on education was the goal toward which all the efforts of the clergy were directed.

The preamble to the 1945 law on secondary education stipulated that the Catholic schools should not be considered private schools but rather Church public schools. [3] Henceforth, therefore, the two systems of education are theoretically on equal footing. No sooner was this equality accepted than control by the State was unjustified. In 1952, the

[2] By a privilege unique to Spain, this tribunal considers cases which for people of any other country are judged in Rome. The Rota tribunal, abolished during the republic, was reinstated in Spain by the pontifical *Motu proprio* of April 7, 1947.
[3] This equality is implicitly established by the April, 1962, measure which places diplomas from Church universities on a par with those of State universities.

episcopacy haughtily refused to submit to the inspection of its schools planned by the young Christian-Democratic minister of education, Ruis Giménez. The Church, so jealous of her rights, is not content to withdraw into her own quarters: in more than one way, she invades the terrain of public education. Religious instruction, compulsory in the primary schools since 1937, was insinuated into secondary education in 1938, and into the university in 1944. Ecclesiastic inspectors named by the bishopric watch over the moral education given in State centers. The Church has a supervisory right in regard to textbooks: her representatives may demand *that books and publications found contrary to Catholic dogma and morals be unauthorized or withdrawn from circulation.* In State schools and universities, the teaching of philosophy is reduced to a defense and illustration of Catholic concepts. Dissident schools of thought are summarized succinctly—only to be instantly refuted and belittled to nothingness. The guiding spirit of this teaching is the same which inspired Father Ripalda, author of the revised and enlarged catechism officially required in all schools, to proclaim such aphorisms as: *Liberalism is a grave sin against the Faith.*

The public educational system treats the Spanish intellectual masters as high explosives. On the occasion of its seventh centennial, the University of Salamanca wished to include among the commemorative ceremonies an homage to Miguel de Unamuno; immediately, the Minister of Education, Ruis Giménez, was summoned to the archbishop's palace in Toledo, and the ceremony was canceled. The Cardinal-Primate, Monsignor Pla y Deniel, has several times expressed his feeling about the work of Unamuno, particularly in his pastoral letter of 1942, when he left his diocese at Salamanca to become primate at Toledo. Monsignor Pla y Deniel reminded the faithful that at the time of the civil war, "in the midst of a crusade, and precisely because the very harmful labors of many Spanish intellectuals had necessitated the having recourse to the supreme remedy, war," he had believed it his duty to publish a pastoral letter—"Misdemeanors of thought and false intellectual idols"—in which he had

sounded the cry of alarm against the "very harmful and un-
deserved idolatry which certain authors inspire." Another
prelate, Monsignor Pildrain, bishop of the Canaries, in a
pastoral letter entitled, "Don Miguel de Unamuno, major
heretic and master of heresy," noted among the works of
the master of Salamanca forty-five statements worthy of condemnation. Episcopal efforts and those of *Opus Dei* succeeded
at last, in 1957, in causing the principal works of Unamuno
to appear on the Index.

The Church stove to keep a generation shut up in cotton
wool, a generation which, all through childhood and adolescence, droned the aphorisms of Father Ripalda and was acquainted with *Del Sentimiento Trágico de la Vida* only in
the form of numbered and refuted statements. The Church
sought to insulate this generation from the temptations of the
mind, from curiosity, from research. By means of its "Committees to Purify the Public Libraries" and its censorship
committees (including delegates from the bishoprics and
representatives of the "Catholic Association of Fathers of
Families"), the clergy rules over the press, rewrites history at
will and imposes its criteria upon science.

The Church has learned nothing and forgotten nothing.
For her nothing has changed since the immediate postwar
era, when children scarcely six or nine years old and still
frightened by the thunder of bombs and revolution which had
rumbled through their childhood, joined hands in a circle in
the courtyards of religious schools and sang: "*Odio al fatal
—y destructor martillo—Gloria al Caudillo—y a la España
imperial.*" [4] And when they reached manhood, they remembered with horror the stifling atmosphere of the religious
boarding schools, the unhealthful exaltations and complexes
to which they were prey. Which is why anti-clericalism is far
more violent among sons of the bourgeoisie—product of
Church schools—than among working-class youth.

Outraged at being compelled to take courses in religious
instruction until they reach the age of 25, the students show

[4] Hate to the fatal—and destructive hammer—Glory to the *Caudillo*—and to
Imperial Spain.

off their impiety and blasphemy. Their opposition to the Church is made even fiercer by ecclesiastical efforts to shut them off from the pleasures of youth. Church censorship controls theater and amusements, dictating the length of a dancer's skirts, the duration of a filmed kiss, the dimensions of a bathing suit. The civil authorities may decree, for instance, that bars and dance halls can close a half-hour later: *Ecclesia*, the official organ of the Church of Spain, intones, "Instead of encouraging licentious amusements, incontinence and libertinage, the government would do better to look after more important matters which await solution" (February, 1952). Concerning prostitution, the development of which is the inevitable consequence of the rigors imposed by the Church and mass poverty, the decisions of the high clergy vary according to the era and the diocese. At one time, the authorities, under pressure from the Church, order the brothels to be closed—the sole result is that the sidewalks are invaded by prostitutes. In other cases, the clerical policy consists in limiting immorality to the "vice neighborhood." Why, in a city like Barcelona, for instance, should a street-corner undistinguished by any border sign mark the limit between extreme license and extreme austerity? Why is that which is prohibited in all countries legal in the *barrio chino?* And why is what is permitted in all countries illegal on the other side of the street?

Paying little attention to these contradictions, prelates and priests issue a flood of pastoral letters and speak a multitude of sermons against short sleeves, and the loosening of morals. The Cardinal-Primate, Monsignor Pla y Deniel, chose the particularly torrid month of July, 1959, in which to cast solemn anathema upon women who went about "without sleeves and with very low necklines." "Public bathing on beaches, in pools or on river banks," he added, "constitutes a prime danger to morality . . . Mixed bathing must be avoided, since it almost always entails chances for sin and scandal. . . ." The virtue of engaged couples was the object of particular concern on the part of the supreme official of the Church in Spain. "They should," he wrote at this same

time, "avoid solitude and darkness . . . It is inacceptable
that they walk arm-in-arm; indeed, it is scandalous and in-
decent to walk about in any sort of embrace whatever." The
persuasive powers of these recommendations inspired so little
confidence in the Cardinal himself that he added, "The engagement should not be very long. . . ."

2. THE UNITY OF THE FAITH

The zeal with which the clergy strives to preserve the purity
of Catholic morality pales into insignificance when compared
with the efforts put forth to stymie the proselytising spokesmen of doctrines opposed to those of the Church, and the
apostles, or ministers, of rival faiths.

A "tribunal for the suppression of Freemasonry" [5] functioned actively during the early years of the regime. In certain instances—exceptional, it is true—Freemasons were
compelled to forswear "their errors" in a medieval ritual: in
church, on their knees and with their faces covered with
cowls.

As for observance of a Protestant religion, in private or
in public, it was simply forbidden until 1945. At this time,
certain measures meant to placate Protestant nations were
adopted in regard to Spain's Protestant minority, which numbers 25,000 persons at most. In July, 1945, the *Fuero of the
Spanish People*, which conferred upon Catholicism the rank
of State religion and forbade "external manifestations" of
other religions, nonetheless promised that "no one would
be persecuted because of his religious beliefs nor in the private observance of his religion." (Article 6.)

But in fact, Protestant chapels were controlled by governors who may order them closed at will. To limit the
effects of this arbitrary authority, most Protestant churches
were declared to be English or American property. The
good or ill fortune of the Spanish Protestant minority was
linked therefore to relations between Spain and the Protes-

[5] This tribunal was also charged with the suppression of communist activities.
It was abolished in May, 1963.

tant powers, whence the anxiety aroused in certain Spanish Catholic milieus by the Hispano-American reconciliation. In February, 1952, Cardinal Segura[6] declared, in a pastoral letter, that it would be better to renounce American economic aid if to accept it meant to submit to tolerance measures liable to favor the propagation of concepts opposed to the "true religion."

In this connection, Cardinal Segura saw fit to reiterate that religious freedom is not a right and that "a conscience gone astray deserves no respect when it comes into conflict with what is just." Thus, the civil authority cannot do otherwise than to defend and support "the true religion, which is the Catholic."

This appeal to the secular arm was not designed to satisfy the government, which was making laborious efforts to wed the moral advantages of its very Catholic etiquette with the tangible profits to be derived from American aid. Since Monsignor Segura persisted in throwing so delicate a machine out of gear, there was but one thing to do: his remonstrances must be edited by censorship. And the great Cardinal continued to write pastoral after pastoral and verbally to crush the little men of the regime whom in Biblical and vehement terms he accused of liberalism, weakness, amorality.

The holy personage found himself at war with the dictatorship, as formerly he had been at war with the republic. From Sevilla, that principality of exile, he continually bawled out the Minister of Education and turned the little gypsy balls of Triana into sodality meetings. Franco, while on an official visit to Sevilla in 1953, wanted to have Mass said in the chapel at his residence, without asking permission of the Archbishop: the Archbishop, outraged, decreed that as punishment for this attempt upon the prerogatives of the hierarchy, the *Caudillo* of the crusade "would be deprived of Mass." But since it would be unthinkable to offer the good pomp-loving people the meagre spectacle of a leading crusader stricken

6 At the time of proclamation of the republic, the Cardinal occupied the office of Cardinal-Primate of Toledo. After the differences which brought him into conflict with the new regime, the Vatican found itself obliged to "accept his resignation." He was then summoned to the archbishopric of Sevilla.

from Sunday Mass, search was hastily made outside the diocese for a novice monk who, both by residence and by position as member of the regular clergy, was not affected by the jurisdiction of the Cardinal-Archbishop.

The *Caudillo* was irritated to the very limits of his endurance by the monarchists' praising and applauding the Cardinal who, from that moment on, appeared as champion of the restoration. By 1955, the conflict had become intolerable and, for the second time, the Holy See abandoned the unbending defender of the primacy of the Church over the temporal power, beginning by naming a coadjutor. This decision provoked a new outburst from the Cardinal. The Nunciate brought new pressure to bear. Age and illness were still more effective in silencing Monsignor Segura, who died in Madrid in the spring of 1957.

This great hieratic figure, who had stupefied his contemporaries, had played no little part in distracting them from the genuine problem of Spanish Catholicism by polarizing their attention. The American leaders, in particular, were —and undoubtedly remain—convinced that it would be an easy matter to come to an agreement with the Church in Spain, if only she were freed from integralist control and put in the hands of the more suave type of prelate, such as Monsignor Angel Herrera. Here at last is a bishop after a progressive's heart. A good guy-prelate, he had only to give up the world to become bishop of Málaga; at the time of his presacerdotal mediocrity, he was very simply editor of a newspaper, just as some important figures in the United States sold newspapers on the corner, as tradition would have it, in their boyhood.[7] An enlightened bishop, who founds a social school for those young priests destined for tasks in the working-class milieu, and who talks as well as any man about democracy and wages . . .

But after the signature of the Concordat which proclaims that "the Catholic religion continues to be the only religion of the Spanish nation" and whose contractual form

[7] Before taking holy orders, Monsignor Herrera was, as we know, editor of the Catholic daily, *El Debate*. (See chapter VII.)

crystallizes the measures of the *Fuero of the Spanish People* prohibiting public observance of other religions, there was no choice but to acknowledge that the opinions broadcast by Monsignor Segura were not his alone but were rather the reflection of an attitude common to all the clergy. And indeed, in the spring of 1963, every prelate vigorously opposed the adoption of the planned Protestants' statute, as drawn up on the advice of the Minister of Foreign Affairs, to please the English and American public.

3. THE NEW ALLIANCE

Associated with the war and with Franco's victory, the Church therefore has blood ties and ties of fear with all that her principles condemn.

The collective letter from the episcopacy, in July, 1937, declared: *We should be the first to deplore the situation if the irresponsible autocracy of a Parliament were replaced by a more terrible dictatorship, without roots in the country.* On June 3, 1951, another collective letter reiterated the condemnation of *modern totalitarianism which bestows absorbing and unlimited powers upon the governmental authority.* And yet the Church upholds the totalitarian State. And insofar as she is linked to the regime, she is blemished by the disrepute attached to a social policy which she condemns.

The episcopacy is well aware of the danger. A report drawn up in 1954 by ecclesiastical appraisers charged with making inquiries in working-class areas noted that "the workers consider both Church and priests as being more in favor of capital than of the humble."

Two years before, the Archbishop of Valencia, Monsignor Olaechea, had given voice to the same conclusions in less diplomatic terms: "The worker looks upon the curates as slackers on the company payroll. He does not know God, does not believe in Him. He considers religion something for women and children." In March, 1952, the Jesuit magazine, *Razón y Fe*, asked in precise terms: *Have we lost the working class in Spain?* The author of this study, Father Florentino del

Valle, then showed with statistics the extent of popular de-christianization: *In Andalusia there are towns of from 15,000 to 20,000 inhabitants where the church, with room for 1,000 or 1,500 persons, is never filled.* If the throng of souls driven off by injustice is to be won back, then the reality of injustice must be altered or at least dissociated from the Church, by sermons or accusations. And indeed there is scarcely a prelate, curate, or monk who does not castigate the racketeers and the evil rich several times each year.

But when the Church attempts to exercise some influence over the policies of the civil authority, she comes up against the tough totalitarian skeleton which exists under the flesh of "democratization." In a State which trumpets its Catholicism, the workers are stripped of the right to form Church-oriented unions. In a Spain governed apparently by the Church, the Catholic press cannot freely express its social principles. Publication of the Catholic magazines, *Tu* and *Razón y Fe* was suspended several times between 1950 and 1952, because they had campaigned against the black market and for just wages.

Demanding freedom of expression for her own publications, the Church was pushed into taking a stand against the principle of State censorship. As a step toward appeasement, the government agreed to remove ecclesiastical publications from the domain of common law, and they have been responsible ever since only to bishoprics. For the most part, however, the prelates continue to criticise the censorship, annoying and inefficient in any case, and to urge its replacement by punitive legislation dealing with misdemeanors of the press.

As far as unions are concerned, the Church has not succeeded in breaking down the Falange monopoly. The Cardinal-Primate, Monsignor Pla y Deniel, had to fight hard to bring the civil authority to accept the constitution of the workers' brotherhoods (H.O.A.C.) within the framework of Catholic Action.

In 1951, when several days were dedicated to the working-class youth of Catholic Action, he recognized the impossibility of reviving the Christian unions formerly tolerated by the anticlerical republic itself: "The only thing possible today," he said, "the only thing that is respected, is the functioning of Catholic Action. Were it not that we respect it, we could not even pretend that a Catholic State exists." Tolerated and nothing more, the workers' brotherhoods were devoid of any power, and membership in these groups in no way cancelled the obligation to membership in the Falangist vertical unions.

Nonetheless, the mere existence of these brotherhoods in fact re-established union dualism, which, as usual, led to competition. In 1951, for instance, the brotherhoods and Catholic press social campaign forced the Falangist unions to adopt a reformist attitude if they were to avoid being outdistanced; this attitude in turn emboldened the underground labor organizations to issue strike appeals.

From their inception, the brotherhoods were supported by a flock of Catholic malcontents: Basque Christian Democrats whose associations had been dissolved, Carlists disappointed by the "crusade's" regime. The pressure from this crowd of fervent and sometimes impatient adherents furnishes at least a partial explanation of the energy with which the episcopacy threw itself into the social crusade. In the uncertain weeks which passed between the "white strike" in Madrid and the opening of Hispano-American negotiations, on June 3, 1951, the episcopacy published a collective letter in which social justice was defined as a higher duty than that of charity: *the alms which God rewards are those which one gives when one has accomplished first all that is just.*

Yet it was at this time that the negotiations toward a Concordat entered a decisive phase. And two years later, in August of 1953, the Church shed her semi-reserve of fourteen years standing and signed a Concordat with the regime. This delayed and surprising decision may be explained by certain diplomatic factors. The Concordat negotiations had proceeded simultaneously with the Hispano-American negotiations. The first exchanges between the Vatican and the then Spanish Ambassador, Ruis Giménez, took place in April, 1951, and secret talks had just begun at about the same time between Madrid and Washington. The negotiations had hung fire while the Hispano-American talks came to a standstill, then were picked up again in January, 1952. And the Concordat was signed a month before the Madrid-Washington pact.

The episcopacy had indeed had reason to fear that the Americans, each day more solidly planted in Spain, would sooner or later require that measures be taken toward religious tolerance. As long as the laws regarding marriage, education, religious observances remained only unilateral measures they could be revoked at any time. If they were to be immune from American influence, they must be clothed in contractual form. To this end the thirty-six articles of the Concordat and the additional Protocol codified the various measures which had been decreed since 1937. *Osservatore Romano* accurately commented upon the signing of these agreements: *The Concordat inaugurates no new order in relations between the Holy Office and Spain, but rather, sanctions and stabilizes an extant de facto situation.*

In order to safeguard her privileges, the Church had not hesitated to conclude yet another alliance with the regime at the risk of definitely alienating the working class.

4. THE SACRED MOUNTAIN

In Cataloña and the Basque country, the clergy has identified itself with popular struggle against centralism. Basques and Cataloñans themselves for the most part, they share the nationalist convictions of their parishioners. Indeed, in villages where the peasants scarcely understand the Castilian language, the curates have no choice but to use the local tongue if they are to fulfill their duties. The same necessity is incumbent even upon the prelates, although most often they are strangers to their respective dioceses. For the government takes advantage of its right to present bishops by assigning prelates of foreign origin to the *fuerista* people. But even the most centralist among them have been obliged to tolerate, at least to some extent, the preaching of sermons in the Basque or Cataloñan tongues. Other bishops deliberately support the regionalist aspirations of these peoples, the better to ally them with the Church.

Only the clergy is sufficiently independent to stand up to the civil prohibition of regional languages, and the churches are the only public places in which speakers may talk in Cataloñan or Euskera. The pulpit is the conservatory of persecuted dialects.

In the Basque country, the bishop of Bilbao, Monsignor Gurpide, authorized preaching in Euskera, and while civil authorities refuse to register Basque first names, these names are recorded in the baptismal registers. Bilingual catechisms and a Bible in Euskera have been brought out under the bishop's auspices.

But this well-intentioned prelate was somewhat embarrassed upon receiving, on May 30, 1960, a collective letter signed by some 339 Basque priests and which constituted a terrible denunciation of the regime. Addressed to the four bishops of the Basque country,[8] this document had been drawn up under pressure of public opinion outraged by centralism, the economic crisis, and repression. "We do not want our silence to lead others to accuse us of complicity." Further, the authors of the petition did not confine themselves to a protest against persecution of Basque cultural values nor to a defense of the principle of "autodetermination . . . of any ethnic group. . . ." Basing their argument upon the postulate of "the inviolability of the conscience," they declared: "Neither torture nor brain-washing is legitimate, nor should public opinion be subjected to the pressure of a super-propaganda . . ." for "the right to truth" is the corollary of the right to freedom. But "the Spanish press is an instrument for the deformation of public opinion . . . In Spain there is neither an authentic parliament, nor political freedom, nor syndical freedom." The signatories denounced the "almost idolatrous cult of the leader" and rose up against oppression. "People are imprisoned for having expressed in public or even in private political opinions counter to those of the

[8] The bishops of Vitoria, Pamplona, San Sebastian, and Bilbao.

government . . . The *Fuero of the Spanish People* is a dead letter . . . A malevolent suspicion is pretext enough for the police or the *Guardia Civil* to beat up most irresponsibly, to torture or to wound any citizen at all. . . ."

In conclusion, the authors of the petition pleaded with the local bishops to intervene and "to find an efficacious formula" to restore "the lost peace" to the Basque people. But the prelates, anxious above all to avoid conflict with the government, strove—in vain—to take this document out of circulation. Copied out by hand or on the typewriter, or distributed as a mimeographed tract, this protest had enormous repercussions not only in the Basque country but throughout Spain.

In Cataloña, the nationalists regrouped about the monastery of Montserrat, which overlooks the valley of the Llobregat, and where the Black Virgin, patron of the locality, is worshipped. When, in a violent speech given at Granollers during a Falangist ceremony (December 1, 1958), the civil governor of Barcelona, General Acedo Colunga, accused the Cataloñan clergy of fomenting secession by preaching in Cataloñan, his words were picked up vigorously by Dom Escarré, abbot of Montserrat. Preaching on December 8 to about a thousand people, the abbot declared: "The Church always speaks the truth. If this truth is not pleasant to the ears of those who govern us, then it is up to them to change."

This text was censored in the newspapers. But thousands of pamphlets reproducing the words of Dom Escarré were passed from hand to hand. Most likely brought into circulation by Catholic Action groups (J.O.C., H.O.A.C., boy scouts) but later recopied by people of every shade of opinion, these tracts urged Cataloñans to support the abbot: "All of us feel that Montserrat is, as always, our Sinai." Two months later, a collective letter circulated by a group of "zealous Catholics" reproached the head of the Church of Cataloña, the Cardinal-Archbishop of Tarragona, Monsignor de Arriba y Castro, as well as the bishops of Lérida and Tortosa, with having "a clearly political and anti-Cataloñan attitude." The signatories stated that unlike the other bishops of the region, these three prelates, obsequious admirers of the Chief-of-State,[9] strove to stamp out the practice of preaching in Cataloñan. And on the following 26th of May, the day of the consecration of the new altarpiece of Montserrat by Eugène Cardinal Tisserant, some fifteen thousand young people went up from Barcelona to Montserrat and acclaimed Dom Escarré.

Agitation was increased after an incident starring Luis de Galinsoga, editor of the important Barcelona daily, *La Vanguardia*. The paper's owner, the Count de Godo, had been forced to accept this Murcian journalist as managing director under the personal protection of the *Caudillo*. The people of Barcelona were infuriated by an affront offered by the intruder who, in the San Ildefonso church, apostrophized a certain priest for preaching in Cataloñan. After a torrent of garbled talk, Galinsoga decided to make his exit from the church shouting: "All the Cataloñans are shits." Pamphlets urging the boycott of the newspaper were issued by the Christian-Democratic groups the following day, June 22, 1959. By the end of the year, the newsstand orders had already dropped 50 per cent and 16,000 subscribers had refused to renew their subscriptions. Stones had been thrown at the newspaper office windows and every day the streets were filled with torn and mutilated issues. A concert of horns and noise makers, scheduled to take place at the end of a soccer game, promised to make the biggest row of the century. But a few hours before the signal was to be given, it was learned that Galinsoga had been dismissed and had left Barcelona on the sly.

This capitulation was but one stage in the policy of "liberalization" adopted in 1956, when the leaders in Madrid

[9] The "zealous Catholics" quoted, among other dithyrambic harangues, that pronounced by the Bishop of Lérida in the presence of General Franco: "The finger of God is here. I believe that no more vigorous, pithy nor accurate expression could be found to give an adequate idea of the character and august person of our beloved Chief-of-State and of his immense work in all areas of human life. Admiration and a dazed marveling—these are the first impressions wrought by the work of this colossus-of-the-mind in any one of his creative acts." (Extract from the official bulletin of the Bishopric of Lérida, September 30, 1955, No. 9, p. 175.)

had acknowledged the danger inherent in the union of certain sectors of the Catholic bourgeoisie with the leftist opposition under the Cataloñanist banner. Thus they tried to win over the privileged to their side. *Opus Dei* and the "third force" who had gained a number of enthusiasts among the Cataloñan upper middle class were forced, in return, to take certain Cataloñan claims under consideration. One Gual Villalbi, representative of Barcelona industrialists, had been named to the Cabinet in February, 1957. At about the same time, the government had ousted the mayor of Barcelona, Simarro, who had turned City Hall into a racketeers' den, and replaced him with one Poricoles, who actively launched a new policy of financial clean-up and important public works.

After the *Vanguardia* boycott, the government attempted to disarm the Cataloñans by making other concessions to them: General Acedo Colunga was removed from office; a code of Cataloñan law was compiled; the fortress of Monjuich was ceded to Barcelona; the municipality of Barcelona was granted a charter guaranteeing a certain degree of financial autonomy and stipulating that the mayor would no longer be named by the Minister of the Interior but by the *Caudillo* himself.

In May, 1960, the *Caudillo* came to stay for some time in Barcelona and made it the seat of government for a month. The annual parade which normally takes place in Madrid to commemorate the 1939 victory was presented that year in Barcelona. Franco presided over a ceremony celebrating the centennial of the birth of the great Cataloñan poet, Maragall; yet the authorities cancelled the singing of the Cataloñan hymn, *Cant de la Senyera* (song of the flag), whose words were written by—Maragall. The ceremony ended, its 3,000 celebrants, crowded into the Hall of Music, arose and in Franco's presence intoned the *Cant de la Senyera*. Chaos and violence ensued. Some militants in the Catholic Action movement were arrested: one of them, Jordi Pujol, a 32-year-old doctor, admitted after being tortured that it was he who had written the pamphlets urging the populace to boycott *La Vanguardia*. In fact, Pujol could have answered the inquisitor who asked him to reveal the author of the pamphlets: "Barcelona, Señor." [10] But the police needed a scapegoat and a hostage. And so on Monday, June 13, 1960, a court-martial including four generals and two colonels sentenced Jordi Pujol to seven years' imprisonment. It was the condemned man himself who had told the audience what lesson should be drawn from his case: "You see me in the dock because I could find no means other than underground action to express what my feelings of responsibility and my Christian beliefs dictate to me when I see so clearly unjust a situation."

5. THE WELFARE PASTORALS

Elsewhere in Spain, priests anxious to break away from the regime led a campaign to raise the workers' standard of living. Many parish priests are all the more prone to defend the humble since they themselves live in such straitened circumstances that they are but one step from absolute poverty, for not only are they poorly paid but too many of their parishioners are either penniless or stingy. Some of these social welfare priests have become very popular in their area. Such is the case of a priest in the Santander region, the abbot Martín Castañeda, Curate of Campuzano. In June, 1958, the governor of the province forced the bishop to dismiss the abbot for having taken up a fund for a group of workers who had been fired. The villagers piled into trucks and went off to demand of the Bishop of Santander that he restore their priest. Having failed to receive justice at the hands of this prelate, whose first care was to avoid provoking an incident with the governor, they sent a delegation to Madrid to complain to the Papal Nuncio—who refused to grant them an audience.

The episcopacy itself had issued more and more pastoral letters on social justice. As early as 1951, the Bishops of Sevilla and Valencia ordered an inquiry into working-class conditions in their respective dioceses. The conclusions could

---

[10] Allusion to a play by Lope de Vega about the communal rebellion of Fuenteovejuna against the Knights of Calatrava. To the inquisitor's: "Who killed the Commander?" the villagers reply: "Fuenteovejuna, Señor."

be summed up under three curt headings: subsistence wages, hunger, slums.[11] The two prelates advised resistance to the high cost of living, punishment for racketeers, and also, above all, a policy for dealing with the housing problem. A modest program. It would undoubtedly have been better to speak, as did the Falangist unions, of a flexible wage scale. "It seems to me," wrote Monsignor Olaechea, Bishop of Valencia, "that what is being talked about is a worker's El Dorado belonging to another place and another age. I think all these things make the workingman smile . . . bitterly." Who is the workingman? Here he is, such as his age-old poverty has fashioned him: he considers himself at war with the ruling classes—employers, the Church, the Army; he has no faith in any regime; at bottom, politics interest him not at all. Sexuality has become his major interest, his only passion: "They think themselves slaves, they seek for pleasure to lighten their yoke . . . They claim that once upon a time slaves were bought and today, they are rented." [12]

The episcopal campaign for a rise in the worker's standard of living was strengthened after the signing of the Concordat. The more the Church was compromised, in the eyes of the masses, the more vital it was for her to dissociate herself from the consequences of the regime's social policy. "If employers would only listen to us," wrote Monsignor Morcillo, then Bishop of Bilbao, after the signing of the Concordat, "we would advise them to increase the workers' share by raising their wages or by an equitable distribution of profits."

Monsignor Olaechea, for his part, urged business heads to "fulfill a duty of the conscience," and accord the worker "absolute familial wages"—that is, double the amount paid at the time. "Any employer who, although able to pay a de-

[11] "Last night a doctor told me that one of his colleagues had been called to see an old woman. He found a hovel about ten yards square wherein six people slept on corn shocks. The old woman was in a corner. As the doctor came toward her, these unhappy people said to him: 'Don Ramón, shall we get up?' 'No, just lift your feet and I'll get by.' One case . . . there are hundreds like it." (Writings of Monsignor Olaechea, *Ecclesia*, December 1, 1951.)

[12] Monsignor Olaechea, *op. cit.*

cent salary, does not do so, is, without doubt, a bad Catholic."

How could an unjust employer reconcile the exercise of his religion with his refusal to obey the exhortations of the episcopacy? Here we hit upon one aspect of that "religious inflation" which is one of the essential themes of the pastoral letters of recent years.

The most characteristic of them is that published by Monsignor Morcillo in the spring of 1954: "Our externalization of religious feeling does not ordinarily include a proportional amount of internal reality. Purely external practice of religion, devoid of pain, of grace, of justice, is worth little and is very often considered scandalous by other persons."

But where then are the Christians in Spain if the practicing minority is made up of bad Catholics whose behavior drives the masses away from religion? Should the Church have recourse to the secular arm to force the faithful into observing her social doctrines? Monsignor Herrera seems to favor this solution: "By preaching alone," he said in the spring of 1954, "we shall not succeed in rapidly guiding men to the fulfillment of their (social) duty. This will take several generations and before the evolution of their consciences is achieved, the social revolution will be accomplished."

But is it reasonable to hope that the government will force the enactment of far-reaching reforms, when after all, it was set up specifically to prevent them? If employers are deaf and the State impotent, what will stop the revolution from being accomplished sooner or later, outside the Church, perhaps even against the Church?

To ward off this danger, Christian Democracy and the H.O.A.C. began, in spring, 1962, to channel the labor movement in their direction by giving clearer support to its demands. The Episcopacy, with its encyclical *Mater et Magistra*, did the same. Paradoxically, the clergy had been driven into opposition just when the regime had granted it the privilege which the Church had been seeking in vain since 1939: the recognition of Catholic centers of higher education as Church universities, whose diplomas are placed on a par with those from State universities. But the Church could hope to preserve the concessions made by an unpopular regime only by breaking away from it.

Early in 1962, the prelates of Spain set forth in precise terms the reforms they considered indispensable. The Bishop of Bilbao urged that the minimum wage be raised from 36 *pesetas* per day to 125 or 140. Soon after, the Archbishop of Sevilla urged agrarian reform and asked that agricultural day laborers be given a daily wage of 110 to 120 *pesetas*. These statements encouraged the strikers—to such a point that in May, the clergy and Catholic Action were led to take a further step: that of coming out clearly in favor of the right to strike.

The daily *Arriba* and other Falangist organs struck back, accusing the Church of meddling in problems of a social nature which were nobody's business but the State's. Echoing the *Caudillo* who, in a speech given on May 28 at Garabitas, had shown the extent of "communist infiltration" into Christian labor organizations, Ullastres accused those groups of "prostituting the Church" by using it as "an instrument in the class struggle." The Cardinal-Primate cut short the dual attack by a letter to the Minister of Foreign Affairs in which he took the responsibility for H.O.A.C. activities, stating that he had given his moral approval to this group's pro-strike manifesto. He further stated that the Church has not only the right but the duty to take a stand on social issues, and that should the State come into conflict with the Church, it is up to the State to alter its position.

A year later, the papal encyclical *Pacem in terris* furnished the lay leaders of Christian Democracy with a chance to formulate openly their political aims. In his speech in early May, 1963, Ruis Giménez, the regime's former Minister of Education, urged that freedom of expression and of association be reinstated, and that the *Cortés'* legislative powers be restored.

Supported by a large portion of the clergy, Christian Democracy had clearly announced its candidacy as Franco's successor.

Chapter Twelve

❧❦❧

FROM GREATER SPAIN
TO LITTLE EUROPE

FRANCO'S DICTATORSHIP has lasted for a quarter-century on the outer margin of a radical transformation of the conditions of international affairs. The United States and the Soviet Union have come into thorough control of their natural and demographic resources, and have filled out their boundaries. The minimum needed for a position of power is a population of about 200,000,000 inhabitants. Furthermore, since the development of industry requires a distribution area more vast than a single nation, the European countries must lower their customs barriers from now on. So it is that economic factors and the need for a common defense have led these nations to come together, to yield up a part of their individual sovereignties for the sake of super-national technical organizations. The cycle of nations is coming to an end; the world is entering the era of super-nations.

Henceforth, association with other nations is of vital necessity for countries of only secondary importance. Spain, subject to this law, was the only country of western Europe in a position to choose its partners and escape the need to consummate an agonizing marriage of convenience with her traditional enemies. For Spain would have had only to strengthen her ties with the Hispano-American nations in order to create a mighty gathering of nearly 200,000,000 people of similar civilization and culture.

But Franco's government did not even try to create new links with *la Hispanidad*.[1] Franco spent over seventeen years in a futile attempt to take over control in Africa, and, in order to escape diplomatic isolation, he was led to sign a pact in 1953 which placed Spain among the satellites of the United States. Apparently taken by surprise when the European Common Market was created five years later, the rulers in Madrid were able to save Spain from economic asphyxia only by cooperation with the European system for which the Spanish economy was totally unprepared.

Throughout this evolution from the Falangist autarchy to the European Common Market, governmental leaders constantly have announced more or less chimerical ambitions, all the while expending a wealth of ingenuity to adapt themselves, *a posteriori*, to the realities which they had allowed to ambush them. Not daring to throw out the imperialist phraseology inherited from the Falange, they have carried out the modest policy forced upon them by the desiderata of the conservative oligarchies, by the realities of the international situation, and by the weakness of their country—a weakness due, simultaneously, to the disharmony of public opinion, to industrial underdevelopment, and to the impotence of the military establishment.

1. THE DOMINATION AND IMPOTENCE OF THE ARMY

Military weakness was the most serious obstacle to the prestige politics dreamed of by the Falange. Furthermore, this

---

[1] *La Hispanidad*, greater Spain. The term refers to the Hispano-American countries.

weakness derived, for the most part, from the fact that Spanish industry was behind the times and unable to mass-produce the modern equipment required by the army.

Yet we cannot help but be struck by the disparity between the funds allotted to national defense and the results obtained. While military expenses accounted for thirteen per cent of the budget in republican times, Franco's government turned over an average thirty-six per cent of the ordinary budget to the armed forces, before signing the pact with Washington.

At the start of Hispano-American negotiations in 1951, after a dozen years of such effort, the American ambassador to Madrid summed up the conclusions reached by United States military experts about the state of Spanish forces. Substantially, he stated that the army is without modern equipment; the Spanish air force is nonexistent; the navy may be described as a "small bunch of ships"—in fact, in twenty years, the dictatorship has not launched a single capital ship.

Four years after the signing of the Hispano-American pact, when Moroccan irregulars attacked the Ifni enclave in November, 1957, Spain had already received some $350,000,-000 for her military establishment: and still she was underequipped. Since the United States did not agree to Spain's using the few modern planes she had against Morocco, Spanish headquarters was forced to make do with 1936 Heinkels.

In the winter of 1958-59, the Minister of War, General Barroso, went to Washington to ask for additional funds of $400,000,000 for the modernization of the army. The plan drawn up during his visit called for the establishment of modern divisions, modeled along American lines. Thus, nineteen years after the inauguration of a military dictatorship which had forced the nation to make unprecedented financial sacrifices, the Spanish army counted on the United States to endow Spain with up-to-date forces which, since they owed everything to the Pentagon—organization, funds, armament —would be able to act only in tight symbiosis with the American army.

Such a ruinous nonexistence of military force stems from the extraordinary waste of energy and money. There are too many officers, so pay is lowered. Ill-paid, the officers cast about for other sources of revenue. The most influential hold desk-jobs and overcrowd offices. Those with the best inside information plunge into an ingenious racket involving supplies and provisions. Others take up a second career on the outside: insurance, brokerage, trade. Involved in plots, rackets, and gossip, the officers have little time left in which to instruct the recruits. As a result, many drafted men have never held a rifle. Each officer is assigned three or four orderlies who not only take their superior officer's children out to play but act in addition as his assistants in his outside job. A captain, spending all his time in his insurance office, may employ four orderlies as typists or office boys.

Who or what will put a stop to these abuses? How can the State, fallen into the hands of a union of army men linked by ties of professional camaraderie, go ahead with military reforms which would require totally opposite conditions: strong power in the hands of men wholly independent of the military caste, dependent on public opinion and stimulated by check-ups in Parliament and the press? As long as the control of Army over State, of executive arm over thinking brain, continues, Spanish and American military expenditures will be made in vain. Their generosity is transformed into canned goods gone bad, into rags, disorder, and nothingness.

2. THE MIRAGE OF POWER
AT A DISCOUNT

Spain's foreign policy at the end of the civil war was set forth in 1941 by Castiella[2] and Areilza, in a work entitled: *The Claims of Spain*. These claims dealt mainly with Gibraltar and l'Oranie, the area around Oran. Furthermore, Franco's government hoped to remove the French presence from Mo-

[2] Fernando María Castiella was then professor of international law at the University of Madrid. He was ambassador to Peru in 1948, to the Vatican in 1951; in February, 1957, he was summoned to take over the Ministry of Foreign Affairs.

rocco and establish a protectorate, which would respect the appearances of the Cherif's sovereignty, over the entire country.

These were to have been some of the fruits of a German victory with which Spain would have been associated, and the public having been flattered, would rally anew about the *Caudillo*. This was the idea broached by Serrano Suñer during a talk with Mussolini, on October 1, 1940. "The war aspect would serve the purpose of tying all the forces of Europe together into one sheaf, since the objectives, Gibraltar and Morocco, are deeply important to all, and especially to youth." [3] Thus Franco, instead of transforming the vital energy of the Spanish people into a conquering weapon, counted on a prestigious success to forge Spanish unity.

But how were these territories to have been conquered? In what way was the Spanish army to have aided the Italo-German effort? As early as the summer of 1939, a military commission sent to Berlin had, with the German command, looked into the conditions of Spain's participation in the war against France. When war was declared in September of that year, Franco's government nonetheless announced its neutrality, which was renamed "non-belligerence" on June 12, 1940. Spanish operations in Africa, begun on June 14, were limited to the occupation of the Tangiers zone. This inaction was accompanied not only by bellicose speeches but also by offers, addressed to the Nazi government, of participation in the war.

These contradictions were accounted for by Spain's situation at the time. Those who had engineered the July, 1939, *pronunciamiento*, whether from the inside or the outside, had not foreseen the obstinacy of republican resistance nor the disintegration of the Spanish productive system, nor even the persistence of a deep-rooted hostility among a large part of the population. They did not realize that the act of force perpetrated in order to bring Spain into the Axis camp would also incapacitate the country so that Spain could do nothing very helpful for her new allies. In any case, the Spanish army's potential for action depended wholly upon Italian

[3] Quoted by Count Ciano in his diary.

and German supplies, since the Spanish command lacked everything, particularly gasoline and provisions. Now, these supplies could not be brought in by land as long as France remained unbeaten; nor again, by sea, because of the Anglo-French blockade.[4]

But as soon as land communications were re-established between Germany and Spain, in June of 1940, Franco made repeated requests for equipment with a view to attacking the French zone of Morocco, an operation which involved the risk of turning over North Africa to de Gaulle and the English. The German veto at this time accounts for Franco's attitude: his warlike utterances and his inaction.

In August, 1940, however, the German command, despairing of ever breaking down English resistance, considered moving against Gibraltar, and, in the next several weeks, there was a series of German-Spanish talks. On September 23, 1940, the two dictators met at Hendaye. But when Franco offered to enter the war on condition that Hitler remove the French from Morocco, the *Führer* was reticent, fearing to alienate Vichy. In the scale of weaknesses, the neutrality of the French fleet outweighed Franco's participation. Nonetheless, although he had not wrung a specific promise from Hitler, Franco undertook to participate in the attack on Gibraltar.

Much later, in December, 1944, Hitler stated in a reproachful letter to Mussolini that an accord "had been reached at Hendaye" between Franco and himself, and that Franco hesitated for the first time only after the Italian defeats in Greece. This hesitation was evident on November 17, 1940, when Serrano Suñer went to Berchtesgaden, three and a half weeks after the Hendaye meeting. Many things had happened in those few weeks: the Italian offensive against Greece (October 28), the first Fascist defeats, and the great blow dealt by the British naval and air forces to the

---

[4] Franco wrote to Mussolini on August 15, 1940: "Ever since the beginning of the present conflict, it has been our intention to intensify our preparations with a view to entering the war at the right moment. The lack of the most essential material and the rupture of our communications with Italy and Germany have, to this day, prevented our every operation. . . ."

Italian fleet anchored off Taranto. While the German command was to direct combined units to Greece in anticipation of a move against Gibraltar, the English army in Egypt was to launch the offensive against Libya, on December 9, which would crush the Graziani army.

At this point, Franco adjourned the carrying out of the plan to attack Gibraltar (December, 1940-January, 1941).[5] Yet all the speeches made by the *Caudillo* during this period indicate that he still believed in an ultimate German triumph. But the Italian defeats had shown him that the war would go on for some time yet, and Spain was in no condition to make a long-term effort. Franco's government was obliged to delay active participation until such time as victory was near for the Germans. Serrano Suñer, disgraced and exiled, admitted to this naïvely Machiavellian reckoning: "My plan was to enter the war at the very moment of the German victory, when the last battles were being decided." [6]

That hour appeared about to strike in the autumn of 1941, the time of the German army's lightning offensive against Russia. Franco therefore adhered, in November, to the anti-Comintern pact. But when operations in Russia slowed to a stalemate in the winter of 1941-42, and the spring and summer campaigns of 1942 produced unspectacular results, Franco saw for the first time that German victory was not certain. Secret negotiations with the English had been undertaken with, at first, no other object than to stall for time; now they yielded some exact promises. By swearing, on November 8, 1942, to remain neutral, Franco allowed the English and Americans to gain a foothold in North Africa. Neutral in the west, Spain was the ally of the Reich on the eastern front, where the Blue Division fought alongside German troops.

[5] When Admiral Canaris, envoy to Madrid, suggested January 10, 1941, as the date for launching the offensive against Gibraltar, Franco had demanded a postponement. But on February 2, in a talk with Mussolini at Bordighera, and on February 26, in a reply to an urgent communiqué from Hitler, Franco declared openly that "circumstances had changed" since Hendaye.

[6] These words were spoken during an interview given in 1945 to a reporter from *Paris-Presse*.

After the Stalingrad fiasco (October, 1942-January, 1943), the *Caudillo* realized that the Reich had lost the war, whereupon Spanish aid to Hitler took the form of a diplomatic offensive intended to convince the leaders in London of the magnitude of the Soviet threat and the need to conclude a separate peace with Germany. Until then, Franco's pretense of neutrality had masked the reality, the aid to Hitler; henceforth, protestations of loyalty to the Nazi cause camouflaged an attempted reconciliation with the Allies.

But such double-dealing did not deceive the leaders either in London or in Washington who, while taking advantage of Spanish neutrality, doubtless had decided to revenge themselves from that point on on the *Caudillo's* trickery.

After the Allied victory, in fact, Franco's government first was excluded from the Dumbarton Oaks conference where the groundwork was laid for the United Nations, and then was solemnly censured by the General Assembly, on February 9, 1946. All of the nations broke off diplomatic relations with Spain. Further, Franco's troops had to evacuate the international zone of Tangiers, occupied in August, 1940. Spain lost even those posts she had held prior to the war in the administration of the international city. The French government decreed the closing of the frontier at the Pyrenees. The program of economic sanctions suggested by the French delegation had been rejected by the United Nations; but during the next five years,[7] the interruption of formal diplomatic relations hindered the circulation of persons and goods and, in short, appreciably diminished the volume of Spanish foreign trade. So it was that these vengeful condemnations, set forth as measures liable to encourage the Spanish people to shake off the yoke of dictatorship, resulted in a still lower standard of living for the masses who actually bore the brunt of economic consequences of the ostracism practiced against a regime they had no part in choosing.

[7] The 1946 censure was repealed by the UN on November 4, 1950. Many nations had already re-established diplomatic relations with Madrid.

3. A BIRD IN THE HAND

Excluded from the western world, Spain could escape isolation only by association with the Arab nations. The eagerness with which the Arabs responded to Spain's advances and the weakening of Anglo-French positions in the Mediterranean soon caused Franco to aspire to a *de facto* protectorate over the Arab world.

But in the spring of 1952, the Minister of Foreign Affairs, Martín Artajo, on a friendly tour through the Near East, was given a rather reserved welcome in Cairo. For Franco, who had been holding out the bait of the Rif's "internal autonomy" since August, 1951, in order to humor his Arab League allies, had refrained from making good his promise.[8]

The "Africanists" in Madrid still believed it possible to pay off the Arabs with seeming concessions. Certainly the new High Commissioner, García Valiño, in 1951, had authorized the Rif nationalist leaders to reorganize their parties and publish their newspapers. But the Reformist Party of Abd-el-Kalek Torres, sponsored and subsidized by the High Commissioner's office, had to adopt the Falange language, the Falange ideology, even the regulation shirt, distinguished by its green dye. By bringing the nationalist leaders into his camp, the *Caudillo* believed he could determine their policies and even apply the brake should they commence to threaten Spanish interests. Moroccan nationalist newspapers, published in Tetuan, could clamor for independence from the French only, while they had to refrain from any criticism of the Madrid government.

Such naïve cunning would have been shot full of holes in no time had it not been for the Sultan's deposition: Moroccans turned their wrath against France. And nationalist fervor simmered down in the Rif where, however, rebel lead-

---

[8] At the time, Franco had already gathered some positive fruit from Arab sympathy. In Tangiers, the Arab riot stirred up by Franco's emissaries had restored to Spain her traditional place in the administration of that international port (spring, 1952).

ers from the adjacent zone, hunted by the French police, took refuge and found subsidies and arms. Indeed, the Moroccan uprising of October, 1955, was prepared in the Rif.

Apparently the *Caudillo* had not foreseen the possibility of the French abandoning to Morocco positions which Madrid's pro-Arab policy had helped to make indefensible. After the Sultan's return, the establishment of an Istiqlal-Democratic Independence Party government in Rabat and renewed assurances from Paris of democratic reforms, Franco's government found itself urged to shape its policies along the lines of those of France.

The Spanish army and the rightists were alarmed. In Tetuan, Moroccan nationalist circles were placed under police surveillance. When in mid-December, 1955, Franco declared that Morocco was not ripe for independence, he was answered by demonstrations, strikes, assassination attempts.

Franco then tried to pressure France into deferring recognition of Moroccan independence (the Dubois-García Valiño talk, on January 10, 1956). The High Commissioner also strove to broaden the local government of Tetuan, to make it more independent of the Rabat government. But France had undertaken too much *vis-à-vis* the Moroccans to be able to postpone the moment for carrying out her promises. The feudal lords of Tetuan, for their part, felt that public opinion in Morocco leaned too much toward a unified country for them to be able to play their personal card. Accordingly, in January, 1956, the "reformist" leader, Abd-el-Kalek Torres, resigned from his post as Minister of Social Affairs in the Tetuan government.

Thus, Franco was obliged to publish, on January 14, 1956, a communiqué which theoretically recognized the unity and independence of Morocco. But the only effect of these purely verbal concessions was to encourage Moroccan opposition. Tension reached its peak after the signing of the Paris agreements by which France formally recognized Moroccan independence. No sooner was the news received in Tetuan than demonstrators thronged in the streets, and great shouts went up for effective independence of the Rif zone. The police opened fire (March 8 and 9, 1956): the dead and wounded could be counted off by dozens.

Had Franco refused to give in, Spain would have had to fight alone, under the worst possible conditions. From here on in, capitulation was inevitable. Early in April of the same year, secret negotiations opened between Spain and the Sultan resulted in the signing of the Madrid accord by which Franco's government gave up all claim to the Rif: the regime's policy of expansion on African soil achieved only the liquidation of the modest yet tangible footholds bought with blood and money, under the reign of Alfonso XIII.

Army officers, irked by this abandonment of the Rif and foreseeing numerous dismissals, began to agitate. Hence, when Franco, yielding to pressure from the military, practically placed his government under the control of the Chiefs-of-Staff in February, 1957, the new team hastened to inaugurate a policy of firmness toward Morocco and rapprochement with France: talks between French and Spanish military figures took place in Madrid in the spring of that year.

The task of carrying out this policy was entrusted to Castiella. At first sight, the former spokesman for Falangist claims on French Morocco seemed ill suited to ally himself with France in order to confine Moroccan nationalism. But Castiella, opportunely recalling the era when he began his career under Angel Herrera, had known how to arouse Catholic and monarchist sympathies.

The new ministerial team refused to concede Moroccan claims to the Ifni enclave. Emboldened by the memory of former instances of abandonment, the Moroccans believed that they could force Franco's hand. In November, 1957, "the Army of the Liberation" attacked Spanish posts of the Ifni enclave. Having sacrificed its genuine positions in the Rif upon the altar of Arab friendship, the dictatorship found itself obliged, if it were to avoid intolerable humiliation, to defend the sand and rocks of Ifni, and thereby aroused the anger of the Arab world.

The prolongation of the state of alert in Africa in the long run entailed certain advantages for Spain, justifying as it did maintenance of troops in Ifni and the creation of a vast camp in the Canary Islands, to which the forces, withdrawn gradually from the Rif, were transferred. Since they continued to receive high active-duty pay, the officers had no reason to conspire against the regime.

But the Madrid government could expect to hang on to its African possessions only insofar as France held on to hers. It was out of the question that Spain, the last colonialist power on Arab soil, stand up alone to pressure from the Arab world, the United Nations, and the United States. Thus the *Caudillo* had to rely on French support to terminate, with a minimum of cost, a policy whose aim was to establish a Spanish sphere of influence in Africa at the expense of the French possessions.

Under such conditions, the talks between General de Gaulle's government and the F.L.N. could not but alarm the leaders in Madrid. Having attempted to support General Salan and the French activists, Franco, with his habitual realism, took stock of the obstacles with which an extreme right *pronunciamiento* would meet in France, and dropped his protégés. Undoubtedly he was resigned to having to abandon further sites: Algerian independence not only implies the eventual departure from Ifni and from Río del Oro, but also means that the Spanish presence in Ceuta and Melilla— cities which have belonged to Spain since the fifteenth and sixteenth centuries—will become an issue.

4. LA HISPANIDAD, YET TO BE BORN

The Falangist ambitions in Africa were the only ones which Franco really tried to carry out. The others on the contrary, particularly those involving Gibraltar and the nations comprised in *la Hispanidad*, were neglected or betrayed by Francoist diplomacy.

It is true that for nearly twenty years, members of the government and spokesmen for the single party did make a number of speeches calling upon England to give Gibraltar back to Spain, while young Falangists, parading through the streets in a spirit of disciplined frenzy, vigorously upbraided the English. These demonstrations never aroused the slightest interest among the people: how can millions of citizens, convinced that Spain is the property of a small clique of profiteers, be made to feel the rightful owners of the rock of Gibraltar? And it was more than unlikely that the *Gibraltareños* would give up the freedom and the high standard of living enjoyed under British rule to take up hand grenades and agitate for Spanish citizenship when, every morning, they could see the inhabitants of the neighboring Spanish villages crush up against the *Linea* barrier to request work in the English arsenals. Total indifference among the masses, not only at Gibraltar but throughout the country, was the chief reason for the failure of the Falange's campaign.

And in fact the Franco government never managed to get negotiations with London off the ground. Until 1951, the British Cabinet pretended to ignore the Falangist claims. The Labor government then supported the plot hatched by Spanish royalists and socialists with a view to restoring the monarchy: for if Don Juan, with his English education, were brought back, Spain would be drawn more than ever into the British sphere of influence.

The wish to prevent exactly this accounts, perhaps, for the promptness with which the United States flew to Franco's aid in July, 1951, when the dictatorship was severely shaken by important strikes in Barcelona, the Basque country, and Madrid.

When the elections in England in November, 1951, returned the Tories to power, Franco's government, shored up by American aid, believed that the time had come to take care of the Anglo-Spanish bone of contention. In an interview granted to the Sunday *Times* [London], Franco suggested a compromise: Gibraltar would be restored to Spain, but the British Admiralty would have a ninty-nine-year lease. This reasonable proposal was not even considered by the Foreign Office which instead brought to bear all possible pressure to delay the conclusion of a pact between Madrid and Washington. The Falange campaign now reached its culmination. It was decided that a "Gibraltar day" would be observed every year on August 4. And during the first few months of 1953, Franco's government consistently refused to authorize the importation of English goods: this boycott was terminated by the English threat to suspend purchases of Spanish fruit.

The Falange was outraged by the announcement, in June, 1954, that Queen Elizabeth II would soon visit Gibraltar. The press abruptly raised its voice, and protest demonstrations appeared in rapid succession. But the government's two-faced manoeuvering was suddenly exposed when Falangist students demonstrated before the British Embassy in Madrid. Because their youthful ardor seemed about to get out of hand and involve them in a genuine incident with the English diplomats, their own organizers about-faced and had them charged by the mounted police.

The young militants' enthusiasm had been dampened once and for all. Speeches claiming Gibraltar for Spain were received with laughter and catcalls, and the imperturbable English continued their preparations for the Queen's visit. The demonstrations scheduled for the day of Her Majesty's entry into Gibraltar had to be cancelled. The Falange could never revive a campaign which had foundered in ridicule. Reconciliation with the rest of Europe necessitated suspension of claims to the *Peñon* (Gibraltar).

The same contradictions are found in Franco's policy concerning Latin America. It is true that the government set up a "Great Council of *la Hispanidad*," endowed with considerable propaganda resources; and on the part of Franco's spokesmen there has been a barrage of commemorative speeches, philological conventions, awarding of decorations to Ibero-American figures. Thanks to generously distributed scholarships, thousands of young Latin Americans were able to spend some time in the mother country. Treaties according dual nationality were reached with several Spanish-speaking nations. When catastrophic acts of nature ravaged Chile and Peru, solidarity appeals launched in Spain helped to strengthen emotional ties between the mother country and those overseas. But the imperialist vocabulary of the Falange offset these positive feelings. In cultural matters, the efforts of the regime are cancelled by the evil reputation of its censorship: overseas readers fear that classic as well as contemporary works have felt the censor's scissors. Consequently, once sought-after Spanish publishers have lost some of their prestige in the Hispano-American book market.

On the political level, Franco's dictatorship has made no effort to realize the Hispanic pretensions once announced by José Antonio Primo de Rivera. Association between the mother country and the Hispanic nations could assume the most varied forms: formation of a consultative committee to fix a behavior pattern compatible with the UN; diplomatic and military alliance; lowering of customs barriers and establishment of free ports; customs union; common market; creation of a common merchant marine and of an inter-Hispanic bank for economic development.

Public opinion would have reacted favorably to a proposal of this sort. Similar living conditions in Spain and in Latin America, created by English and American economic colonization, have aroused the same wrath and the same demanding fervor on both sides of the Atlantic. From the iron of Bilbao and the mercury of Almadén to Chilean copper, Venezuelan petroleum, and Bolivian tin, all the raw materials from the Spanish-speaking world are monopolized by preponderantly American or English international cartels. The same is true of the Hispanic nations' sea and air transports. A goodly part of the value of the raw materials is therefore channeled directly to London or New York in the form of dividends, freightage, insurance, reinsurance. As foremost purchasers of raw materials and agricultural produce, and as foremost suppliers of manufactured goods, the English-speaking countries set buying and selling prices at will. The nations of the Spanish-speaking world receive only a small fraction of what their exports are worth—in a market whose low level is artificially maintained—yet they must pay sky-high prices for imported industrial products. In this way they are sentenced to a low standard of living by a trade balance with a consistently large deficit.

A common sense of economic frustration engenders a reflex of Hispanic nationalism on both sides of the Atlantic. Anxious to eliminate Washington's domination, the Spanish-American countries look for extra-continental supporters—and the first possibility they see is Spain. The members of the Spanish family of nations have thus rediscovered the warmth of a forgotten blood tie. Spain could have taken a peaceful revenge on Washington. In the nineteenth century, the United States took advantage of the Spanish-American nations' struggle against Madrid's centralism and brought them under outright economic control. Spain, in turn, could have benefited from the rebellion provoked by these abuses and, amid the ardor of a common struggle, could have recreated political ties that had been broken for over a century.

All that was needed to cause the Hispanic peoples to rise up against Washington was to spread nationalist propaganda, to stir up xenophobia and revolt everywhere, to support all who rebelled against the United States, and to show that a rise in the general standard of living depended upon the seizure of *yanquí* property.

Authentic Falangists would undoubtedly have put this policy into action. But the gap between the Falangist program and the government's conduct was brought to light between 1946 and 1950 by the failure of the Hispano-Argentine alliance. The Peronist and Falangist programs included the same objectives: to expropriate the property of the big foreign companies, limit foreign investments, create industries and transport which would allow both countries to develop their own resources. It is this identity of circumstances and aims which explains Perón's effort to create a Madrid-Buenos Aires axis. By issuing his solemn "declaration of economic independence" in 1947, Perón felt that he was applying—and indeed he was—the Falange doctrine.

Within the framework of this ideological family relationship, the Argentine dictator attempted to weave economic and diplomatic ties. The Hispano-Argentine commercial protocol, signed in October, 1946, after Perón's first election to the presidency of the republic, was succeeded by the Franco-Perón protocol, in the wake of Evita Perón's triumphal visit to Madrid. But as early as January, 1950, the Argentine government decided to suspend this treaty. Hispano-Argentine relations grew noticeably cooler. In two years, the Argentine funds allocated to Spain had been exhausted by mass importation of wheat, and Franco's regime was in no condition to pay back its debt.

Still another reason for the failure of the alliance was the ill will on the part of Spanish leaders with regard to Perón's proposed economic collaboration. The Argentine *Caudillo* was dreaming of an Hispanic customs union, with Cádiz as its free port in Europe—an ambitious plan which would have made Spain the nerve center of communications between Europe and Latin America. But far from jumping at this unhoped-for chance, Franco's diplomacy used every dilatory tactical resource to avoid any positive realization of the project and gradually to make Argentina relinquish it. This ill will may be accounted for partially by the routine negligence of the Madrid authorities; but there were also specifically deeper-lying reasons having to do with the character of the two regimes. At the very time when assertive nationalism had come to power in Buenos Aires, a government in Madrid dominated by representatives of the conservative oligarchies had usurped the Falangist label.

At the time, these privileged castes ruled all of the Ibero-American nations—except Argentina. The policy they carried out, on both shores of the Atlantic, was necessarily oriented toward the English-speaking powers. The foremost of these oligarchies is that which includes landowners, exporters of agricultural produce, shipowners, and banks linked with agrarian capital. Representatives of these interests fear that measures biased against foreign capital would incite the great industrial powers to cut their purchases of Hispanic agricultural produce. For their part, the great mining or banking companies directly controlled by English or American capital have given rise all about them, in Spain as well as in Latin America, to another privileged caste: administrators, ghost- or dummy-partners, counsels on retainers, engineers, civil servants under bribes, politicians or generals who sit on the boards of directors of these companies. In the shade of these beneficiaries-at-first-hand of foreign exploitation, the luxury industries—hotels, restaurants, amusement spots—thrive; and these establishments, in turn, provide a living for a privileged proletariat.

Thus, in Spain as in Latin America, the oligarchies at the top of government can live and prosper only in symbiosis with a great industrial power, be it England or the United States. A certain community of ideology and way of life was destined to link the privileged Spanish to the Ibero-American oligarchies. Thus, for fifteen years, Franco's dictatorship strove with all the power at its command to uphold the Latin-American dictatorships which represented the same economic structures. The Peruvian dictator, Odría; the Colombian, Rojas Pinilla; the Venezuelan, Pérez Jiménez; all, and Trujillo as well, received police assistance, army instructors, and Spanish *Guardia Civil*, who helped them put down Hispanic nationalist movements.

But there were only very limited possibilities of collaboration with this type of regime. And those governments which would abide by U.S. State Department orders each time an important act or a trade treaty, a military pact, or a United Nations vote came up, could not be considered as linked firmly to the destiny of Spain. The results of Franco's "Hispanic policy" were in fact confined to academic verbiage in which for two decades the two *Caudillos* uttered transatlantic, imperturbable assurances that they mourned the passing of former power and all the while demonstrated their firm intention to perpetuate as long as possible the disintegration of *la Hispanidad*, the poverty of the peoples it comprised, and their common submission to the United States.

The phase of tacit abandon of the Falange's Hispanic ambitions was followed in 1953 by the phase of the Madrid-Washington alliance, an imbalance which actually implied recognition of Yankee sovereignty over Spain itself. This phase-to-phase evolution was but a local episode in the general relaying of English capital by American capital.

The Spain-U.S. pact naturally had the effect of accentuating the pro-Yankee aspect of Franco's politics. Spain was one of the few countries to applaud the 1954 invasion of Guatemala by United Fruit mercenaries; and the *Caudillo* refrained from making a move when Costa Rica's nationalist government was threatened, in 1955, by armed bands in the pay of the fruit company.

The mother country's submission to Washington's policies angered the nationalist and democratic parties which came to power between 1954 and 1959 in the majority of the Spanish-American countries, in the wake of a sweeping tide of rebellion which deposed the *caudillos* who were vassal to Washington, one after the other. When Pérez Jiménez and Batista fell, in January, 1958, and January, 1959, respectively, Franco's regime did nothing more than record passively the *fait accompli*. Madrid by now had practically no Latin American policy.

The Spanish-American peoples themselves hate in Franco the two central ideas against which they have accomplished their revolution: totalitarianism, and submission to Washington. Although the new democratic governments have not followed Mexico's example—that is, have not consistently refused to recognize Franco's government—they are anxious nonetheless, despite the purely formal diplomatic relationships, to see an anachronistic regime disappear, since it constitutes the major obstacle to Spain's participation in the Hispanic renascence.

5. CONTRACT FOR BONDAGE

Opposed to the United States by its interests in Latin America and to Russia by the preoccupation with security in Europe, Spain could wriggle out of the dilemma in which the two rival imperialists strive to box in all other peoples only by working wholeheartedly toward the creation of a third force uniting the industrial potential of western Europe with the vast raw-material resources of Latin America. But a feeble government, devoid of international prestige, could not take on such a role.

This being the case, security considerations required that Spain join the western military system. Further, the anti-communist crusade was the only tactic able to guarantee Franco's diplomacy a minimum of continuity by casting the *Caudillo* as the unsung precursor of the anti-Bolshevik struggle.

When negotiations were opened officially between Madrid and Washington, in the autumn of 1951, the *Caudillo* expected that a genuine military alliance would be concluded by which Spain and her armed forces would be incorporated, sooner or later, into the western military system. For nearly two months, Franco's spokesmen refused to recognize that the pact proposed by Washington was nothing more than a contract for the leasing of bases. After wasting several months in futile manoeuvres to broaden negotiations, Franco fought only to win certain minor concessions, all the while trying to conceal his loss of face from public opinion at home. This accounts for the bitter and endless bargaining which dragged on for a year and a half, until the signing of an accord in September, 1953.

It was American backing which enabled Franco's government to gain an entry into the international assemblies— first UNESCO, and then, in 1955, the United Nations; but Spain no longer occupied the place she had held prior to the civil war. Whereas Spain, rightful member of the League of Nations from that organization's inception, had become permanent member of its directive committee in 1926, Franco's Spain was barely voted into the UN after an eleven-year exclusion, and then only as an ordinary member of the General Assembly.

In the economic field, the need to continue feeding Franco driblets of aid forced the leaders in Washington to expend far more than had been foreseen in the initial promises. In 1963, a decade after the Madrid-Washington pact was signed, $1,183,000,000 had been poured into the civilian sector alone of Franco's regime. But by that time, through the Marshall plan, France had received $5,186,000,000, and Italy, $3,447,000,000. Thus, in financial as in diplomatic matters, the 1953 pact was confined to assuring Spain tardily of a small portion of the advantages which that country could have enjoyed earlier and in full under another government, one less concerned with grandeur.

And even the small advantages of the 1953 pact had been obtained at the cost of onerous and perilous conditions. For the pact completely disparaged the measures formerly adopted under Falangist influence with a view to preventing the economic colonization of Spain by foreign capital. American stockholders were exempt from the obligation to reinvest their profits in Spain. On the other side of the picture, the law prohibiting Spanish firms from accepting foreign contributions equal to more than twenty-five per cent of their capital was not officially annulled until 1959.[10] But certain firms were authorized nonetheless, as early as 1954, to receive foreign capital up to forty-five or fifty per cent of their corporate assets.

The cession of three air bases and the Rota naval base (near Cádiz) to the United States is a source of anxiety and dissatisfaction among the Spanish. American troops sent to Spain were, it is true, advised to act discreetly, and Washington guaranteed that in time of peace, no more than the personnel strictly necessary to their surveillance and maintenance would be stationed at these bases. In case of an openly declared or even threatened war, however, American authorities would have the right to increase the personnel and adopt any measures they might judge useful to defense. And the Spanish command, while exercising theoretical authority over the ceded bases, could only countersign the orders issued by U.S. headquarters.

Further, in case of war, the presence of American bases

[10] This law was not really enforced against foreign companies established prior to its promulgation, particularly those developing the Almadén mercury. The Peñarroya lodes were, however, nationalized by mutual agreement. The foreign company involved was given an indemnity far greater than the actual value of the half-exhausted deposits (1954).

in Spain implies danger of whose extent the population is not even aware. If the first missiles aimed toward the U.S.S.R. were to have been launched from the Torrejón de Ardoz base, not even ten miles from Madrid, that capital could have been the first target of Soviet missiles and become the Hiroshima of Europe. Even if the bases could be used only for classic-style bombardments, the *Caudillo,* by agreeing to their establishment *despite the advice of the technical committee consulted,* had exposed the capital to serious danger.

While Spain shares the perils of the western world, the country has no part in the elaboration of the west's policy and strategy. Spain's entry into NATO is still opposed, especially by Belgium and the Scandinavian countries. Spanish representatives have not participated in any international conference, nor were they admitted to the diplomatic talks begun in the spring of 1959 with the aim of resolving the Berlin crisis. Yet had war broken out over this issue, had American planes taken off from Spanish territory to bomb Russia, Madrid would have been placed in mortal danger of reprisals.

Franco's government appeared to become suddenly aware of this altogether abnormal situation early in 1963, when it began talks with Washington for a renewal of the 1953 pact. By then, the considerable changes in American strategy had stripped the air bases in Spain of all importance. But Spanish military leaders felt that the Rota port could serve as a stop-over and supply base for American submarines carrying Polaris missiles. In exchange for a continued lease of this base, Franco hoped to be granted a certain role in the councils of the Atlantic alliance. On February 2, 1963, Spain's ambassador to Washington, Antonio Garrigues, declared that Spain would not consent to being a "second-class partner," a passive ally who could not take part in the making of decisions which it was obliged nevertheless to carry out. [*Ed. note:* On September 26, 1963, the 1953 agreement on American air and naval bases in Spain was extended for five years. New measures of increased defense cooperation were also announced.]

6. THE "EUROPEANIZATION" OF SPAIN

The conservative ministerial team which came to power in February, 1957, launched a policy of reconciliation with "Little Europe," particularly with France and West Germany. During the winter of 1958-59, when the era of the Common Market began, the question of Spain's joining European groups came under discussion in the political circles of Madrid.

The little groups of the "tolerated" opposition—particularly liberal monarchists and Christian Democrats—were "Europeans" for sentimental reasons and also because they hoped that Spain's entry into the European community would entail a political and economic "liberalization." Spokesmen for the agricultural export interests campaigned for the same thing, so that the European market would not exclude Spanish produce. But most industrialists, on the other hand, fought the "integration" movement, for fear of competition of European manufactured products.

The arguments of the pro-"Europeanization" figures had more weight, in Cabinet meetings, than did those of their adversaries. The *Caudillo* and his ministers saw clearly that Spain could not be anything more than a poor relation in the Atlantic alliance and that Spain would be admitted to NATO membership only insofar as backing from the three "greats" of western Europe—England, Germany, France—could overcome the veto of the small Scandinavian states.

Furthermore, the Spanish economy, victim of acute inflation, needed European funds; and the *Caudillo*'s economic advisors believed that Spain could obtain the tangible benefits of adherence to the European alliance while postponing until a hazy future period the moment so feared by the industrialists, the moment when Spanish production should meet the challenge of European industry on her own markets.

Franco's government did indeed obtain, by joining the Organization of European Economic Community in 1959, substantial funds which allowed it to carry out its "stabilization plan." The cancellation of import quotas and licenses brought satisfaction to Spanish economic circles and to the member nations of the OEEC. But this partial "liberation" of imports was accompanied by an appreciable rise in customs duties, protecting Spanish industry from foreign competition.

For the next two years, however, Franco's government was the target of a "Europeanist" offensive which reached its culmination in the spring of 1961, when, during an official visit to Madrid, German Vice-Chancellor Erhard strove to convince Spain of the need to join the Common Market. In a speech delivered at the end of a banquet offered by the Bank of Spain, he declared that Germany was "disposed to contribute both materially and financially to the reconstruction and expansion of the Spanish national economy." But he left no doubt that this aid was dependent upon both Spain's participation in the Common Market and removal of her "protectionist barriers." The Federal Republic was attempting in fact to bring as many of the European nations as possible over to its side, in order to isolate England and thereby force the British to join the Common Market; and German industry was aiming to take over the Spanish market.

A few days before Erhard's visit, the Spanish "Europeanists" had launched a new offensive. The monarchists distributed a clandestine manifesto demanding a "tightening of the links with Europe," while the Spanish Committee of the OEEC set aside "European integration days" in Madrid. Both of these moves were backed by all the interests having to do with production and/or exportation of agricultural and mineral produce, these sectors being gravely concerned by the possibility of England's entry into the Common Market.

At this point, Alberto Ullastres, Commerce Minister, opened talks—directly or through the G.A.T.T.—with various European nations to assure, in any case, the preservation of conditions favorable to Spanish agricultural exports. But his interlocutors demanded that in return Spain lower her duties on imported manufactured goods.

In January, 1962, when England requested admission

into the Common Market and when the six nations of "little Europe" signed the Brussels accord setting up an agricultural common market, Franco's government realized that resistance was no longer possible. By remaining on the fringe of western Europe, Spain was in danger of being ousted, not only from Germany and the Benelux countries but also from the English market—vital to the Spanish economy—by similar producing nations: Italy, the French *midi*. On February 9, 1962, Castiella bowed to the inevitable and sent to M. Couve de Murville, then presiding over the Cabinet of the European Economic Community, a letter requesting that negotiations be opened for Spain's entry into the Common Market.

When, in January, 1963, General de Gaulle vetoed England's inclusion in "little Europe," France's five partners refused to take any other candidacy under consideration; Spain's request was shelved. This did not alter the plans of Franco's government which, realistically, had prepared for lengthy negotiations: Greece was associated with the Common Market in July, 1961—after two years of negotiations. Moreover, it is felt in Madrid that the will of only one man cannot exclude England for any considerable length of time. Once England is admitted, other candidacies can be taken up; and Spain will do her utmost not to be outdistanced by other citrus-fruit producers already linked with Europe (Algeria) or having requested admission (Israel).

The policy of a government unable either to build *la Hispanidad* or to foresee the creation of Europe, or even to prepare national industry for that event, has driven Spain into this abrupt "Europeanization" involving the need to carry out a gigantic drive toward industrial modernization at breakneck pace.

The Hispanic and African dreams of the Falange are a far cry from the bitter reality of membership in a European community triply dominated by London, Paris, and Bonn.

Chapter Thirteen

※

FROM AUTARCHY TO THE COMMON MARKET

IN LESS THAN a quarter-century, Spain has evolved from the autarchical economic planning of the Falange to the liberalism prevalent in the councils and conferences of "Little Europe."

Until 1951, the country suffered from scarcity of basic goods and from underproduction, both due to some extent to civil wartime demolitions. But this first phase dragged on beyond the normal time. The slow pace of reconstruction stemmed less from the isolation of Spain and the slowing down of her exchanges with other nations than from the opposition of the classic right's conservatism to the reformism of the Falange.

On the other hand, the period 1951-59 is notable for a relatively rapid increase in national income. The regime, no longer ostracized by the United Nations, entered into many exchanges with western nations. Furthermore, since the government of "technicians" installed in 1951 was anxious to appease public opinion, Falangist economic planning has become less rigid; and American aid gave the government the means to carry out the policies required by the evolution of public opinion. The period of achievement which began at this time resulted nonetheless in an inflationary crisis such that a "stabilization plan" had to be adopted, in 1959.

For the sake of obtaining funds from abroad and safeguarding agricultural exports, the regime was driven to joining first the OEEC, then to try to enter the Common Market, and in this way to inaugurate a new phase of adaptation to European reality.

1. FINANCIAL STATEMENT

The national income, which had risen consistently from the start of the twentieth century until 1935, went into a brutal decline after the civil war. In terms of 1929 *pesetas:* the income dropped from 24,880,000,000 *pesetas*—the yearly average in the period 1931-35—to 22,652,000,000 in the period 1940-44. The decrease becomes more apparent when we consider the demographic rise. The average yearly per capita income, which in 1931-35 reached 1,036 *pesetas,* did not go beyond 883 *pesetas* in the 1940-44 period. Not until 1951 did global and individual incomes return to and outstrip the corresponding averages for 1931-35. The civil war and the immobility of the 1940-50 decade were paid off by a lag of some fifteen or twenty years.

Progress was fairly rapid from 1951 on. The annual average of national income reached 28,949,000,000 *pesetas* between 1950 and 1954 and 34,735,000,000 between 1955 and 1957. Yet even these figures were not very satisfactory when the 1950-58 period was put back into the context of Spanish development. For in fact, during the twenty years which separate the 1911-15 period from the five immediate post-civil war years, the national income rose by 39.6 per cent. Had this rise continued at the same rate, income would have reached an annual average of 34,732,000,000 *pesetas* by 1950-

54. This figure was not reached, however, until 1955-57.[1] Yet, by that time, a normal economic evolution at the prewar rate would have raised national income to over 36,500,000,000 *pesetas*.

Thus Spain, on the eve of the adoption of her stabilization plan had not yet—despite American aid—reached the level to which she would have risen had the war not taken place and had her economy continued to develop at the leisurely rhythm of the first three decades of the twentieth century.

2. THE SAD STATE OF THE RURAL AREAS

In 1951—twelve years after the end of the civil war—the observer could note three factors which point to a definite sag in agricultural production: an overwhelming increase in food imports, as well as a drop in agricultural exports and in individual consumption. Indeed, the wheat harvest which, in the pre-civil war years, had risen to an average of 43 million *quintals* had dropped, between 1948 and 1951, to an average of only 25 million. Neither drought nor civil war

1	Average yearly national income		Average income
Five-year periods	In *pesetas* at the current rate of the period	In 1929 *pesetas*	Per year & per capita in 1929 *pesetas*
1911-15	10,854,000,000	17,848,000,000	884
1916-20	22,462,000,000	19,928,000,000	981
1921-25	22,774,000,000	21,326,000,000	981
1926-30	23,609,000,000	23,571,000,000	1,031
1931-35	24,401,000,000	24,880,000,000	1,036
1940-44	50,929,000,000	22,652,000,000	883
1945-49	93,472,000,000	23,074,000,000	913
1950-54	211,000,000,000	28,949,000,000	1,125
Three-yr. period 1955-56-57 }	321,710,000,000	34,735,000,000	1,189
1958	440,219,000,000	38,311,000,000	1,291
1959	463,387,000,000	39,490,000,000	1,320
1960	469,118,000,000	39,293,000,000	1,304
1961	516,274,000,000	41,997,000,000	1,368
1962*	573,628,000,000	44,389,000,000	1,434

* Provisional figures.

could justify so prolonged a period of diminished productivity, whose cause may be more legitimately considered the lack of the auxiliaries of agriculture—fertilizers, livestock, farming implements.[2]

The funds allocated to farmers were indeed ridiculous; and imports of fertilizers and implements had diminished appreciably in comparison with the prewar volume. These deficiencies exposed the negligence of which the organisms in charge of production were guilty. These faults appear all the more serious when we realize that these autonomous organisms monopolized currency, aspired to be the sole purveyors in grain, equipment, and fertilizer, fixed sales prices, and, finally, collected the harvested grain and took charge of distributing produce. The Wheat Institute ordered farmers to conform to extremely low sales prices; preferring inaction to unremunerative toil, farmers let part of their fields lie fallow.

Grumblings against bureaucratic tyranny reached a peak in 1949. In September, there were disturbances in Aragon, where the peasants refused to deliver their harvests to the Wheat Institute collectors. Thereupon, in its first departure from the planning principles of the Falange, the government inaugurated the "double sector." Henceforth, farmers would be required to turn over only a part of their harvest to the Wheat Institute. This measure, as well as a rise in grain prices, stimulated increased production beginning in 1951.

Furthermore, as a result of the stormy strikes which had occurred some weeks before in Barcelona and Madrid, the government was forced to improve the system of provisions for the large urban centers and, therefore, to review its agricultural policy. The elimination of rationing came about as the first progressive steps were taken and wholesale grain imports were financed by American funds. Grain collecting was no longer necessary. And a return to free trade induced better harvests in the next few years.

[2] Of the 3,383,000 plows counted in a 1946 census, 2,121,000 were of the Roman type. In 1949, there were but 9,260 tractors throughout the country, and 4,500 of these dated from the civil war. Agriculture in Spain could count on one tractor for every 2,430 *hectares*, whereas in Western Germany, for example, the proportion was one tractor for every 14 *hectares*.

Nonetheless progress was made more slowly than in industry. The delay may be partly explained by the immobility of the agrarian structure. The surface of the newly irrigated and "colonized" lands in the Ebro region and in Badajoz province[3] is not extensive enough for the effect of these reforms to be felt throughout Spain. Agricultural development is further hindered by the continuance of certain of the factors which caused the drop in production between 1939 and 1951.

It is true that the regime has increased slightly the allotments to agriculture, and that the development of the chemicals industry makes up for the lack of fertilizers. But government allotments are still insufficient, equipment is still archaic, there is still not enough livestock. The monopolization of wholesale trade (especially in oranges) by certain cartels is not an incentive to production. Middlemen, reaping a fat profit—and thus causing prices to rise—leave the producer only a small return for his labor.

The harmful action of these private monopolies is underlined by that of the State. Rationing was abolished only to make way for taxes. Inflation, which continued until 1959, forced the government to tax essential articles at low prices in order to contain the rise. Cultivation of grains and leguminous plants became so unprofitable to the farmer that the potato was replaced by industrial plants.

Certain crops, new to Spain—cotton, tobacco, flax, sugar beets and sugar cane—made rapid progress after 1951. On the other hand, it was not until a few years ago that the great classic categories of Spanish agriculture—fruit trees, grapes, olive oil—climbed back to the prewar averages. Grain and potato production is still below the level of 1931-36.[4] As for wheat, the yearly average between 1956 and 1961 did not go

---

[3] The Badajoz plan provides for the irrigation of a total of 129,500 *hectares*. The work of catching and diverting the Guadiana waters is to take fourteen years (1952-66). According to statistics published in 1961, some 36,000 *hectares* had already been irrigated and parcelled out by December 31, 1960.

[4] The average annual production of potatoes, which rose to 46,478,000 *quintals* in 1931-35, did not surpass 27,556,000 between 1946 and 1950, 40,186,000 for 1951-55, and 43,606,000 for 1956-60.

beyond 42.5 million *quintals,* which figure is nearly one million less than the 1931-35 average. This drop in production is worsened by the fact that Spain now has 5,000,000 more mouths to feed than before the civil war. Thus, the average annual wheat production per capita today is only 150 kilograms as against 170 kilograms prior to the war.[5] But the decreased consumption of the most costly goods—meat and sugar—by comparison with pre-1936 figures, was to increase consumption of the cheaper food products—bread and potatoes. The gap of about 20 per cent which thereby is created between production and consumer needs, can be filled only by importation.

And in fact, in the five years following the signing of the Washington-Madrid pact, some forty-eight per cent of American aid, or $529,000,000, was devoted to the importation of foodstuffs and products for immediate consumption. In other words, nearly half of the funds granted for industrial development was absorbed by day-to-day food needs. Underproduction in agriculture in this way was an obstacle to the progress of industrial production.

Yet the first years of the application of the Hispano-American pact corresponded to a period of regular rainfall and normal yield. The very small harvest of 1961, on the other hand, brought famine and unemployment to certain provinces. In the vast Tierra de Campos region, extending from the borders of León and Castile to the north of the

[5]

WHEAT PRODUCTION

	Total production (annual average in *quintals*)	Production per capita (annual average in kilograms)
1931-35	43,637,000	170
1941-45	31,798,000	120
1946-50	33,989,000	120
1951-55	40,307,000	140
1956-61 (6 Years)	42,520,000	150

For the period 1931-35, we have taken the production figure as it appeared in all the statistics of the time and in the Statistical Yearbook of Spain up to and including 1955. Since then, the National Institute of Statistics has felt that it should "rectify," twenty years late, the 1931-35 figures. This trickery deceived the OEEC experts.

Douro valley, a region noted for its fertility, 318 villages were virtually ruined. In October of 1961, the government had to decree a moratorium on payment to the landowners of the region, and sizeable public works projects were undertaken, to give work to the unemployed. Throughout the country, food prices rose considerably. Once again, this instance showed that Spain, with her defective agrarian distribution and archaic methods of cultivation, is at the mercy of a dry season.

3. THE FEAT OF THE N.I.I.

Although much less affected than was agriculture, nonetheless industry went through a crisis of underproduction between 1939 and 1951.

It was not until 1954 that metallurgy was able to reach its 1929 level. The extraction of iron and metals was on the decline, and in consumer goods industries, the 1950 production level was clearly below that of the prewar period. The hardest hit was the textile industry, foremost in the nation by virtue of the number of workers it employs: over 300,000, including nearly 225,000 in Cataloña alone. The drop in textile production was occasioned by worn-out equipment, restrictions on electricity, and the fact that imports of cotton had dropped from an average of 103,000 tons before the civil war to 38,000 in 1948.

Spanish industry also lacked outlets. Since the regime was internationally ostracized, foreign markets were closed to Spanish products; at the same time the home market was very limited, resulting from fixed salaries and a lowered standard of living.

Sales were further discouraged by high prices. Although wages and direct taxes were very low, manufacturing prices were necessarily high, because production was scattered, equipment worn, and because the regime burdened industry with indirect taxes. The State forbade layoffs; for example, at certain times the factories in Barcelona operated only eight hours a week because of power cuts—yet they were forced to pay wages to their workers for a normal forty-hour week. When genuine activity was lacking, the State maintained the appearance of full activity, at the employers' expense, in order to economize on unemployment benefits.

Because of the bureaucratic control of private enterprise, all sorts of extortion occurred. The autonomous offices created on Falangist initiative held a monopoly on currencies, on the granting of import licenses, on the distribution of raw material "coupons." A factory could not expand or open a new workshop without permission from the National Institute of Industry. The bribe was the clinching argument which allowed industrialists to speed up formalities and obtain the necessary permission. The I.E.M.E. (Spanish Institute of Foreign Currency), by its "systems of multiple exchanges," exacted a veritable tribute from private enterprise. This organism was free to fix exchange rates and was the only one empowered to handle foreign moneys; it placed a usurer's price on imports and pushed through exports at a scandalously low rate of exchange. In 1953, there was the case of a producer of canned goods who had to import a certain type of can; the I.E.M.E. paid the foreign suppliers of cans in dollars and billed the manufacturer for a sum calculated on a basis of 54.20 *pesetas* to the dollar. But the price of exported canned foods, received by the Office, was paid the producer on a scale of 27.37 *pesetas* to the dollar; hence, for every dollar of exchange, the government made a net profit of 26.83 *pesetas*—at the manufacturer's expense.

But beginning in 1951, American aid, the reopening of outside markets, and a rise in the standard of living fostered an industrial revival. If we are to appreciate the conditions under which the great industrialization effort of 1951-58 was carried out, we must take into account the role played by José Antonio Suanzes. A native of El Ferrol, like Franco, he was also the childhood friend of the *Caudillo*. In 1932, as a naval engineer, he became director of a large shipbuilding concern. When he offered his services to Franco at the outset of the civil war, he was warmly welcomed. Named Minister of Industry in 1938, he soon gave up this post and, in 1941, became director of the National Institute of Industry, which had been set up on his advice. After another stint in the Cabinet between 1945 and 1951, he left the government to give himself wholly to the N.I.I.

Suanzes' conservative background and Catholicism made him lean toward the classic right. But like the Falangists he felt that in an underdeveloped nation, improvement in basic areas—metallurgy and power—must take preference over the rise of transformational industries, and that only the State, with strict planning, could bring off this first step in industrialization.

The N.I.I.'s achievements under Suanzes' direction, between 1951 and 1958, were considerable. But if we look at the results in an international context, we can see that the "Francoist miracle" is far from comparable with the "German miracle." Let us take, for example, the brief and particularly active period, 1953-56: on the base of 100 in 1953, the index of Spanish industrial production rose to 129 in 1956. This increase is certainly superior to that in the great western nations which, before that period, had already reached a high standard of living and production; their index of industrial development wavered between 107 (U.S.A.) and 114 (Sweden). But in those countries which, like Spain, had been under-industrialized until then or seriously hurt by the war, the index wavered between the minimum of 133 (France) and the maxima of 139 (Western Germany), 142 (Japan), and 145 (Yugoslavia). Considered to be in the reconstruction category, the Francoist economy may be ranked according to its results roughly halfway between the leisure economies and the reconstruction economies.

The greatest effort had been put forth in the field of electricity (hydraulic and thermal), which rose from the annual average of 2,936,000,000 kilowatt hours (index: 100) for 1931-36 to 13,663,000,000 kwh. in 1956 (index: 465). But the other western nations had advanced still more rapidly, and the gap between their electricity output and that of Spain had widened. Indeed, Spain's yearly per capita electricity output had been equivalent, in 1944, to thirty-two per cent of the English output; in 1956, it was equal only to twenty-seven per cent of the English per capita average.[6]

Spanish steel production per capita in 1954 was far below the 1929 figures: 38.2 kg. as against 43.77, and the 1929 level was not reached again until 1957.[7] In the other key-sectors which received N.I.I. funds—cement, pig-iron, chemicals—the progress achieved has slightly, but never substantially, narrowed the gap between Spain and western Europe.[8]

Further, it was only to the detriment of other areas of national production that this progress was made. Throughout the mining industries, except in coal and potassium salts, the terribly low figures of 1939-51 have risen very slowly.

The production of consumer goods industries had been systematically restricted in order to turn over all available resources to the basic industries. In 1954, for instance, the textile production index was below the 1929-31 average (96 instead of 100); having climbed to 106 in 1957, it sagged again in 1958.[9]

While N.I.I. funds were reserved exclusively for new large-scale enterprises, the equipment of the old factories had been completely neglected. Seventy-three per cent[10] of this equipment dated from before 1931; hence, it was so wanting as to be

---

[6] Average electric output in per capita kwh.: Spain—1944: 146; 1956: 467. West Germany—1944: 340; 1956: 1,659. England—1944: 455; 1956: 1,701.
[7] From 1953 to 1956, the per capita steel production had risen as follows: Spain: 35.4 per cent (31.3 kg. to 42.4). England: 16.5 per cent (351.7 kg. to 409.8). France: 31.9 per cent (233 kg. to 307.4). West Germany: 44.8 per cent (314.7 kg. to 456). Italy: 66.2 per cent (73.7 kg. to 122.5). At this rate, it would take Spain eighty years to catch up with England.
[8] For the 1953-56 period, rise in per capita production:

Cement:	Spain:	39 per cent (96.9 to 135)	Pig-iron:	14 per cent (28-32)
(in kg.)	England:	13 per cent (224-253)	(in kg.)	16 per cent (224-260)
	France:	24 per cent (210-261)		27 per cent (204-262)
	W. Ger:	24 per cent (314-387)		46 per cent (239-348)
	Italy:	42 per cent (165-235)		46 per cent (28-41)

[9] The production of cotton goods is rising, but only insofar as these cheap fabrics replace the more costly wool and silk fabrics.
[10] According to a report drawn up in 1958 by the Economic and Social Council, forty-five per cent of Spain's industrial plants dated from before 1920; twenty-eight per cent had been installed between 1920 and 1931; and only twenty-seven per cent had been equipped since 1931.

largely responsible for the low yield of most transformational industries.

Except for certain frequented touristic routes, the system of roadways had not been repaired nor even kept up since the civil war. Similarly, the dilapidated state of the railways (R.E.N.F.E.)—the obsolescence of tracks and rolling stock, the lack of cars or their comfortless and overcrowded condition, the slowness, the inaccuracy of arrival and departure times—had become common themes in every Spaniard's jokes and complaints. The number of accidents rose, and it appeared likely that the whole railroad system would become paralyzed. Sixty-five per cent of the merchant marine consisted of vessels of retirement age—twenty-five years, and there were even ships known to be a century old.

The precipitousness of industrialization sheds some light upon the gap between the results obtained and the sacrifices forced upon the nation. The program of economic development was put into action in eight years, with the aim of making up for the delay caused by civil war destruction and by a dozen years of incompetence.

Furthermore, the costs of industrialization were increased by corruption in N.I.I. agencies and by misconceptions. Hence the desire to hamper the development of Basque and Cataloñan industry led the government to build several dams —not in the rainy Pyrenees regions but, rather, in the center (Douro basin) and on the southeast coast. Since there was little rainfall in these regions, production was lower than forecast, while the distance between the dams and the industrial areas required transfers of current which entailed heavy losses, as the transmission cables wore out. In this way, Cataloñan industry was paralyzed every winter—again in February, 1958—by power cuts, while unused energy accumulated in other regions.

The "giantism" complex is another source of waste. Its most perfect expression is found at Aviles. In this Asturian village, the government had decided to build the largest metallurgical plant in the world, and installed the most modern and expensive machines from the United States, England, France, Germany. Seven years' work, several thousands of workers housed in makeshift quarters, the expenditure of $350,000,000: this, in 1956, was what the Aviles builders had to show. Of the four blast furnaces scheduled to be created, only one was operational. In 1958—the first year of activity in the Aviles metallurgical complex—production reached 70,000 tons: according to the initial plan, the factory should have produced some 4,000,000 tons by that time.

Political pressure or bribes often led the N.I.I. to award public works contracts to firms that had swelled their estimates scandalously. Everyone in the government wanted to own a firm or sit on one or several of the executive boards. Unprofitable businesses were born: airplane factories were erected at great cost and had to close down after producing perhaps twenty machines incapable of flying; automobile plants put out such expensive trucks—at 800,000 *pesetas*— that it was impossible to dispose of them on the market. The State was driven to forcing cities to buy up the chassis for use in garbage collecting.

Many and various factors—drawn-out delays, poor quality supplies, technical errors, accidents, unusable products— tended to raise the manufacturing price, put off the moment of amortization, and eat into returns. Every ton of output cost the Spanish community dear.

The structure of industry also played a role in limiting production and keeping manufacturing prices high. Formerly, Spanish industry had been very decentralized; but in 1950, a trend began toward concentration. The change occurred under very particular conditions; the State and the large banks were the moving forces. Through the N.I.I. the State controls a great number of firms running the gamut of types of production. Some of these companies, like the *Empresa Nacional Siderúrgica*, are immediately dependent on the N.I.I.; others are mixed enterprises, financed both by the State and by private capital, as in the case of the powerful chemicals company, *Sociedad Ibérica del Nitrogeno*.

For their part, the six great banks—Central Bank, Spanish Credit Bank, Hispano-American Bank, Bank of Bilbao, Bank of Vizcaya, and Urquijo Bank—dominate a vast sector of economic life. Shares in the Bilbao Blast Furnaces are in the hands of the Banks of Vizcaya and of Bilbao. The latter also holds a controlling interest in the *Iberduero* hydro-electric company and manages naval shipyards, coal mines, and chemicals industries, as well as a veritable paper cartel: *Papelera Española*. The Hispano-American Bank (which has the largest annual turnover—more than 2,000,000,000 *pesetas*) has a hand in smaller banks and in insurance companies (*Estrella*). The Spanish Credit Bank has a part interest in cement production, while the Central Bank prefers to invest in electrical and metallurgical firms (*Cia Minerosiderúrgica de Ponferrada*).

Because of the State's and banking groups' financial investments in a number of varied firms, the concentration of capital and of economic power goes far beyond the size of the firm. And even in the major industries, the extreme concentration of capital goes along with a relative decentralization of production.

The concentration of capital is still further underlined by several circumstances, primarily, the rarity of the small personal savings account. For all of the capital which keeps production going comes from a privileged minority, with a monopoly both on capital and on higher education. The same personalities appear on every board of directors—politicians and generals, important landowners, bankers, technocrats. Obviously, those who sit on these boards of directors have no reason to place any one of the various businesses they govern in opposition to any of the others. And elsewhere, certain companies neither financially nor administratively related one to another have reached agreements among themselves. These ties and pacts hamper competition and enable the firms which do share the market to keep consumer prices artificially high.

Now, such prices deprive the large company of its principal advantage in the struggle with the average or small business. But it is not in the interest of the large firms, dominating a considerable slice of the market, and endowed with a generous profit margin, to lower their prices abruptly and close out the small businesses which do them no harm. So the N.I.I.-nurtured big businesses and the banks coexist with a horde of little family or handwork enterprises. In the electrical industry in 1961, for instance, there were some 3,000 firms dealing in a total production of 20,775,000,000 kwh.; of these only 25 large private companies and the installations directly dependent upon the N.I.I. create 89 per cent of the energy used in Spain. In the automobile industry, the same decentralization is to be found. In 1957, 12 firms with 9,390 workers, had a total output of 30,385 vehicles. Such scattered production is reflected in the number of makes and of kinds of spare parts. In 1960, production had risen to 56,000 vehicles—the output of 16 factories, each making an average of 11 cars per workday; but most of the cars licensed in Spain are made by the three or four big concerns (especially Pegaso and S.E.A.T.). Nonetheless, since these firms insist on excessive profit margins and since automobiles bring exorbitant prices in Spain, the little shops are able to go on producing a car a day, under anti-economic conditions. Paradoxically, the super-concentration of capital guarantees the day-to-day survival of the isolated small business.

In 1959, the government announced that steps were to be taken against monopolies. "The law of banking organization," passed in February, 1962, makes a timid effort to crack down on the first of these monopolies, the bankers, by nationalizing the Bank of Spain while allowing it to examine other banks, and by restricting the right of private banks to buy industrial shares.

Thus, at the very moment of its attempted entry into the Common Market, Franco's government realized that the lowering of manufacturing prices and the struggle against foreign competition imply not only retooling, mergers, and the elimination of isolated businesses, but also the need to bust trusts and disperse hyperconcentrated capital.

4. RACKETEERS' PARADISE

Without any doubt, the black market is the most prosperous branch of the Spanish economy.

Until 1951, food shortages, rationing, poverty, economic planning kept the gates to fraud wide open. Farmers, required to turn over their harvest to a State-run bureau at a price which left profit out of the question, simply hid part of their grain. In other cases, the grain duly collected by the State office was redistributed to pseudo-official agencies—bursaries, military commissariats—which proceeded to resell it in the black market. Sometimes these redistributions never took place and the agents of the State office saw to it that the grain was sold clandestinely to certain millers. In this way thousands of *quintals* were stolen every year from rationing provisions, and were to be rediscovered in restaurants—in the form of white bread sold *de estraperlo*[11] at fifteen or eighteen *pesetas* the kilogram, or about three fourths of a worker's daily wages at the time.

All goods of prime importance were priced both at an official rate and another, parallel; that is, a taxable price and a black market price. From the farmer's silo to the consumer's table, the route was long and devious, making detours through a number of middlemen. These maneuvers required official collaboration and the participation of manual labor; countless persons became involved in the black market: the big racketeers and the little sharpies, the police inspectors paid for holding their tongues, truckers, workers in clandestine mills. And each middleman took his slice, which is why olive oil at Jaén, where it was produced, cost six *pesetas* the quart but was sold at thirty-five and forty *pesetas* in the large northern cities. A considerable minority of the population battened on the impoverished majority.

There was further opportunity for corruption in the distribution of imported raw materials by the autonomous agencies. Racketeers created nonexistent businesses, for the

[11] *Estraperlo:* black market.

sake of obtaining raw materials which they then resold *de estraperlo*.

Thus was born a sort of feudal multi-level hierarchy in the black market. Parasites in Falangist jobs adept in the illicit sale of import licenses, large-scale racketeers and venal policemen, heads of nonexistent companies and fraudulent shopkeepers—in short everyone who throve on shady deals feared above all that a new regime would come to power and look into the sources of wealth. Thus, the regime's staunchest supporters were to be found among such racketeers.

In 1951, rationing was lifted and free trade was partially restored: these moves spelled the collapse of the black market in comestibles. Fraud, expelled from dealings higher up, moved in with the shopkeepers in the form of "under the counter" sales. Only inferior goods were sold at legitimate prices: customers who wanted something better had to pay the shopkeeper a percentage. Today, however, this practice is tending to disappear.

The black market is no longer a one-man operation. As the field of action open to fraud grew narrower, fraud took on more complex forms. The countless little manipulators have given way to a few teams of "technicians" to whom industrial prosperity and N.I.I. operations have opened the vista of "big deals." Public works contracts awarded on the strength of bribes, stepped-up estimates, low-grade materials sold at top quality prices—were the means which launched the sharks who loitered about the N.I.I. in eight years of soaring prosperity. But in 1959 imports were partially "liberalized" and the powers of the Falangist agencies restricted; the bureaucrats were thereby cut off from most of the means they had used to pressure others into paying tribute to private enterprise. The recession which followed the stabilization plan and the cut in funds allotted to the N.I.I. have been fatal to many racketeers. And the government, moved by the "purity" of the *Opus Dei* devout, is making an effort to combat administrative fraud, which has, however, left traces not easily eradicated in all branches of public office.

5. THE RISE OF INFLATION

Until the enactment of the stabilization plan in 1959, the Spanish economy was sapped by inflation, whose causes were underproduction and excessive public expenditures.

If the basic State budget were examined alone, expenses were seen to be lower, in real value, than those in the republican period. But income was still lower, for the classic right opposed any and all increases in income taxes as well as any really effective fiscal checkup. Double-dealing was the order of the day. Tributary pressure was less than before the war. Indirect taxes accounted for fifty-four per cent of the fiscal intake. This increase in indirect taxes accelerated the rise in prices, while it did not compensate for the diminished receipts from direct taxes. The economic imbalance in the basic budget forced the State to ask the Bank of Spain for advances and finally to issue new bonds.

Inflation was abetted by the autonomous agencies' spending. The State in fact concealed part of its expenses by assigning all of its investment costs to the budgets of such agencies, which proliferated in proportion to the greed of the Falangist *jerarcas*.[12] Their global budget in 1951 had risen to 8,100,000,000 *pesetas*. The expenses tabulated in the State's basic budget (21,400,000,000) represented no more than three fourths of the real total of administrative costs. Taking into account the 5,300,000,000 *pesetas* budgeted by regional and municipal governments, we see that public expenditures reached nearly 35,000,000,000.

In order to meet their excessive expenses, the authorities were obliged to borrow, to such an extent that the administration absorbed sixty-three per cent of the available capital.

---

[12] The government had created some singular and superfluous organisms. Let us note especially the "Institute of Ministerial Automobile Fleets" which in 1951 absorbed 99,000,000 *pesetas* (nearly $4,000,000), far more than the funds allotted to the Grain Institute (73,000,000 *pesetas*). The people of Madrid facetiously translated the agency's initials (P.M.M.) as *para mis mujeres*—for my wives.

And the State had recourse to practices which looked very much like forced loans.[13]

Fiduciary circulation, which rose every month, had already risen to 36,645,000,000 *pesetas* by December 31, 1952, as compared with 13,556,000,000 in 1939.[14] With rising inflation, the currency was deflated and prices swelled. Between 1936 and 1951, the cost of living index rose from 100 to 572.

Beginning in 1951, increased investments caused a spectacular rise in governing expenses. In the five-year period, 1951-56, the total of State, local, and autonomous agency expenses more than doubled, rising from 33 to 78 billion *pesetas*. Including indirect levies, overall administrative expenses in 1956 were equal to about twenty-six per cent of national income.

Fiscal receipts covered only seventy per cent of these expenses. The deficit was made up by American aid and by loans. In 1952, the issuance of government bonds covered nineteen per cent of administrative expenses; in 1956, twenty-five per cent. The national debt doubled between 1951 and 1959. And on December 31, 1956, the amount of money in circulation had reached 55,821,000,000 *pesetas* at the rate of that period, as against 36 billion in 1952.

The chronic commercial deficit encouraged currency depreciation. While food imports remained very high, the concentration of money in the hands of a privileged class stimulated luxury imports: whisky, cigarettes, automobiles, gasoline. Industrialization, for its part, caused a rapid increase in imports of equipment and machine-tools. The flow of foreign money into Spain, due to American aid [15] and the develop-

[13] The banks were asked to invest forty per cent of their capital in State bonds. And a decree issued in March, 1951, increased from thirty to sixty per cent the portion of Savings Deposits compulsorily invested in government bonds.

[14] These 36,000,000,000 represented 7,000,000,000 prewar, and in 1935 there were only 4,836,000,000 in circulation.

[15] Funds from the United States up to and including 1958-59 rose to $1,096,-000,000. This global figure, which does not include military allocations, may be broken down as follows: Aid as such: $407,000,000; loan from the Export-Import Bank: $138,000,000; funds for the purchase of agricultural produce: $392,000,000; value of food-gifts: $117,000,000; special funds for grain purchases: $20,000,000; development loan: $22,600,000.

ment of the tourist trade, did not suffice to offset the deficit in the balance of trade.

Capitalists, alarmed by the currency depreciation, were of course leery of investing their funds in Spain. Hence, a large part of the national income was channeled out of the country or into the underground market, in the form of purchases of gold or of foreign currencies. By withdrawing their capital from the Treasury and from productive investments, the wealthy aggravated the two root-causes of inflation: imbalance of public finances and underproduction.

This state of affairs could not continue. The State had to adopt a policy in accord with its means, or else acquire the means befitting its policy. The Falangists demanded that income tax be increased to finance industrialization. The classic right favored making economies. The government had to choose between industrial expansion on the one hand, and deflation on the other.

In March, 1957 pressure brought to bear on Franco by conservative elements forced him to withdraw the Falange from what control it still had of economic affairs. The naming as Minister of Commerce of the young professor Alberto Ullastres, member of *Opus Dei,* and the creation of various agencies of economic coordination dominated by representatives of capitalist interests, put economic responsibility in the hands of spokesmen for the classic right. No sooner had it come to power than the new ruling element hastened to slow down industrialization by cutting the funds earmarked for the N.I.I.

Treasury receipts were swelled by a new "general tax on money spent" (*i.e.,* on one's manner of living) and by increased indirect taxes. This rise in taxes on current consumer products entailed a further rise in prices.

But the State was forced to devote to hitherto neglected branches of the economy—railroads, merchant marine, agriculture, housing—sums equivalent to those formerly allotted to industrialization. And in most cases, political pressure prevented the layoffs which had been foreseen. Thus, expenditures continued to mount in 1957 and 1958. By virtue of greater receipts, the Treasury was able to include part of the expenses which formerly had burdened the autonomous agencies in its regular budget. But part of administrative costs was still financed by loans (22 per cent in 1957, 16.2 per cent in 1958, compared with 24 per cent in 1956).

The inexorable increase in fiduciary circulation pursued its course. Whereas some 55 billion *pesetas'* worth of bills were in circulation in December, 1956, at last count in 1958 there were 69 billion. Thus, in his report to the government early in 1959, Fernández Araoz, councillor to the Bank of Spain, confirmed that henceforth the *peseta* was worth only as much as the prewar five-*céntimo* piece called the *perrilla* (little she-dog).

The commercial deficit grew worse. A slight reduction in machine purchases had been more than outweighed by a drastic rise in motor-fuel purchases. The deficit for the year 1958 was the most sizeable that had yet been recorded in Spain: $386,000,000. Gold and currency reserves were being depleted.

Panic reigned among the property-owning classes. Great sums were sent out of the country, and this hastened the collapse of the *peseta*,[16] to such a point that in spring, 1959, the economic situation appeared desperate—and without further help from abroad, Spain would be unable to meet even her most pressing import obligations. American aid was not enough, and hopeful eyes turned toward Europe and the International Monetary Fund. But this hypothetical source of loans demanded that Spanish finances be placed on a sounder footing, and the European governments were ready to help Spain only insofar as the Iberian market would let in their exports. Further, the ties being created at that time among the European nations were a threat to Spanish imports. A

[16] The accidental arrest of a Swiss broker furnished Franco's police with the list of Spaniards who had money deposited in Switzerland. The Falangist press, determined to make this a weapon against the oligarchies, revealed the incident. Newspapers abroad estimated the Spanish money illegally deposited in Switzerland at $280,000,000. In June, 1959, money had become so scarce that banks were obliged to give black market interest of 4 per cent on short-term deposits, while the legal rate was 1.5 per cent.

lowering of customs barriers among the member nations of the European organizations, liberalizations of imports, credit possibilities granted by the European monetary agreement —all of these measures making for easier exchanges among the member nations of the O.E.E.C. could not help but exclude Spain from European markets, if she remained aloof.

The *Caudillo* gave way to necessity. In July, 1959, he resigned himself to effecting a radical reform in his economic policy. Admitted to the O.E.E.C., Spain received $418,000, 000 of new funds. The devalued *peseta* was freely convertible henceforth. The abolition of the system of multiple exchanges caused the majority of the State's indirect levies on production to disappear. Fifty per cent of imports were freed, whereas the O.E.E.C. had bound the member nations to "liberalize" ninety per cent of their imports. This external "liberalization" was accompanied by a corresponding internal "liberalization." Industrialists were dispensed from asking N.I.I. authorization for expansion into new shops or increasing production. Falangist economic planning had lost its last battle.

6. THE DILEMMA

The stabilization plan quickly restored the equilibrium of public finance and the trade balance. Tax increases and fewer investments allowed the State to limit bond issues. When the funds accorded by the banks to business were lessened, economic paralysis and unemployment followed; these in turn caused demand to drop. Lack of sales and limited credit forced business firms to throw their stock on the market. Prices dropped.

Elsewhere, the recession caused a spectacular decrease in imports; the industrial "pause" particularly hurt purchases of raw materials and machinery. The cancellation of import licenses and quotas had been counter-balanced by the adoption of new customs tariffs. The overall value of imported goods, having risen to $872,000,000 in 1958, fell to $721,000, 000 in 1960. Exports, on the other hand, were favored by a new and more realistic rate of exchange: between 1958 and 1960, the value of exports rose from $486,000,000 to $725,000,000. In 1958, the foreign trade balance was, for the first time, slightly in the black.

Investments by foreign capital—which, government leaders believed, should guarantee an economic revival—were less than expected. A July, 1959, Order in Council had annulled however a Falangist-inspired law which limited foreign participation to twenty-five per cent of the capital assets of Spanish firms: henceforth foreigners could own fifty per cent of the shares. The exportation of dividends was tolerated up to a maximum of six per cent. And those companies recognized by the Cabinet as being "in the national interest" might be authorized to receive foreign backing of more than fifty per cent and to export their entire profits. Many foreign capitalists nonetheless felt that this softening of measures formerly taken to prevent economic colonization of Spain was insufficient. Accordingly, such investments did not go higher than $36,000,000 in 1960 and $37,500,000 in 1961. This disappointment was more than compensated for in three ways: an advancing tourist industry brought in foreign currencies, emigrant Spaniards sent money back home, and Spanish capital abroad was repatriated. The balance of payments for 1960 showed an excess of $372,000,000. The currency reserve, in the process of being built up again, had already risen to $700,000,000 in July, 1961.

But these gains had been achieved at the cost of a serious recession. There were numerous bankruptcies as the result of sacrifice sales, plummeting prices, and cuts in the funds granted by banks to private concerns. In most industries, production indices showed a sharp drop in 1959 and rose only slightly the following year. This was the case especially in most consumer-goods industries (textiles, shoes, tobacco). And others, particularly the building industry, in the long run felt the repercussion of the deflationary measures.

The number of unemployed, on a rise beginning in the second quarter of 1959, increased in 1960 especially, as the building industry was crippled. While at the end of 1959 there were 90,000 registered unemployed, at the end of the following year there were 132,000. The increase is relatively small, and is only a partial reflection of the slowdown in activity, which was most apparent in the elimination of overtime work. Furthermore, many unemployed, who should normally have been among those registered, had gone abroad to seek work—particularly in West Germany—or were still being paid by their employers even though they were virtually idle. For the government, while permitting the textile factories to fire surplus personnel in 1959, had refused to extend this measure to all areas of production.

The government was sufficiently alarmed by the unlooked-for duration of the recession to step up its investments for 1961. Further, the capitalists were reassured by monetary stability. Brought back from abroad or taken out of hiding, capital was once again in circulation. Consequently, production indices began to rise at the end of 1960, although in certain sectors, the 1961 indices were lower than those for 1958. But the basic industries—electricity, cement, steel—made rapid progress.

Demand rose, as did the cost of government investments; these factors were immediately translated by a rise in the cost of living. Wholesale prices shot up in 1961 and winter 1961-62, and this development was reinforced by the disastrous harvest of 1961. Economic revival encouraged imports of raw material and machinery, while the bad harvest made the bottom drop out of exports. Whereas the trade balance had been favorable in 1960, in 1961 it again showed a deficit, of $250,000,000. The precarious equilibrium achieved by two recession years was cancelled by the slightest increase in government investments and a poor harvest.

Under such conditions, the Spanish economy has to meet the crucial challenge of adaptation to the European Common Market. Government leaders hoped to postpone the decision. For Ullastres and his colleagues could not but realize that the industrialists would put up a resistance, since they produced at non-competitive prices and had reason to fear that Spain's entry into the Common Market and a gradual lowering of customs barriers would cause Spain to be overrun by European manufactured goods.

But early in 1962, after the member nations of the Common Market reached an accord on agricultural policy, it was clear that if Spain remained aloof, she would see her agricultural produce increasingly shut out from the European markets, item by item. Should Spain refuse to be integrated and thereby sacrifice her agricultural exports, which account for over half of her total sales abroad ($385,000,000 in 1960, out of the overall sum of $725,000,000)? Or was it better to take down frontier barriers and sacrifice home industry in order to preserve the traditional outlets for agricultural produce?

The pressure brought to bear by landowners, exporters, and capitalists linked with foreign interests proved the strongest. "The citrus fruit panic" broke down the last resistance and caused Spain to rush toward the Common Market in 1962. Some weeks earlier, in December, 1961, when it was evident that this decision must inevitably be taken, Ullastres spoke before the members of the Barcelona Chamber of Commerce; his talk was intended to calm the fears of Catalonian industrialists. He explained that the lowering of customs barriers, hence the admission into Spain of foreign manufactured articles, would be done very slowly. "Short-term peace of mind," he promised them, but added, "long-term uneasiness."

A Development Plan has been worked out and is to become effective beginning in January, 1964. The most modest estimates place the initial sum needed for the first four years of its execution at $1,000,000,000. Eight years of industrialization have brought Spain to the verge of bankruptcy, yet have not enabled the country to close the gap between her level and that of Europe; and a precarious equilibrium could be bought only with two years of stagnation and poverty. How can Spain, in the next few years, carry out a far greater effort if she refuses the strongly progressive tax, quotas for sumptuary imports, and the mobilization of all of the country's resources toward the one goal of economic development? But how can such a neo-socialist policy be put into action by governments which are spokesmen for mighty conservative interests?

Industrial collapse in the near or more remote future, or structural reform: this is the dilemma by which Spain is boxed in today, and from which she may escape only by means of vast funds from abroad. Spain has received sizeable loans from the International Monetary Fund and from other governments. As of November, 1962, the percentage of foreign capital in the corporate assets of Spanish firms has been unlimited, and the same is now true of the percentage of their profits which may be exported. Consequently, the following January saw a tide of foreign capital—chiefly English and German—flow into Spain. But such aid implies the risk of placing Spanish industry under the yoke of foreign capital. Spanish producers may be allowed to evade the fatal competition of European industry only by a virtual abdication in favor of alien industry—born in Spain, an "extra-territorial" industry which would function for the sake of shareholders abroad.

Chapter Fourteen

❧

DAILY LIFE

THE CHIEF characteristics of present-day Spain are a low standard of working-class living, pauperization of the middle class, and exceptionally heavy peasant migrations.

It would seem that such social conditions would be conducive to revolution, but the Spanish masses are curiously indifferent to politics. Sports or spectacles of a violent nature absorb all of their attention, and soccer, the movies, bicycles are the new idols of this people who has lost its political faith.

1. WORKING-CLASS LIVING CONDITIONS

Living conditions among the urban proletariat have improved slowly under the two and a half decades of dictatorship but without, however, rising to their prewar level.

The scanty harvest which came in the wake of the civil war brought on a famine, whose principal victims were the workers in the large urban centers. After 1945, agricultural output rose somewhat; but the rationing which had been instituted to cope with food shortages actually worsened labor's living conditions by stimulating the birth of the black market. Inflation was felt elsewhere in the rapidly rising cost of living. Statistics published early in 1951 expressed salary increases by the index 281 (based on the index of 100 for 1936), while the rise in the cost of living was expressed in the index 572.

Those articles the most severely affected by the price rise were the most basic ones: food products. The foodstuffs index reached 746.9 in the spring of 1951 while, as we have seen, the general price index was at 572. While the worker's pay had tripled, he paid out seven and a half times more for his food than he had in 1936. Rationing allowed a daily average of 554 calories per person, whereas the basic minimum for a worker is 2,500 to 3,000 calories. This meant that some 2,000 daily calories must be obtained from articles whose sale was unrestricted and which came from the black market. Workers could not manage to supply their families with the minimum daily food needs, and rachitic children, clothed in rags, roamed through the slums of Madrid and Barcelona. Fifty per cent of them in the capital had never gone to any school; and the municipal statistics bulletin of Madrid admitted, in its 1949 summary, that 71.68 per cent of the children in the capital city were tubercular.

The disturbances which broke out in the spring of 1951, under the stress of incessant privation, convinced the governing elements that henceforth they must purchase the resignation of the masses by underwriting their basic food needs. Increased agricultural production due to a relaxation of economic planning, mass imports financed by American aid, the abolition of rationing and shrinking of the black market— these caused food prices to drop and the workers' standard of living to rise. But it was not long before inflation and a new currency depreciation stimulated another rise in prices, so that at the end of 1955, the price index was 607.5, as against the 1951 figure of 572. This new increase had been countered however by the salary increases decreed in 1954. The period 1955-56 is consequently the sunniest the Spanish proletariat has known since 1936; after that brief interval, the very rapid rise in prices was compensated for only partially by the salary adjustments which the rebirth of social agitation, in spring and autumn of 1956, forced the government to make.[1]

The improvement in labor-class conditions during the industrialization era (1951-59) had lagged far behind the increase in national income.

In the 1955-56 period—the optimum interval in the life of a Spanish worker since the civil war—salary income accounted for only 42.8 per cent of national income whereas at the same moment, the ratio varied from 48 per cent in Italy, 59 per cent in France, 63.6 per cent in Germany, to 73.2 per cent in England.

This salary income is most unevenly distributed; the salaries of qualified workers—much sought after among new industries—rose much more quickly than did those of ordinary hands. If we refer once again to 1955-56, we see that the standard of living among miners and certain categories of highly qualified workers was almost equal, at the time, to that of 1936. But in other categories, the real value of salaries remained between 15 per cent and 35 per cent lower than before the war.[2]

Overtime work, being very well paid, creates considerable inequality between those salaried workers who have the opportunity to do some, and the others who can count on nothing but their salaries. During the era of concerted industrialization, almost all of the big firms gave their workers the chance to earn an hour or two a day of overtime pay. Many men worked ten or eleven hours, sometimes in two different factories. There were metallurgists who, upon leaving one factory at the end of the day, worked the night shift in a garage, managing thus to work a fourteen-hour day.

1 Daily wage of an ordinary laborer: in 1936, 8.25 *pesetas*; in the winter of 1958-59, 48.11 *pesetas* (including bonuses and allotments). The price of meat per kilogram had gone up ten times (60 *pesetas* in 1958-59, 6 in 1936); bread, 12 times (8 *pesetas*, as against .65 in 1936); potatoes, 18 times (3.65 *pesetas*, as against .20 in 1936).
2 Taking the 1936 standard of living as a basis (index 100), that of 1955 gives the following indices: agricultural day laborers: 61; metallurgists: 66; textile workers: 82; carpenters: 83; masons: 85.

Circumstances of family life and the number of dependents create other inequalities among workers. The young bachelor is of course in the best position in this regard, while the single woman, the old or sick person is particularly unfortunate because of the low pay scale for women's labor and gaps in the Social Security system. Young couples with small children are also badly off, since family allotments are wanting. During the relatively "good times" of spring, 1956, the ecclesiastical magazine, *Pax*, showed that the monthly wages of a married metallurgist with two children (that is, 1,273 *pesetas*, including bonuses and allotments)[3] was some 817 *pesetas* below the minimum required to purchase the essentials of living for this category of family (2,090 *pesetas*). The deficit could be made up only by working overtime hours: the father would have to work ten or eleven hours a day if his family, by spending eighty-five per cent of its income, could guarantee each member a quasi-normal daily ration of 2,700 calories.

Those in the most fortunate position are the families whose children are old enough to go out to work. Let us take an average case. The father is a semi-qualified worker—a master mason, for example; the daughter works in a factory, as a cleaning woman, or as a seamstress at home; the two sons work out an apprenticeship and receive only a small wage. The mother remains at home. These five or six persons are crowded into two or three dim, ill-furnished rooms. The rent is negligible. The mistress of the house sternly rations the amount of electric light, of oil and sugar. But the father goes out to the café every evening—by buying one cheap drink he has the right to linger for hours. Each of the sons has one threadbare suit and their mother wears herself out trying to piece and salvage it. Nonetheless every Sunday the young worker is impeccably dressed in clean suit, very white shirt, polished shoes, and his hair is elaborately slicked down. Once a week he goes to the movies, on Sundays to a soccer

---

3 It must be noted that *Pax*, as a clerical publication, was subject only to Church censure. The 1,273-*peseta* wage which this worker earned averaged out to 318 *pesetas* per person or, in relative worth, to about $5.20.

game. The young man who has already been working for several years manages to scrimp and save enough to make good the ultimate ambition of Spanish working-class youth: ownership of a bicycle or even a scooter, in which case, the young man, if he lives in Madrid, takes his *novia*[4] dancing on Sundays in the taverns on the banks of the Río Jarama.

The 20- or 25-year-old worker has vague recollections of hard times during the first decade of Franco's dictatorship. But when asked if he feels the pinch of hunger today, he shakes his head: *No, no, pasa hambre* (no, he is not hungry). He can eat all the bread he wants, all the potatoes and *garbanzos* (chick peas). Fortunate are the families that eat meat once a week: the traditional *cocido* (stew) appears on the Sunday table.

The diet of the masses remains low in nutritive value. Sugar, milk, meat, eggs are still considered semi-luxury items. In 1955-56, annual sugar consumption—while three times higher than in 1943 but twenty per cent lower than during the republican period—ranked after that in Greece, Egypt, and Pakistan. The Spaniard ate less meat than did the Greek.[5]

Living conditions among the working classes were seriously affected by the enactment of the stabilization plan. Spanish economists calculate that when overtime work was abolished between 1959-61, the proletarian's purchasing power dropped some twenty-five to thirty-five per cent.

[4] A vague term which can mean friend, girl friend, or fiancée.
[5] Annual per capita consumption in 1955

	Spain	Greece	India	Egypt	Pakistan	Italy	France	England
Sugar (Kg.)	9.4	11	14	14	15	17	28	50
Milk (L.*)	86	86	—	—	—	106	160	205
Meat (Kg.)	17.47	18	—	—	—	20	78	67
Calories per day	2,330	2,590	—	2,560	—	2,595	2,930	3,330

* L. = Litre = 1.06 quarts.
Increase over Spanish consumption prior to 1951:
Sugar: 9.4 kg. in 1955 as against 4.51 kg. in 1941 and 3.44 in 1943.
Decrease as compared with pre-1936 period:
Sugar: 9.4 kg. in 1955 as against 11.02 in 1929 and 11.50 in 1933.
Meat: 17.47 kg. in 1955 as against 28.40 in 1933 and 29.74 in 1835.

(Report by Miguel Sánchez Mazas on the nourishment of the Spanish people.)

The circumstances in which the industrial revival was carried out in 1951 discriminated still further among the workers. While the recession continues in certain branches of industry, other factories, benefiting from government funds and bank loans, work at full capacity. The inequalities thus created within the proletariat are further emphasized by collective labor contracts; they became more common after 1958, particularly in 1959, but certain professional categories are still deprived of them.

The Minister of Commerce, Ullastres, has estimated that in the year which followed the strikes (May-June, 1962–May-June, 1963), the overall pay of salaried workers rose by 30 per cent compared with the 1961-1962 figures. But the rise was cancelled partly by an accompanying rise in prices, which dated from 1961. Retail prices in the first half of 1963 rose 6 per cent.

Despite collective labor contracts and salary raises, the Spanish worker's standard of living is still far lower than that of workers in other western European nations;[6] a moderately qualified worker, for instance, who is married and has one or two children, earns roughly 3,000 *pesetas* ($50.00) a month. Government spokesmen have admitted again and again that Spain, on joining the Common Market, would be obliged to shore up salaries and Social Security benefits. But they did not explain how an industry which, despite the minimal extent of its social obligations, has not managed to catch up with Europe in the past decade, will abruptly be able to bear further welfare burdens and achieve simultaneously in an incredibly short time, the enormous goal of modernization which will be incumbent upon it in view of Spain's entry into the Common Market.

[6] The Geneva office of Información-Española-UGT has drawn up this table comparing the amount of time a mechanic in Spain, in England, and in France must work in order to purchase certain goods.

	1 kg. bread	1 kg. meat	1 kg. potatoes
Spain	35 min.	5 hr. 54 min.	15 min.
Great Britain	12 min.	1 hr. 46 min.	9 min.
France	11 min.	3 hr. 05 min.	4 min.

2. THE TWO BOURGEOISIES

The economic conditions which have created a relatively privileged proletariat and a sub-proletariat have also widened the distance between the ways of living of the wealthy bourgeoisie and of the middle class.

The difference is less noticeable in the little towns of "intermediary Spain" and in the cities of 10,000 to 100,000 inhabitants than in the large urban centers, for they have a virtual monopoly on the increased yield of the national income. Further, the small-city bourgeoisie has little chance to speculate and amass sizeable sums.

The small-city middle class, for its part, has not grown appreciably poorer. This class has, in fact, always lived in more or less straitened circumstances. Not only are their salaries small but also they almost never have an opportunity to take on supplementary work. The percentage of active population has never been very high; today it averages about thirty-five per cent, thanks to the idleness of a part of this bourgeoisie. The head of the family is compelled therefore to support an abnormal number of dependents. A married woman simply does not work—the very idea is scandalous; unmarried girls seldom take jobs. Furthermore, a certain number of rustic petits bourgeois feel it their duty to live "nobly," in idleness, even though their meagre income melted away during the inflationary rise. And the social decorum of even the most modestly-situated families requires the presence of a servant.

Such heavy expenses force serious privation on families with such scanty budgets. But the soil is close at hand, the cost of living is low, there is no genuine black market, and so the small-town middle class has almost always managed to procure its basic food needs.

In short, the upper middle class is a little richer and the lower middle class a little poorer; but each one "knows his station." Stagnant social concepts are reflected in manners and morals, carried over from the last century. The women, being idle, are punctilious about their religious duties and their activities in the local priest's charitable works. There are but two amusements: gossip and the movies. Even so, the unmarried girl cannot go to a movie theatre unless accompanied by at least one other woman. When a girl has gone out once with a young man, she is considered either engaged or compromised. The man's day-to-day life follows the relaxed time-honored rhythm. Business is transacted in the morning or late in the afternoon, after the *siesta*. The cocktail hour brings together the local small-time industrialist, the mayor, the notary public, the lieutenant of the *Guardia Civil* at a table in the central café.

But in the great urban centers, the post-civil war years were marked by a profound change in social structure. A new class appeared, whose members waxed fat on fraud. Shady speculators lived as showily as bankers. The traditional upper middle class was the element which profited most from the industrial expansion of 1951-58. The industrial accords, the cartels set up at that time, guarantee the large firms exaggerated profit margins. A Bank of Vizcaya[7] study shows that in 1960, despite the recession, some 228 important companies, with total assets of 72,800,000,000 *pesetas,* made some 15,265,000,000 *pesetas'* profit; in other words, a 20.9 per cent return monopolized by a privileged minority. For in the absence of small savings accounts, a restricted group of bankers, big capitalists, and landowners, shares corporate stocks and seats on the Boards of Directors. Their ubiquity, born of the concentration of capital, makes the great fortunes grow still greater by geometric progression.

The upper class—whether brash *parvenus* or moneyed names of long standing—often travels abroad, mingles with American diplomats in Madrid, apes the foreign tourists at Torremolinos, in the Baleares, on the beaches of the Costa Brava. Hence the taste for the American or Italian cars, the downing of whisky after whisky, the English phrases which lard their conversation; the women go in for the latest Paris fashion, the most flagrant make-up, hang about the cafés,

7 Cited by *Tribuna Socialista,* January-March, 1962, number 4.

smoke American cigarettes, and make a great show of airy indifference, for fear of seeming *cursis*[8] to their foreign friends.

Much less influenced by exotic ways, the lower middle class and the middle class in the big cities were severely shaken when the *peseta* dropped and their little incomes were depreciated. Salaries lagged far behind the rise in prices. During the black market period, a man with a family, a retired person or a single woman could get enough to eat only by selling furniture, renting out rooms, pawning jewelry. When the trade in food products was normalized and when, some years later, inflation was arrested, middle-class living conditions improved. But even now, a man must have a second job if his family is to live in relative comfort. So in the evening the bank clerk goes over the accounts of some firm, the high-school teacher gives lessons and corrects papers in a private school.

Outside work and the American-style workday[9]—adopted three years ago by civil servants, office workers, and salesmen —have upset their whole way of life. In the beginning, there were strong protests against the new schedules. Employees of the Bank of Barcelona for several weeks picnicked in the street and scattered greasy wrappings on the sidewalk to point out how little time they were allotted for lunch. Gradually the new ways became new habits and the leisurely pleasures of the old days—long *siestas*, a long chat in a café—have become mere memories.

Small industrialists and businessmen have been hard hit since 1959 by the recession, by increased taxes, sacrifice sales, and restricted bank loans—all of which affected only small companies. They are still in a precarious position and the very existence of this class is threatened by Spain's joining the European economic community and the consequent competition from foreign manufactured articles.

These problems notwithstanding, the bureaucrat and the small manufacturer in the big city try to live up to what their

---

[8] *Cursis*: ridiculous.
[9] As opposed to the traditional Spanish day, with time out for a prolonged lunch and a *siesta*.

standing makes incumbent upon them. Their wives are forbidden any sort of employment, their sons—if it is at all possible—are put through college. With these expenses to meet, the lower-middle-class Spaniard is rarely able to reach his two essential goals: a television set and a second-hand car. Today in Spain there are only ten automobiles for every thousand inhabitants.[10]

The Spanish lower middle class feels bitter and frustrated, but looks upon Franco's dictatorship as the least of possible evils. The history of the last hundred-fifty years shows nonetheless that the middle class is not equipped with unlimited patience. The lower middle class—one moment favoring the left, the next favoring the party of special interests—is the beam in the balance scale and as such was at the source of two typically Spanish phenomena in the nineteenth and early twentieth centuries: abrupt reversals of the parliamentary majority and contradictory *pronunciamientos*. If tomorrow big industry and foreign competition should wipe out the small businessman, then the lower middle class, shifting suddenly toward a new liberalism, could once again create such circumstances as were at the root of all *pronunciamientos*.

3. THE GREAT MIGRATIONS

For two decades now, the large-scale migrations typical of twentieth-century Spain have taken a serious turn. Spokesmen for the present regime blame this on an abnormal demographic growth. The population is in fact increasing by 350,-000 a year, or 12 for every thousand inhabitants. This figure places Spain in the western European group, wherein demographic growth is the least noticeable. And at that, Spain is not in first place in this group: that rank must go to Holland, whose population annually increases by 13 or 14 per thousand inhabitants.

Moreover, it would seem that even this moderate degree

10 The corresponding ratios are: France: 111 cars for every 1000 inhabitants; England: 88 per 1000; United States: 382 per 1000.

of growth should drop in the years to come since its cause is not so much an increased birth rate as lowered mortality rate. The Spanish birth rate at the start of this century had risen to 35 per 1,000; it has recently gone down to 20 per 1,000. In the early twentieth century, Spain was comparable to the high-birth-rate countries of Asia and Latin America; she is now on the level of the low-birth-rate countries of western Europe, between France (18.8 per 1,000) and the Netherlands (21.6 per 1,000). The decrease is explained particularly by the exodus from country to city—where young peasant couples quickly shed their traditional beliefs—and by the fact that people marry older and after abnormally long engagements—a situation most apparent in the large cities and attributable to the housing shortage.

Although the Spanish population has increased by some 12,000,000 since the start of the century, the present total of newborn infants is 60,000 lower than the annual yearly figure of the 1901-05 period. But every year there are 200,000 fewer deaths to record than there were 60 years ago. In Spain, as in every other country in the world, the mortality rate—and especially the infant-mortality rate—has decreased continually since 1900. Even so, the decrease is less marked in Spain than in most other western European nations.

The fact that Spain's demographic evolution has changed its trend relatively recently—thirty or forty years ago—implies some exact and formidable facts for the future. The Spain of 1920-30 was characterized by a high birth rate, a high death rate, and a short life expectancy, all of which still make themselves felt today. Most of the adults of that period are gone, their disappearance hastened by war, famine, repression, emigration. On the other hand, the children born during that time are now about 30 or 40 years old. It follows that Spain now has few old people and many young adults, and that the death rate is low. The singular thing is that the birth rate is also low, given so high a proportion of young men and young women.

This young and abundant population, which reproduces relatively little, is growing old; in fifteen or twenty years, when it will have reached the age of sterility and death, it will be replaced by the skeletal post-civil war generations: the population will begin to decline. Demographers estimate that the population figure will reach its maximum of 35,000,000 between 1975 and 1980 and will diminish thereafter—unless the present tendencies undergo radical change.

The post-civil war birth rate, low though it was, did not affect the labor market until 1950-55. For the young people who had previously taken places in active life were born during the years of the high birth rate, before 1936. The adolescents who came of age to work after 1950, on the other hand, and particularly after 1955, belong to the skeletal civil war and immediately postwar generations. The swelling exodus to the city—far more evident today than before 1950—and the new current of emigration abroad which began at mid-century, therefore and without the shadow of a doubt, expose the two veritable causes of this massive population transfer: the static agrarian system and industry's inability to absorb the excess rural birth rate.

The phenomenon of migration begins in the rural areas and most of all in the regions of the *latifundio*: Andalusia, Extremadura, Murcia. The overall surface occupied by the great plantations has not changed since 1936. Cattle raising and extensive cultivation, the two ways of working the large holdings, require only a minimum number of hands; at the same time, the birth rate continues to be very high among the southern peasantry. Every day the gap grows wider between labor supply and demand, between the openings for workers and the number of applicants. Full employment is reached only at harvest time. A large portion of the rural proletariat therefore is doomed to seasonal unemployment, to an extent which varies from one region to another. The Governor of Badajoz, in a declaration made in the summer of 1951, admitted that in this province alone there were 100,000 unemployed tillers of the soil—"which leaves us to deduce," he continued, "the enormous figure of 450,000 persons who cannot be sure of obtaining their daily bread." In view of this disquieting situation, Franco's government de-

cided to carry out the "Badajoz plan." The irrigation work is
to be completed within a fourteen-year span (1952-66). At
the end of 1960, eighth year of construction, 3,347 day-
laborers had already been settled on the irrigated land. The
total number of peasants who will have benefited from the
irrigation work is forecast at 9,000. At this rate, it would take
a century and a half to resettle the 100,000 seasonally unemployed of Badajoz.

How do they manage to live all year long on what they
earn during the brief weeks of work? The *Revista Socialista*[11]
published, in July, 1961, the answers made by a certain
number of emigrants, one-time peasants. One of them, from
a village in the Badajoz region, declared that he was one of
four children and that he had begun to work at the age of
ten. Both parents and children went into the woods to
gather firewood and acorns which they sold to villagers who
were better off. The mother also gathered medicinal herbs
for the druggist. "With what we earned all together," this
emigrant declared, "we still could not buy bread, nor rice,
nor oil. Every other evening we went to bed without dinner.
When we ate, it was always the same things: boiled grasses,
which bloat but do not nourish you, olives, acorns, beans
and from time to time—a real feast—boiled potatoes, without oil."

Such living conditions led to two types of emigration,
the first of which were seasonal migrations. During the
slack season, the young people look for work elsewhere, going
on foot, sleeping on the ground, bartering work for a meal.
When they tire of this vagabond life, many young people
decide to leave their home towns once and for all. Migratory
workers aim for the rich agricultural provinces of the Mediterranean coast. It used to be true that Valencia received
emigrants from Badajoz, Andalusia and Murcia; but in 1956,
Valencians themselves began to migrate, a fact which was
first imputed to the frost, which wiped out the orange trees.
But emigration from Valencia continued and was intensified

[11] This periodical is published in Paris. The article in question was entitled,
"Reports by Emigrated Workers."

in the years that followed, for a normal demographic growth coupled with immigration had brought the labor force to such numbers that for the first time it exceeded the demand for labor. Today Cataloña, alone among the agricultural areas, can still absorb some emigrants; but emigration from Valencia took on such proportions that the municipality of Barcelona was forced to place *Guardia Civil* in the railroad stations to turn back the hopeful.

For the most part the migratory current moves toward the big cities. Since the civil war, the population of Barcelona has climbed by 500,000. That of Madrid rose from 953,000 in 1936 to 2,378,934 on January 1, 1963. Between 1950 and 1963, the capital gained 760,434 inhabitants. In 1962, 28,758 of the 73,000 new residents were emigrants from the provinces of Cuenca and Guadalajara, from Toledo and other agricultural areas. An average of 2,200 emigrant farm laborers settled in the capital every month during 1962.[12]

This incoming population tide confronts the bigger cities with a housing problem aggravated by the notorious insufficiency of State funds earmarked for its solution. Between 1951-58, the yearly average of housing units constructed reached only 26,531, whereas the minimum needs were estimated at 70,000. The cumulative deficit at the end of 1957 therefore stood at 1,067,452. To catch up with this delay in twenty years, all the while taking care of the additional day-to-day needs of newly married couples and the rate of demographic growth, it would have been necessary to build 200,000 housing units each year. But in 1958 only 115,000 were finished. Thereafter the construction rate sagged for two years and did not pick up until 1961, when some 125,000 housing units were made available. In the four-year period, 1958-61, therefore, the initial deficit had risen by an annual average of 100,000.[13] Since private capital is invested in luxury or medium-price housing and since the law—which

[12] If the exodus continues at the rate of the past decade and a half, it is estimated that Spain's population which, in 1900, was 51 per cent rural and 49 per cent urban will, in the year 2000, be only 20 per cent rural and 80 per cent urban.

[13] All of these figures are taken from official statistics. The situation was serious

places ceilings on old rents—tolerates almost unlimited rent increases in new buildings, the needy classes remain the chief victims of the housing shortage. Immigrants from the country camp on the outskirts of the big cities in wood or corrugated iron shacks, in tents or caves. In an article published on September 22, 1952, *Pueblo*, the Falangist unions' newspaper, revealed that in "the belt of filth and poverty" which rings Madrid, some 11,000 caves had been adopted as shelter by "immigrant" families. A document published in 1958 by the Bishopric of Barcelona estimated that 300,000 people were living in such shacks, that most of these measured only a very few yards square, and that some of them housed up to ten or a dozen persons spanning three generations.

Those whom the countryside cannot nourish and the city cannot employ are driven to expatriate themselves. During the first decade of Franco's regime, emigration was out of the question, since diplomatic relations with other countries had been broken off. Beginning in 1949, however, the yearly average number of emigrants once again rose to a very high level, comparable with that at the start of the century. By 1959, some 585,000 persons had left for the Americas. Thereafter, emigration overseas tapered off because of the economic problems presently afflicting Latin America. But the tide of emigrants to Europe swelled very quickly.

Once the stabilization plan was adopted, unemployment increased and emigration to Europe became a veritable exodus. Spaniards became miners in Belgium, restaurant waiters in Switzerland or Holland, building workers and farm laborers in France, while Spanish women were hired as maids and cleaning women in French and English families. Between 1958 and 1960, an estimated 20,000 Spanish workers, on the average, settled in France; in the first three quarters of 1961, this number had already risen to 27,764. In the same year, 100,000 migratory workers entered France as farm hands in

---

enough to make the government announce, in December, 1961, the enforcement of a plan to construct 3,700,000 housing units in the next fifteen years.

the *Midi*. And at the end of December, 1961, there were some 600,000 Spaniards settled in France in one capacity or another.

Shamelessly, the Spanish government goes about regulating and encouraging the emigration of surplus labor. To this end a treaty was signed with West Germany in 1960, and, by the following June, 30,146 Spanish workers had already gone to Germany under contract. This number doubled by the end of 1961. Nearly all of the Spaniards settled in Germany are qualified workers.

This exodus of specialized labor, unique in the history of Spanish emigration, sprang from a momentary recession but strengthened a trend of emigration the permanence of which no one in Spain can any longer refuse to recognize. The Falangist newspaper *Arriba* stated, on April 1, 1961, that given the ratio between demographic growth and employment possibilities, Spain must "be drained of at least 80,000 to 100,000 individuals per year" [*sic*]. But the leaders of Franco's government realize that the European labor market will not be able to absorb Spanish workers indefinitely and that therefore in the years to come the large urban centers in Spain will be in danger of being overrun by a horde of unemployed peasants, a potential revolutionary force. Accordingly the Falangist leader, José Solis, urged, in a speech delivered at Alicante in 1961, that 2,500,000 new jobs be created. And the Convention of Falangist unions, which met in Madrid in March, 1962, declared itself strongly in favor of agrarian reform. The majority of conservative leaders realize that the peasant exodus can be held back only by the institution of agrarian reform. Franco, yielding to necessity, announced—in veiled terms—an agrarian law. Speaking on July 24, 1961, at Monte San Cristobal in Valladolid, he declared that "we will do all that is humanly possible to restore and to free the lands and the fields of Spain"; and in the next few weeks all of the newspapers harmonized on the theme of agrarian reform. But on August 2, 1960, the agricultural engineer, Font de Mara, stipulated in A.B.C. that agrarian reform is not necessarily a matter of parcelling out land. He urged landowners to work in association with farm labor. Further, to convince the *terratenientes* of the need to abandon their "paternalist protectionism," he declared that he counted upon "an authentic economic and Christian sense of cooperation." [14]

We could find no clearer affirmation that for present-day Spain, agrarian reform is of vital necessity and that a conservative government, supported by *terratenientes*, is not capable of carrying it out.

4. THE NEW IDOLS

The pre-revolutionary social conditions prevalent in Spain have not inspired a spirit of rebellion. To some extent we may account for this indifference by the policy of a regime which deliberately persists in depriving the masses, and even the middle-class Spaniard, of any and all means of information and judgment which would permit them to grasp the real state of affairs. The government has carried out a policy of "disintellectualization" in Spanish life. During the first decade of Franco's reign, public education was neglected; since then it has not been given the attention which has been turned on other branches of national activity. The funds allotted to education are absurdly insufficient and today, as yesterday, teachers are the least well paid of all civil servants. Things had come to such a pass by 1958 that 10,000 teachers resigned to take better-paying jobs elsewhere. Yet the following year the government appointed only 3,084 teachers, even though 12,820 new graduates had applied for jobs. Such a situation may well seem astonishing in a country where everyone deplores the lack of schoolmasters; but the lack of schools is even greater than the lack of teachers. The director of primary education declared, in 1959, that 25,000 schools

---

[14] On April 13, 1962, the *Cortés* approved three laws which, respectively, protected the sort of farming carried on as a family enterprise, compelled large landowners to work uncultivated lands in a normal way, and regulated land distribution in zones being irrigated.

would have to be built if all the population of school age (6 to 12 years) were to be enabled to receive schooling—at a rate of 40 pupils per class. And if nursery schools were to be set up for children aged 3 to 6 years and if the compulsory minimum school-leaving age were to be raised to 14, the State would have to erect 73,000 schools (since 56,000 are nonexistent and 17,000 on the verge of total dilapidation). The construction rate (which in the past few years has wavered between 3,000 and 5,000 schools yearly) cannot cancel out a deficit which with each passing year is made worse by demographic progression and increasing wear-and-tear on extant buildings. It is estimated that thirty per cent of children of school age simply do not go to school, that this figure is still higher in certain impoverished agricultural areas, and stands at fifty-seven per cent at Jaén (Andalusia).

The percentage of illiteracy is nonetheless relatively low, since it does not exceed ten per cent—thanks to the army, which remains the people's principal school. Drafted men are put through an ultra-rapid course which allows the army to strike them from the list of illiterates. Most of these men, even though they have learned to spell correctly, cannot really read fluently.

In secondary schools and universities, research gives way to dogma. Intellectual curiosity is systematically stifled. Students are made to learn a certain number of notions by heart and thus to acquire a diploma and take up a more or less lucrative career. Censorship discourages the reading of newspapers, magazines, and serious books since their potential audience knows that there is no authentic information to be gleaned here. In all events, intellectual works only tire or bore most Spaniards of our day. Once they no longer have to worry about where their daily bread might come from, they look only for amusement, for escape from reality.

The present-day Spaniard reads little. Circulation figures for books and newspapers are exceptionally low, and preference for escape literature is evident. Between 1936 and 1951, the number of political, scientific, and literary publications fell from 1,365 to 562 per year; at the same time, sports and movie magazines have spawned rapidly. Novel- and theater-fans seek every form of distraction: in time, in space, in the unreal. Historical or folkloristic novels, love stories, murder mysteries, light comedy, or spectacular shows that are more or less *aflamencadas*—all of the fashionable *genres* are remarkable for their superficiality.

Official circles at last showed some concern about the dearth of literary output. In 1946, a chorus of complaints was heard, first in the magazines and the literary weeklies. Publishers, rich patrons, public and private institutions established a flurry of prizes, somewhat in the French manner, in an attempt to revive literary life; hence, the *Premio Nadal,* the *Premio Planeta, Premio Café-Gijón.* These awards had no influence on the appearance of a new generation of novelists, but they were instrumental in making some of them known. Thanks to the *Premio Nadal, El Jarama* by Sánchez Ferlosio, *Primera Memoria,* by Ana María Matute and other novels went into printings of 20,000 or even 25,000 copies—extraordinary for Spain. But for the most part, the new generation of novelists are strangers to the majority of readers. The public is considerably swayed however by foreign influences. The "Anglo-Saxon" novel is all the rage among the leisure classes, while young people of all social levels are ardent fans of a detective story magazine, *El Caso,* and of comic strips along the lines of those in the United States.

The movies arouse tremendous enthusiasm on every social level. The ex-farm laborers who have emigrated to Madrid and camp on the city's outskirts in tents or caves would not for the world miss going to the movies on Sunday. They demand that the show be a diversion in the true sense of the word; that is, something which diverts, distracts them from reality. And they want this moment of escape to last as long as possible; consequently shows may go on generously for four or five hours and include three or four films. The more removed from reality its subject, the more success a movie will have, and old westerns, historic melodramas, Spanish genre operettas, more or less dominated by bullfights, and *aflamencadas* are the favorites.

The dictatorial regime has promoted every form of sport —not, however, the effort-sport which elevates, ennobles, but the spectacle-sport which polarizes man's natural aggressiveness and habituates him to identifying himself with an active "other." Since the regime is a faithful mirror for the *terratenientes'* oligarchy—for the bull-raising interests—it tried first to channel public passion into the *corrida*. But the hecatombs of the circus are a costly affair, no longer within the people's reach. While at one time the *corrida* was reserved for the lumpen-proletariat and considered despicable by the upper classes, now it is the darling of the snobs, the foreign aesthetes, the tourists. As late as the nineteenth century, the *corrida* played the role of public holiday; that distinction has devolved now upon the bicycle races and soccer games. Feverishly the people follow the progress of the *Vuelta* (a major bicycle race and Spain's answer to the *Tour de France*). Soccer is more than a passion; rather, an idol. The excitement of last Sunday's game is kept up all week long by the *quinielas:* open betting in all the cafés on the outcome of the next game.

On the international level, sports act as catalyst for Spanish passions. When the *Real Madrid* comes to Paris for a game, squads of supporters converge on the capital by bus and once in the stadium shout and stamp and wave their little Spanish flags. And if the national team is triumphant, the Spanish press gives itself over to delirious joy. For lack of rank in world affairs, Spain has captured a rank on the playing field.

The imaginary violence of sport and the remembered violence of war, escape literature, and the absorbing reality of the daily struggle—all help to remove the Spaniard from the sphere of politics and to maintain the social status quo.

Chapter Fifteen

❦

YOUNG SPAIN

FOR TWENTY YEARS the regime connived to last, to survive for the sake of bringing up an entire new generation according to its doctrines. The regime has indeed lived on—only to see the new generations of students rise in opposition to it. Student participation in the streetcar boycott in Barcelona, in 1951, was the first symptom of the dissatisfaction imperceptibly ripening among the young. In 1956, the students broke out in open rebellion and ever since there has been an undercurrent of agitation.

1. MOTIFS OF DISCONTENT

Causes of this exasperation, most of them pragmatic, throw some light on the crisis of the middle class, from which most students come. Workers' sons almost never manage to go on to higher education. Tuition costs and the price of books force the middle class to heroic sacrifices, since monetary depreciation was very hard upon these families. The number

of students continues nonetheless to go higher,[1] as sons of
both bourgeoisies coexist in the universities: the old and established bourgeoisie, which refused to be downgraded, and the
new, product of civil war and black market, which considers
a university diploma as a social step up.

Overcrowding was the first complaint of the "mid-
century generation." Madrid students have since left the old
quarters in the *calle* San Bernardo and moved into the new
university buildings, whose wide bay windows look out over
the Sierra de Guadarrama. And a modern edifice now houses
the law school in Barcelona. But in most provincial universities, students are still packed into outgrown and outdated
quarters.

Libraries are understocked, laboratories old-fashioned,
playing fields almost universally lacking, the teaching body
understaffed, overworked and ill-paid,[2] the food in student
restaurants sub-standard. Each of these conditions not only
points up the extent to which the regime has neglected education,[3] but also hampers all of the students and means an unbearable burden for the poorer among them.

Already dissatisfied with present circumstances, the

[1] In 1956, first year of student rebellion, there were 57,030 students; in 1931-
1936, there had been only 32,013 on the average. Men (81 per cent of the
total) flock to the law school, which takes 35 per cent of them, and to medicine and science. Women, for the most part, take up pharmacology, philosophy,
and letters. The percentage of drop-outs because of money problems is high:
41.6 per cent in law, 53 per cent in medicine, 22 per cent in science. Scholarships are few indeed: of the 1,600 students registered at the law school in
Barcelona in 1956, for example, only six had scholarships. And at that, most
scholarships take care of only a tiny part of school expenses. There are no
reduced fares for students in public transport, on railways or at the movies.
And they are expected to observe a certain decorum.
[2] Because their salaries are not enough, professors take on extramural activities:
lectures, consultations. Their chronic absenteeism is so well-known that in 1957
the government put through a law setting up a new category of professors
"totally devoted to teaching": upon their arrival at the university, they check
in with the secretary, as workers punch a time-clock, and are rewarded with a
bonus.
[3] According to a study published by *Arriba* on November 20, 1955, the State's
per capita expenditures for education came to $2.22. The corresponding figure
in Argentina is $4.99 and in Egypt $3.98. In the important western European
countries, the per capita sum varied from the low point of $8.27 (Italy) to
the high of $28.15 (Sweden), with $16.20 (France) as a median.

young people look anxiously, pessimistically to the future. Given the economic under-development of the country, the increased number of diplomas needed to secure a decent job and the "traffic jam" in career hunting,[4] young people are haunted by fear of unemployment or repulsed by the dismal salaries to be had in the administration and private concerns.

There are not only material reasons for dissatisfaction but spiritual sources as well. In their awareness of political reality, young people notice the perpetual contradiction between the government's optimistic allegations and the actual state of affairs, between official phraseology and the facts. The result is an absolute scepticism. Any information from an official source is immediately suspect in the eyes of youth. Everything is shaded with doubt, even the truth.

A young man asking questions of himself will look for the answers in foreign publications and heterodoxical Spanish works. But such works are found neither through regular trade channels nor in libraries; there is an active black market in them, but their prices are out of reach of most students. Should the young intellectual attempt to expose his doubts publicly, he comes up against similar prohibitions.

Censorship of material intended for students is far more lenient now than before. The "liberalization" began between 1951 and 1956, when official education was in the charge of Christian-Democrats; Ruiz Jimenez was Minister of Education and Laín Entralgo was Rector of the University of Madrid. It was at this time that non-conformist magazines —*Umbral, Alcalá, El Ciervo, Laye*—came into being. The Falangist party label, uniformly thrust upon students, journalists, writers, all who work openly was good enough for the censors who in most cases did not even glance at the documents submitted to them by the young party members. In

---

[4] The hecatombs of war and repression have forced the government to call upon very young people—mostly those who fought in Franco's forces—to fill the gaps. At every level of administrative hierarchy, therefore, and in the various positions in banking, industry, and trade, are to be found men who are obviously far younger than such work would normally require. Their relief is proceeding only very slowly.

this way the little coteries which tried to undermine official doctrine were born in the shadow of the Falange.

The authorities adopted strict measures when they became aware of the new generation's revolt. But scepticism had already gone too far among the young for the government even to consider a return to such conformism as was *de rigueur* in the aftermath of the civil war. Today the authorities calculate that it is wiser to give youth a certain margin of freedom, and tolerate literary clubs, seminars, avant-garde magazines, poets' conferences insofar as they serve as safety valves and allow the students to let off steam. Certain philosophical and social problems of altogether relative boldness can be worked over in such magazines as *Índice* and *Ínsula*. Films which would never have got past the censors in 1951 are given public showings today.

But only the readers of literary reviews and viewers in certain movie theaters are aware of even such slim triumphs. The popular press and theater, commercial films and novels, are still subject to crippling scrutiny.

Thus, youth yearns above all to beat down the prohibitions which cut off its pursuit of truth: to bring about suspension of censorship, opening of frontiers, free exchange of books and newspapers, to obtain the right to express its ideas in the press and in public.

2. THE MID-CENTURY GENERATION

In its chafing at restrictions, the old liberalism fleetingly recovered the ardor of its adolescence. This thirst for freedom was revealed by the demonstrations which took place at the death of Ortega y Gasset.

There had been a series of demonstrations in the University of Madrid between December, 1955, and January, 1956.[5] The students' anger was reaffirmed by the official bur-

---

[5] These "corporative" demonstrations aimed to force the improvement of student living conditions. At the end of December, Franco was struck by the results of a semi-official referendum carried out at the University of Madrid under the Rector's auspices: 82 per cent of students interviewed declared that they no longer had confidence in the government leaders.

ial of Ortega y Gasset in a farcical rite by which a totalitarian regime tried to cover itself with the world-wide renown and glory of the theoretician of political liberalism. The day after this new hoax had been perpetrated, the university's students marched in procession through the streets of Madrid to place on the master's tomb a laurel wreath with a ribbon inscribed, "To Don José Ortega y Gasset, Spanish liberal philosopher." When their act was answered by threats of punishment and the prohibition of any further demonstration in Ortega's memory, exasperation reached its height. The students demanded the abolition of the S.E.U.'s union monopoly; this was the Falangist union in which they were all automatically registered upon entering the university. Early in February, 1956, at the time of elections for delegates to the S.E.U., the students of Madrid on their own initiative made up an independent list which won a landslide victory. The University of Madrid had thereby departed from Francoist "legality" since the lists of candidates were supposed to be submitted to the S.E.U. authorities for approval. The election was therefore annulled. This decision gave rise to further student demonstrations and to Falangist counter-demonstrations in which a Falangist student was seriously wounded.

These incidents in turn gave rise to the adoption of the first repressive measures against the students. Not only were a certain number of them suspended from the University and others dismissed outright, but also the leaders of their opposition movement were arrested and made to appear in court. Nearly all of the accused belonged to the winning side of the civil war; one of them, Francisco Bustelo, was the nephew of Calvo Sotelo.

The 1956 demonstrations actually had no political aspect. The spring of 1951 had seen the opening of a five-year period of "depoliticization" of intellectual youth. The many young monarchist students in the university between 1945 and 1950 had finished their studies and lost their enthusiasm. The Falange, which had been tottering since 1945, lost the remnants of its prestige. The eighteen- and twenty-year-olds who entered the University in about 1951 had never paid more attention to the courses in Falangist doctrine than to their catechism classes. While all of them were automatically members of the Falangist S.E.U., only two per cent of them were genuine Falangists by conviction.[6]

Yet rightist convictions were still not supplanted by leftist ones. There were, of course, in all of the universities, little literary groups which took heretical stands on philosophical issues. In the absence of a collective myth attractive enough to serve as a pretext, if for nothing more than an expenditure of energy, other young people put on a sort of despairing bravado. This was the time of nihilism, of studies scorned, lengthy palavers, gratuitous gestures, dirty hands and bushy beards, nocturnal noise-making and "leper evenings." This was the time of *Juegos de Manos*.[7] Whether victor or vanquished, decadent or a failure, the father was made responsible for all evil, for the ridiculous war, unjust society, futile life. He stood for the established order, for authority submitted to but not respected. On the other hand, woman—sister, girl friend, potential fiancée—irked the young nihilist by her docility, her pragmatic conformism aimed toward marriage. The mother was respected, as ever, but considered incapable of understanding the "problems" tormenting her son. Solitary, lost in a present without horizon, without guide lines, the young man of the mid-century lived in the company of his comrades, formed a "group" with them, a little secret republic of which adults saw only the bravado and the scorn.

Nihilism and the new literary theories did not affect more than a small minority of the young. Sceptical or indifferent to political happenings, most students were interested only in soccer, movies, girls, *quinielas*, and in the price which must be paid for such pleasures: the university degree,

---

[6] At the law school in Barcelona, the regime's "bosses" could not find enough "reliable" young people to fill the lists of candidates for S.E.U. posts and, in order to fill the vacancies, had to call upon students in other colleges.
[7] Allusion to Juan Goytisolo's novel of the same name and from which the term "leper evening" (orgiastic evening) is also borrowed.

then professional success. Yet the minority and the majority had certain things in common: to begin with, lack of political training, scornful mistrust of any form of political action, and a prejudice against the old republican parties. Both the young nihilist and the most anti-conformist intellectual were at that time a thousand miles from imagining any leftist action. Had they possessed some faith, they would not have been desperate. Whether members of the majority or of the minority, whether indifferent or rebellious, they also shared the dissatisfaction inspired by the conditions of student life, by their anxiety for the future, their scorn of comfortable politicians, their hatred of the S.E.U. bosses who arrogated to themselves the right to represent them; finally, by their conviction that their life would be transformed if only they could succeed in placing elected delegates of their own choosing in positions of power. At this time their activities were not aimed at bringing down the regime but were solely to draw attention to their particular grievances. Ignorant of repression since their class had not had to suffer it, unaware of the danger, the students believed that the public speech, ruckus-raising, and strikes would force the government to take their complaints under consideration. Therefore the first tumultuous student demonstrations united the non-conformist minority and the indifferent masses.

The repression in 1956 was the springboard for the university's "repoliticization." The students had realized that if their voices were to be heard, the regime must be overthrown. While this idea had not gone beyond the germinal stage before February, 1956, and at that only in a few rebellious minds, with the disturbances in Madrid and Barcelona in 1956 and 1957, it became widespread. The Cataloñan university once again became the scene of such incidents as had occurred the year before: students in an uproar, impromptu meetings in the lecture halls, chanting, processions, police charges, arrests, domiciliary searches, beatings, temporary closing of the university, dismissal or suspension of some 600 students.

Suddenly aware of the risks they ran, the students realized that they must work underground and their opposition became a silent campaign. The stormy demonstrations of 1956-57 have not recurred, nor has such unanimity been seen since. The majority shrink from the risks involved in action and still more from an alliance with the left, while the minority organizes and tends at once toward the left and toward clandestine action.

3. THE EYEWITNESS NOVEL

The anxiety of the new generation had found its voice in the novel, in poetry, theater, and the movies themselves which, influenced by Italian neo-realism, have become—thanks to Berlanga and especially to Bardem—a type of analysis and criticism of social reality. Novelists of sober and classic gifts —Ricardo Fernández de la Reguera, Camilo José Cela, Luis Romero, Miguel Delibes—were becoming famous about 1951 when public attention was suddenly focused on the products of the mid-century: Juan Goytisolo, the most representative of these writers, published *Juegos de Manos*, which became the novelized manifesto of the new generation.

Today, adolescent writers are legion in Spain. There is nothing surprising about this. Since the most generous and most gifted of those who were twenty in or about 1950 no longer held to the old social myths, their need for affirmation of the "self" could not be satisfied by their playing the leading roles in a farce in which they had lost faith. Since revolutionary action had not prestige enough in their eyes, then the only way left to give vent to their rebellion and their criticism, their hopes and despair was to write. In a society from which politics are banished, all activities tend to become "politicized." And because opinion could find no direct expression, it was inevitable that the novel become the sole reflection of social life.

Obsessed by an overly burdensome social reality, today's novelists in Spain have killed off the protagonist, and take an interest only in collective life; they seek indeed to be the impassive witnesses of it. The mid-century novelists have in fact already painted a complete picture of modern Spanish society: the dismal poverty of working-class youth in the Barcelona suburbs, as seen in the works of the brothers Goytisolo, Juan and Luis; the difficulties, love affairs and leisure activities of young middle-class Madrileños in Sánchez Ferlosio's *El Jarama*; the life of the Basque fishermen in Ignacio Aldecoa's *El Gran Sol*; the rudimentary existence of Castilian peasants in *Los Bravos* by Fernández Santos; and the great ache of men without land in Ana María Matute's *Fiesta al Noroeste*. While these young novelist-reporters aim only for meticulous clinical description of the social fact, nonetheless they feel the need to elude it in an unreal atmosphere of holiday, masks, and disguises. Since the fairy-tale world *par excellence* is the childhood world, most Spanish novels of recent years take for their protagonists children or adolescents who, mentally and imaginatively living in a phantasmagorical realm, are caught up in the harsh reality of war or social conflict.

The young novelist-witnesses share their tendencies and preoccupations with the poets of the new generation: Gil de Biedma, Agustín Goytisolo, Carlos Barral, who, like their immediate elders—Gabriel Celaya and Blas de Otero (*Pido la paz y la palabra*, "I demand peace and the right to speak") —use poetry to express social needs. The group's theoretician is the Cataloñan critic, José María Castellet; but the members of the "group" have never sat down together around a table. This does not prevent them taking a place in the history of Spain under the common title, "mid-century generation."

4. YOUNG SPAIN FACING THE FUTURE

Between 1956 and 1959, the underground networks led by the "under-30-year-olds" advanced at the expense of the "apolitical" masses, but never stopped beyond the minority stage. The first groups organized in Madrid and Barcelona—the Christian Democrats, the Social Democrats and the A.S.U. —soon had followers in Sevilla, Valencia, Salamanca. Free from the rancor which the civil war had bequeathed to the left, the young set an example of unity for their elders. Under A.S.U. guidance, the various groups came together in a federation in the autumn of 1957, forming the Democratic Student Union, from which the small communist element was nonetheless excluded. While the regime promulgated a new law by which students could be hauled up before a court-martial—in order to uncover and break up underground units —a new underground group, the People's Liberation Front, was created by leftist Christians and swiftly moved toward advanced social ideas, winning over the 18- to 22-year-olds.

When in June, 1959, resistance elements launched a propaganda campaign for a general strike, students—sons of the bourgeoisie—went from door to door in the working-class neighborhoods of Madrid and Barcelona, urging participation in the strike. The workers did not answer this summons. The police cracked down on the students, who were further disappointed by the workers' apathy; student resistance suffered a serious setback. The abortive strike on June 18, 1959, was the Waterloo of the mid-century generation. Its underground networks were very much subdued for the next three years, its leaders in jail (like Cerón and Pujol) or in exile (Sánchez Mazas and Girbau). Many young activists were discouraged enough to abandon resistance. Furthermore, the young people who had taken part in underground activities between 1956 and 1959 had for the most part finished their studies, become securely middle-class citizens or underpaid employees. Yesterday, hot-headed students; today sober prisoners of their professional and familial obligations. The children of the mid-century are growing old.

But rebellion reawoke in the universities of Barcelona and Madrid in February, 1962, producing the same sort of scene as in 1956 and 1957. A "poetic colloquy" at the University of Barcelona gave rise to such incidents that the police burst into the school of medicine and arrested several students.[8] Student groups proceeded to demonstrate several times

[8] The students destroyed a portrait of Franco and covered the walls with anti-Franco slogans.

before police headquarters, while a sympathy strike decreed by the students in Madrid had a substantial following.

Virtually all of the demonstrators who were put under arrest at this time were between 18 and 20 years old: hence, unborn at the time of the civil war, only 8 or 10 years old in the spring of 1951, and unfamiliar with police oppression and the disappointments of the 1956-59 period.

Drunk with hope and oblivious to the risks involved, a new generation of Spaniards broke into active life by smashing a portrait of Franco, at the very moment when Basque workers in Beasain and Irun were demonstrating to cries of "A hundred *pesetas* a day!" In Madrid, in the imposing edifice on the *Paseo del Prado*, where the union convention was taking place, José Solis Ruiz and Fernández Cuesta, spokesmen of the Falangist old guard, were holding out against a Christian Democrat offensive since members of the group had infiltrated the "vertical unions." In the Madrid night, movie theater and café lights were going out for the first time between midnight and one A.M., at the same time as the lights in all the capitals of Europe.[9] The European hour had just struck on the clock of *Puerta del Sol:* a few days before, Spain had requested admission into the European community.

With the Common Market and Castrism, two new themes have been brought into young intellectuals' discussions. Yet most of the problems which besiege the young people of 1962 are those which aroused their predecessors: those who died young, who were twenty in the spring of 1936, and the rebels of 1951 whose hopes live on within university walls. The sacrificed generation and the mid-century generation have willed their failures to the adolescents of today. Everything in this ancient country must be rebuilt. Agrarian reform must be put through at last and production raised to a level on which needs can be met. A new formula for communal life must be conceived so as to rec-

---

[9] This departure from the traditional closing hour of public places in Spain (3 or 4 A.M.) was decreed as a step toward putting Spain on the same time-table as the Common Market countries.

oncile governmental power and the personality of the Iberian nations, the discipline indispensable to society and the
freedoms which are part of the inalienable patrimony of the
Spanish people.

The time allotted to Spain for the accomplishment of
this task is severely limited. Since the regime lost its chance
to build *la Hispanidad*, Spain is condemned to sharing the
fate of Europe. Spain must raise her industrial level and
standard of living—or else become a mere stockpile of raw
materials for her European partners and a source of cheap
labor.

The new generations in Spain, present and to come,
must achieve in ten years what their forebears attempted in
vain. The task is enormous, the months are numbered. But
all the great things that have ever been accomplished in this
venerable nation, so often suspended halfway between annihilation and triumph, have always been accomplished in
haste, in anguish, in a flame of fervor.

ÉLÉNA FRANCISCA DE RIBERA Y LA SOUCHÈRE, born in Barcelona in 1916, is of both French and Spanish heritage. She had earned the Bachelor of Law degree and was working toward the Doctorate in Law and Political Science, when civil war cut her studies short. She had lived in Barcelona during the heavy bombings and in besieged Madrid as well (1937-38), before she was entrusted—first by the Catalonian Generalidad, then by the Spanish republican government—with various diplomatic missions and lecture tours abroad.

From 1940 to 1943, in London, under the direction of Don Manuel de Trujo, former Minister of Justice under the Republic, she helped to set up a unit of Spanish and South American volunteers. To avoid diplomatic complications between London and Franco's government, this unit was placed within the framework of the Free French Navy. Throughout that period, the author was in charge of liaison between the Spanish delegation and Free French Forces headquarters. The Spanish battalion was dissolved during the winter of 1942-43, when Franco gave England his assurance of neutrality. She was subsequently responsible for the liberated Spanish refugees who had been held under the Pétain regime.

When the Spanish republican government was reestablished in 1945, in exile, the author was director of that government's unofficial press agency. Since 1946, when hopes for resurrection of the republic in the near future were abandoned, the author has devoted herself to literature and journalism. She regularly contributed the leading article to El Socialista Espanol. The author also took charge of the Spanish and Latin American affairs department of Les Temps Modernes, and of the corresponding part of the weekly France-Observateur. These articles, and her contributions to Les Lettres Nouvelles,

Paris literary review, introduced the new generation of Spanish novelists, whose first works date from 1951, to the French public. She continues to contribute to a number of publications in several countries. Mlle. de La Souchère lives in Paris.

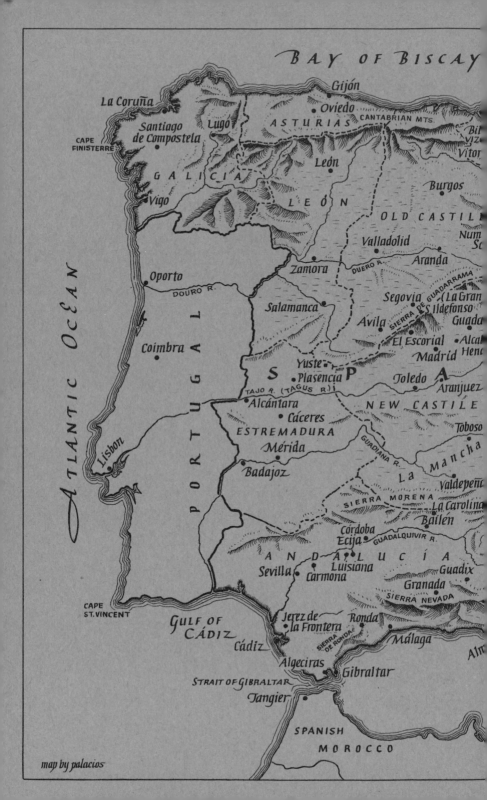